Betty Crocker's International Cookbook

Betty Crocker's
International Cookbook

Random House   New York

Library of Congress Cataloging in Publication Data

Crocker, Betty, pseud.
Betty Crocker's International cookbook.

Includes index.
1. Cookery, International.   I. Title.
II. Title: International cookbook.
TX725.A1C66   641.59   80-5311
ISBN 0-394-50453-4

Manufactured in the United States of America
6 8 9 7

Our thanks to the following for their invaluable help in the making of this book:

Design: Robert Aulicino

Illustrations: Pat Stewart

Director of Photography: Barbara Gorder Sims

Editorial Research: Michael Dorn

Foreword

Betty Crocker's International Cookbook was inspired by the escalating interest of Americans in foreign foods. Through travel and communications, we have all been brought into closer contact with people of other places, their customs, celebrations and traditional foods.

This is basically a book of country cooking, although it includes some of the classic and more sophisticated recipes where tradition and authenticity dictate. All of these recipes are "from scratch" rather than from convenience foods, and they have all been tested in the Betty Crocker kitchens. We have adhered faithfully to the original concept of each recipe, retaining its authentic flavors while simplifying and streamlining wherever possible. Occasionally we have adapted centuries-old recipes to modern tastes and cooking techniques—just as homemakers throughout the world have always done.

You will find more than 450 recipes from the cuisines of more than 50 countries. The color photographs include "how-to" pictures and suggest the ambience of the countries represented.

For us, the making of this book has been like taking a journey around the world. It has given us fascinating glimpses of great cultures past and present, broadened our knowledge of geography, enriched our travels and, of course, opened up a whole new sphere of cooking and entertaining.

Join us, now, in our voyage around the world of great tastes—some familiar from your own family's heritage, others perhaps new and exotic but notable. As you turn the pages, plan your personal itinerary. Adventure awaits you.

Betty Crocker

Contents

Setting the Scene for Your International Dinner

The Equipment

Since this is primarily a book of country recipes which can be prepared with standard pans, skillets and baking dishes found in every adequately stocked American kitchen, you will need no special equipment for any of these recipes. Of course, there are some utensils that can make your cooking easier, more fun and more international—an oriental wok, for instance. A food processor, pasta machine, *lefse* baker and other such gadgets can be useful too, if you have a large budget and sufficient space to store them for ready use. But since you need only basic equipment to get maximum appreciation from international cooking, you may want to concentrate more on attractive, colorful serving dishes, linens and stemware with a bright international flair.

The Ingredients

The national enthusiasm for international cooking has not gone unnoticed by your neighborhood grocer. Most large supermarkets and many small groceries carry all of the ingredients found in this book. Sometimes the ingredients you are looking for may be displayed in what seem to be unlikely places: Capers, for example—piquant little salad garnishes—might be placed with salad dressings; with pickles and olives; with "gourmet" foods; or even with party accessories and cocktail mixes! Tortillas might be found canned in the Mexican food section; frozen in the dairy section; or even fresh, tucked among the oriental and Spanish vegetables. But don't be discouraged. If you have questions about foreign ingredients or anticipate difficulty in finding them, consult your supermarket home economist or store manager. For best results, choose recipes with ingredients that are in season.

The Mood

When planning a dinner party with an international theme, set the scene for the party just as you would set the stage for a play. If it's a very important party—a celebration or a once-a-year gala—it's a good idea to let your guests know of the theme you have in mind and perhaps invite them to dress accordingly. Even if it's a simple dinner for four or six, plan to have suitable background music, an oriental flower arrangement, a bowl of tropical fruit or a Scandinavian centerpiece—such simple touches do much to create a foreign or international atmosphere and thus enhance the appeal of your dishes and the enjoyment of your guests or family. The photographs in this book will provide you with ideas.

The Menu

The most important part of your evening will be the meal itself. For your menu-planning convenience, you will find occasional serve-with suggestions throughout the book. In the indexes there are listings of recipes by country of origin as well as by name and food category. If you have found a delectable Mexican casserole or French stew that you want to feature as your main course, consult the Index by Country or Region for Mexican or French appetizers, salads, side dishes, breads and desserts.

And feel free to break away from single-country menus. A dinner that is "purely Chinese" from start to finish is a most satisfying experience. But just as satisfying, and perhaps even more exciting, is a dinner that begins with a crisp, warm Greek appetizer or a light, simple Japanese soup, moves on to a sprightly Mexican chicken dish accompanied by a colorful Italian salad and a crisp Indian bread, and concludes with a glorious French dessert.

Betty Crocker's International Cookbook

Clockwise from top: Cheese Puffs (page 7), Gazpacho (page 31) and Bean-and-Tuna Salad (page 13).

Starters

To start the evening with a savory snack ... to start a gala party with a colorful tray of appetizers ... to start a formal dinner party with an elegant soup, or a buffet supper with a crisp, colorful salad ... and most of all, to start you on an exciting adventure in international cooking!

In this chapter we have collected a tasty sampling of international appetizers. You'll find succulent hot nibbles, such as Crisp Wontons from China, Cheese Puffs from Greece, Deep-Fried Indian Pastries and Little Latin Meatballs.

There are cold appetizers, too—ideal for entertaining, since they can be prepared well in advance of the party. Try our spicy African Red Dip when you want to serve a memorable shrimp cocktail ... or our applause-winning Country Terrine from France when planning an important walkabout party ... or our Bean-and-Sesame Seed Spread when you want to recapture the invigorating atmosphere of the Middle East!

Select from a number of light, refreshing international soups to serve as a first course at formal dinner parties. (The heartiest of these soups can be served as a main dish for a light lunch or supper.) Glance through the recipes in this chapter, and we know you'll want to begin your adventures in international cooking right away!

South-of-the-Border Turnovers

(Empanaditas)

Empanaditas *are tiny versions of* empanadas— *meat-filled baked pastries served throughout Mexico and in many South American countries. They go well with Avocado Dip (page 18).*

About 24 appetizers

⅔   cup shortening
2   tablespoons margarine or butter, softened
2   cups all-purpose flour
½   teaspoon salt
4   to 6 tablespoons cold water
      Ham Filling or Chicken Filling (below)
1   egg, separated
1   tablespoon milk

Cut shortening and margarine into flour and salt until particles are size of small peas. Sprinkle in water, 1 tablespoon at a time, tossing with fork until all flour is moistened and pastry almost cleans side of bowl. Gather pastry into a ball; divide into halves. Shape one half into flattened round on lightly floured cloth-covered board. Roll pastry into rectangle, 13 x 10 inches; cut into 3-inch circles. Place on ungreased cookie sheet.

Prepare filling. Beat egg white slightly; brush on edges of pastry circles. Place 1 teaspoon filling on center of each circle. Fold pastry over filling; press edges with fork to seal securely. Repeat with remaining half pastry. Heat oven to 375°. Mix egg yolk and milk; brush turnovers with egg yolk mixture. Bake until light brown, 18 to 20 minutes.

Ham Filling
1   can (4½ ounces) deviled ham
¼   cup grated Cheddar cheese
1   teaspoon prepared mustard
⅛   teaspoon pepper

Mix all ingredients.

Chicken Filling
½   cup finely chopped cooked chicken
2   tablespoons taco or chili sauce
2   tablespoons chopped stuffed olives
¼   teaspoon salt

Mix all ingredients.

Do-Ahead Tip: After baking, turnovers can be covered and refrigerated several hours. Heat in 375° oven until hot, about 8 minutes.

Shrimp Balls

(Hsia Ch'iu)

A Cantonese specialty, Shrimp Balls are best served piping hot; provide bamboo skewers or wooden picks for ease in dipping balls into Sweet-and-Sour Sauce.

About 24 shrimp balls

2   cans (4½ ounces each) shrimp, drained and finely chopped
4   water chestnuts, finely chopped
1   green onion, finely chopped
1   teaspoon cornstarch
1   teaspoon sesame seed oil
¼   teaspoon ground ginger
      Dash of white pepper
1   egg white
      Vegetable oil
      Sweet-and-Sour Sauce (page 8)

Mix shrimp, water chestnuts, green onion, cornstarch, sesame seed oil, ginger and white pepper. Beat egg white until foamy; stir into shrimp mixture. Shape mixture into 1-inch balls.

Heat vegetable oil (1½ to 1¾ inches) to 360°. Fry 6 to 8 shrimp balls at a time until golden brown, turning 2 or 3 times, about 2 minutes. Drain on paper towels. Serve with Sweet-and-Sour Sauce.

Little Russian Pastries (Pirozhki)

These savory pastries are traditional appetizers throughout the Soviet Union and Eastern Europe. Often pirozhki *are served as a light supper, with a steaming bowl of Shredded-Cabbage Soup (page 28) or* Borscht *(page 130).*

About 42 appetizers

½   pound ground beef
1   small onion, finely chopped
1   hard-cooked egg, finely chopped
1   tablespoon snipped dillweed or parsley*
½   teaspoon salt
⅛   teaspoon pepper
     Sour Cream Pastry (right)
1   egg yolk
1   tablespoon cold water

Cook and stir beef and onion in 10-inch skillet until beef is light brown; drain. Stir in egg, dillweed, salt and pepper.

Prepare pastry; divide into fourths. Cover with damp towel to prevent drying. Roll each fourth into 12-inch circle on well-floured cloth-covered board. Cut pastry into 3-inch circles. Place rounded teaspoonful filling on center of each circle. Fold one side of pastry over filling; fold in two opposite sides ½ inch. (See diagram.)

Moisten fourth side with water; fold over to seal. Place seam sides down on ungreased cookie sheet. Repeat with remaining pastry. (Pastries can be covered and refrigerated no longer than 24 hours at this point.) Heat oven to 400°. Mix egg yolk and water; brush pastries with egg yolk mixture. Bake until golden brown, 15 to 20 minutes.

* 1 teaspoon dried dillweed or dried parsley flakes can be substituted for the fresh dillweed or parsley.

Sour Cream Pastry

¾   cup margarine or butter, softened
2   cups all-purpose flour
1   teaspoon salt
½   cup dairy sour cream

Cut margarine into flour and salt until particles are size of small peas; stir in sour cream. Gather pastry into a ball.

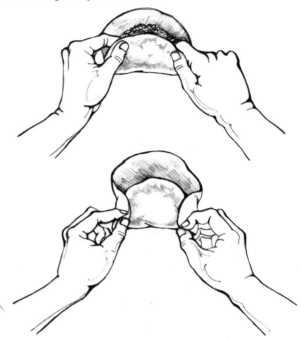

Fold one side of pastry over filling; fold in two opposite sides ½ inch.

Spices and Herbs

Did You Know?

Spices and herbs should enhance the food, not overpower it. Keep in mind that tastes differ and seasonings in some foreign foods are characteristically hot, so you may want to start with a smaller amount and increase to personal and family preference.

Dried herbs are more concentrated than fresh. As a general rule, if a recipe calls for 1 tablespoon snipped fresh herbs and you need to substitute, use only ½ to 1 teaspoon dried herbs and ¼ teaspoon ground herbs.

Deep-Fried Indian Pastries

Deep-Fried Indian Pastries

(Samosas)

India's version of the stuffed fried pastries popular throughout the world. Mango chutney is the traditional dip for samosas. *Plain yogurt garnished with snipped parsley or coriander leaves is often served as an additional dip.*

About 60 appetizers

1	pound ground lamb or beef
1	medium onion, finely chopped
1	clove garlic, finely chopped
1	teaspoon salt
½	teaspoon ground coriander
¼	teaspoon ground cumin
¼	teaspoon ground ginger
¼	teaspoon pepper

Pastry (page 7)
Vegetable oil
Chutney

Cook and stir lamb, onion and garlic in 10-inch skillet until lamb is light brown; drain. Stir in salt, coriander, cumin, ginger and pepper. Cool.

Prepare pastry; divide into fourths. Cover with damp towel to prevent drying. Roll each fourth into 12-inch circle (dough will be springy and may be slightly difficult to roll). Cut into 4-inch circles; cut circles into halves. Moisten edges with water. Place 1 teaspoon filling on each half circle. Fold pastry over filling to form triangle. Press edges to seal securely. Repeat with remaining pastry.

Heat oil (1 to 1½ inches) to 375°. Fry about 5 pastries at a time until light brown, turning 2 or 3 times, 3 to 4 minutes. Drain on paper towels. Keep warm in 200° oven. Serve warm with chutney.

Pastry

2   tablespoons margarine or butter
1   tablespoon shortening
2   cups all-purpose flour
½   teaspoon salt
1   egg yolk
½   cup cold water

Cut margarine and shortening into flour and salt until mixture resembles fine crumbs; stir in egg yolk. Sprinkle in water, 1 tablespoon at a time, tossing with fork until all flour is moistened and pastry almost cleans side of bowl. Gather pastry into a ball; knead on lightly floured cloth-covered board until smooth, about 1 minute.

Cheese Puffs

(Tiropetes)

Filo (or phyllo) leaves, also called strudel leaves, are paper-thin pastry sheets used throughout the Middle East in many dishes, including Baklava (page 317). The leaves can be purchased at fine groceries and shops carrying Middle Eastern foods. These little pastries are a great favorite in Greece.

About 30 appetizers

1   pound feta cheese*
2   eggs, slightly beaten
¼   cup finely chopped chives
¼   teaspoon white pepper
1   pound frozen filo leaves, thawed
¼   cup margarine or butter, melted

Crumble cheese in small bowl; mash with fork. Stir in eggs, chives and white pepper until well mixed. Cut filo leaves lengthwise into 3 strips. Cover with waxed paper, then with damp towel to prevent drying. Use 2 layers filo leaves for each strip. Place 1 heaping teaspoon filling on end of strip; fold end over end, in triangular shape, to opposite end.

(See diagrams.) Place on greased cookie sheet. Repeat with remaining filling. (Puffs can be covered and refrigerated no longer than 24 hours at this point.)

Heat oven to 350°. Brush puffs with margarine. Bake until puffed and golden, about 20 minutes.

* Finely shredded Monterey Jack cheese can be substituted for the feta cheese.

Place a heaping teaspoon filling on end of strip.

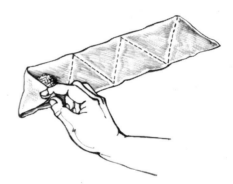

Fold end over end, in triangular shape, to opposite end.

Filo (Fillo, Phyllo)

Did You Know?

Frozen filo leaves should be thawed completely before using so that the paper-thin sheets can be separated without tearing. Thaw them overnight in the refrigerator or several hours at room temperature. The soft leaves dry quickly; keep them covered with waxed paper and a damp towel until they are shaped and brushed with margarine. They bake into flaky, crisp, golden pastry.

Egg Rolls
(Chi Tan Chuan)

Traditional egg roll skins can be purchased at many American supermarkets; but for more delicate, light-as-a-feather egg rolls, look for spring roll skins, sometimes called Shanghai spring roll skins. As thin as crêpes, they are usually found only in oriental groceries or in gourmet shops carrying an extensive line of Chinese food.

16 to 18 egg rolls

1	pound ground pork
3	cups finely shredded cabbage
1	can (8½ ounces) bamboo shoots, drained and chopped
½	cup chopped mushrooms
4	medium green onions, sliced
2	tablespoons soy sauce
1	teaspoon cornstarch
1	teaspoon five spice powder
1	teaspoon salt
½	teaspoon sugar
1	pound egg roll skins (16 to 18)
	Vegetable oil
	Sweet-and-Sour Sauce and Hot Mustard Sauce (right)

Stir-fry pork in wok or 10-inch skillet until brown. Remove pork from wok; drain, reserving 2 tablespoons fat. Stir-fry cabbage, bamboo shoots, mushrooms and onions in reserved fat. Mix soy sauce, cornstarch, five spice powder, salt and sugar; pour over vegetable mixture. Stir-fry 1 minute; cool.

Mix pork and vegetables. Cover egg roll skins with damp towel to prevent drying. Place ¼ cup pork mixture on center of each egg roll skin. Fold one corner of egg roll skin over filling; overlap the two opposite corners. (See diagram.) Moisten fourth corner with water; fold over to make into roll. (See diagram.)

Heat oil (1½ to 1¾ inches) to 360°. Fry 3 to 5 egg rolls at a time until golden brown, turn-ing once, about 3 minutes. Drain on paper towels. Serve hot with Sweet-and-Sour Sauce and Hot Mustard Sauce.

Sweet-and-Sour Sauce
Heat ¼ cup plum or grape jelly and ¼ cup chili sauce in small saucepan, stirring constantly, until jelly is melted.

Hot Mustard Sauce
Mix 3 tablespoons dry mustard, 2 tablespoons water and 1 tablespoon soy sauce until smooth.

Do-Ahead Tip: After frying, egg rolls can be covered and refrigerated no longer than 24 hours. Heat uncovered in 375° oven until hot, about 15 minutes.

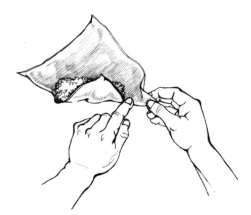

Fold one corner of egg roll skin over filling; overlap the two opposite corners.

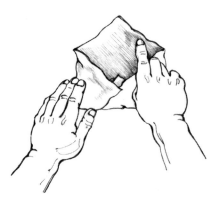

Moisten fourth corner with water; fold over to make into roll.

Chinese Barbecued Ribs
(Shao Pi K'u)

For ease in eating, provide an ample supply of paper napkins and bowls for depositing bones.

About 42 appetizers

1½	to 2 pounds fresh pork spareribs
¼	cup soy sauce
¼	cup hoisin sauce or chili sauce
2	tablespoons honey
2	tablespoons sake or dry sherry
1	small clove garlic, crushed

Have spareribs cut crosswise into 1½-inch pieces. Place ribs in shallow glass or plastic dish. Mix remaining ingredients; spoon over ribs. Cover and refrigerate at least 2 hours.

Remove ribs from marinade, reserving marinade. Arrange ribs meaty sides up in single layer on rack in foil-lined broiler pan. Brush with reserved marinade. Cover and cook in 325° oven 1 hour. Brush ribs with marinade. Cook uncovered, brushing occasionally with marinade, until done, about 45 minutes. Brush with marinade.

Glazed Chicken Wings

Inexpensive chicken wings make a delectable appetizer when marinated in honey and soy sauce; for a pungent Chinese accent, serve with Hot Mustard Sauce (page 8).

About 30 appetizers

3	pounds chicken wings (about 15)
⅔	cup soy sauce
½	cup honey
2	tablespoons vegetable oil
2	teaspoons five spice powder
2	cloves garlic, crushed

Cut each chicken wing at joints to make three pieces; discard tips or save for use in making stock (page 101). Place chicken wings in shallow glass or plastic dish. Mix remaining ingredients; pour over chicken. Cover and refrigerate, turning chicken occasionally, at least 1 hour.

Arrange chicken on rack in foil-lined broiler pan; reserve marinade. Brush chicken with reserved marinade. Cook in 375° oven 30 minutes. Turn chicken and cook, brushing occasionally with marinade, until done, about 30 minutes.

Do-Ahead Tip: After cooking, chicken wings can be covered and refrigerated no longer than 24 hours. Heat uncovered in 375° oven until hot, about 15 minutes.

Rumaki

These classic Japanese kabobs are often served with one or more dips—soy sauce, teriyaki sauce, Hot Mustard Sauce (page 8) or Tempura Sauce (page 69).

20 appetizers

½	pound chicken livers
½	can (8-ounce size) water chestnuts
¼	cup soy sauce
2	tablespoons packed brown sugar
2	thin slices fresh ginger root or ⅛ teaspoon ground ginger
1	clove garlic, crushed
10	slices bacon

Cut chicken livers into halves; cut water chestnuts crosswise into halves. Mix soy sauce, brown sugar, ginger root and garlic in glass or plastic bowl; stir in chicken livers and water chestnuts. Cover and refrigerate at least 2 hours. Drain.

Cut bacon slices into halves. Wrap piece of liver and piece of water chestnut in each bacon piece. Secure with wooden pick. Arrange on rack in broiler pan. Cook in 400° oven, turning once, until bacon is crisp, 25 to 30 minutes.

Crisp Wontons

Crisp Wontons
(Cha Yun T'un)

Wontons such as those added to Wonton Soup (page 24) assume a bold, crisp character when fried golden brown and served as hot appetizers with a spicy dip. Chinese plum sauce, barbecue sauce and teriyaki sauce can be used as well as the sauces suggested below.

About 48 wontons

½   pound ground pork
1   can (4½ ounces) shrimp, drained and chopped
6   water chestnuts, finely chopped
2   green onions (with tops), chopped
1   tablespoon soy sauce
1   teaspoon cornstarch
½   teaspoon salt
1   pound wonton skins*
   Vegetable oil
   Sweet-and-Sour Sauce or Hot Mustard Sauce
    (page 8)

Stir-fry pork in wok or 10-inch skillet until brown; drain. Stir in shrimp, water chestnuts, green onions, soy sauce, cornstarch and salt. Stir-fry 1 minute.

Place 1 teaspoon filling on center of each wonton skin. Moisten edges with water. Fold each skin in half to form triangle; press edges to seal. (See diagram.) Pull bottom corners of triangle down and overlap slightly. (See diagram.) Moisten one corner with water; press to seal.

Heat oil (1 to 1½ inches) to 360°. Fry 6 to 8 wontons at a time until golden brown, turning occasionally, about 2 minutes. Drain on paper towels. Serve with Sweet-and-Sour Sauce.

* 12 to 14 egg roll skins can be substituted for the wonton skins; cut each skin into fourths.

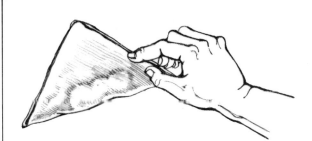

Fold each wonton skin in half to form triangle; press edges to seal.

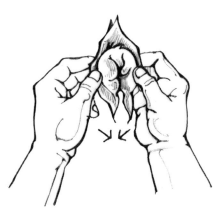

Pull bottom corners of triangle down, as arrows indicate, overlapping slightly.

Deep-Fat Frying

Did You Know?

Deep-fat frying can be done in a wok (standing the wok on the adapter ring over the burner for stability), a saucepan, a skillet or a fondue pot; but a deep, heavy saucepan or wok is preferable because the thermometer can rest against the side of the pan and the high sides give less possibility of spattering. For best results, use a thermometer. If the oil is too hot, food will be too brown on the outside before the center is cooked, and if the oil is too cool, the food will absorb grease. The smaller the area of the pan, the less oil will be necessary to reach the specified depth.

Little Latin Meatballs
(Albondiguitas)

Served as appetizers in many Latin American countries and in Spain, these perky meatballs can be made in advance and kept warm in the chafing dish. For ease in eating, provide guests with bamboo skewers or decorative party picks.

36 meatballs

2	jalepeño chilies
1	pound ground beef
1	egg
½	cup dry bread crumbs
¼	cup milk
¼	cup shredded Monterey Jack or Cheddar cheese
1	small onion, finely chopped
1	teaspoon salt
¼	teaspoon pepper
	Salsa (below)

Remove stems, seeds and membranes from chilies; chop chilies. Mix chilies, beef, egg, bread crumbs, milk, cheese, onion, salt and pepper. Shape mixture into 1-inch balls. Place meatballs in ungreased oblong pan, 13 x 9 x 2 inches. Cook uncovered in 400° oven until brown, 15 to 20 minutes. Place meatballs in chafing dish. Pour Salsa over meatballs.

Salsa

1	can (8 ounces) tomato sauce
1	medium tomato, chopped
2	cloves garlic, finely chopped
2	tablespoons snipped parsley
1	tablespoon vinegar
⅛	teaspoon ground cumin
⅛	teaspoon salt

Heat all ingredients in 1-quart saucepan, stirring occasionally, until hot.

Chicken Kabobs with Peanut Sauce

(Saté Ajam)

These Indonesian kabobs are eaten right off the skewer. Serve the zesty Peanut Sauce in shallow bowls so that the skewers can be turned easily.

About 16 appetizers

2	large whole chicken breasts
¼	cup soy sauce
1	tablespoon vegetable oil
1	teaspoon packed brown sugar
¼	teaspoon ground ginger
1	clove garlic, crushed
	Peanut Sauce (below)

Remove bones and skin from chicken breasts. Cut chicken into ¾-inch pieces. (For ease in cutting, partially freeze chicken.) Mix chicken, soy sauce, oil, brown sugar, ginger and garlic in glass bowl. Cover and refrigerate, stirring occasionally, at least 2 hours.

Prepare Peanut Sauce. Remove chicken from marinade; reserve marinade. Thread 4 or 5 chicken pieces on each of 14 to 16 bamboo skewers. Brush chicken with reserved marinade. Set oven control to broil and/or 550°. Broil skewers with tops about 4 inches from heat 4 to 5 minutes; turn. Brush with marinade. Broil until chicken is done, 4 to 5 minutes. Serve with Peanut Sauce.

Peanut Sauce

1	small onion, finely chopped
1	tablespoon vegetable oil
⅓	cup peanut butter
⅓	cup water
1	tablespoon lemon juice
¼	teaspoon ground coriander
3	to 4 drops red pepper sauce

Cook and stir onion in oil in 1½-quart saucepan until tender. Remove from heat. Stir in remaining ingredients; heat over low heat just until blended (sauce will separate if overcooked).

Cheese-Stuffed Mushrooms

(Funghi alla Parmigiana)

Select firm white or creamy-beige mushrooms with caps that are closed or slightly open around the stem for this hot hors d'oeuvre from Italy.

About 24 appetizers

1	pound medium mushrooms (about 24)
¼	cup finely chopped green onions (with tops)
1	clove garlic, finely chopped
¼	cup margarine or butter
½	cup dry bread crumbs
¼	cup grated Parmesan cheese
2	tablespoons snipped parsley
½	teaspoon salt
½	teaspoon dried basil leaves
¼	teaspoon pepper

Cut ends from mushroom stems. Remove stems from mushrooms; chop stems finely. Cook and stir mushroom stems, green onions and garlic in margarine over medium heat until tender, about 5 minutes. Remove from heat; stir in remaining ingredients.

Fill mushroom caps with stuffing mixture. Place mushrooms filled sides up in greased baking dish. Cook in 350° oven 15 minutes. Serve hot.

Marinated Mushrooms
(Antipasto di Funghi Crudi)

The word "antipasto" simply means before the meal. Antipasto trays in Italy include a wide range of foods, from anchovies to zucchini. These marinated sliced mushrooms are prized antipasto offerings throughout Italy, and are especially loved in Rome.

8 to 10 appetizer servings

1   pound mushrooms
¼   cup lemon juice
½   cup olive or vegetable oil
2   green onions (with tops), thinly sliced
¼   cup snipped parsley
1   clove garlic, finely chopped
¾   teaspoon salt
¼   teaspoon freshly ground pepper
    Paprika
    Parsley sprigs
    Grissini (see Note)

Cut mushrooms into ⅛-inch slices. Mix mushrooms and lemon juice in large bowl. Stir in oil, green onions, ¼ cup parsley, the garlic, salt and pepper; toss. Cover and refrigerate, stirring occasionally, at least 3 hours.

Just before serving, remove to salad bowl with slotted spoon. Sprinkle with paprika; garnish with parsley. Serve with grissini.

Note: Grissini (very long thin breadsticks) are available at Italian bakeries, gourmet shops, and some supermarkets.

Bean-and-Tuna Salad
(Insalata di Fagioli e Tonno)

The plump white beans of Tuscany have been prized by Italians since ancient times. In Florence, the chilled bean salad is included among the antipasto trays of many restaurants. At posh Florentine restaurants, fresh caviar is sometimes used instead of tuna!

12 servings (about ¾ cup each)

3   cups water
½   pound dried white kidney, Great Northern or navy beans*
⅓   cup olive or vegetable oil
3   tablespoons red wine vinegar
1   teaspoon salt
    Freshly ground pepper
1   medium Spanish, Bermuda or red onion, thinly sliced
1   can (6½ ounces) tuna, drained
    Snipped parsley

Heat water and beans to boiling; boil 2 minutes. Remove from heat; cover and let stand 1 hour. Add enough water to cover beans if necessary. Heat to boiling; reduce heat. Cover and simmer until tender, 1 to 1½ hours (do not boil or beans will burst). Drain and cool.

Mix oil, vinegar, salt and pepper; pour over beans and onion in shallow glass or plastic dish. Cover and refrigerate, stirring occasionally, at least 1 hour. Transfer bean mixture to serving platter with slotted spoon. Break tuna into chunks; arrange on bean mixture. Sprinkle with parsley.

* 2 cans (15 to 20 ounces each) cannellini or other white beans, drained, can be substituted for the cooked dried beans.

Greek Appetizer Salad

Greek Appetizer Salad
(Salata Meze)

A medley of traditional Greek vegetables, briefly cooked and marinated in a lemony dressing. The Greeks often sprinkle a few tablespoonfuls of crumbled feta cheese over each salad before serving.

8 servings

8	ounces green beans
3	small zucchini, cut into ½-inch slices
1	small cauliflower, separated into flowerets
½	cup olive or vegetable oil
¼	cup lemon juice
1	teaspoon salt
½	teaspoon sugar
½	teaspoon dried oregano leaves
1	clove garlic, finely chopped
	Lettuce leaves
1	small onion, sliced and separated into rings
	Cherry tomatoes, cut into halves
	Ripe olives

Heat 1 inch salted water (½ teaspoon salt to 1 cup water) to boiling in 3-quart saucepan. Add beans; cover and simmer 5 minutes. Add zucchini and cauliflower. Heat to boiling; reduce heat. Cover and cook just until tender, about 5 minutes. Drain. Place vegetables in shallow glass or plastic dish.

Mix oil, lemon juice, salt, sugar, oregano and garlic; pour over vegetables. Cover and refrigerate, spooning marinade over vegetables occasionally, at least 2 hours. Remove vegetables to lettuce-lined plates with slotted spoon; top with onion rings. Garnish with cherry tomatoes and olives.

Mixed Salad with Anchovy Dressing
(Insalata Mista)

Ripe olives and a robust Anchovy Dressing lend a memorable Neapolitan flavor to this aromatic first-course salad.

8 servings

	Anchovy Dressing (below)
1	can (8 ounces) pitted ripe olives, drained
1	jar (6 ounces) marinated artichoke hearts, drained
1	head curly endive
½	head iceberg lettuce
½	bunch romaine

Prepare Anchovy Dressing; refrigerate at least 2 hours. Pour dressing into 5-quart salad bowl. Slice ¼ cup of the olives. Cut artichoke hearts into halves. Add remaining olives and the artichoke hearts to dressing. Tear greens in bite-size pieces into salad bowl; refrigerate at least 1 hour. Toss just before serving; garnish with olive slices.

Anchovy Dressing

½	cup olive or vegetable oil
1	can (2 ounces) anchovy fillets, drained
2	tablespoons lemon juice
2	tablespoons white wine vinegar
½	teaspoon salt
½	teaspoon sugar
¼	teaspoon onion salt
¼	teaspoon dried oregano leaves
¼	teaspoon dry mustard
¼	teaspoon paprika
⅛	teaspoon dried thyme leaves
1	clove garlic, crushed

Place all ingredients in blender container. Cover and blend on medium speed until smooth and creamy, about 45 seconds.

Cucumbers and Shrimp

Add interest to this Japanese appetizer: Partially pare the cucumber in alternate lengthwise strips before slicing, leaving portions of bright green peel.

6 servings

1   can (4½ ounces) shrimp, drained
2   medium cucumbers, thinly sliced
¼   cup vinegar
1   tablespoon sugar
1   teaspoon soy sauce
½   teaspoon salt
     Lettuce leaves
1   tablespoon toasted sesame seed (see Note)

Place shrimp and cucumbers in 1½-quart glass bowl. Mix vinegar, sugar, soy sauce and salt; pour over shrimp and cucumbers. Toss. Cover and refrigerate at least 1 hour. Remove salad to lettuce-lined salad bowls with slotted spoon. Sprinkle with sesame seed.

Note: To toast, heat sesame seed in ungreased skillet over medium heat, stirring occasionally, until golden, about 2 minutes.

Marinated Gingered Shrimp

Sake—Japan's traditional rice wine—can be purchased at many liquor stores. If sweet sake is unavailable in your area, substitute sweet sherry.

60 to 65 appetizers

1½   pounds frozen shrimp, shelled and deveined
¼   cup soy sauce
3   ounces ginger root, chopped
¼   cup vinegar
2   tablespoons sugar
2   tablespoons sweet sake
1½   teaspoons salt
      Dash of monosodium glutamate (optional)
2   to 3 tablespoons thinly sliced green onion

Cook shrimp as directed on package; drain. Arrange shrimp in single layer in oblong baking dish, 12 x 7½ x 2 inches. Heat soy sauce to boiling; add ginger root. Reduce heat; simmer uncovered until most of the liquid is absorbed, about 5 minutes. Stir in vinegar, sugar, sake, salt and monosodium glutamate; pour over shrimp. Cover and refrigerate at least 2 hours.

Remove shrimp from marinade with slotted spoon; arrange on serving plate. Garnish with green onion.

Anchovy-and-Garlic Dip (Bagna Cauda)

Bagna cauda *(from Italy's Piedmont region) means hot bath. The dip was originally served warm with bread and vegetables as a main dish in late autumn and early winter.*

⅔ cup dip

2   cans (2 ounces each) anchovy fillets
½   cup margarine or butter, softened
2   cloves garlic, cut into halves
     Snipped parsley
     Vegetable Dippers (below) or Italian bread sticks

Drain anchovies; reserve 1 tablespoon oil. Place anchovies, reserved oil, the margarine and garlic in blender container. Cover and blend on medium speed, scraping sides of blender frequently, about 1 minute. Garnish with parsley. Serve at room temperature with Vegetable Dippers.

Vegetable Dippers: Carrot sticks, cauliflower or broccoli flowerets, celery sticks, cucumber or zucchini sticks, green onion pieces, small whole mushrooms, red or green pepper strips, radishes with stems.

Mexican Bean Dip
(Frijoles para Sopear)

Canned refried beans can be found in the Mexican foods section of supermarkets. When in season, sweet red pepper strips make a colorful addition to the vegetable dippers.

About 2 cups dip

1   can (15 ounces) refried beans
2   tablespoons milk
½   cup shredded Monterey Jack cheese
     Carrot and celery sticks

Heat beans and milk in 1-quart saucepan, stirring constantly, until hot. Stir in cheese; cook and stir until cheese is melted. Serve in fondue pot or chafing dish with carrot and celery sticks.

Flaming Cheese
(Saganaki)

Few hot appetizers are easier or more glamorous than this Greek specialty. Kasseri and Kefalotiri cheese can be found at fancy cheese shops and in groceries specializing in Middle Eastern food. Wedges of pita bread or sesame crackers can be served in place of rye bread.

6 servings

½   pound Kasseri or Kefalotiri cheese*
1   tablespoon margarine or butter, melted
2   tablespoons brandy
½   lemon
     Cocktail rye bread or assorted crackers

Cut cheese into 3 wedges; place in shallow heatproof serving dish. Brush cheese with margarine. Set oven control to broil and/or 550°. Broil cheese with top 4 to 6 inches from heat until bubbly light brown, 5 to 6 minutes. Heat brandy until warm; pour over cheese.

Ignite immediately. Squeeze lemon over cheese. Cut wedges into halves. Serve with rye bread.

* Mozzarella cheese can be substituted for the above cheeses.

Chilies with Cheese
(Chiles con Queso)

A rich, spicy Mexican version of the much-admired cheese fondue. Crisp vegetable dippers and tortilla chips can be served in addition to corn chips.

About 3 cups

1   small onion, finely chopped
2   tablespoons margarine or butter
1   cup drained solid pack tomatoes
1   can (4 ounces) peeled green chilies, seeded and chopped
½   teaspoon salt
     Dash of pepper
½   pound Monterey Jack cheese*
¾   cup half-and-half
     Corn chips

Cook and stir onion in margarine in 10-inch skillet until tender, about 5 minutes. Stir in tomatoes, chilies, salt and pepper. Simmer uncovered 15 minutes.

Cut cheese into ½-inch cubes; stir into tomato mixture. Stir in half-and-half when cheese begins to melt. Cook and stir until cheese is melted; cook uncovered 10 minutes. Serve dip in fondue pot or chafing dish with corn chips.

Chilies and Peppers

Did You Know?

The medieval quest for the black pepper of India led to the discovery of the Americas and a whole new world of "peppers." But the peppers found thriving in Latin America bore no relation to India's peppercorns. All Western Hemisphere peppers are members of the capsicum family and include sweet red and green bell peppers, long yellow banana peppers, pimientos and fiery chilies—of which there are many varieties.

Chile is the word used by Spanish-speaking Mexicans for capsicum. *Pimento* is the Spanish word for allspice. *Pimientos* are sweet red peppers developed in Europe. *Paprika* is a variety of sweet red pepper developed in Hungary and Austria.

In our book we use the expressions "ground red pepper," "red pepper flakes" and "red pepper sauce" to indicate fiery chilies. These products are available in all large supermarkets. Jalepeño chilies—green, yellow or red—are popular Mexican chilies found fresh, canned and dried in many supermarkets. They vary considerably in degree of hotness and are generally labeled "hot" or "mild" on the package.

Avocado Dip

(Guacamole)

Food historians believe that guacamole *was served in Mexico many centuries ago, when the Aztec civilization was in flower. Today the dip is featured on restaurant menus from Acapulco to Jerusalem—and modern recipes are much like the old Aztec ones.*

1½ cups dip

2	very ripe medium avocados, mashed
1	small onion, finely chopped
1	green jalepeño chili, finely chopped
1	tablespoon lemon or lime juice
1	teaspoon snipped coriander leaves or ¼ teaspoon ground coriander (optional)
½	teaspoon salt
1	medium tomato, chopped
	Tortilla chips

Mix avocados, onion, chili, lemon juice, coriander and salt. Stir in tomato. Cover and refrigerate at least 1 hour. Serve with tortilla chips.

Eggplant Dip

(Baba Ghannooj)

Eggplant Dip is served in many Mediterranean countries; along the French Riviera, it is often called poor man's caviar. In the Middle East, a few tablespoons of sesame seed paste or plain yogurt are often blended into the dip for extra flavor.

About 2 cups dip

1	medium eggplant (about 1 pound)
1	small onion, cut into fourths
1	clove garlic
¼	cup lemon juice
1	tablespoon olive or vegetable oil
1½	teaspoons salt
	Raw vegetable dippers

Prick eggplant 3 or 4 times with fork. Cook in 400° oven until tender, about 40 minutes. Cool. Pare eggplant; cut into cubes. Place eggplant, onion, garlic, lemon juice, oil and salt in blender container. Cover and blend on high speed until smooth. Serve with vegetable dippers.

Eggplant Dip

Country Terrine

Country Terrine
(Terrine de Campagne)

The introduction of turkey breast keeps cost down in our version of a traditional French country pâté. The terrine is ideal for important walkabout parties.

About 50 servings

1	frozen turkey breast (6 pounds), thawed
½	cup dry white wine
2	teaspoons monosodium glutamate (optional)
2	teaspoons salt
½	teaspoon ground cloves
½	teaspoon ground nutmeg
½	teaspoon ground allspice
1	pound pork boneless loin or leg
1	pound fully cooked smoked ham
1½	pounds sliced bacon or side pork
½	pound chicken livers
6	eggs
1	tablespoon salt
	Wine Aspic (page 21)

Remove bones and skin from turkey breast, leaving skin intact. Cut ¼ of the turkey breast into thin slices; cut slices into ¼-inch strips. Place in shallow glass or plastic dish. Mix wine, monosodium glutamate, 2 teaspoons salt, the cloves, nutmeg and allspice; pour over turkey strips. Cover and refrigerate 1 hour.

Grind remaining turkey, the pork, ham and 1 pound of the bacon.* Place chicken livers, eggs and 1 tablespoon salt in blender container. Cover and blend on high speed until smooth; stir into ground meats. Drain turkey strips, reserving marinade. Stir marinade into ground meat mixture.

Line 2 loaf pans, 9 x 5 x 3 inches, with aluminum foil, leaving about 3 inches overhanging sides. Line pans with turkey skin if desired. Place remaining bacon slices across bottoms and up sides of pans, letting slices overhang edges of pans. Pack ¼ of the ground meat mixture (about 3½ cups) in each pan. (See diagram.) Place half the turkey strips on mixture in each pan. Cover each with half the remaining ground meat mixture; fold bacon over top. (See diagram.) Place loaf pans in large shallow pan; pour very hot water (1 to 2 inches) into pan. Cook uncovered in 425° oven 2 hours.

Remove pans from hot water; fold foil over top. Place weights on terrine. (See diagram.) Press down firmly 2 minutes. Leave weights on pans; refrigerate loaves in pans. (Do not remove weights until terrine is completely cool.) Prepare Wine Aspic.

Remove terrine from pans by grasping ends of aluminum foil; remove foil. Place terrine on platter; cut into thin slices. Cut slices into halves if desired. Cut aspic into tiny squares; place around terrine.

* Follow directions in food processor manual for chopping raw meats, or use coarse blade of hand grinder.

Wine Aspic

1   envelope unflavored gelatin
2   tablespoons cold water
2   teaspoons instant beef bouillon
1   cup dry white or red wine
1   cup water

Sprinkle gelatin over 2 tablespoons cold water in saucepan; stir in bouillon and wine. Cook over medium heat, stirring constantly, until gelatin is dissolved. Remove from heat. Stir in 1 cup water. Place pan with wine mixture in bowl of ice and water; stir until mixture begins to thicken, 5 to 10 minutes. Pour into jelly roll pan, 15½ x 10½ x 1 inch. Cover and refrigerate until set.

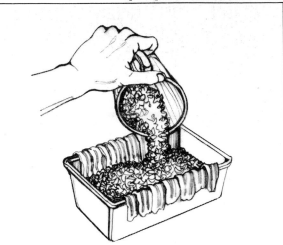

Pack a quarter of the ground-meat mixture in each pan.

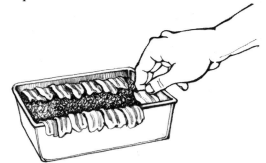

Fold bacon over turkey strips and ground-meat mixture in pans.

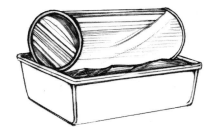

An unopened 46-ounce juice can makes a good weight.

Storage of Spices and Herbs

Did You Know?

Spices and herbs are perishable, so store them in a cool, dark place, as heat will destroy the flavors. Be sure to keep all containers tightly closed to seal in the flavors. Expect whole and leaf spices to keep fresh and flavorful longer than ground ones.

Date all new containers with a waxed pencil or felt-tipped pen. Then check each container for freshness and flavor at least once a year. Test by rubbing a bit of spice or herb between your palms, and if there is no aroma, it's time to replace your supply.

African Red Dip

(Ata Sauce)

From West Africa—a fiery red pepper dip used in many ways. When served with shrimp, as suggested, African Red Dip adds a new dimension to one of America's favorite appetizers—the shrimp cocktail.

1 cup dip

Mix 1 cup chili sauce and 2 tablespoons Red Pepper Paste (below). Serve with 1 dozen chilled cooked shrimp.

Red Pepper Paste

¼   cup dry red wine
1   teaspoon ground red pepper
¾   teaspoon salt
¼   teaspoon ground ginger
⅛   teaspoon ground cardamom
⅛   teaspoon ground coriander
⅛   teaspoon ground nutmeg
⅛   teaspoon ground cloves
⅛   teaspoon ground cinnamon
⅛   teaspoon black pepper
⅛   of a medium onion
1   small clove garlic
¼   cup paprika

Place all ingredients except paprika in blender container. Cover and blend on high speed until smooth, scraping sides of blender frequently.

Heat paprika in 1-quart saucepan 1 minute. Add spice mixture gradually, stirring until smooth. Heat, stirring occasionally, until hot, about 3 minutes. Cool.

Pink Dip

Mix ⅔ cup mayonnaise or salad dressing, 2 tablespoons Red Pepper Paste and 1 tablespoon lemon juice. Serve with celery sticks.

African Red Dip

Bean-and-Sesame Seed Spread

(Hummus)

This is the most famous of all Middle Eastern appetizers. There are many variations of hummus, *which may be served as a dip, a spread, and even in lettuce cups as a salad.*

2 cups spread

1   can (15 ounces) garbanzo beans (chickpeas), drained (reserve liquid)
½   cup sesame seed
1   clove garlic, cut into halves
3   tablespoons lemon juice
1   teaspoon salt
    Snipped parsley
    Pita bread, crackers or raw vegetable sticks

Place reserved bean liquid, the sesame seed and garlic in blender container. Cover and blend on high speed until mixed. Add beans, lemon juice and salt; cover and blend on high speed, scraping sides of blender if necessary, until of uniform consistency. Garnish with parsley. Serve as spread or dip with wedges of pita bread.

Cauliflower Soup
(Blomkaalssuppe)

Popular throughout Scandinavia, Cauliflower Soup can be served hot or cold. The Danes often accent the soup with a few teaspoons of madeira, a Portuguese wine similar to sherry.

8 servings (¾ cup each)

2   cups water
1   medium head cauliflower (1 to 1½ pounds), separated into flowerets
1   medium onion, sliced
2   tablespoons margarine or butter
2   tablespoons flour
1   cup water
1   tablespoon instant chicken bouillon
½   teaspoon celery salt
¼   teaspoon salt
⅛   teaspoon pepper
1   cup half-and-half
    Ground nutmeg

Heat 2 cups water to boiling in 3-quart saucepan; add cauliflower and onion. Heat to boiling; reduce heat. Cover and simmer until tender, about 10 minutes; do not drain. Pour cauliflower and onion with water into blender container. Cover and blend on high speed until smooth.

Heat margarine in 3-quart saucepan until melted; stir in flour. Cook, stirring constantly, until mixture is smooth and bubbly; remove from heat. Stir in 1 cup water. Heat to boiling, stirring constantly; boil and stir 1 minute. Stir in cauliflower mixture, bouillon, celery salt, salt and pepper; heat just to boiling. Stir in half-and-half; heat just until hot. Sprinkle each serving with nutmeg.

Cream of Mushroom Soup
(Potage Crème de Champignons)

Fresh mushrooms are the tasty key to success with this soup from France. To prepare the mushrooms, just rinse under cold water and pat dry—never soak them.

6 servings (¾ cup each)

8   ounces mushrooms
4   tablespoons margarine or butter
1   medium onion, chopped
¼   cup all-purpose flour
1   teaspoon salt
¼   teaspoon white pepper
1   can (10¾ ounces) condensed chicken broth
1   soup can water
1   cup half-and-half
    Snipped parsley

Slice enough mushrooms to measure 1 cup; chop remaining mushrooms. Cook and stir sliced mushrooms in 2 tablespoons of the margarine in 3-quart saucepan over low heat until golden brown. Remove mushrooms with slotted spoon.

Cook and stir chopped mushrooms and onion in remaining margarine until onion is tender; stir in flour, salt and white pepper. Cook over low heat, stirring constantly, about 1 minute; remove from heat. Stir in chicken broth and water. Heat to boiling, stirring constantly; boil and stir 1 minute. Stir in half-and-half and sliced mushrooms. Garnish each serving with parsley.

Wonton Soup
(Hun T'un T'ang)

This is our homemade version of the popular Chinese restaurant soup. In China, a hearty wonton soup is often served as a main dish. To make your own Wonton Soup supper to serve four, simply increase serving sizes, allowing six wontons for each bowl.

8 servings

½	pound ground pork
1	green onion (with top), chopped
2	teaspoons soy sauce
½	teaspoon cornstarch
¼	teaspoon ground ginger
¼	teaspoon salt
24	wonton skins
5	cups water
3	cans (10¾ ounces each) condensed chicken broth
3	soup cans water
1	tablespoon soy sauce
1	cup spinach, torn into small pieces, or 1 cup watercress

Cook and stir pork and green onion until pork is brown; drain. Mix pork, green onion, 2 teaspoons soy sauce, the cornstarch, ginger and salt. Place 1 teaspoon filling on center of each wonton skin. Moisten edges with water. Fold each skin in half to form triangle; press edges to seal. Pull bottom corners of triangle down and overlap slightly. Moisten one corner with water; pinch to seal. (Wontons can be covered and refrigerated no longer than 24 hours.)

Heat 5 cups water to boiling in Dutch oven; add wontons. Heat to boiling; reduce heat. Simmer uncovered 2 minutes. (Wontons will break apart if overcooked.) Drain. Heat chicken broth, 3 cans water and 1 tablespoon soy sauce to boiling in 3-quart saucepan; add spinach. Heat just to boiling. Place 3 wontons and 1 cup hot broth in each soup bowl.

Clear Japanese Soup

Clear Japanese Soup
(Suimono)

The fresh vegetables you select and carefully prepare will create the "eye appeal" so essential to the success of many Japanese dishes. If you use lemon peel as a garnish, pare only the "zest" or yellow part of the peel.

4 servings (¾ cup each)

Heat 3 cups water, 1 tablespoon instant chicken bouillon and 1 teaspoon soy sauce to boiling, stirring occasionally. Serve in small bowls; top with 1 to 3 Garnishes (below).

Garnishes: Thinly sliced mushrooms, green onion strips, celery leaves, thinly sliced lemon or lime, thinly sliced carrot, strips of lemon peel.

Avocado Broth

This easy soup from East Africa can be prepared in a trice. If slicing avocados in advance, sprinkle lightly with lemon juice to prevent discoloration.

10 servings (½ cup each)

2   cans (10½ ounces each) condensed beef broth
2   soup cans water
3   to 4 drops red pepper sauce
2   tablespoons lemon juice
1   large ripe avocado, thinly sliced

Heat beef broth, water, red pepper sauce and lemon juice just to boiling. Add avocado.

Watercress Soup
(Pi Chi T'ang)

A light, ginger-flavored soup from China. Fresh watercress and a garnish of green onions add the distinctive color and texture.

6 servings (about 1 cup each)

1   can (46 ounces) chicken broth
3   thin slices peeled fresh or canned ginger root
1   teaspoon monosodium glutamate (optional)
    Dash of salt
1½ to 2 cups snipped watercress
2   green onions (with tops), thinly sliced

Heat chicken broth, ginger root, monosodium glutamate and salt to boiling in 2-quart saucepan. Cook uncovered over high heat 5 minutes. Remove ginger root from broth; stir in watercress. Cook uncovered over medium heat 15 minutes. Garnish each serving with green onions.

French Onion Soup

Slow simmering of onions and an irresistible topping of melted Swiss and Parmesan cheese bring a rich homemade flavor to the much-admired French Onion Soup. Our recipe makes an ideal first course for an intimate dinner for four. Individual ovenproof soup bowls or casseroles make service easy.

4 servings

4   medium onions, sliced
2   tablespoons margarine or butter
2   cans (10½ ounces each) condensed beef broth
1½ cups water
1   bay leaf
⅛   teaspoon pepper
⅛   teaspoon dried thyme leaves
4   slices French bread, ¾ to 1 inch thick
1   cup shredded Swiss cheese (about 4 ounces)
¼   cup grated Parmesan cheese

Cover and cook onion in margarine in 3-quart saucepan over low heat, stirring occasionally, until tender, 20 to 30 minutes. Add beef broth, water, bay leaf, pepper and thyme. Heat to boiling; reduce heat. Cover and simmer 15 minutes.

Set oven control to broil and/or 550°. Place bread slices on cookie sheet. Broil with tops about 5 inches from heat until golden brown, about 1 minute. Turn; broil until golden brown. Place bread in 4 ovenproof bowls or individual casseroles. Add broth; top with Swiss cheese. Sprinkle with Parmesan cheese.

Place bowls on cookie sheet. Broil with cheese about 5 inches from heat just until cheese is melted and golden brown, 1 to 2 minutes. Serve with additional French bread or rolls if desired.

Clockwise from top: Finnish Summer Vegetable Soup (page 27), French Onion Soup (page 25) and Cream of Lettuce Soup (page 27).

Finnish Summer Vegetable Soup

(Kesäkeitto)

Crisp fresh vegetables add color and delicious flavor to kesäkeitto—*which requires less than twenty minutes cooking time! Served in larger portions with Finnish Rye Bread (page 267) and cheese, it makes a superlative soup supper.*

10 servings (¾ cup each)

2	cups water
2	small carrots, sliced
1	medium potato, cubed
¾	cup fresh or frozen green peas
1	cup cut fresh or frozen green beans
¼	small cauliflower, separated into flowerets
2	ounces spinach, cut up (about 2 cups)
2	cups milk
2	tablespoons flour
¼	cup whipping cream
1½	teaspoons salt
⅛	teaspoon pepper
	Snipped dillweed or parsley (optional)

Heat water, carrots, potato, peas, beans and cauliflower to boiling in 3-quart saucepan; reduce heat. Cover and simmer until vegetables are almost tender, 10 to 15 minutes.

Add spinach; cook uncovered about 1 minute. Mix ¼ cup of the milk and the flour; stir gradually into vegetable mixture. Boil and stir 1 minute. Stir in remaining milk, the whipping cream, salt and pepper. Heat just until hot. Garnish each serving with dill.

Cream of Lettuce Soup

(Potage Crème de Laitue)

This delicate French soup is traditionally served in the spring or early summer, when lettuce is in abundant supply in kitchen gardens and markets.

6 servings (about ¾ cup each)

1	small onion, chopped
¼	cup margarine or butter
2	large heads Boston lettuce or 2 small bunches romaine, finely shredded (about 7 cups)
¼	cup all-purpose flour
3	cups water
1	tablespoon instant chicken bouillon
1	cup half-and-half
½	teaspoon salt
⅛	teaspoon pepper
	Mint leaves or parsley

Cook and stir onion in margarine in 3-quart saucepan over low heat until tender. Reserve 1 cup lettuce; stir remaining lettuce into onion. Cover and cook over low heat until lettuce wilts, about 5 minutes. Stir in flour; cook and stir 1 minute. Add water and bouillon. Heat to boiling, stirring constantly. Boil and stir 1 minute.

Pour mixture into blender container. Cover and blend on high speed until smooth, about 30 seconds; pour into saucepan. Stir in reserved lettuce, the half-and-half, salt and pepper. Heat just to boiling. Garnish with mint.

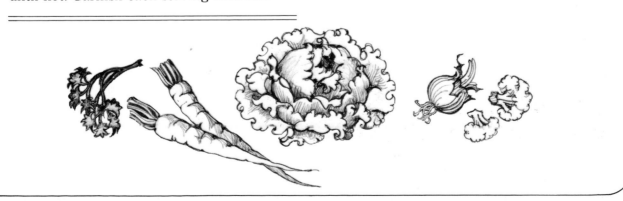

Tortilla Soup
(Sopa de Tortilla)

Corn tortillas—available fresh, frozen or canned in most supermarkets—provide this soup with both its characteristic flavor and its texture. Tortilla Soup is a special favorite in central Mexico.

8 servings (¾ cup each)

6   six-inch corn tortillas
¼   cup vegetable oil
¼   cup water
1   medium tomato, cut into fourths
1   small onion, cut into fourths
1   clove garlic
2   cans (10¾ ounces each) condensed chicken broth
1   soup can water
¼   teaspoon ground coriander
¼   teaspoon salt
⅛   teaspoon pepper
1   sprig mint (optional)
      Shredded Monterey Jack or Cheddar cheese

Cut tortillas into ¼-inch strips. Heat oil in 10-inch skillet until hot. Fry one fourth of the tortilla strips at a time over medium heat, stirring occasionally, until crisp and brown, about 3 minutes. Drain on paper towels.

Place ¼ cup water, the tomato, onion and garlic in blender container. Cover and blend on high speed until smooth. Heat tomato mixture, chicken broth, 1 can water, the coriander, salt, pepper and mint sprig to boiling in 3-quart saucepan. Cook uncovered 3 minutes. Sprinkle each serving with cheese and tortilla strips.

Shredded-Cabbage Soup
(S'chee)

There are many versions of this country-style soup from the Soviet Union—but cabbage is always the identifying ingredient.

12 servings (about ¾ cup each)

2   medium onions, thinly sliced
3   tablespoons bacon fat, margarine or butter
2   cans (10½ ounces each) condensed beef broth
2   soup cans water
1   small head green cabbage, coarsely shredded (5 cups)
2   carrots, sliced
2   medium potatoes, cubed
1   stalk celery (with leaves), sliced
2   tomatoes, cut up
1   teaspoon salt
      Freshly ground pepper
      Dairy sour cream
      Dillweed or parsley

Cook and stir onions in bacon fat in Dutch oven until tender. Add beef broth, water, cabbage, carrots, potatoes and celery. Heat to boiling; reduce heat. Cover and simmer until vegetables are tender, about 20 minutes. Stir in tomatoes, salt and pepper. Simmer uncovered about 10 minutes. Top each serving with sour cream; garnish with dill.

Dairy Sour Cream
Did You Know?

Dairy sour cream should be stored in the original carton in the coldest part of the refrigerator. When sour cream is used in cooking, as for Beef Stroganov (page 128), it should be added just before serving and heated carefully. Overcooking causes curdling, which will affect the appearance but not the taste. Although sour cream does not freeze well, many foods that are prepared with it can be frozen with excellent results.

Egg-Drop Soup
(Tan Hua T'ang)

One of the easiest of all Chinese dishes—it can be prepared in minutes and is a fine light first-course soup for any meal.

6 servings (about ¾ cup each)

5	cups water
1	tablespoon plus 2 teaspoons instant chicken bouillon
½	teaspoon salt
½	teaspoon monosodium glutamate (optional)
3	tablespoons cold water
1	tablespoon plus 1½ teaspoons cornstarch
1	egg, slightly beaten
2	scallions or green onions (with tops), diagonally sliced

Heat 5 cups water, the bouillon, salt and monosodium glutamate to boiling in 2-quart saucepan. Mix 3 tablespoons water and the cornstarch; stir gradually into broth. Boil and stir 1 minute. Slowly pour egg into broth, stirring constantly with fork, to form shreds of egg. Remove from heat; stir slowly once or twice. Garnish each serving with scallions.

Egg-and-Lemon Soup
(Soupa Avgolemeno)

The Greeks claim soupa avgolemeno *as their very own—but this fragrant broth is prized in many areas of North Africa and the Middle East, from Casablanca to Beirut. The Arabic name for Egg-and-Lemon Soup is* bied bi lamoun.

6 servings (about 1 cup each)

1	can (46 ounces) chicken broth
⅓	cup uncooked regular rice
¼	teaspoon salt
2	eggs, beaten
3	tablespoons lemon juice
2	tablespoons snipped parsley, chives or mint

Heat chicken broth, rice and salt to boiling in 3-quart saucepan, stirring once or twice; reduce heat. Cover and simmer until rice is tender, about 14 minutes.

Mix eggs and lemon juice. Stir ¼ cup of the hot broth into egg mixture; stir into broth mixture in saucepan. Cook and stir over low heat until slightly thickened, 2 to 3 minutes. (Do not boil or eggs will curdle.) Garnish each serving with parsley.

Food Safety Tips
Did You Know?

1. When you shop for groceries, plan to pick up perishable foods last. Refrigerate or freeze them as soon as possible after purchase.
2. Remember that the most perishable foods are those containing eggs, milk, seafood, poultry and meat (such as creamed foods, sauces, seafood salad and custards).
3. Use fresh meat within 3 days, ground meat and variety meats (such as tongue and liver) within 24 hours. Use fresh fish and poultry within 2 days. Freeze for longer storage. Keep frozen food at 0°F.
4. Eggs, fish and meat should always be cooked rather than eaten in a raw state.
5. Foods that require marinating should be covered and marinated in the refrigerator rather than at room temperature.
6. A hard plastic cutting board is safer than a wooden chopping board for cutting up raw meat and poultry, as it is less porous and easier to clean. Surfaces used for cutting up raw meat or poultry should be thoroughly cleaned before using for cutting other food. To sanitize, wash surface with a mixture of 2 teaspoons chlorine bleach and 1 teaspoon vinegar to a gallon of water.

Gazpacho

Gazpacho is made in many ways, but always includes tomatoes and green peppers—both native to the Western Hemisphere. Some food historians believe the soup originated in Latin America (it is popular in Mexico today), but Gazpacho truly rose to fame in Spain, where each city takes pride in its own version of the dish.

6 servings (about ½ cup each)

4   slices bread, torn into pieces
4   large ripe tomatoes, chopped
2   medium cucumbers, chopped
1   medium green pepper, chopped
1   medium onion, chopped
1   cup water
¼   cup olive or vegetable oil
⅓   cup red wine vinegar
2   cloves garlic, finely chopped
2   teaspoons salt
1   teaspoon ground cumin
⅛   teaspoon freshly ground pepper

Mix bread, ¾ of the tomatoes, ½ of the cucumber, ¼ of the green pepper, ½ of the onion, the water and oil in large bowl. Cover and refrigerate 1 hour.

Place half the mixture in blender container. Cover and blend on high speed 8 seconds. Repeat with remaining mixture. Stir in vinegar, garlic, salt, cumin and pepper. Cover and refrigerate at least 2 hours.

Place remaining chopped vegetables in small bowls. Cover and refrigerate; serve as accompaniments.

Cold Yogurt-Cucumber Soup

(Tarator)

This light, no-cook soup from the Middle East is a treat for both cook and guests in the summer when the weather is warm and cucumbers are crisp and young. Garnish the soup with sprigs of fresh mint when available.

7 servings (about ½ cup each)

2   medium cucumbers
1½   cups unflavored yogurt
½   teaspoon salt
¼   teaspoon dried mint flakes
⅛   teaspoon white pepper

Cut 7 thin slices from cucumber; reserve. Cut remaining cucumber into ¾-inch chunks. Place half the cucumber chunks and ¼ cup of the yogurt in blender container. Cover and blend on high speed until smooth.

Add remaining cucumber, the salt, mint and white pepper. Cover and blend until smooth. Add remaining yogurt; cover and blend on low speed until smooth. Cover and refrigerate at least 1 hour. Garnish with reserved cucumber slices.

Clockwise from center bottom: Mediterranean Fish Soup (page 43), Fish with Green Grapes (page 35), Glazed Salmon Steaks with Green Mayonnaise (page 56).

Fish and Seafood

Today modern distribution methods have made both fresh-water fish and seafood available all year round, in all areas of the country. Live lobster and sea-breeze-fresh oysters and shrimp can be purchased at specialty markets thousands of miles from the sea, and of course frozen and canned fish are available everywhere.

In this chapter you'll find dozens of ways to bring an exciting international flair to fish and seafood dishes. There are robust fish soups and stews from France, Africa, Latin America . . . chilled seafood dishes from Scandinavia, the Caribbean, Japan, Russia, France . . . do-ahead party dishes that can be prepared a day in advance (ideal for carefree entertaining).

We have included quick, stir-fry recipes from the Orient . . . subtly seasoned Middle Eastern favorites . . . off-the-shelf specials (like Linguini with White Clam Sauce and Indonesian Fried Rice). Make them in minutes with ingredients easily stored "for emergencies" on the kitchen or refrigerator shelf—perfect for spur-of-the-moment entertaining!

There are easy-on-the-budget recipes for family and friends, and dramatic party dishes to delight distinguished guests—Seafood Crêpes, our prize Paella, graceful Fish with Green Grapes!

Deep-fried seafood is much admired throughout the world, and can be done in many ways. Try Japan's famed Tempura, Jamaican Codfish Fritters, China's Sweet-and-Sour Fish, and that British all-time favorite, Fish and Chips!

To help you realize full value from this chapter, we have included for your convenience special tips on how to select, care for and store fresh and frozen fish, and illustrated instructions for filleting fish.

Aegean Baked Fish
(Psari Plaki)

Plaki, *a method of cooking using a variety of vegetables, seafood and seasonings, is found in many parts of the Middle East. It is especially prized in the countries surrounding the Aegean Sea—Greece and Turkey. In Greece, lemon and oregano are often added as flavor enhancers; in Turkey,* plaki *is frequently served cold.*

10 servings

2	tablespoons olive or vegetable oil
½	cup dry bread crumbs
2	pounds fish fillets
1	teaspoon salt
1	teaspoon dried oregano leaves
¼	cup lemon juice
1	can (8 ounces) tomato sauce
½	cup snipped parsley
2	cloves garlic, finely chopped
2	tablespoons olive or vegetable oil
½	teaspoon salt
¼	teaspoon pepper
¼	cup dry bread crumbs
	Lemon slices
	Ripe olives

Pour 2 tablespoons oil evenly into oblong baking dish, 13½ x 9 x 2 inches. Sprinkle ½ cup bread crumbs evenly over oil. Pat fish dry with paper towels. Arrange fish in single layer in baking dish; sprinkle with 1 teaspoon salt and the oregano. Pour lemon juice over fish.

Mix tomato sauce, parsley, garlic, 2 tablespoons oil, ½ teaspoon salt and the pepper; spoon over fish. Sprinkle with ¼ cup bread crumbs. Cook uncovered in 350° oven until fish flakes easily with fork, 30 to 40 minutes. Serve on heated platter. Garnish with lemon slices and olives.

Baked Fish, Spanish Style

From sunny Spain, a colorful, low-calorie fish dish garnished with a traditional Spanish medley of green peppers, tomatoes, onions and subtle seasonings.

6 servings

1½	pounds fish steaks or fillets
1½	teaspoons salt
¼	teaspoon paprika
¼	teaspoon pepper
1	green pepper, cut into rings
1	tomato, sliced
1	small onion, sliced
2	tablespoons lemon juice
2	tablespoons olive or vegetable oil
1	clove garlic, finely chopped
	Lemon wedges

If fish pieces are large, cut into serving pieces. Arrange fish in ungreased square baking dish, 8 x 8 x 2 inches; sprinkle with salt, paprika and pepper. Top with green pepper rings and tomato and onion slices. Mix lemon juice, oil and garlic; pour over fish. Cover and cook in 375° oven 15 minutes. Uncover and cook until fish flakes easily with fork, 10 to 15 minutes. Garnish with lemon wedges.

Fish with Green Grapes
(Poisson Véronique)

Seedless green grapes—a "must" for any recipe including the term Véronique—*bring to this dish an elegance reminiscent of Versailles.*

6 to 8 servings

2	pounds fish fillets
1½	teaspoons salt
¼	teaspoon pepper
¾	cup dry white wine
1	cup water
2	tablespoons finely chopped shallots or green onion
1	tablespoon lemon juice
8	ounces (about 1⅓ cups) seedless green grapes*
2	tablespoons margarine or butter
2	tablespoons flour
½	cup whipping cream
2	tablespoons margarine or butter

Sprinkle fish with salt and pepper; fold in half. Place fish in 10-inch skillet; add wine, water, shallots and lemon juice. Heat to boiling; reduce heat. Cover and simmer until fish flakes easily with fork, 4 to 5 minutes. Remove with slotted spatula to heatproof platter; keep warm. Add grapes to liquid in skillet. Heat to boiling; reduce heat. Simmer uncovered 3 minutes. Remove grapes with slotted spoon.

Heat liquid in skillet to boiling; boil until reduced to 1 cup. Pour liquid into measuring cup; reserve. Heat 2 tablespoons margarine in skillet until melted; stir in flour. Cook and stir 1 minute; remove from heat. Stir in reserved liquid and the whipping cream. Heat to boiling, stirring constantly.

Boil and stir 1 minute. Add 2 tablespoons margarine; stir until melted. Drain excess liquid from fish; spoon sauce over fish. Set oven control to broil and/or 550°. Broil fish 4 inches from heat just until sauce is glazed, about 3 minutes. Garnish with grapes.

* 1 can (16 ounces) seedless green grapes, drained (reserve liquid), can be substituted for the fresh grapes. Substitute the reserved liquid for 1 cup water. Increase wine to 1 cup.

Fish with Sour Cream
(Betyár Fogas)

In Hungary as in Austria, small "boiling" potatoes served in their bright red skins often accompany betyár fogas. *For dessert, try Apple Strudel (page 316).*

4 to 6 servings

1	pound fish fillets
4	ounces mushrooms, sliced
1	small onion, chopped
1	tablespoon margarine or butter
½	teaspoon salt
⅛	teaspoon pepper
½	cup dairy sour cream
3	tablespoons grated Parmesan cheese
2	tablespoons dry bread crumbs
	Paprika
	Snipped parsley

If fish fillets are large, cut into serving pieces. Pat fish dry with paper towels; arrange in ungreased oblong baking dish, 12 x 7½ x 2 inches. Cook and stir mushrooms and onion in margarine until mushrooms are golden, about 3 minutes. Spoon mushroom mixture over fish; sprinkle with salt and pepper.

Mix sour cream and cheese; spread over mushroom mixture. Sprinkle with bread crumbs. Cook uncovered in 350° oven until fish flakes easily with fork, 25 to 30 minutes. Sprinkle with paprika and parsley.

Fish and Chips

Fish and Chips

Serve this beloved British dish "pub style"—accompanied by mugs of ale.

4 servings

	Vegetable oil
4	or 5 potatoes, cut lengthwise into ½-inch strips
1	pound fish fillets, cut into 2 x 1½-inch pieces
⅔	cup all-purpose flour
½	teaspoon salt
½	teaspoon baking soda
1	tablespoon vinegar
⅔	cup water
	Malt or cider vinegar
	Salt

Heat oil (2 to 3 inches) in deep fat fryer to 375°. Fill basket ¼ full with potatoes; slowly lower into hot oil. (If oil bubbles excessively, raise and lower basket several times.) Use long-handled fork to keep potatoes separated. Fry potatoes until golden, 5 to 7 minutes. Drain potatoes; place in single layer on cookie sheet. Keep warm; repeat.

Pat fish dry with paper towels. Mix flour and ½ teaspoon salt. Mix baking soda and 1 tablespoon vinegar. Stir vinegar mixture and water into flour mixture; beat until smooth. Dip fish into batter; allow excess batter to drip into bowl. Fry 4 or 5 pieces at a time (see Note) until brown, turning once, about 3 minutes. Drain on paper towels.

Set oven control to broil and/or 550°. Broil potatoes 6 inches from heat until crisp, 2 to 3 minutes. Sprinkle with vinegar and salt.

Note: Do not use basket for fish.

Fish Stew with Vegetables

Fish stews that include okra and cabbage are popular throughout the African continent, from Cairo to Johannesburg. Okra is thought to have been introduced to the United States by African slaves in the eighteenth century—it is as essential to the gumbos of Louisiana as it is to the fish stews of Africa.

8 servings

1   can (15 ounces) tomato sauce
4   cups water
1   cup uncooked regular rice
3   carrots, thinly sliced
1   onion, thinly sliced
1   tablespoon salt
½   teaspoon ground red pepper
1   package (10 ounces) frozen okra pods
1   package (10 ounces) frozen green beans
3   cups sliced cabbage
1½ pounds catfish, perch, bass or trout fillets, cut into serving pieces

Heat tomato sauce, water, rice, carrots, onion, salt and red pepper in Dutch oven to boiling; reduce heat. Cover and cook 10 minutes.

Rinse okra and green beans under running cold water to separate; drain. Cut okra lengthwise into halves. Add okra, green beans, cabbage and fish to Dutch oven. Heat to boiling; reduce heat. Cover and cook until fish flakes easily with fork and vegetables are tender, 10 to 12 minutes.

Fish and Collard Greens

This fish stew comes from the Congo region of central Africa, where it is often served with yams or sweet potatoes. Use fresh collard greens when in season.

4 servings

2   medium onions, sliced
1   green pepper, sliced
¼   cup margarine or butter
1   package (10 ounces) frozen collard greens
2   tablespoons water
1   pound fish fillets
1½ teaspoons salt
½   teaspoon paprika
¼   teaspoon pepper

Cook and stir onions and green pepper in margarine in 3-quart saucepan until onion is tender, about 3 minutes. Add collard greens and water. Heat to boiling; separate greens with fork. Reduce heat. Cover and simmer 5 minutes.

Cut fish into strips, 4 x ¾ inches each; add to vegetables. Sprinkle with salt, paprika and pepper. Heat to boiling; reduce heat. Cover and simmer until fish flakes easily with fork, about 5 minutes. Garnish with lemon wedges if desired.

Collards

Did You Know?

This mild-flavored green so popular in the South is one of the oldest members of the cabbage family, a close relative of kale. Look for a healthy green color and tender, young, unblemished leaves. Collards are best cooked just until done with very little water.

Fish Fillets with Spinach (Filets de Poisson Florentine)

In French cooking, florentine *indicates the use of spinach—but in Italy* alla fiorentina *simply means a recipe that is a specialty of Florence, and may or may not include spinach. Crusty Potato Cake (page 242) makes a splendid side dish to serve with* filets de poisson florentine.

4 servings

2	tablespoons margarine or butter
2	tablespoons flour
1	teaspoon instant chicken bouillon
	Dash of ground nutmeg
	Dash of ground red pepper
	Dash of white pepper
1	cup milk
⅔	cup shredded Swiss or Cheddar cheese
1	package (10 ounces) frozen chopped spinach, thawed and well drained
1	tablespoon lemon juice
1	pound fish fillets, cut into serving pieces
½	teaspoon salt
2	tablespoons grated Parmesan cheese
	Paprika

Heat margarine over low heat until melted; stir in flour, bouillon, nutmeg, red pepper and white pepper. Cook over low heat, stirring constantly, until mixture is smooth and bubbly; remove from heat. Stir in milk. Heat to boiling, stirring constantly. Boil and stir 1 minute. Add Swiss cheese; cook, stirring constantly, just until cheese is melted.

Place spinach in ungreased oblong baking dish, 12 x 7½ x 2 inches, or square baking dish, 8 x 8 x 2 inches; sprinkle with lemon juice. Arrange fish on spinach; sprinkle with salt. Spread sauce over fish and spinach. Cook uncovered in 350° oven until fish flakes easily with fork, 20 to 25 minutes. Sprinkle with Parmesan cheese and paprika.

Fish in Cream Sauce with Mushrooms (Poisson Bonne Femme)

French chefs use the expression bonne femme *(literally "good woman") to denote home cooking or "women's cooking" as opposed to restaurant cooking. But there is nothing "homely" about our version of the French classic* sole bonne femme. *French-style green beans go well with this dish.*

8 servings

8	ounces mushrooms, sliced
2	green onions, finely chopped
2	tablespoons margarine or butter
2	pounds fish fillets, cut into serving pieces
¾	cup dry white wine
1	tablespoon lemon juice
2	tablespoons margarine or butter
2	tablespoons flour
½	cup whipping cream
1	teaspoon salt
¼	teaspoon white pepper
¼	cup shredded Swiss cheese

Cook and stir mushrooms and green onions in 2 tablespoons margarine in 10-inch skillet until mushrooms are tender, about 3 minutes; remove from skillet. Place fish in skillet; add wine, lemon juice and just enough water to cover fish. Heat to boiling; reduce heat. Cover and simmer until fish flakes easily with fork, 4 to 5 minutes. Remove fish with slotted spoon to platter; keep warm.

Heat liquid in skillet to boiling; boil until reduced to 1 cup, 7 to 8 minutes. Pour liquid into measuring cup; reserve. Heat 2 tablespoons margarine in skillet until melted; stir in flour. Cook and stir 1 minute; remove from heat. Stir in reserved liquid and the whipping cream. Heat to boiling, stirring constantly. Boil and stir 1 minute. Stir in mushrooms, green onions, salt and white pepper.

Drain excess liquid from fish. Spoon sauce over fish; sprinkle with cheese. Set oven control to broil and/or 550°. Broil fish 2 to 3 inches from heat just until cheese is melted, 2 to 3 minutes.

How to Fillet a Fish

To fillet a fish, turn fish on its side and make a cut back of the gills straight down to the backbone.

Turn the knife blade flat and cut the flesh along the backbone almost to the tail. (Except for the tail portion, the top fillet will be separated from the rest of the fish with the narrow rib cage still attached.) Without removing knife, lift the still-attached fillet away from backbone and entrails and flip it to the right so the flesh side is on top and the skin side on bottom.

Cut the fillet away from the skin in one piece by sliding the knife between the skin and the flesh.

Cut the rib cage from the fillet. Turn the fish over and repeat the above steps. If you like, scoop out the "cheek" of the fish (the little morsel of flesh under the eye) with a knife.

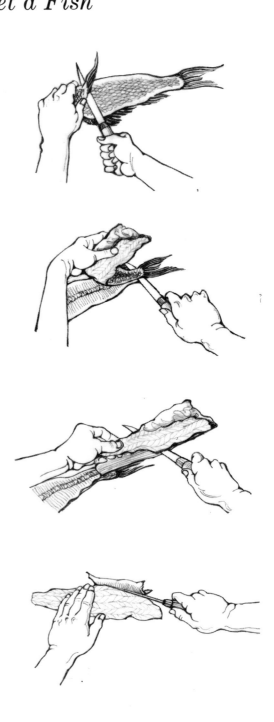

Fried Fish in Pungent Sauce

(Escabeche de Pescado Frito)

The word escabeche *means "pickled" in Spanish. The dish* escabeche *takes many forms. It is found in Spanish-speaking countries throughout Latin America and is often served cold, as an appetizer or a first course.*

8 servings

¼	cup olive or vegetable oil
1½	pounds fish fillets, cut into serving pieces
¾	cup water
2	carrots, thinly sliced
2	small onions, sliced
1	small green pepper, cut into rings
1	clove garlic, finely chopped
1	tablespoon packed brown sugar
½	teaspoon salt
¼	teaspoon ground ginger
⅓	cup vinegar
2	teaspoons cornstarch

Heat oil in skillet until hot. Pat fish dry with paper towels. Cook over medium heat until fish flakes easily with fork, turning carefully, 8 to 10 minutes.

Heat water, carrots, onions, green pepper, garlic, brown sugar, salt and ginger to boiling in 1½-quart saucepan; reduce heat. Cover and simmer 5 minutes. Mix vinegar and cornstarch; stir into vegetables. Heat to boiling, stirring constantly. Boil and stir 1 minute. Pour over fish.

Sweet-and-Sour Fish

(Tien Shuen Yu)

One of America's favorite Chinese dishes. Serve with bowls of Egg-Drop Soup (page 30).

6 servings

2	carrots, cut diagonally into thin slices
½	cup water
1½	pounds fish fillets, cut into 1-inch pieces
½	cup packed brown sugar
⅓	cup vinegar
2	tablespoons cornstarch
2	tablespoons soy sauce
1	can (13½ ounces) pineapple chunks
1	green pepper, cut into 1-inch pieces
	Vegetable oil
	Batter (below)

Heat carrots and water to boiling. Cover and cook until crisp-tender, 8 to 10 minutes. Pat fish dry with paper towels. Mix brown sugar, vinegar, cornstarch and soy sauce in 2-quart saucepan. Stir in carrots (with liquid), pineapple (with syrup) and green pepper. Heat to boiling, stirring constantly. Boil and stir 1 minute. Keep warm.

Heat oil (1 to 1½ inches) to 360°. Prepare batter. Dip fish into batter with tongs. Allow excess batter to drip into bowl. Fry 7 or 8 pieces at a time until golden brown, about 1 minute on each side. Drain on paper towels. Arrange on platter; pour sauce over fish.

Batter

¾	cup water
⅔	cup all-purpose flour
1¼	teaspoons salt
½	teaspoon baking powder

Mix all ingredients.

Do-Ahead Tip: Cool fried fish quickly. Freeze no longer than 2 weeks. Heat on ungreased cookie sheet in 400° oven 8 to 10 minutes.

Fish Soup Provençale
(Bourride)

Once considered peasants' fare, bourride *appears today on the menus of many of the finest restaurants that dot the French Riviera.*

6 servings

1½	cups mayonnaise or salad dressing
3	cloves garlic, mashed
½	cup margarine or butter
12	slices French bread
1	clove garlic, cut into halves
1	pound fish fillets, cut into 1-inch pieces
1½	cups dry white wine
6	slices onion
3	slices lemon
5	sprigs parsley
1	bay leaf
1	teaspoon salt
	Paprika

Mix mayonnaise and 3 cloves garlic; cover and refrigerate. Heat ¼ cup of the margarine in 12-inch skillet until melted. Toast 6 of the bread slices in skillet over medium heat until brown on both sides; rub one side of bread with half clove garlic. Remove from skillet; keep warm. Repeat with remaining bread.

Place fish in single layer in skillet. Add wine, onion and lemon slices, parsley, bay leaf, salt and just enough water to cover. Heat to boiling; reduce heat. Simmer uncovered until fish flakes easily with fork, about 6 minutes. Remove fish with slotted spoon; keep warm.

Strain fish broth. Pour 1½ cups of the broth into 2-quart saucepan; gradually beat in mayonnaise mixture. Cook over low heat, stirring constantly, until slightly thickened. Place 2 slices of the French bread upright in each soup bowl; spoon fish between slices. Pour soup over fish; sprinkle with paprika.

Latin American Fish Soup
(Sopa de Pescados)

Chicken broth provides a rich, full-bodied flavor to this Latin American interpretation of the fish soups found throughout the Mediterranean countries.

8 servings

2	medium onions, chopped
2	cloves garlic, crushed
2	tablespoons olive or vegetable oil
1½	pounds fish fillets, cut into 1-inch pieces
2	cans (10¾ ounces each) condensed chicken broth
2	soup cans water
3	tomatoes, coarsely chopped
2	green peppers, chopped
½	teaspoon salt
½	teaspoon dried oregano leaves
½	teaspoon ground red pepper

Cook and stir onions and garlic in oil in Dutch oven until onion is tender; add remaining ingredients. Heat to boiling; reduce heat. Cover and simmer until fish flakes easily with fork, about 5 minutes.

Fish Terms to Know

Whole fish: just as it comes from the water.

Drawn fish: whole but eviscerated.

Dressed or pan dressed: ready to cook.

Steaks: cross-section slices, about ¾ inch thick, from large dressed fish.

Fillets: sides of fish cut lengthwise away from the backbone—almost boneless.

Butterfly fillets: double fillets held together by skin.

Sticks: cuts from frozen blocks of fish fillets, breaded, partly cooked and frozen.

Mediterranean Fish Soup

Each bustling Mediterranean seaport has a traditional seafood soup or stew. Within each city, recipes vary according to the day's catch and family tradition. Often shellfish and even squid and eel are added! Our recipe suggests how to recall the memorable flavors of the Mediterranean with fresh or frozen fish purchased at your neighborhood market.

8 servings

12	slices French bread, cut ¾-inch thick
2	medium onions, chopped
3	cloves garlic, crushed
¼	cup olive or vegetable oil
3	medium tomatoes, chopped
1	bottle (8 ounces) clam juice
6	cups water
2	teaspoons salt
1	teaspoon finely chopped fresh thyme or ½ teaspoon dried thyme leaves
½	teaspoon crushed fennel seed
½	teaspoon ground turmeric
⅛	teaspoon pepper
1	bay leaf
2	pounds assorted white fish (halibut, haddock, pollack, red snapper, whiting, bass, cod, flounder)

Place bread in single layer on cookie sheet. Bake in 325° oven until crisp, about 30 minutes. Cook and stir onions and garlic in oil in Dutch oven over medium heat until onions are tender. Add tomatoes, clam juice, water, salt, thyme, fennel seed, turmeric, pepper and bay leaf. Heat to boiling; reduce heat. Cover and cook 5 minutes.

Cut fish into 1-inch chunks; add to tomato mixture. Heat to boiling; reduce heat. Cover and cook until fish flakes easily with fork, about 5 minutes. Pour soup into tureen. Serve with the French bread.

Stuffed Rolled Fish Fillets
(Huachinango Relleno)

These Latin American fish rolls are appropriately complemented with Sweet Potatoes with Apples (page 243) or Zucchini-Avocado Salad (page 209).

6 to 8 servings

2	pounds fish fillets
2	medium onions, chopped
¼	cup margarine or butter
2	cups soft bread crumbs
½	cup snipped parsley
2	teaspoons salt
½	teaspoon ground nutmeg
2	eggs, slightly beaten
2	tablespoons margarine or butter, melted
1	tablespoon lemon juice
	Paprika
	Snipped parsley

If fish fillets are large, cut into serving pieces. Cook and stir onions in ¼ cup margarine until tender. Stir in bread crumbs, ½ cup parsley, the salt, nutmeg and eggs. Spread mixture evenly over fish fillets. Roll up fish fillets; fasten with wooden picks. Place seam sides down in ungreased oblong baking dish, 10 x 6 x 1½ inches, or square baking dish, 8 x 8 x 2 inches. Mix melted margarine and lemon juice; drizzle over fish. Sprinkle with paprika. Cook uncovered in 350° oven until fish flakes easily with fork, about 25 minutes. Garnish with parsley.

Red Snapper with Tomato Sauce and Olives

Red Snapper with Tomato Sauce and Olives

(Huachinango Veracruzano)

Olives—introduced to Mexico by early Spanish settlers—and native sweet and fiery peppers are the hallmarks of the cooking of Veracruz, Mexico's principal seaport.

8 servings

1	or 2 jalapeño chilies
2	medium onions, chopped
1	clove garlic, chopped
2	tablespoons olive or vegetable oil
1	can (15 ounces) tomato sauce
1	tablespoon lime or lemon juice
1	teaspoon salt
½	teaspoon sugar
⅛	teaspoon ground cinnamon
⅛	teaspoon ground cloves
⅛	teaspoon pepper
¼	cup all-purpose flour
1	teaspoon salt
⅛	teaspoon pepper
2	pounds red snapper fillets,* cut into serving pieces
¼	cup olive or vegetable oil
¼	cup sliced pimiento-stuffed olives
	Parsley

Remove stems, seeds and membranes from chilies; cut chilies lengthwise into thin strips. Cook and stir onions and garlic in 2 tablespoons oil until onion is tender. Add chilies, tomato sauce, lime juice, 1 teaspoon salt, the sugar, cinnamon, cloves and ⅛ teaspoon pepper. Heat to boiling; reduce heat. Simmer uncovered 5 minutes. Keep warm.

Mix flour, 1 teaspoon salt and ⅛ teaspoon pepper; coat fish with flour mixture. Heat ¼ cup oil in skillet until hot. Cook fish over medium heat until golden brown, turning carefully, 4 minutes on each side. Garnish with olives and parsley. Spoon sauce over fish.

* 2 pounds cod, haddock, halibut or yellow pike fillets can be substituted for the red snapper fillets.

Lemon-Baked Cod

(Ovnsstekt Torsk med Sitron)

In Norway this dish is often served with parsleyed potatoes and a crisp cucumber salad.

4 servings

1	pound cod fillets
¼	cup margarine or butter, melted
2	tablespoons lemon juice
¼	cup all-purpose flour
½	teaspoon salt
⅛	teaspoon white pepper
	Paprika

If fish fillets are large, cut into serving pieces. Mix margarine and lemon juice. In another bowl, mix flour, salt and white pepper. Dip fish into margarine mixture; coat fish with flour mixture. Place fish in ungreased square baking dish, 8 x 8 x 2 inches. Pour remaining margarine mixture over fish; sprinkle with paprika. Cook uncovered in 350° oven until fish flakes easily with fork, 25 to 30 minutes. Garnish with parsley sprigs and lemon slices if desired.

Jamaican Codfish Fritters

(Stamp and Go)

Light, spicy codfish fritters—as popular in Jamaica as Fish and Chips (page 36) is in Britain—are known locally as "stamp and go." According to one version, before electricity became commonplace in Jamaican homes, the fritters were purchased at takeout stands, wrapped in brown paper, stamped "paid" and taken home or to the beach for eating. Our recipe is an adaptation of the original, which uses salt cod.

About 36 fritters

8	ounces cod fillets
2	medium onions, chopped
2	tablespoons olive or vegetable oil
	Vegetable oil
1	cup all-purpose flour
¾	cup milk
1	egg
1	teaspoon baking powder
1	teaspoon salt
1	teaspoon vegetable oil
¼	teaspoon ground red pepper

Heat fish and just enough water to cover to boiling; reduce heat. Cover and simmer until fish flakes easily with fork, 5 to 7 minutes; drain. Cool and flake. Cook and stir onions in 2 tablespoons oil until tender.

Heat oil (1 to 1½ inches) to 360°. Beat remaining ingredients with hand beater until smooth. Stir in fish and onions; drop by level tablespoonfuls into hot oil. Fry 5 or 6 at a time until golden brown, turning once, about 4 minutes. Drain on paper towels. Serve with tartar sauce and lemon wedges if desired.

Cod-and-Vegetable Bake (Kalakasvisvuoka)

A favorite family dish from Finland—nice with baked potatoes and coleslaw. Finnish Cranberry Whip (page 300) would provide a delicious traditional Finnish finish.

6 servings

2	pounds cod fillets
3	tablespoons lemon juice
1½	teaspoons salt
⅛	teaspoon pepper
2	carrots, coarsely shredded
1	large stalk celery, finely chopped
1	onion, chopped
5	slices bread (crusts removed), cubed
½	cup margarine or butter, melted
½	teaspoon salt
½	teaspoon ground sage
½	teaspoon ground thyme
3	tablespoons dry bread crumbs
2	tablespoons snipped parsley
½	teaspoon paprika

If fish fillets are large, cut into serving pieces. Arrange fish in ungreased oblong baking dish, 12 x 7½ x 2 inches, or square baking dish, 8 x 8 x 2 inches. Sprinkle with lemon juice, 1½ teaspoons salt and the pepper.

Mix carrots, celery, onion, bread cubes, margarine, ½ teaspoon salt, sage, and thyme. Spread evenly over fish. Mix bread crumbs, parsley and paprika; sprinkle over vegetables. Cover and cook in 350° oven until fish flakes easily with fork, about 35 minutes.

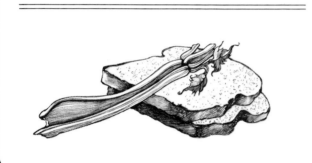

Caribbean Codfish Salad

Native to Dominican Republic, Trinidad and Tobago, Caribbean Codfish Salad can be served hot or cold. In Trinidad it is even served for breakfast!

6 servings

1	pound salt cod fillets
1	avocado
2	tomatoes, coarsely chopped
1	onion, chopped
¼	cup pitted green olives, sliced
¾	cup olive or vegetable oil
⅓	cup lemon or lime juice
	Dash of pepper

Place fish and enough cold water to cover in 1½-quart glass bowl. Cover and refrigerate 12 to 24 hours, changing water 3 or 4 times. Drain. Remove bones and skin if necessary. Cut into 1-inch pieces. Heat fish and just enough water to cover to boiling in 2-quart saucepan; reduce heat. Cover and simmer until fish flakes easily with fork, about 10 minutes. Drain.

Cut avocado into bite-size pieces. Place fish, avocado, tomatoes, onion and olives in salad bowl. Shake oil, lemon juice and pepper in tightly covered jar. Pour over salad; toss.

Salt Cod

Did You Know?

Salt cod is not uniform in its saltiness. The farther from land it is caught, the more salt it needs to preserve it. Before cooking, all salt cod must be soaked in several changes of cold water, but the size of the fish and the amount of salting determine the length of soaking. A small fillet that can be easily bent doesn't need as much as a large piece that is stiff with salt.

Salt Cod in Tomato Sauce

Salt Cod in Tomato Sauce
(Bacalhau com Tomatada)

The Portuguese have many ways of preparing salt cod, or bacalhau *(in Spanish,* bacalao; *in French,* morue*). Salt cod can be found in fish shops and in markets carrying Spanish foods.*

8 servings

1½	pounds salt cod fillets
2	medium onions, sliced
1	tablespoon olive or vegetable oil
2	tomatoes, chopped
1	clove garlic, chopped
⅛	teaspoon pepper
2	hard-cooked eggs, sliced
¼	cup pitted ripe olives, sliced
	Snipped parsley

If fish fillets are large, cut into serving pieces. Place fish in enamel or stainless steel pan or glass bowl. Cover with cold water; refrigerate 12 to 24 hours, changing water 3 or 4 times.

Cook and stir onions in oil until tender. Add tomatoes, garlic and pepper. Cover and simmer 5 minutes. Pour into ungreased oblong baking dish, 12 x 7½ x 2 inches.

Drain fish. Remove bones and skin if necessary; rinse fish in cold water. Arrange fish on tomato mixture. Cover and cook in 350° oven until fish flakes easily with fork, 20 to 30 minutes. Garnish with eggs, olives and snipped parsley.

Smoked Haddock with Rice

(Kedgeree)

There are many versions of kedgeree—a dish the British serve for brunch or a light supper. According to British tradition, the dish originated in India; a hint of curry powder is included in many recipes for kedgeree.

8 servings

4	hard-cooked eggs
2	cups water
1	cup uncooked regular rice
1	teaspoon salt
1	pound smoked haddock or cod
1	large onion, chopped
¼	cup margarine or butter
¼	teaspoon salt
⅛	to ¼ teaspoon ground red pepper
	Snipped parsley

Separate egg yolks from whites. Press yolks through sieve; chop whites. Heat water, rice and 1 teaspoon salt to boiling, stirring once or twice; reduce heat. Cover and simmer 14 minutes. (Do not lift cover or stir.) Remove from heat. Fluff rice lightly with fork; cover and let steam 5 to 10 minutes.

Cover fish with cold water. Heat to boiling; reduce heat. Cover and simmer 10 minutes; drain. Break fish into large flakes with fork, removing any bones and skin. Keep warm.

Cook and stir onion in margarine in 10-inch skillet until tender. Stir in chopped egg white, rice, ¼ teaspoon salt and the red pepper. Stir in flaked fish carefully. Serve on heated platter; sprinkle with egg yolk and parsley.

Smoked Haddock with White Sauce

(Finnan Haddie with White Sauce)

Finnan haddie is virtually the national dish of Scotland, where it is often served for breakfast. The name comes from Findon (a Scottish village famous for curing fish) and from haddock ("haddie" is Scottish slang for haddock). Either smoked haddock or smoked cod can be used in the dish—both are available canned or in packages at delicatessens, fish stores and many supermarkets.

4 servings

1	pound smoked haddock or cod fillets
2	tablespoons margarine or butter
1	small onion, chopped
¼	teaspoon salt
⅛	teaspoon pepper
¾	cup milk
2	teaspoons cornstarch

Cut fish into 1-inch pieces, removing any bones and skin. Heat margarine in skillet until melted; add fish and onion. Sprinkle with salt and pepper. Cook and stir 5 minutes.

Stir milk gradually into cornstarch in 1-quart saucepan; heat to boiling, stirring constantly. Boil and stir 1 minute. Pour over fish. Simmer uncovered until fish flakes easily with fork, 3 to 5 minutes. Serve with boiled or baked potatoes if desired.

Herring Salad

Herring Salad

(Sillsallad)

Easy to make, sillsallad *is cherished throughout northern Europe. In Scandinavia it often
appears on the smorgasbord (it is a traditional
Christmas dish). The Germans often serve* sillsallad *as an appetizer.*

6 to 8 servings

1	jar (22 ounces) herring cutlets in wine sauce, drained
3	medium potatoes, cooked and cubed (2 cups)
1	jar (16 ounces) pickled beets, drained and cubed
2	small dill pickles, chopped
1	apple, cut up
1	small onion, chopped
¼	cup vinegar
2	tablespoons sugar
2	tablespoons water
⅛	teaspoon pepper
	Dilled Sour Cream (below)

Place herring, potatoes, beets, chopped
pickles, apple and onion in glass or plastic
bowl. Mix vinegar, sugar, water and pepper;
pour over herring mixture. Toss lightly.
Cover and refrigerate, stirring once or twice,
at least 2 hours. Serve with Dilled Sour
Cream. Garnish with parsley and wedges of
hard-cooked egg if desired.

Dilled Sour Cream
Mix 1 cup dairy sour cream, 2 tablespoons
milk and ½ teaspoon dried dillweed.

Trout Baked Irish Style

Trout Baked Irish Style

A savory stuffing enhances the flavor of Trout Baked Irish Style; try it with creamed carrots and warm Irish Soda Bread (page 259).

4 servings

4	green onions, sliced
1	green pepper, chopped
¼	cup margarine or butter
1	cup soft bread crumbs
¼	cup snipped parsley
1	teaspoon lemon juice
1	teaspoon salt
¼	teaspoon dried basil leaves
4	drawn whole trout (about 8 ounces each)
	Salt

Cook and stir onions and pepper in margarine until onions are tender; remove from heat. Stir in bread crumbs, parsley, the lemon juice, 1 teaspoon salt and the basil.

Rub cavities of fish with salt; stuff each with about ¼ cup stuffing. Place fish in greased oblong baking dish, 13½ x 9 x 2 inches. Cook uncovered in 350° oven until fish flakes easily with fork, 30 to 35 minutes. Garnish fish with cherry tomatoes and parsley if desired.

Trout Fillets with Almond Sauce

(Filets de Truite Amandine)

At formal dinners, the French often serve this dish as a first course. Our recipe, which uses trout fillets rather than small whole trout, makes a fine main dish served with French Garden Peas (page 233) and Butter-Steamed New Potatoes (page 245).

4 servings

¼   cup all-purpose flour
½   teaspoon salt
⅛   teaspoon pepper
1   pound trout fillets, cut into serving pieces
¼   cup milk
    Vegetable oil
¼   cup margarine or butter
¼   cup slivered almonds
    Lemon wedges
    Snipped parsley

Mix flour, salt and pepper. Dip trout in milk; coat with flour mixture. Heat oil (⅛-inch) in skillet until hot. Cook fish over medium heat until golden brown, turning carefully, about 5 minutes on each side. Remove trout to platter; keep warm.

Drain oil from skillet; add margarine and almonds. Cook over low heat until margarine starts to brown. Spoon over trout; garnish with lemon wedges and sprinkle with parsley.

Trout with Bacon

(Brithyll a Chig Moch)

The Welsh are enthusiastic fishermen, prizing trout caught from the clear rivers of Wales above nearly all other fresh-water fish. Bacon adds the distinctively Welsh flavor to this dish, which is often served with buttered lima or broad beans.

6 servings

12   slices bacon
6   drawn whole trout (about 5 ounces each)
2   tablespoons snipped parsley
1½   teaspoons salt
¼   teaspoon freshly ground pepper
    Snipped parsley

Arrange bacon in single layer in broiler pan. Cook uncovered in 400° oven 10 minutes; drain on paper towels.

Sprinkle inside of fish with 2 tablespoons parsley, the salt and pepper. Arrange fish in single layer on bacon in pan. Cover and cook until fish flakes easily with fork, about 20 minutes. Split fish down center along backbone; remove as many bones as possible. Serve each fish with 2 bacon slices. Garnish with parsley.

How to Select Fresh or Frozen Fish

For whole fresh fish, look for bright, clear eyes that bulge, firm flesh that springs back when you press it, reddish-pink gills, shiny bright-looking scales that are close to the skin, and a fresh (not too strong) odor.

In choosing frozen fish, look for fish that is frozen solid, not discolored, has little or no odor, is tightly wrapped, and has little or no air space between fish and wrapping.

Stuffed Pike

Stuffed Pike
(Gefüllter Hecht)

In Austria's golden age, when all Vienna danced to the music of Strauss, pike was a delicacy only the rich could afford and was prized as dearly as fresh caviar. Often a gala pike dinner was topped with Austria's heavenly dessert, Salzburger Nockerln *(page 313).*

8 servings

2-	to 2½-pound pike,* cleaned
½	teaspoon salt
⅛	teaspoon pepper
1	small onion, chopped
½	cup sliced mushrooms
2	tablespoons margarine or butter
1	cup soft bread crumbs
3	anchovy fillets, mashed
3	tablespoons milk
1	tablespoon snipped parsley
¼	cup margarine or butter, melted
2	tablespoons lemon juice
1	clove garlic, chopped

Rub cavity of fish with salt and pepper. Cook and stir onion and mushrooms in 2 tablespoons margarine until onion is tender. Mix onion, mushrooms, bread crumbs, anchovies, milk and parsley. Spoon into cavity of fish. Close opening with skewers; lace with string. Place fish in shallow roasting pan.

Mix ¼ cup margarine, the lemon juice and garlic; brush fish with margarine mixture. Cook uncovered in 350° oven, brushing occasionally with margarine mixture, until fish flakes easily with fork, about 1 hour. Garnish with parsley sprigs and thinly sliced lemon if desired.

* Salmon, red snapper, lake trout, bass or whitefish can be substituted for the pike.

Fish Baked with Sesame Seed
(Samak Tahini)

Toasted sesame seed and red pepper bring the fragrant flavors of the Middle East to samak tahini. *Although many kinds of fish fillets can be used in this dish, we recommend perch for the American kitchen. Saffron- or turmeric-flavored rice is often served with* samak tahini.

4 servings

1	medium red onion, sliced
1	tablespoon vegetable oil
⅓	cup sesame seed, toasted (see Note)
¼	cup water
1	small clove garlic, finely chopped
½	teaspoon salt
2	tablespoons lemon juice
	Dash of ground red pepper
	Olive or vegetable oil
2	tablespoons dry bread crumbs
2	tablespoons snipped parsley
1	pound perch fillets
	Parsley
	Ripe olives

Cook and stir onion in 1 tablespoon oil until tender. Mix sesame seed, water, garlic, salt, lemon juice and red pepper. Lightly brush square baking dish, 8 x 8 x 2 inches, with oil; sprinkle with bread crumbs and 2 tablespoons parsley. Pat fish dry with paper towels; arrange in baking dish. Pour sesame seed mixture over fish; top with onion. Cook uncovered in 400° oven until fish flakes easily with fork, 20 to 25 minutes. Garnish with parsley and ripe olives.

Note: To toast, heat sesame seed in ungreased skillet over medium heat, stirring occasionally, until golden, about 2 minutes. Or bake sesame seed on ungreased cookie sheet in 350° oven until golden, about 10 minutes.

Russian Salmon Loaf (Coulibiac)

Over the years, enterprising French chefs have added many embellishments to this favorite Russian dish. We prefer one of the original Russian versions—a mixture of rice cooked in broth, mushrooms, dill and salmon, wrapped in a light, golden pastry. Kasha (buckwheat groats) is often used instead of rice. Serve this splendid dish at a cold buffet.

8 to 10 servings

	Pastry (page 55)
1	medium onion, sliced
1	bay leaf
5	peppercorns
2	teaspoons salt
2	pounds salmon steak*
1	cup water
½	cup uncooked regular rice
1	teaspoon instant chicken bouillon
8	ounces mushrooms, thinly sliced
3	large onions, finely chopped
¼	cup margarine or butter
3	hard-cooked eggs, chopped
2	tablespoons snipped dill
1	teaspoon salt
1	egg yolk
1	tablespoon water
	Melted margarine or butter or dairy sour cream

Russian Salmon Loaf

Prepare pastry. Heat 1½ inches water, 1 onion, the bay leaf, peppercorns and 2 teaspoons salt to boiling in 12-inch skillet; reduce heat. Arrange fish in single layer in skillet. Simmer uncovered until fish flakes easily with fork, 4 to 6 minutes. Drain and cool. Remove bones and skin from fish; flake fish.

Heat 1 cup water, the rice and bouillon to boiling in 1-quart saucepan, stirring once or twice; reduce heat. Cover and simmer 14 minutes. (Do not lift cover or stir.) Remove from heat. Fluff rice lightly with fork. Cook and stir mushrooms and 3 onions in margarine until onions are tender. Gently stir rice, mushrooms, onions, eggs and dill into flaked salmon. Sprinkle with 1 teaspoon salt.

Heat oven to 400°. Shape one-half pastry into flattened rectangle on well-floured cloth-covered board. Roll pastry with floured stockinet-covered rolling pin into rectangle, 16 x 7 inches. Trim edges evenly. Place on ungreased cookie sheet. Mound salmon mixture over pastry to within 1 inch of edges. (See photograph.) Roll other half pastry into rectangle, 18 x 9 inches. Moisten edges of pastry on cookie sheet with water. Carefully place second half pastry over filling. Press edges with fork or flute to seal. (See photograph.) Leftover pastry can be cut into a variety of shapes to trim top of pastry.

Cut 1-inch circle in center of top crust or cut slits so steam can escape. Mix egg yolk and 1 tablespoon water; brush pastry with egg yolk mixture. Bake until golden brown, 50 to 60 minutes. Serve with melted margarine, butter or dairy sour cream.

Pastry

1   cup margarine or butter
⅓   cup shortening
4   cups all-purpose flour
1   teaspoon salt
10 to 12 tablespoons cold water

Cut margarine and shortening into flour and salt until particles are size of small peas. Sprinkle in water, 1 tablespoon at a time, tossing with fork until all flour is moistened and pastry almost cleans side of bowl. Gather pastry into a ball. Divide into halves; shape into 2 rounds. Cover and refrigerate until firm, about 3 hours.

* 2 cans (16 ounces each) salmon, drained and flaked, can be substituted for the salmon steak; omit cooking step.

Mound salmon mixture on pastry to within 1 inch of edges.

Press edges with fork to seal.

Riviera Salad Bowl
(Salade Niçoise)

From the shining city of Nice, perched on the glamorous French Riviera, comes this refreshing salad, ideal for warm-weather entertaining. For a hearty meal, serve salade niçoise with French Potato Salad (page 208) and crusty French bread.

4 servings

1   package (10 ounces) frozen French-style green
       beans
1   head Boston lettuce, torn into bite-size pieces
2   tomatoes, cut into sixths
2   hard-cooked eggs, cut into fourths
1   can (6½ ounces) tuna, drained
8   ripe olives
1   can (about 2 ounces) anchovy fillets
     Snipped parsley
     Vinaigrette Dressing (below)

Cook beans as directed on package; drain. Cover and refrigerate at least 1 hour. Place lettuce in salad bowl; arrange beans, tomatoes and eggs around edge. Mound tuna in center. Garnish with olives, anchovies and parsley. Serve with Vinaigrette Dressing.

Vinaigrette Dressing

½   cup olive or vegetable oil
¼   cup white wine vinegar
½   teaspoon salt
½   teaspoon dried basil leaves
¼   teaspoon dry mustard
⅛   teaspoon pepper

Shake ingredients in covered jar; refrigerate.

Glazed Salmon Steaks with Green Mayonnaise

(Côtelettes de Saumon Glacées)

This French masterpiece can be prepared the day before and refrigerated until party time. The chilled salmon steaks, glazed with aspic, artfully garnished and served with Green Mayonnaise, make this a dish especially suited to summer entertaining.

8 servings

1½	cups dry white wine
1	cup water
1	small onion, sliced
1	stalk celery (with leaves) cut up
4	sprigs parsley
1	teaspoon salt
5	peppercorns
1	bay leaf
¼	teaspoon dried thyme leaves
¼	teaspoon dried tarragon leaves
8	salmon steaks, 1 inch thick (about 4 pounds)
1	envelope unflavored gelatin
2	cups dry white wine
	Pitted ripe olives
	Pimiento
	Green onion tops
	Parsley sprigs
	Green Mayonnaise (right)

Heat 1½ cups wine, the water, onion, celery, 4 sprigs parsley, the salt, peppercorns, bay leaf, thyme and tarragon leaves to boiling in 10-inch skillet; reduce heat. Cover and simmer 5 to 10 minutes. Place 4 of the salmon steaks in wine mixture; add enough water to cover steaks. Heat to boiling; reduce heat. Simmer uncovered until fish flakes easily with fork, 12 to 15 minutes. Remove fish with slotted spatula; drain on cooling racks. Remove skin and discard. Add remaining fish to wine mixture; add equal parts wine and water to cover fish.

Repeat. Place racks in shallow pan. Cover and refrigerate until cold.

Sprinkle gelatin on ½ cup of the 2 cups wine in small bowl. Place bowl in pan of hot water over low heat until gelatin dissolves, about 5 minutes. Stir in remaining wine. Place bowl in pan of ice and water, stirring occasionally, until mixture begins to thicken, 20 to 25 minutes. (Mixture should be consistency of unbeaten egg white.)

Cut olives lengthwise into fourths. Cut circles from pimiento; use green onion tops for stems. Spoon ⅔ of the glaze over salmon steaks until completely coated. Arrange decoration on glaze; spoon remaining glaze on decorations. (If glaze begins to thicken, place bowl in pan of hot water.) Refrigerate until glaze is firm. Remove salmon steaks from racks; place on serving plates. Garnish with parsley. Serve with Green Mayonnaise.

Green Mayonnaise

2	cups mayonnaise or salad dressing
½	cup finely chopped spinach
½	cup snipped parsley
2	to 3 teaspoons snipped fresh dill or 1 tablespoon dried dillweed
1	tablespoon tarragon vinegar
1	tablespoon snipped chives

Place all ingredients in blender container. Cover and blend on high speed until smooth. Refrigerate at least 2 hours.

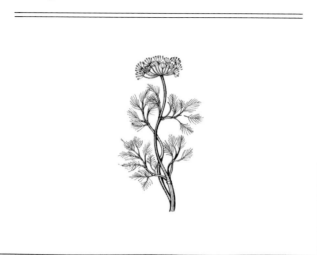

Seafood Crêpes
(Crêpes Fruits de Mer)

Crêpes, really just thin, elegant pancakes, are well known for their versatility. They are used for appetizers, main dishes and desserts. Seafood Crêpes are featured on the menus of great restaurants throughout Europe and America. The creamy sauce used in our recipe is inspired by the cuisines of Normandy and Brittany, in northern France. In Normandy, the crêpes are often served with chilled apple cider. For convenience, make the crêpes ahead (see Do-Ahead Tip) and keep them on hand for carefree entertaining.

8 servings (2 crêpes each)

	Crêpes (right)
6	medium mushrooms, chopped
3	tablespoons chopped green onion
3	tablespoons margarine or butter
3½	cups (about 18 ounces) cooked seafood, cut into bite-size pieces
3	packages (3 ounces each) cream cheese, cubed
⅓	cup half-and-half
3	tablespoons snipped parsley
2	tablespoons sherry (optional)
1	cup shredded Swiss cheese
¼	cup chopped green onion

Prepare crêpes; keep covered to prevent drying. Cook and stir mushrooms and 3 tablespoons green onion in margarine until onion is tender. Stir in seafood, cream cheese, half-and-half and parsley. Cook, stirring constantly, until cream cheese is melted. Stir in sherry.

Place about ¼ cup filling on center of each crêpe; roll up. Place 8 crêpes seam sides down in each of 2 ungreased oblong baking dishes, 12 x 7½ x 2 inches, or ovenproof serving platters. Sprinkle each with ½ cup Swiss cheese. Cover and heat in 350° oven until crêpes are hot, about 20 minutes. Garnish each dish with 2 tablespoons green onion.

Crêpes

2¼	cups all-purpose flour
¾	teaspoon salt
½	teaspoon baking powder
3	cups milk
3	eggs
2	tablespoons margarine or butter, melted

Mix flour, salt and baking powder; stir in milk, eggs and margarine. Beat with hand beater until smooth. For each crêpe, lightly brush 8-inch skillet or crêpe pan with margarine; heat over medium heat until bubbly. Pour scant ¼ cup batter into skillet; immediately rotate skillet until thin film covers bottom. Cook until top is dry and bottom is light brown; turn. Cook other side until light brown. Stack crêpes as they are removed from skillet; cool. (Cover crêpes with plastic wrap to prevent drying.)

Do-Ahead Tip: Stack crêpes with waxed paper between each. Wrap and refrigerate no longer than 2 days or freeze no longer than 3 months. Thaw wrapped frozen crêpes at room temperature about 3 hours.

Seafood Crêpes

Shrimp Curry, Caribbean Style

East Indians began emigrating to the West Indies in the mid-nineteenth century to fill a labor shortage created by the abolition of slavery. The Indians brought their traditional curry recipes with them. Today many natives of Jamaica, Trinidad and Tobago continue to make their "curries" from scratch, using their favorite combinations of spices. Thus commercial curry powder does not appear in the recipe ingredients below.

6 servings

1   medium onion, chopped
2   tablespoons margarine or butter
4   tomatoes, chopped, or 2 cans (16 ounces each) tomatoes, drained and chopped
½   teaspoon salt
½   teaspoon ground coriander
½   teaspoon ground turmeric
¼   teaspoon ground ginger
¼   teaspoon ground cumin
⅛   teaspoon ground red pepper
2   cups clean cooked shrimp
    Hot cooked rice (page 253)
    Chutney

Cook and stir onion in margarine in 10-inch skillet until tender, about 3 minutes. Add tomatoes, salt, coriander, turmeric, ginger, cumin and red pepper. Heat to boiling; reduce heat. Cover and simmer 15 minutes. Stir in shrimp; heat until shrimp is hot, 3 to 5 minutes. Serve with rice and chutney.

Shrimp in Spicy Sauce (Sambal Goreng Udang)

On festive occasions, Indonesians serve sambal goreng udang *with separate bowls of rice cooked in coconut milk and flavored with curry powder. The shrimp can be garnished with crisp cucumber slices and roasted peanuts.*

4 servings

¼   cup vegetable oil
1   pound small raw shrimp, shelled and deveined
2   small onions, sliced
1   clove garlic, chopped
½   to ¾ teaspoon crushed red pepper
1   cup Coconut Milk (below)
1   tomato, coarsely chopped
1   green pepper, thinly sliced into rings
1   tablespoon packed brown sugar
½   teaspoon salt
    Freshly ground pepper

Heat oil in 10-inch skillet until hot. Cook and stir shrimp, onions, garlic and red pepper until shrimp starts to turn pink, 2 to 3 minutes. Stir in remaining ingredients. Simmer uncovered until shrimp is tender, about 5 minutes. Serve in bowls.

Coconut Milk
Place 1 cup chopped fresh coconut and 1 cup hot water in blender container. Cover and blend on high speed until coconut is finely chopped. Strain through several layers of cheesecloth. Refrigerate no longer than 48 hours.

Note: To open coconut, puncture eye of coconut with ice pick; drain liquid. Bake coconut in 375° oven 12 to 15 minutes. Remove from oven. Tap shell with hammer to open. Cut meat out of shell. Pare brown skin from coconut meat.

Shrimp with Lobster Sauce

(Tou Shih Hsia Jen)

A Cantonese specialty, lobster sauce contains no lobster—the sauce was created to serve with lobster, but is now used with many Chinese dishes. Salted black beans can be found at oriental groceries and at some gourmet shops and natural food stores.

4 servings

2	cloves garlic, finely chopped
2	tablespoons soy sauce
1	tablespoon salted black beans, washed, drained and mashed
1	teaspoon finely chopped ginger root
½	teaspoon sugar
½	teaspoon salt
2	tablespoons vegetable oil
1	pound raw shrimp, shelled and deveined
2	green onions (with tops), chopped (reserve tops)
½	cup hot water
1	tablespoon cornstarch
1	tablespoon cold water
2	eggs, slightly beaten
	Hot cooked rice (page 253)

Mix garlic, soy sauce, beans, ginger root, sugar and salt. Heat oil in 10-inch skillet until hot. Stir in shrimp, bean mixture and green onions. Cook and stir 1 minute. Stir in ½ cup water. Cover and cook until shrimp is pink, about 2 minutes.

Mix cornstarch and 1 tablespoon water; stir into shrimp mixture. Cook and stir until thickened. Add eggs; cook and stir just until eggs are set. Sprinkle with reserved green onion tops; serve with rice.

Shrimp with Tomato Sauce on Rice

(Camarones a la Criolla)

This quick and easy recipe from Mexico is a fine one to keep in mind for impromptu entertaining. A tossed green salad or our Mexican Fruit Salad (page 211) is all you need to complete the menu.

4 to 6 servings

1	jalapeño chili
1	medium onion, chopped
1	clove garlic, chopped
3	tablespoons margarine or butter
1	can (16 ounces) tomatoes
1	stalk celery, chopped
1	tablespoon lemon or lime juice
1	teaspoon salt
½	teaspoon sugar
¼	teaspoon pepper
1	package (10 ounces) frozen quick-cooking shrimp
	Hot cooked rice (page 253)
2	tablespoons snipped parsley

Remove stems, seeds and membranes from chili; chop chili. Cook and stir chili, onion and garlic in margarine in 2-quart saucepan until onion is tender. Add tomatoes, celery, lemon juice, 1 teaspoon salt, the sugar and ¼ teaspoon pepper. Heat to boiling; reduce heat. Simmer uncovered 15 minutes, stirring occasionally.

Stir shrimp into tomato sauce. Heat to boiling; reduce heat. Cover and simmer 5 minutes; serve over rice. Garnish with parsley.

Chilled Shrimp, Pea Pods and Bean Curd

Chilled Shrimp, Pea Pods and Bean Curd

Bean curd (tofu) can be purchased in oriental groceries, natural food stores, and in many supermarkets carrying fresh oriental produce. To whet your appetite for this pleasant Japanese dish, we suggest starting the meal with a steaming bowl of our easy-to-make Clear Japanese Soup (page 24).

6 servings

8   ounces bean curd
8   ounces fresh or frozen raw shrimp
4   cups water
2   tablespoons salt
1   package (6 ounces) frozen Chinese pea pods
1   green onion, finely chopped
2   tablespoons soy sauce
¼   teaspoon monosodium glutamate (optional)
1   tablespoon sesame oil

Cut bean curd into 3 slices; carefully place in sieve. Blanch bean curd in boiling water 30 seconds; drain. Cut each slice into 3 strips; cut each strip diagonally into 1-inch pieces.

Peel shrimp. (If shrimp is frozen, do not thaw; peel under running cold water.) Make a shallow cut lengthwise down back of each shrimp; wash out sand vein. Heat water to boiling. Add shrimp and salt. Cover and heat to boiling; reduce heat. Simmer until shrimp is pink, about 5 minutes; drain.

Cook pea pods as directed on package; drain. Place bean curd, shrimp, pea pods, and green onion in bowl. Mix soy sauce, monosodium glutamate and sesame oil; pour over shrimp mixture. Toss lightly. Cover and refrigerate at least 1 hour.

Indonesian Fried Rice (Nasi Goreng)

This Indonesian version of "fried rice" bears little resemblance to Chinese-restaurant fried rice. Often the recipe begins with leftover rice, which is enhanced by the addition of ham, shrimp and oriental spices.

6 servings

2   medium onions, chopped
3   tablespoons vegetable oil
4   cups cold cooked rice (page 253)
1   cup finely chopped fully cooked smoked ham
2   teaspoons curry powder
¼   teaspoon ground coriander
¼   teaspoon ground cumin
¼   teaspoon salt
1   can (5 ounces) tiny shrimp, drained
2   tablespoons snipped parsley

Cook and stir onions in oil in 12-inch skillet until tender. Add rice, ham, curry powder, coriander, cumin and salt. Cook and stir until rice is golden brown, 10 to 15 minutes. Stir in shrimp and parsley. Cover and cook 1 minute.

Oyster Casserole
(Ostiones en Cazuela)

From Mexico's dramatic Pacific Coast—a creamy oyster-and-tomato casserole flavored with cumin, allspice and red pepper.

4 servings

1	pint shucked select or large oysters, drained
2	tomatoes, chopped
½	cup half-and-half
2	cups cracker crumbs (about 20 crackers)
½	cup margarine or butter, melted
½	teaspoon salt
½	teaspoon ground cumin
¼	teaspoon ground allspice
⅛	teaspoon ground red pepper
	Lemon or lime wedges

Mix oysters and tomatoes; arrange in ungreased oblong baking dish, 11 x 7 x 1½ inches. Pour ¼ cup of the half-and-half over mixture. Mix remaining ingredients except lemon wedges; sprinkle over oysters and tomatoes. Pour remaining half-and-half over crumb mixture. Cook uncovered in 375° oven until light brown, about 30 minutes. Garnish with lemon wedges.

Oyster Stew Nippon
(Kaki No Nikomi)

The artfully composed dishes served in fine Japanese restaurants bear little resemblance to Japanese country cooking. In rural Japan the evening meal often consists only of a bowl of nourishing soup or stew and a serving of boiled or steamed rice.

4 servings

1	can (10¾ ounces) condensed chicken broth
1	soup can water
2	tablespoons soy sauce
¼	teaspoon grated ginger root
1	pint shucked select or large oysters
2	cups chopped Chinese cabbage
8	ounces sliced mushrooms
½	cup bean sprouts*
4	green onions (with tops), cut into 1-inch pieces

Heat chicken broth, water, soy sauce and ginger root to boiling in 3-quart saucepan. Add oysters (with liquid), cabbage, mushrooms and bean sprouts. Heat to boiling; reduce heat. Cover and simmer until cabbage is crisp-tender, about 2 minutes. Ladle soup into bowls; garnish with green onions.

* Pea pods can be substituted for the bean sprouts.

Oysters
Did You Know?

Oysters, which have been cultivated in some parts of the world for thousands of years, vary in size, thickness, saltiness and flavor. They are available canned, fresh in the shells, shucked (fresh or frozen), dried and smoked. Fresh edible oysters have shells tightly closed; the liquor around fresh shucked oysters is clear, not milky.

To open or shuck an oyster, gently chip away the thin end of the shell with a hammer. Then hold the oyster tightly and force a table knife or shucking knife between the shells at the broken end; pull the halves of the shell apart over a strainer in a bowl to separate the shell fragments and catch the liquor for use in cooking.

Crab Soufflé Roll
(Soufflé de Crabe Roulé)

From France—a soufflé-type base spread with a creamy crabmeat filling and rolled. Serve as a light main dish accompanied by a tossed green salad, or use smaller servings for appetizers.

8 servings

¼   cup margarine or butter
½   cup all-purpose flour
2   cups milk
4   egg yolks
½   teaspoon salt
     Dash of ground red pepper
2   teaspoons snipped chives
4   egg whites
¼   teaspoon cream of tartar
⅓   cup grated Parmesan cheese
     Crabmeat Filling (right)

Grease jelly roll pan, 15½ x 10½ x 1 inch. Line bottom of pan with waxed paper; grease lightly and flour. Heat margarine over medium heat until melted. Remove from heat; stir in flour. Cook over low heat, stirring constantly, until smooth and bubbly. Remove from heat; stir in milk. Heat to boiling, stirring constantly. Boil and stir 1 minute. Remove from heat. Beat in egg yolks, one at a time. Stir in salt, red pepper and chives. Cool at room temperature, stirring occasionally. (Cover mixture to prevent formation of film.)

Heat oven to 350°. Beat egg whites and cream of tartar in large mixer bowl until stiff but not dry. Stir about ¼ of the egg whites into egg yolk mixture. Gently fold egg yolk mixture and cheese into remaining egg whites. Pour into pan. Bake until puffed and golden brown, about 45 minutes. Immediately loosen soufflé from edges of pan; invert on cloth-covered cooling rack. Spread soufflé with Crabmeat Filling; roll up from narrow end. Cut into 1¼-inch slices. (See photographs for assembling soufflé.)

Crabmeat Filling

4   green onions, finely chopped
2   tablespoons margarine or butter
2   packages (6 ounces each) frozen crabmeat, thawed, drained and flaked, or 2 cans (6 ounces each) crabmeat, drained and cartilage removed
1   package (3 ounces) cream cheese, softened
⅓   cup half-and-half
2   tablespoons snipped parsley
     Dash of red pepper sauce
     Salt and pepper

Cook and stir green onions in margarine until tender. Stir in remaining ingredients; heat until hot.

Spread soufflé with crabmeat filling.

Roll up from narrow end.

Crab Soufflé Roll

Scallops and Mushrooms in Wine Sauce

Scallops and Mushrooms in Wine Sauce

(Coquilles Saint-Jacques à la Parisienne)

One French name for scallops is coquilles Saint-Jacques. *In Paris the scallops are often poached in wine, mixed with a cream and mushroom sauce, and then sprinkled with cheese and bread crumbs and broiled in scallop shells. Oven-to-table scallop shells (either authentic shells or porcelain reproductions) are available.*

6 servings

2	packages (12 ounces each) frozen scallops, thawed, or 1½ pounds fresh scallops
1	cup dry white wine
¼	cup snipped parsley
½	teaspoon salt
2	tablespoons margarine or butter
4	ounces mushrooms, sliced (about 2 cups)
2	shallots or green onions, chopped
3	tablespoons margarine or butter
3	tablespoons flour
½	cup half-and-half
½	cup shredded Swiss cheese
1	cup soft bread crumbs
2	tablespoons margarine or butter, melted

If scallops are large, cut into 1½-inch pieces. Place scallops, wine, parsley and salt in 3-quart saucepan. Add just enough water to cover scallops. Heat to boiling; reduce heat. Simmer uncovered until scallops are tender, about 8 minutes. Remove scallops with slotted spoon; reserve liquid. Heat reserved liquid to boiling. Boil until reduced to 1 cup. Strain and reserve.

Heat 2 tablespoons margarine in 3-quart saucepan until melted. Cook and stir mushrooms and shallots in margarine until tender, 5 to 6 minutes. Remove from pan. Add 3 tablespoons margarine; heat until melted. Remove from heat; stir in flour. Cook over low heat, stirring constantly, until smooth and bubbly. Remove from heat; stir in reserved liquid. Cook and stir 1 minute. Stir in half-and-half, scallops, mushrooms, shallots and ¼ cup of the cheese; heat until hot.

Toss bread crumbs in melted margarine. Lightly brush 5 or 6 baking shells or ramekins with margarine. Divide scallop mixture among baking shells. Sprinkle with remaining cheese and the crumbs. Set oven control to broil and/or 550°. Broil 5 inches from heat until crumbs are toasted, 3 to 5 minutes.

Scallops Provençale

Western chefs often include a purée of tomatoes and green peppers in any dish labeled provençale. *Traditionally the word simply indicates that garlic has been added (tomatoes and green peppers were unknown in Provence until modern times). Serve with a vegetable salad and Scalloped Potatoes with Cheese (page 240).*

8 servings

12	ounces fresh scallops or 1 package (12 ounces) frozen scallops, thawed
¼	cup all-purpose flour
¼	teaspoon salt
	Dash of pepper
¼	cup vegetable oil
1	small clove garlic, finely chopped
2	tablespoons margarine or butter
	Snipped parsley
	Lemon wedges

If scallops are large, cut into 1½-inch pieces; pat dry with paper towels. Mix flour, salt and pepper; coat scallops with flour mixture. Heat oil in 10-inch skillet. Cook scallops until light brown, turning carefully, 4 to 5 minutes.

Cook and stir garlic in margarine over low heat in 1 quart saucepan about 2 minutes; pour over scallops. Sprinkle with parsley; serve with lemon wedges.

Lobster with Chinese Vegetables

(Ch'ao Lung Hsia)

A little lobster goes a long way when cooked Chinese style. If planning a Chinese dinner party, begin the meal with Crisp Wontons (page 10). A light, easy-on-the-cook dessert suggestion: fresh pineapple cubes skewered on wooden picks.

8 servings

1½	pounds frozen lobster tails
1	package (6 ounces) frozen Chinese pea pods
3	medium stalks bok choy
2	tablespoons vegetable oil
2	cloves garlic, finely chopped
2	thin slices ginger root, crushed
1	can (8½ ounces) water chestnuts, drained and thinly sliced
1	can (8½ ounces) bamboo shoots, drained
4	ounces mushrooms, sliced
1	can (10¾ ounces) condensed chicken broth
2	tablespoons cornstarch
2	tablespoons soy sauce
1	teaspoon salt
1	teaspoon sugar
¼	teaspoon white pepper
2	green onions, thinly sliced
	Hot cooked rice (page 253)

Cook lobster tails as directed on package; drain. Cut away thin undershell (covering meat of lobster) with kitchen scissors. Remove meat; cut into 1-inch pieces.

Rinse pea pods under running cold water to separate; drain. Separate leaves from bok choy stems; reserve leaves. Cut stems into ¼-inch slices. Heat oil in 12-inch skillet, Dutch oven or wok until hot. Cook and stir garlic and ginger root over medium heat until brown. Add pea pods, bok choy stems, water chestnuts, bamboo shoots and mushrooms. Cook and stir over medium heat 2 minutes.

Stir in ¾ cup of the chicken broth; reduce heat. Cover and simmer 1 minute.

Mix remaining chicken broth, the cornstarch, soy sauce, salt, sugar and white pepper; stir into vegetable mixture. Cook and stir until thickened, about 30 seconds. Tear bok choy leaves into bite-size pieces; add leaves and lobster to vegetable mixture. Heat until hot. Garnish with green onions; serve with rice.

Care of Fresh and Frozen Fish

Store fresh fish in the coldest part of the refrigerator; freeze fish you don't plan to cook within a day or two. Keep frozen fish solidly frozen. If any kind of frozen fish becomes thawed, use it right away.

To freeze fresh fish, clean and scale it, then wash under running cold water. Drain and pat dry with paper towels, then wrap tightly in freezer wrap. Or place in a freezer container and cover with cold water. Separate steaks and fillets with a double thickness of foil, then tightly wrap, label and freeze.

Thaw frozen fish in the refrigerator—only long enough for easy handling (about 24 hours for a 1-pound package). Do not thaw fish at room temperature.

To speed up thawing, immerse fish (in a sealed package) in cold water. Use the fish as soon as it is thawed, drying with paper towels before cooking. Fillets or steaks can be fried, broiled or poached before they are completely thawed; they will take a little longer to cook. After they are cooked, fish can be covered and refrigerated no longer than three days or frozen no longer than three months.

Paella

Paella

The pride of Spain's Costa Brava (the rugged Mediterranean coast of southeastern Spain), Paella derives its name from the shallow two-handled dish in which it is served.

8 to 10 servings

¼	cup olive or vegetable oil
1	to 1½ pounds broiler-fryer chicken pieces
1	medium onion, chopped
1	clove garlic, chopped
3	cups water
1½	cups uncooked regular rice
1	can (16 ounces) tomatoes
2	teaspoons salt
1	tablespoon paprika
1	tablespoon instant chicken bouillon
½	teaspoon pepper
⅛	teaspoon saffron or ground turmeric
½	teaspoon ground red pepper
1	pound clean raw shrimp

1	can (24 ounces) steamed clams in shells, drained
1	can (15 ounces) artichoke hearts, drained and cut up
1	package (10 ounces) frozen peas, thawed
1	jar (2 ounces) sliced pimiento, drained

Heat oil in Dutch oven until hot. Cook chicken over medium heat until brown on all sides, about 15 minutes. Remove chicken. Cook and stir onion and garlic in oil until onion is tender. Drain fat from Dutch oven. Stir in water, rice, tomatoes, salt, paprika, bouillon, ½ teaspoon pepper, saffron and ½ teaspoon red pepper; add chicken. Heat to boiling; reduce heat. Cover; simmer 20 minutes.

Stir shrimp and clams into chicken mixture. Cover and simmer 5 minutes. Add artichoke hearts and peas; cover and heat until hot, 5 to 10 minutes. Serve in paella pan or large shallow baking dish; garnish with pimiento.

Linguini with White Clam Sauce

(Linguini con Vongole Bianco)

The use of butter and cheese indicates that this recipe comes from northern Italy. If you prefer, substitute a favorite pasta for linguini—spaghetti, fettuccini or spinach egg noodles.

5 or 6 servings

1	medium onion, chopped
1	clove garlic, finely chopped
3	tablespoons margarine or butter
1	tablespoon flour
3	cans (6½ ounces each) minced clams
½	teaspoon salt
½	teaspoon dried basil leaves
⅛	teaspoon pepper
1	tablespoon salt
3	quarts water
8	ounces uncooked linguini
¼	cup snipped parsley
	Grated Parmesan cheese

Cook and stir onion and garlic in margarine in 2-quart saucepan until onion is tender; stir in flour. Add clams (with liquid), ½ teaspoon salt, the basil and pepper. Heat to boiling; reduce heat. Cover and simmer 5 minutes.

Add 1 tablespoon salt to rapidly boiling water in Dutch oven. Add linguini gradually so that water continues to boil. (If linguini strands are left whole, place one end in water; as they soften, gradually coil them into water.)

Boil uncovered, stirring occasionally, just until tender, 7 to 10 minutes. Test by cutting several strands with fork against side of Dutch oven. Drain quickly in colander or sieve. Add parsley to clam sauce. Serve sauce over hot linguini; sprinkle with cheese.

Tempura

Tempura—an assortment of fish and vegetables dipped in batter, fried and served with a special sauce—has nearly as many fans in America as in Japan. Special tempura equipment can be purchased at department stores and oriental shops. Do not let the long list of ingredients discourage you from trying Tempura; select, according to personal preference and recipe instructions, those that most appeal to your taste.

4 servings

	Shrimp with tails, shelled and deveined
	Scallops, cut into halves
	Fish fillets, cut into bite-size pieces
1	cup 1-inch pieces asparagus
1	cup ¼-inch slices carrots or celery
1½	cups cauliflowerets
1½	cups 2 x ¼-inch eggplant sticks
1	cup 2-inch pieces green beans, partially cooked
1	cup 2-inch pieces green onions
1	green pepper, cut into ¼-inch rings
1	medium onion, sliced and separated into rings
1	bunch parsley
1	cup pea pods
1	sweet potato, cut into ⅛-inch slices
	Vegetable oil
	Tempura Batter (right)
	Tempura Sauce (right)

Tempura

Choose 1 pound seafood (about 4 ounces per person). If serving shrimp, make several crosswise slits on undersides to prevent curling. Choose 3 or 4 vegetables from selection above. Pat seafood and vegetables dry; arrange attractively on platter. Cover and refrigerate until serving time.

Heat oil (1 to 1½ inches) in wok to 360° (see Note). Prepare Tempura Batter. Dip seafood and vegetables into batter with tongs, fork or chopsticks; allow excess batter to drip into bowl. Fry a few pieces at a time until golden brown, turning once, 2 to 3 minutes.

Drain. Serve with Tempura Sauce.

Tempura Batter

2   eggs, beaten
1   cup cold water
¾   cup all-purpose flour
1   tablespoon cornstarch
½   teaspoon baking powder
½   teaspoon salt

Mix all ingredients with fork just until blended. (Batter will be thin and slightly lumpy.)

Tempura Sauce

¼   cup chicken broth
¼   cup water
¼   cup soy sauce
1   teaspoon sugar

Heat all ingredients until hot. Serve in small individual bowls.

Note: A wok is recommended for this recipe because of its large surface area and slanted sides, which protect against splattering.

Clockwise from top: Lemon Chicken, Hunan Style (page 108); Chicken Tacos with Avocado and Cheese (page 106); Stuffed Cornish Hens, Hamburg Style (page 72).

Poultry

In this chapter we have collected several of the world's favorite poultry recipes ... festive Roast Goose with Apple Stuffing from northern Europe ... sumptuous Duckling with Orange Sauce from France ... Mexico's exuberant Turkey Mole. But mainly this chapter is concerned with chicken, an international favorite since ancient times.

Chefs throughout the world have long appreciated the versatile chicken. It is adaptable to nearly every kind of cooking, from quick stir-frying to slow simmering or oven roasting. Its price remains relatively stable when meat and fish prices soar. It is prized for its flavor by nearly every ethnic group in the world.

In the following pages you will find recipes for tasty main-dish soups, such as Mulligatawny Soup from India, Chicken Soup with Tortellini from Italy, and Chicken-and-Leek Soup from Scotland ... plus fragrant fricassées from France ... hearty chicken and dumplings from Hungary and Latin America ... robust stews from the Caribbean and Africa ... fried and roasted chicken from Mexico, Spain and the Middle East.

There are the all-time international favorites, such as Chicken Cacciatore and Chicken Curry (ideal for casual get-togethers and fancy party fare too), Chicken Cordon Bleu from Switzerland, Chicken Kiev from the Soviet Union and the delightful Chicken with Flaming Pineapple from Cuba. For warm-weather entertaining we have included several chilled chicken dishes from the Orient.

Instructions are included for cutting up whole chickens and boning chicken breasts, and there are tips for making your own best-ever chicken broth from chicken trimmings.

Stuffed Cornish Hens, Hamburg Style

(Gebratene Hähnchen)

Stubenküken—small chickens no more than four weeks old—are a great specialty of the German city of Hamburg. We use a close equivalent—Cornish game hens, available in most supermarkets. Try the dish with German Potato Pancakes (page 247) and marinated cucumbers.

6 servings

6	slices bacon
1	medium onion, chopped
⅓	cup margarine or butter
1¾	cups soft bread cubes
1	stalk celery (with leaves), chopped
2	tablespoons snipped parsley
½	teaspoon poultry seasoning
⅛	teaspoon pepper
3	Rock Cornish hens (about 1¼ pounds each)
	Margarine or butter, melted
1	tablespoon flour
1	cup water
1½	teaspoons instant chicken bouillon
½	cup dairy sour cream

Fry bacon until crisp; drain on paper towels. Crumble bacon. Drain fat, returning 2 tablespoons fat to skillet. Cook and stir onion in bacon fat until tender. Add ⅓ cup margarine; heat until melted. Add bacon, bread cubes, celery, parsley, poultry seasoning and pepper; toss.

Stuff each hen with about 6 tablespoons stuffing. Secure opening with skewer. Fasten neck skin to back with skewer. Tie legs together with string. Place hens breast sides up on rack in shallow roasting pan. Brush with margarine. Roast hens uncovered in 350° oven, brushing with margarine 3 or 4 times, until golden brown and done, about 1 hour.

Remove hens from pan; keep warm. Spoon 2 tablespoons pan drippings into 1-quart saucepan; stir in flour. Cook over low heat, stirring constantly, until mixture is smooth and bubbly; remove from heat. Stir in water and bouillon. Heat to boiling, stirring constantly. Boil and stir 1 minute. Stir in sour cream. To serve, cut hens with kitchen scissors, cutting through the breast and along backbone from tail to neck. Serve with dressing and gravy.

Roast Goose with Apple Stuffing

(Gänsebraten mit Apfelfüllung)

Roast goose is traditional Christmas fare in many northern European countries. The apple stuffing is characteristic of both Austria, where the goose is often served with puréed chestnuts, and Germany, where red cabbage or sauerkraut and applesauce are traditional Christmas accompaniments.

6 to 8 servings

1	ready-to-cook goose (8 to 10 pounds)
2	cups water
1	small onion, sliced
1¼	teaspoons salt
6	cups soft bread crumbs
3	tart apples, chopped
2	stalks celery (with leaves), chopped
1	medium onion, chopped
¼	cup margarine or butter, melted
2	teaspoons salt
1	teaspoon ground sage
½	teaspoon ground thyme
¼	teaspoon pepper
1	teaspoon salt
¼	cup all-purpose flour

Trim excess fat from goose. Heat giblets, water, sliced onion and 1¼ teaspoons salt to

Roast Goose with Apple Stuffing

boiling; reduce heat. Cover and simmer until giblets are done, about 1 hour. Strain broth; cover and refrigerate. Chop giblets; toss with remaining ingredients except 1 teaspoon salt and the flour.

Rub cavity of goose with 1 teaspoon salt. Fold wings across back with tips touching. Fill neck and body cavities of goose lightly with stuffing. Fasten neck skin of goose to back with skewers. Fasten opening with skewers; lace with string. Tie drumsticks to tail. Prick skin all over with fork. Place goose breast side up on rack in shallow roasting pan.

Roast uncovered in 350° oven until done, 3 to 3½ hours, removing excess fat from pan oc-

casionally. Place a tent of aluminum foil loosely over goose during last hour to prevent excessive browning. Goose is done when drumstick meat feels very soft. Place goose on heated platter. Let stand 15 minutes for easier carving.

Pour drippings from pan into bowl. Return ¼ cup drippings to pan. Stir in flour. Cook over low heat, stirring constantly, until smooth and bubbly. Remove from heat. Add enough water to reserved broth if necessary to measure 2 cups. Stir into flour mixture. Heat to boiling, stirring constantly. Boil and stir 1 minute. Serve goose with apple stuffing and gravy.

Duckling with Orange Sauce

(Caneton à l'Orange)

One of the most famous of all French culinary triumphs, duckling à l'orange *was originally made with a complex sauce based on caramelized sugar and vinegar, duck stock, orange juice and orange liqueur, and madeira wine. Our version reflects the spirit of France's nou-velle cuisine,* or new cooking, *which eliminates costly, time-consuming steps without sacrificing flavor.*

4 servings

1	ready-to-cook duckling (4 to 5 pounds)
2	teaspoons grated orange peel
½	cup orange juice
¼	cup currant jelly
1	tablespoon lemon juice
⅛	teaspoon dry mustard
⅛	teaspoon salt
1	tablespoon cold water
1½	teaspoons cornstarch
1	orange, peeled and sectioned
1	tablespoon orange-flavored liqueur (optional)

Fasten neck skin of duckling to back with skewers. Lift wing tips up and over back for natural brace. Place duckling breast side up on rack in shallow roasting pan. Prick skin with fork. Roast uncovered in 325° oven until done, about 2½ hours, removing excess fat from pan occasionally. (If duckling becomes too brown, place piece of aluminum foil lightly over breast.) Duckling is done when drumstick meat feels very soft. Let stand 10 minutes for easier carving.

Heat orange peel, orange juice, jelly, lemon juice, mustard and salt to boiling. Mix water and cornstarch; stir into sauce. Cook over medium heat, stirring constantly, until mixture thickens and boils. Boil and stir 1 minute. Stir in orange sections and liqueur. Brush duckling with some of the orange sauce; serve with remaining sauce.

Danish Stuffed Duckling

(Stegt And)

In Denmark duck is prepared in many ways and served throughout the year. This recipe, which uses a stuffing made from apples, prunes or raisins, and rye bread, is a favorite family meal. The Danes often serve it with dumplings, or with boiled potatoes and red cabbage.

4 servings

1	ready-to-cook duckling (4 to 5 pounds)
3	cups rye bread crumbs
1	apple, chopped
1	small onion, chopped
½	cup cut-up prunes or raisins
1	teaspoon salt
½	teaspoon dried marjoram leaves
1	egg, beaten

Fasten neck skin of duckling to back with skewers. Lift wing tips up and over back for natural brace. Mix bread crumbs, apple, onion, prunes, salt, marjoram and egg. Fill body cavity of duckling lightly with stuffing. Fasten opening with skewers. Place remaining stuffing in small greased baking dish. Cover and refrigerate; place in oven with duckling during last 30 minutes of roasting. Place duckling breast side up on rack in shallow roasting pan. Prick skin with fork.

Roast duckling uncovered in 350° oven until done, about 3 hours, removing excess fat from pan occasionally. (If duckling becomes too brown, place piece of aluminum foil lightly over breast.) Duckling is done when drumstick meat feels very soft. Place duckling on heated platter. Let stand 10 minutes for easier carving. Serve with stuffing.

Turkey Mole
(Pavo en Mole Poblano)

The surprise ingredient in Turkey Mole is chocolate! In Mexico, chocolate has been used to flavor stews and ragouts since ancient times. The Aztecs served it at Montezuma's royal court.

Turkey Mole is a substantial dish for an important occasion. Menu suggestions: Begin with Tortilla Soup (page 28); serve Christmas Eve Salad (page 214) as a side dish; and for dessert serve a light, do-ahead Caramel Custard (page 307).

10 servings

8-	to 10-pound turkey, cut up
2	medium onions, chopped
3	cloves garlic, finely chopped
¼	cup margarine or butter
4	six-inch tortillas, torn into pieces and dried (see Note)
4	squares unsweetened chocolate, chopped
⅓	cup slivered almonds
⅓	cup peanuts
⅓	cup shelled pumpkin or sunflower seeds
¼	cup toasted sesame seed
½	to ¾ cup chili powder
2	to 3 tablespoons sugar
2	teaspoons ground cumin
1	teaspoon salt
¼	teaspoon anise seed
1	two-inch stick cinnamon, broken

Heat turkey and enough salted water to cover (1 tablespoon salt to 1 quart water) to boiling; reduce heat. Cover and simmer until thickest pieces are done, about 1½ hours. Drain; reserve 4 cups broth. Place turkey in 2 ungreased baking dishes.

Cook and stir onions and garlic in margarine until onions are tender. Place 1 cup of the reserved broth, the tortilla pieces and onion mixture in blender container. Cover and blend on high speed until smooth. Pour into large bowl. Place 1½ cups of the turkey broth,

the chocolate, almonds, peanuts, pumpkin and sesame seeds in blender container. Cover and blend until smooth. Add to onion mixture in bowl.

Place remaining 1½ cups turkey broth, the chili powder, sugar, cumin, salt, anise seed and cinnamon in blender container. Cover and blend until smooth. Add to onion mixture in bowl. Mix all ingredients thoroughly. (Mixture will be consistency of chocolate sauce.) Pour sauce over turkey. Heat in 300° oven until hot, 30 to 40 minutes.

Do-Ahead Tip: After pouring sauce over turkey, cover and refrigerate no longer than 24 hours.

Note: To dry tortillas, let pieces stand at room temperature until dry and brittle, 1 to 2 hours.

Carving a Goose
Did You Know?

Carving a goose is different from carving other poultry; the leg joint is much farther down on the bird and harder to get at. The wings must be taken off in order to carve the breast, and unless the goose is large, there will not be enough meat on the wings to serve. When carving, it is better to start out in the kitchen, using a small or medium-sized carving knife and fork. Remove the wings and legs, and cut away each of the two sections of breast meat in one piece. To remove the stuffing easily, enlarge the opening by cutting from the keel bone (the wide center bone between the rib cages) to the tail, thus exposing the stuffing. To serve the goose, arrange the parts around the stuffing, then slice the breast meat, thighs and drumsticks (if the goose is large) into smaller portions at the table.

Roast Chicken with Spiced Yogurt

(Tandoori Murghi)

A tandoor is a clay oven with a live coal or wood fire. Archeologists have found evidence suggesting that the tandoori method of cooking may have been developed by the ancient civilization that thrived along the Indus River valley nearly four thousand years ago. Today tandoori cooking is popular throughout Pakistan and India, and is rapidly gaining fans in Europe and America. You need no special oven or coals to prepare our version of tandoori murghi.

8 to 10 servings

3-	to 4-pound broiler-fryer chicken
½	teaspoon water
¼	teaspoon dry mustard
1	cup unflavored yogurt
¼	cup lemon juice
1	clove garlic, chopped
1½	teaspoons salt
½	teaspoon ground cardamom
¼	teaspoon ground ginger
¼	teaspoon ground cumin
¼	teaspoon crushed red peppers
¼	teaspoon pepper
¼	cup water

Place chicken in large glass or plastic bowl. Mix ½ teaspoon water and the mustard in 1-quart bowl; stir in yogurt, lemon juice, garlic, salt, cardamom, ginger, cumin, red peppers and pepper. Pour over chicken; turn to coat well with marinade. Cover and refrigerate 12 to 24 hours.

Place chicken on rack in shallow roasting pan, reserving marinade. Roast uncovered in 375° oven, spooning reserved marinade over chicken during last 30 minutes of roasting, until thickest pieces are done, 1¾ to 2¼ hours. (Place a tent of aluminum foil loosely over chicken during last 30 minutes to prevent excessive browning.) Remove chicken from pan; stir in ¼ cup water. Heat just until hot. Serve with chicken.

Country-Style Chicken

(Poulet en Cocotte à la Paysanne)

When France's King Henry IV dreamed of "a chicken in every Frenchman's pot," it was probably a dish like this he had in mind—a simple pot-roasted chicken flavored with aromatic vegetables, white wine and thyme.

8 servings

3-	to 4-pound broiler-fryer chicken
2	tablespoons margarine or butter
1	can (10¾ ounces) condensed chicken broth
1	teaspoon salt
¼	teaspoon pepper
¼	teaspoon dried thyme leaves
8	medium carrots, cut into fourths
8	small whole white onions
4	medium turnips, cut into fourths
½	cup dry white wine
2	tablespoons cold water
1	tablespoon cornstarch

Fold chicken wings across back with tips touching; tie drumsticks to tail. Heat margarine in Dutch oven until melted. Cook chicken in margarine over medium heat until brown on all sides, 20 to 30 minutes. Pour broth over chicken; sprinkle with salt, pepper and thyme. Cover and cook in 375° oven 45 minutes. Arrange carrots, onions and turnips around chicken. Cover and cook until thickest pieces of chicken are done, 1 to 1½ hours.

Remove chicken and vegetables to warm platter; remove string. Keep chicken warm. Stir wine into chicken broth. Heat to boiling. Mix water and cornstarch; stir into wine broth. Heat to boiling, stirring constantly. Boil and stir 1 minute; skim fat. Serve sauce with chicken.

Spanish Chicken with Vegetables and Olives

Spanish Chicken with Vegetables and Olives

(Pollo a la Chilindrón)

An old Spanish saying holds that "in the South they fry, in central Spain they roast, in the North they stew." Thus pollo a la chilindrón *is typical of the cooking of central Spain. Chilindrón refers to a method of combining smoked ham with vegetables, popular in the Aragon region of Spain, northeast of Madrid.*

6 to 8 servings

3-	to 4-pound broiler-fryer chicken
¼	cup margarine or butter, melted
3	tomatoes, cut into wedges
2	green peppers, cut into rings
2	medium onions, sliced
1	clove garlic, chopped
¼	pound fully cooked smoked ham, cut up (1 cup)
8	pitted ripe olives, cut into halves
1	teaspoon salt
¼	teaspoon pepper

Fasten neck skin of chicken to back with skewer. Fold wings across back with tips touching. Tie or skewer drumsticks to tail. Brush with margarine. Place chicken breast side up in Dutch oven. Cook uncovered in 375° oven, brushing with margarine every 30 minutes, until thickest pieces of chicken are done, about 1½ hours.

Add tomatoes, green peppers, onions, garlic, ham and olives. Sprinkle chicken and vegetables with salt and pepper. Cover and cook until green pepper is tender, about 20 minutes. Place chicken on serving platter; arrange vegetables and ham around chicken. Serve with hot cooked rice if desired.

Chicken with Sesame Sauce

(Pipián Rojo de Ajonjoli)

Pipián is a Mexican expression for a spicy to-mato sauce containing seeds or nuts—in this recipe, sesame seed, introduced to Mexico by Spanish *conquistadores in the seventeenth century. "Toasting" the sesame seeds in a skil-let adds a rich, nutty flavor to the dish. Try* pipián *with our Zucchini-and-Avocado Salad (page 209).*

6 to 8 servings

2½-	to 3-pound broiler-fryer chicken, cut up
1	cup water
1	clove garlic, finely chopped
1	teaspoon salt
½	cup sesame seed
1	can (8 ounces) tomato sauce
1	small onion, chopped
2	teaspoons chili powder
2	teaspoons paprika
¼	teaspoon ground cinnamon
⅛	teaspoon ground cloves
	Snipped parsley

Heat chicken, water, garlic and salt to boiling in Dutch oven; reduce heat. Cover and sim-mer until thickest pieces of chicken are done, 35 to 45 minutes. Remove chicken from broth; keep warm. Reserve ½ cup broth.

Heat sesame seed in ungreased skillet over medium heat until golden brown, 2 to 3 min-utes. Place in blender container. Cover and blend on medium speed until finely chopped, about 5 seconds. Mix sesame seed, tomato sauce, onion, chili powder, paprika, cinna-mon and cloves in 2-quart saucepan. Cook and stir 5 minutes. Stir in reserved broth; pour over chicken. Sprinkle with parsley.

African Chicken-and-Rice Casserole

(Jollof Rice Ghana)

Jollof rice comes from West Africa and is thought to be named after the Jollof region of Senegal, although the word may come from "Wolof"—one of the peoples of Senegal. "Jollof" always indicates that the rice is cooked in the dish rather than served separately. The use of chicken (rather than fish) is characteristic of Ghana.

8 servings

2½-	to 3-pound broiler-fryer chicken, cut up
2	cans (16 ounces each) stewed tomatoes
2	cups water
2	teaspoons salt
¼	teaspoon pepper
1	cup uncooked regular rice
¼	pound fully cooked smoked ham, cubed (¾ cup)
¼	teaspoon ground cinnamon
¼	to ½ teaspoon ground red pepper
3	cups coarsely shredded cabbage
8	ounces green beans*
2	onions, cut into ½-inch slices
½	teaspoon salt

Heat chicken, tomatoes (with liquid), water, 2 teaspoons salt and the pepper to boiling in 5-quart Dutch oven; reduce heat. Cover and simmer 30 minutes. Remove chicken. Stir in rice, ham, cinnamon and red pepper. Add chicken, cabbage, green beans and onions. Sprinkle with ½ teaspoon salt. Heat to boil-ing; reduce heat. Cover and simmer until thickest pieces of chicken are done, 20 to 30 minutes.

* 1 package (10 ounces) frozen French-style green beans, thawed, can be substituted for the green beans.

Chicken-and-Vegetable Stew

Chicken-and-Vegetable Stew

(Saucochi di Gallinja)

Here is another classic Caribbean stew—this one a favorite in the Dominican Republic and popular throughout the Caribbean. Saucochi di gallinja *combines whole ears of sweet corn cut into thirds with such colorful vegetables as sweet potatoes, tomatoes and peas. A touch of hot chili makes the stew as tongue-tingling as it is eye-appealing.*

8 or 9 servings

2½-	to 3-pound broiler-fryer chicken, cut up
6	cups water
2	tablespoons instant beef bouillon
2	medium tomatoes, chopped
2	medium onions, chopped
2	medium potatoes, cut into ½-inch slices
2	medium sweet potatoes or yams, cut into ½-inch slices
3	ears sweet corn, cut into 3 pieces
¼	pound winter squash, pared and cut into ½-inch pieces (about 1 cup)
½	cup fresh or frozen green peas
1	small hot chili, stemmed, seeded and sliced
2	teaspoons salt
¼	teaspoon pepper
	Snipped chives

Heat chicken, water and bouillon to boiling in Dutch oven; reduce heat. Cover and simmer 30 minutes. Skim off fat. Add remaining ingredients except chives. Heat to boiling; reduce heat. Cover and simmer until thickest pieces of chicken are done and vegetables are tender, about 20 minutes. Garnish each serving with chives.

Storing and Freezing Poultry

Did You Know?

Fresh poultry is very perishable and should be stored loosely wrapped in the coldest part of the refrigerator. Use within 1 or 2 days. For longer storage wrap tightly in freezer wrap (giblets separately). Label, date and freeze at 0°F or lower.

For optimum quality, freeze chicken no longer than 9 months, ducks and geese 6 months and giblets 3 months. For best results, freeze cut-up cooked poultry in chicken broth or gravy and use within 3 weeks.

Thaw frozen poultry, still freezer-wrapped, in the refrigerator, allowing about 2 hours per pound. For faster thawing at room temperature, place the wrapped poultry in a brown paper bag on a tray, allowing about 1 hour per pound. Or immerse wrapped poultry in cold water, allowing ½ to 1 hour per pound.

Tarragon Chicken

Tarragon Chicken

(Poulet à l'Estragon)

Tarragon—an anise-flavored perennial herb—is highly regarded in the Burgundy region of southeastern France, famed for its fine wine and superb food. Tarragon Chicken goes well with noodles and buttered green beans or peas, and is usually served with a light red or a rosé wine.

6 to 8 servings

2½- to 3-pound broiler-fryer chicken, cut up
1   cup chicken broth or bouillon
3   medium carrots, sliced
1   tablespoon snipped fresh tarragon or 1 teaspoon dried tarragon leaves
1½   teaspoons salt

⅛   teaspoon pepper
1   bay leaf
4   ounces mushrooms, sliced
2   stalks celery, sliced
1   medium onion, sliced
½   cup dry white wine
½   cup half-and-half
3   tablespoons flour
1   egg yolk
     Hot cooked noodles

Heat chicken, chicken broth, carrots, tarragon, salt, pepper and bay leaf to boiling in 12-inch skillet or Dutch oven; reduce heat. Cover and simmer 30 minutes. Add mushrooms, celery and onion. Heat to boiling; reduce heat. Cover and simmer until thickest pieces of chicken are done, about 15 minutes.

Remove chicken and vegetables to warm platter with slotted spoon; keep warm. Drain liquid from skillet; strain and reserve 1 cup. Pour reserved liquid and the wine into skillet. Mix half-and-half, flour and egg yolk until smooth; stir into wine mixture. Cook, stiring constantly, until thickened. Serve with chicken, vegetables and noodles.

Chicken in Groundnut Sauce

In Africa, peanuts are called groundnuts. They were introduced to Africa from the New World by the Spanish in the early seventeenth century. Groundnuts flourished in the lush tropical climate and quickly became a staple food of many of the peoples of Africa. This recipe is a specialty of West Africa, and is served in homes and resaurants from Senegal to the Congo.

8 servings

1	can (1 ounce) anchovy fillets
2	tablespoons peanut or vegetable oil
2½-	to 3-pound broiler-fryer chicken, cut up
1	cup hot water
2	tablespoons tomato paste
1	can (14½ ounces) whole tomatoes
1	medium onion, sliced
1	clove garlic, finely chopped
3	to 4 dried chilies, crumbled
1	tablespoon chopped candied ginger or ¼ teaspoon grated ginger root
1½	teaspoons chili powder
½	teaspoon salt
1	to 1½ cups crunchy peanut butter Accompaniments (right) Whole chilies

Drain oil from anchovies into Dutch oven; add peanut oil. Heat until hot. Cook chicken over medium heat until brown on all sides, about 15 minutes. Remove chicken. Drain fat from Dutch oven. Heat anchovies, water, tomato paste, tomatoes (with liquid), onion, garlic, dried chilies, ginger, chili powder and

salt to boiling in Dutch oven; reduce heat. Cover and simmer 10 minutes. Add chicken; cover and simmer 45 minutes.

Stir some of the hot liquid into peanut butter; stir into chicken mixture. Turn chicken to coat with sauce. Cover and cook until chicken is done, 10 to 15 minutes. Serve with a selection of Accompaniments; garnish with whole chilies.

Accompaniments: Fried sliced plantains, chopped raw peanuts, chutney, chopped tomatoes, diced green pepper, chopped onion, diced cucumber.

Zesty Chicken Oregano (Kotopoulo Riganato tis Skaras)

The flavors of lemon and oregano predominate in many Greek dishes. For a refreshing Greek supper, serve Zesty Chicken Oregano with our Athenian Salad (page 203) and Pocket Bread (page 272).

6 to 8 servings

2½-	to 3-pound broiler-fryer chicken, cut up
½	cup olive or vegetable oil
¼	cup lemon juice
2	teaspoons dried oregano leaves
1	teaspoon salt
½	teaspoon pepper
1	clove garlic, chopped Lemon slices

Place chicken in ungreased oblong pan, 13 x 9 x 2 inches. Mix remaining ingredients except lemon slices; pour over chicken. Cook uncovered in 375° oven, spooning oil mixture over chicken occasionally, 30 minutes. Turn chicken; cook until thickest pieces are done, about 30 minutes. Garnish with lemon slices.

Chicken Fricassée
(Fricassée de Poulet)

In France, a fricassée *is a combination of a fried dish and a stew. First the vegetables and chicken are cooked in margarine or butter; then liquid is added; and finally the sauce is thickened with a rich, velvety combination of egg yolks and cream.* Fricassée de poulet—*a "white" fricassée—has been cherished by the French for centuries.*

6 to 8 servings

2	medium carrots, sliced
1	medium onion, sliced
1	stalk celery, sliced
6	tablespoons margarine or butter
2½-	to 3-pound broiler-fryer chicken, cut up
2	cups water
1	cup dry white wine
2	teaspoons instant chicken bouillon
½	teaspoon salt
2	Bouquets Garnis (below)
16	small white onions
8	ounces mushrooms, sliced
1	tablespoon lemon juice
2	egg yolks
½	cup whipping cream
2	tablespoons snipped parsley
	Hot cooked rice (page 253)

Cook and stir carrots, sliced onion and the celery in 4 tablespoons of the margarine in 12-inch skillet or Dutch oven until onions are tender; push to side. Add chicken; cook uncovered until light brown, about 10 minutes. Add water, ½ cup of the wine, the bouillon, salt and 1 Bouquet Garni. Heat to boiling; reduce heat. Cover and simmer until thickest pieces of chicken are done, about 40 minutes.

Heat 16 onions and the remaining margarine, wine and Bouquet Garni to boiling; reduce heat. Cover and simmer until onions are tender, about 25 minutes. Remove chicken and onions to warm platter with slotted spoon. Strain bouillon and onion liquid together; discard carrots, onion and celery slices. Skim fat from broth. Heat broth, mushrooms and lemon juice to boiling; reduce heat. Simmer uncovered until reduced to 2½ cups.

Mix egg yolks and whipping cream. Beat 1 cup broth by tablespoonfuls into whipping cream mixture. Beat in remaining broth. Heat to boiling, stirring constantly. Boil and stir 1 minute; pour over chicken and onions. Sprinkle with parsley. Serve with rice.

Bouquets Garnis
For each Bouquet Garni, tie 2 sprigs parsley, ½ bay leaf and ⅛ teaspoon dried rosemary leaves in cheesecloth bag.

Chicken with Spanish Garden Vegetables
(Pollo a la Jardinera)

The Spanish have been growing and enjoying cauliflower since the twelfth century, when several varieties of the vegetable were introduced to Spain by Moorish invaders from North Africa. In Spanish cooking, a la jardinera *means using fresh garden vegetables.*

6 to 8 servings

⅓	cup all-purpose flour
1	teaspoon salt
⅛	teaspoon pepper
2½-	to 3-pound broiler-fryer chicken, cut up
2	tablespoons olive or vegetable oil
⅓	cup water
1	medium onion, cut into 8 wedges
1	clove garlic, chopped
½	teaspoon dried basil leaves
½	small head cauliflower, separated into flowerets
1	package (10 ounces) frozen green peas
2	medium tomatoes, coarsely chopped
1	teaspoon salt

Mix flour, 1 teaspoon salt and the pepper; coat

chicken with flour mixture. Heat oil in Dutch oven or 12-inch skillet until hot. Cook chicken over medium heat until brown on all sides, about 15 minutes. Drain fat from Dutch oven. Add water, onion, garlic and basil. Heat to boiling; reduce heat. Cover and simmer 25 minutes.

Add cauliflower, peas and tomatoes to chicken mixture; sprinkle with 1 teaspoon salt. Add 2 to 3 tablespoons water if necessary. Cover and simmer until thickest pieces of chicken are done and vegetables are tender, about 15 minutes. Garnish with snipped parsley if desired.

Crunchy Almond Chicken

In ancient times Pakistan, like Afghanistan, served as a crossroads for spices and gems moving from China and India to the Middle East. This delicately spiced Pakistani dish reflects the flavors of several worlds—ginger root from China, cumin from the Middle East, paprika from the New World by way of Hungary, and almonds, native to Pakistan.

6 to 8 servings

1	cup blanched slivered almonds
1	clove garlic
1	thin slice ginger root
1	teaspoon salt
1	teaspoon paprika
¼	teaspoon ground cumin
¼	teaspoon pepper
2½-	to 3-pound broiler-fryer chicken, cut up
⅓	cup margarine or butter, melted

Place almonds, garlic and ginger root in blender container; cover and blend until finely ground. Mix almond mixture, salt, paprika, cumin and pepper. Dip chicken into margarine; roll in almond mixture. Place chicken skin sides up in ungreased oblong pan, 13 x 9 x 2 inches. Cook uncovered in 375° oven until thickest pieces are done, 55 to 60 minutes.

Chicken Creole

The word "creole" originally meant a person of European descent who was born and raised in the West Indies, Spanish America, or the French colonies of southern North America. Creole cooking reflects this mixed heritage. This recipe, which comes from Haiti, includes tomatoes and peppers (native to Latin America) and okra, which was introduced to the West Indies in the seventeenth century by European settlers and their African slaves.

6 to 8 servings

2	tablespoons vegetable oil
2½-	to 3-pound broiler-fryer chicken, cut up
2	medium onions, chopped
1	clove garlic, chopped
1	green pepper, chopped
1	can (16 ounces) stewed tomatoes
1	can (8 ounces) tomato sauce
1	teaspoon salt
½	teaspoon ground thyme
½	teaspoon red pepper sauce
¼	teaspoon ground red pepper
1½	cups sliced okra*
	Hot cooked rice (page 253)

Heat oil in 12-inch skillet or Dutch oven until hot. Cook chicken over medium heat until brown on all sides, about 15 minutes. Drain fat from skillet. Stir in remaining ingredients except okra and rice. Heat to boiling; reduce heat. Cover and simmer 30 minutes.

Stir in okra. Heat to boiling; reduce heat. Cover and simmer until thickest pieces of chicken are done and okra is tender, about 10 minutes. Serve with rice.

* 1 package (10 ounces) frozen okra can be substituted for the fresh okra.

Chicken Curry

Chicken Curry

The regional cooking of the Indian subcontinent is as diverse as the cooking of Western Europe—yet a Western-style "curry" is rarely found in India. Our easy, tasty Chicken Curry brings you a taste of Indian cooking without requiring you to purchase, grind and blend many exotic Indian spices.

6 to 8 servings

2	tablespoons vegetable oil
2½-	to 3-pound broiler-fryer chicken, cut up
1	teaspoon salt
1	medium onion, chopped
2	tablespoons water
1	cup dairy sour cream
2	teaspoons curry powder
⅛	teaspoon ground ginger
⅛	teaspoon ground cumin
	Mango Chutney (right)
	Hot cooked rice (page 253)

Heat oil in 12-inch skillet or Dutch oven until hot. Cook chicken over medium heat until brown on all sides, about 15 minutes. Drain fat from skillet. Sprinkle chicken with salt, onion and water. Cover and simmer until thickest pieces of chicken are done, 30 to 40 minutes.

Remove chicken from skillet; keep warm. Pour liquid from skillet into bowl; skim fat. Return ¼ cup liquid to skillet; stir in sour cream, curry powder, ginger and cumin. Heat, stirring constantly, just until hot. Pour sauce over chicken. Serve chicken with Mango Chutney and rice.

Mango Chutney

1	mango (about 1 pound), coarsely chopped
1	cup golden raisins
1	cup packed brown sugar
¾	cup vinegar
1	jar (2⅞ ounces) crystallized ginger, finely chopped
1	clove garlic, chopped
1	teaspoon salt

Heat all ingredients to boiling; reduce heat. Simmer uncovered until slightly thickened, about 45 minutes.

Mangos

Did You Know?

Mangos—plump, juicy, deep-gold tropical fruits with reddish-yellow skins—come in a variety of shapes, including round and oval. They are ripe when the fruit yields to soft pressure, but they can be bought green and ripened at room temperature. Mangos are refreshing for desserts or salads, and are sometimes used in sauces and preserves. The skins are thicker than apple skins, and firm. Pare mangos just before you serve them and slice against the pit, as with peaches.

Caribbean Chicken with Limes

The food of the Caribbean is nearly always international in nature, reflecting the influence of the many peoples who have colonized the islands since Columbus discovered them. This recipe includes Worcestershire sauce and lime (introduced by the British), cabbage and onion (introduced by the first Spanish settlers), and tomatoes (which may have reached the Caribbean from Mexico in pre-Columbian times).

6 to 8 servings

2½-	to 3-pound broiler-fryer chicken, cut up
1	teaspoon salt
3	tablespoons lime juice
2	tablespoons vegetable oil
¼	cup water
2	tomatoes, chopped
1	large onion, chopped
1	stalk celery, sliced
1	clove garlic, chopped
2	teaspoons Worcestershire sauce
1	teaspoon salt
⅛	teaspoon pepper
4	cups shredded cabbage
2	cups water
1	cup uncooked regular rice
1	tablespoon snipped parsley
2	teaspoons instant chicken bouillon
½	teaspoon grated lime peel (optional)

Place chicken in shallow glass or plastic dish; sprinkle with 1 teaspoon salt. Pour lime juice over chicken. Cover and refrigerate about 1 hour. Heat oil in Dutch oven or 12-inch skillet until hot. Cook chicken over medium heat until brown on all sides, about 15 minutes.

Drain fat from Dutch oven. Add water, tomatoes, onion, celery, garlic, Worcestershire sauce, 1 teaspoon salt and the pepper. Heat to boiling; reduce heat. Cover and simmer 30 minutes. Add cabbage. Cover and simmer until thickest pieces of chicken are done, 10 to 15 minutes.

Heat water, rice, parsley, bouillon and lime peel to boiling, stirring once or twice; reduce heat. Cover and simmer until liquid is absorbed, about 14 minutes. (Do not lift cover or stir.) Fluff rice lightly with fork; cover and let steam 5 to 10 minutes. Serve chicken and vegetables with juices over rice. Garnish with celery leaves and lime slices if desired.

Five Spice Chicken (Wu Hsiang' Chi)

Wu hsiang means five spices—a favorite Chinese spice combination for many centuries. The traditional five spices used by the Chinese were whole star anise, fennel, Chinese anise pepper, cloves and cassia (Chinese cinnamon). Our recipe uses five similar spices available at supermarkets. Several modern versions of Chinese five spice seasoning can be found at oriental groceries and large supermarkets.

6 to 8 servings

2½-	to 3-pound broiler-fryer chicken, cut up
⅓	cup soy sauce
2	tablespoons vegetable oil
1	small onion, chopped
1	clove garlic, finely chopped
½	teaspoon ground ginger
¼	teaspoon ground cinnamon
¼	teaspoon crushed anise seed
⅛	teaspoon ground nutmeg
⅛	teaspoon ground cloves

Place chicken in shallow glass or plastic dish. Mix remaining ingredients; pour over chicken. Cover and refrigerate, spooning marinade over chicken occasionally, at least 1 hour.

Remove chicken from marinade; reserve marinade. Place chicken in ungreased oblong baking dish, 12 x 7½ x 2 inches. Brush marinade on chicken. Cook uncovered in 350° oven, brushing once or twice with marinade, until thickest pieces of chicken are done, about 1 hour.

Honey-Spiced Chicken with Orange Sauce

Honey-Spiced Chicken with Orange Sauce

The food of modern Israel reflects both the traditional flavors of the Middle East and the influence of the many peoples who have made Israel their new home. This splendid recipe is most characteristic of the age-old cooking of the eastern Mediterranean countries.

6 to 8 servings

2	tablespoons vegetable oil or chicken fat
2½-	to 3-pound broiler-fryer chicken, cut up
2	medium onions, sliced
1	teaspoon salt
1	teaspoon paprika
⅛	teaspoon pepper
1	cup orange juice
¼	cup honey
2	tablespoons lemon juice
½	teaspoon ground ginger
¼	teaspoon ground nutmeg
½	cup pitted ripe olives
1	tablespoon cold water
2	teaspoons cornstarch
	Orange slices

Heat oil in skillet until hot. Cook chicken over medium heat until brown on all sides, about 15 minutes. Place chicken in ungreased oblong baking dish, 11 x 7 x 1½ inches; top with onions. Sprinkle with salt, paprika and pepper. Mix orange juice, honey, lemon juice, ginger and nutmeg; pour over chicken. Add olives. Cover and cook in 350° oven until thickest pieces of chicken are done, 45 to 60 minutes.

Arrange chicken, onions, and olives on platter. Pour pan juices into saucepan; heat to boiling. Mix water and cornstarch; stir into juices. Cook and stir until slightly thickened, 1 to 2 minutes. Garnish chicken with orange slices; serve with orange sauce.

Chicken Cacciatore
(Pollo alla Cacciatora)

Cacciatora usually spelled cacciatore on American restaurant menus—means "hunter's style" in Italian. Although the dish rarely includes game, it is always served with generous portions of spaghetti, making it a favorite of sportsmen with hearty appetites. One Italian legend holds that the dish was invented by a hunter's wife when the unlucky hunter returned home with only a few mushrooms and olives.

6 to 8 servings

½	cup all-purpose flour
1	teaspoon salt
¼	teaspoon pepper
2½-	to 3-pound broiler-fryer chicken, cut up
¼	cup olive or vegetable oil
1	can (16 ounces) tomatoes
1	can (8 ounces) tomato sauce
1	cup mushrooms, sliced
¼	cup water
¼	cup sliced pitted ripe olives
1	medium onion, chopped
2	cloves garlic, crushed
1	teaspoon salt
1	teaspoon crushed dried oregano leaves
¼	teaspoon pepper
1	bay leaf
	Snipped parsley
	Hot cooked spaghetti

Mix flour, 1 teaspoon salt and ¼ teaspoon pepper. Coat chicken with flour mixture. Heat oil in 12-inch skillet or Dutch oven until hot. Cook chicken over medium heat until brown on all sides, about 15 minutes. Drain fat from skillet.

Mix tomatoes, tomato sauce, mushrooms, water, olives, onion, garlic, 1 teaspoon salt, the oregano, ¼ teaspoon pepper and the bay leaf; break up tomatoes with fork. Pour over chicken. Heat to boiling; reduce heat. Cover and simmer until thickest pieces of chicken are done, about 30 minutes. Sprinkle with parsley; serve with spaghetti.

Mexican Fried Chicken
(Pollo en Jugo de Limones)

Lime juice is the secret flavoring agent in this recipe; combined with a touch of chili powder, it brings a refreshing tropical flavor to familiar fried chicken. Our Quick Mexican Potato Salad (page 208) adds a colorful and nourishing touch to a summery south-of-the-border supper.

6 to 8 servings

1	clove garlic
½	teaspoon salt
2½-	to 3-pound broiler-fryer chicken, cut up
¼	cup lime juice
1	small onion, finely chopped
	Vegetable oil
½	cup all-purpose flour
1	teaspoon salt
1	teaspoon chili powder

Mash garlic and ½ teaspoon salt until pasty. Rub chicken with garlic mixture. Arrange chicken in shallow glass or plastic dish. Sprinkle with lime juice and onion. Cover and refrigerate, turning occasionally, at least 3 hours. Remove chicken from marinade; pat dry.

Heat oil (¼ inch) in skillet until hot. Decrease heat to medium. Mix flour, 1 teaspoon salt and the chili powder. Coat chicken with flour mixture. Place chicken in skillet skin sides down. Cover and cook 5 minutes. Uncover and cook 15 minutes. Turn chicken. Cover and cook 5 minutes. Uncover and cook until thickest pieces are done, 10 to 15 minutes. Drain on paper towels.

Chicken with Golden Pilaf

Chicken with Golden Pilaf

(Kabuli Pelau)

Pilaf is a rice dish basic to Greece, the Middle East and southern Asia. There are many ways to prepare it and many spellings (see page 99). This recipe comes from Afghanistan, a crossroads for the luxury trade in spices, gold and gems in ancient times. Today the food of Afghanistan still reflects a mingling of Middle Eastern and Indian flavors.

6 to 8 servings

2	tablespoons vegetable oil
2½-	to 3-pound broiler-fryer chicken, cut up
1	teaspoon salt
2	medium carrots
1	medium onion, chopped
¼	cup margarine or butter
2¼	cups water
1	cup uncooked regular rice
½	cup raisins
1	tablespoon instant chicken bouillon
½	teaspoon curry powder
¼	teaspoon salt
¼	teaspoon dried thyme leaves
¼	cup toasted slivered almonds

Heat oil in 12-inch skillet or Dutch oven until hot. Cook chicken over medium heat until brown on all sides, about 15 minutes; reduce heat. Sprinkle with 1 teaspoon salt. Cover and cook over low heat until thickest pieces are done, 30 to 40 minutes. (Add water if necessary.) Uncover during last 5 minutes of cooking to crisp chicken.

Cut carrots lengthwise into ¼-inch strips; cut into 1-inch pieces. Cook and stir onion in margarine in 2-quart saucepan until tender. Add carrots, water, rice, raisins, bouillon, curry powder, ¼ teaspoon salt and the thyme. Heat to boiling, stirring once or twice; reduce heat. Cover and simmer 14 minutes. (Do not lift cover or stir.)

Remove from heat. Fluff rice lightly with fork; cover and let steam 5 to 10 minutes. Serve chicken with rice; top with almonds.

Chicken with Flaming Pineapple

(Pollo con Piña a la Antigua)

From Cuba comes an old and simple chicken dish flavored with lime juice and oregano. The real excitement comes at the last minute, when warm pineapple chunks are flamed with dark rum and spooned over the chicken! Flame the dish at table and be prepared for enthusiastic applause.

6 to 8 servings

2½-	to 3-pound broiler-fryer chicken, cut up
3	tablespoons lime juice
1½	teaspoons salt
¼	teaspoon pepper
2	tablespoons vegetable oil
2	medium tomatoes, cut up
1	medium onion, sliced
1	clove garlic, finely chopped
¼	cup raisins
½	teaspoon dried oregano leaves
3	or 4 drops red pepper sauce
¼	cup water
1	can (20 ounces) pineapple chunks, drained (reserve syrup)
2	tablespoons dark rum

Sprinkle chicken with lime juice, salt and pepper. Cover and refrigerate 30 minutes. Heat oil in 12-inch skillet or Dutch oven until hot. Cook chicken over medium heat until brown on all sides, about 15 minutes. Drain fat from skillet. Add tomatoes, onion, garlic, raisins, oregano, red pepper sauce and water. Heat to boiling; reduce heat. Cover and simmer until thickest pieces of chicken are done, 30 to 40 minutes.

Remove chicken mixture to warm platter with slotted spoon. Heat pineapple and ¼ cup of the reserved syrup to boiling. Heat rum until warm; ignite. Pour flaming rum over pineapple. Spoon flaming pineapple mixture over chicken.

Pilaf

Did You Know?

One basic method of cooking rice in Europe and Asia that often causes confusion among Western cooks is *pilaf*. There are many spellings (including pilau, pilaw, pilav, pilaff) and many recipes, which vary from country to country and even from family to family within a community.

Basically "pilaf" indicates rice that is first cooked briefly in oil or butter and then cooked in bouillon or broth. The initial cooking in butter is sometimes omitted, and a wide variety of seasonings and even vegetables, fruits and nuts may be included in pilaf.

"Pilaf" can also indicate a rice dish that is cooked or served with fish, poultry or meat (as in our Chicken with Golden Pilaf, page 88). To add to the complexity of this simple word, "pilaf" can even be used to describe non-rice dishes (made with grains, such as cracked wheat and buckwheat) that are flavored with broth.

Couscous

Couscous

The word "couscous" applies both to a finished stew and to the grain that serves as a primary ingredient in the stew—in our recipe, wheat-grain semolina. Semolina is available at natural food stores and many supermarkets, and is often sold simply as "couscous."

Couscous is popular throughout North Africa; usually it is prepared in a vessel known as a couscoussière. *The grain is placed on a special rack and steamed over the stew.* Couscoussières *are expensive and often difficult to find; our streamlined recipe requires no special equipment.*

8 servings

2	tablespoons olive or vegetable oil
2½-	to 3-pound broiler-fryer chicken, cut up
4	small carrots, cut into 2-inch pieces
2	medium onions, sliced
2	medium turnips, cut into fourths
2	cloves garlic, finely chopped
2	teaspoons ground coriander
1½	teaspoons salt
1	teaspoon instant chicken bouillon
¼	teaspoon ground red pepper
¼	teaspoon ground turmeric
1	cup water
3	zucchini, cut into ¼-inch slices
1	can (about 16 ounces) garbanzo beans (chickpeas), drained
	Couscous (right)

Heat oil in Dutch oven until hot. Cook chicken in oil until brown on all sides, about 15 minutes. Drain fat from Dutch oven. Add carrots, onions, turnips, garlic, coriander, salt, bouillon, red pepper and turmeric. Pour water over vegetables. Heat to boiling; reduce heat. Cover and simmer 30 minutes.

Add zucchini to chicken mixture. Cover and cook until thickest pieces of chicken are done and vegetables are tender, about 10 minutes. Add beans; heat 5 minutes.

Prepare Couscous. Mound on center of heated platter; arrange chicken and vegetables around Couscous.

Couscous

1⅓	cups couscous (wheat-grain semolina)
¾	cup raisins
½	teaspoon salt
1	cup boiling water
½	cup margarine or butter
½	teaspoon ground turmeric

Mix couscous, raisins and salt in 2-quart bowl; stir in boiling water. Let stand until all water is absorbed, 2 to 3 minutes. Heat margarine in 10-inch skillet until melted; stir in couscous and ground turmeric. Cook and stir 4 minutes.

Chicken with Cornmeal Dumplings

(Bolitas con Pollo)

Bolitas— *"little balls," or dumplings made with cornmeal and flavored with onion and thyme— are popular throughout Latin America. In the recipe below, the chicken is enhanced by the flavor of bacon and cooked with tomato sauce and whole-kernel corn, which accents the cornmeal flavor of the* bolitas.

6 to 8 servings

4	slices bacon
⅓	cup all-purpose flour
1	teaspoon salt
1	teaspoon paprika
¼	teaspoon pepper
2½-	to 3-pound broiler-fryer chicken, cut up
1	can (8 ounces) tomato sauce
½	teaspoon ground marjoram
¼	to ½ teaspoon ground red pepper

1	can (16 ounces) whole-kernel corn
2	tablespoons cold water
1	tablespoon flour
	Cornmeal Dumplings (below)
2	zucchini, sliced
½	teaspoon salt

Fry bacon in 12-inch skillet or Dutch oven until crisp; drain on paper towels. Crumble bacon; reserve. Mix 1/3 cup flour, 1 teaspoon salt, the paprika and pepper; coat chicken with flour mixture. Cook chicken in bacon fat until brown on all sides. Drain fat from skillet. Add tomato sauce, marjoram and red pepper. Heat to boiling; reduce heat. Cover and simmer 30 minutes.

Remove chicken from skillet; keep warm. Skim fat from skillet if necessary. Add corn (with liquid); heat to boiling. Mix 2 tablespoons water and 1 tablespoon flour; stir into corn. Heat to boiling, stirring constantly. Boil and stir 1 minute. Return chicken to skillet. Prepare Cornmeal Dumplings; drop by spoonfuls onto hot chicken mixture. Arrange zucchini slices around dumplings; sprinkle with ½ teaspoon salt. Cover and simmer 20 minutes. Garnish each serving with bacon.

Cornmeal Dumplings

½	cup all-purpose flour
½	cup yellow cornmeal
¼	cup milk
1	egg
1	small onion, finely chopped
2	tablespoons vegetable oil
1	teaspoon baking powder
½	teaspoon salt
¼	teaspoon ground thyme

Mix all ingredients.

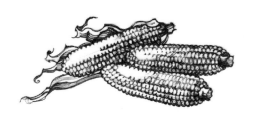

Chicken Paprika with Dumplings

Chicken Paprika with Dumplings

(Csirke Paprikás)

This creamy Hungarian version of chicken and dumplings is most tasty and colorful when made with fine-quality sweet Hungarian paprika, which can be purchased at some large supermarkets and at shops carrying German and Austrian specialty foods.

6 to 8 servings

2	tablespoons vegetable oil
2½-	to 3-pound broiler-fryer chicken, cut up
2	medium onions, chopped
1	clove garlic, chopped
1	tomato, chopped
½	cup water
½	teaspoon instant chicken bouillon
2	tablespoons paprika
1	teaspoon salt
¼	teaspoon pepper
1	green pepper, cut into ½-inch strips
	Dumplings (below)
1	cup dairy sour cream

Heat oil in 12-inch skillet until hot. Cook chicken over medium heat until brown on all sides, about 15 minutes. Remove chicken. Cook and stir onions and garlic in oil until onions are tender; drain fat from skillet. Stir in tomato, water, bouillon, paprika, salt and pepper; loosen brown particles from bottom of skillet. Add chicken. Heat to boiling; reduce heat. Cover and simmer 20 minutes. Add green pepper; cover and cook until thickest pieces of chicken are done, 10 to 15 minutes. Prepare Dumplings.

Remove chicken to heated platter; keep warm. Skim fat from skillet. Stir sour cream into liquid in skillet; add Dumplings. Heat just until hot. Serve chicken with Dumplings and sour cream sauce.

Dumplings

8	cups water
1	teaspoon salt
3	eggs, well beaten
½	cup water
2	cups all-purpose flour
2	teaspoons salt

Heat 8 cups water and 1 teaspoon salt to boiling in Dutch oven. Mix eggs, ½ cup water, the flour and 2 teaspoons salt; drop dough by teaspoonfuls into boiling water. Cook uncovered, stirring occasionally, 10 minutes. Drain. (Dumplings are chewy, not fluffy and tender as in American version.)

Cutting Up a Chicken

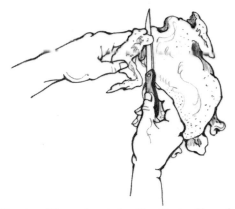

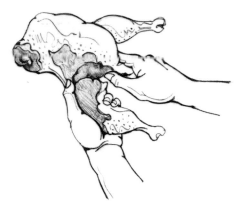

Start with a sharp knife. Cut off each wing by cutting the wing joint, then rolling knife to let blade follow through at the curve of the joint.

Cut off each leg by cutting skin between leg and body; cut through the meat between the tail and hip joint. Pull leg away to separate meat from bone, then cut through remaining skin.

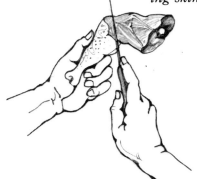

Cut each drumstick away from thigh by cutting ⅛ inch from the thin fat line that runs crosswise at the joint between drumstick and thigh.

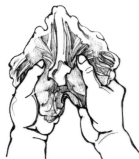

Separate backbone by holding body, neck end down, and cutting along each side of the backbone through the rib joints.

Place breast skin side down, neck end away from you and cut through cartilage at the **V** of the neck. Bend back both sides to pull, and pop out the bone and cartilage. Pull out bone and cartilage. Cut breast in half; for 8 servings, cut each breast half in halves.

Spicy Chicken Stew with Fruit

Spicy Chicken Stew with Fruit

(Mancha Manteles)

The Mexican name for this hearty cinnamon-and-chili-powder-flavored stew means table-cloth stainers. The unusual combination of chicken, pork, fruit and vegetables suggests a dish for an important party.

8 to 10 servings

2	tablespoons vegetable oil
2	pounds chicken legs and thighs
1	pound pork boneless shoulder, cut into ¾-inch pieces
1	medium onion, chopped
1	green pepper, chopped
¼	cup blanched almonds
1	can (8 ounces) tomato sauce
1	can (about 8½ ounces) sliced pineapple, drained (reserve syrup)
½	cup water
2	teaspoons chili powder
1	teaspoon salt
½	teaspoon ground cinnamon
2	sweet potatoes, cut into 1-inch pieces
2	apples, sliced
2	bananas, sliced
	Parsley

Heat oil in Dutch oven or 12-inch skillet until hot. Cook chicken over medium heat until brown on all sides, about 15 minutes. Remove chicken. Cook and stir pork until brown, about 10 minutes. Remove pork. Cook and stir onion, green pepper and almonds until onion is tender. Place onion, green pepper, almonds and tomato sauce in blender container. Cover and blend until of uniform consistency.

Drain fat from Dutch oven. Mix tomato mixture, reserved pineapple syrup, the water, chili powder, salt and cinnamon in Dutch oven. Add chicken, pork and sweet potatoes.

Heat to boiling; reduce heat. Cover and simmer until sweet potatoes are tender, 45 to 60 minutes. (Add ¼ cup water if necessary.)

Cut pineapple slices into halves; add pineapple and apples to chicken mixture. Cover and simmer until apples are tender, about 10 minutes. Add bananas. Serve in soup bowls; garnish with parsley.

Chicken-and-Leek Soup

(Cock-a-Leekie)

Recipes for this country-style soup from Scotland appeared in British cookbooks in Elizabethan times, when prunes were often included in the soup. Since the time of Napoleon, cock-a-leekie has been prized by British and French peasants and princes. Our easy version can be made in about an hour. Serve with Scottish Oatcakes (page 263) or Crumpets (page 280).

7 servings (about 1 cup each)

2½	pound broiler-fryer chicken, cut up
4	cups water
1	medium carrot, sliced
1	medium stalk celery, sliced
½	cup barley
2	teaspoons instant chicken bouillon
2	teaspoons salt
¼	teaspoon pepper
1	bay leaf
1½	cups sliced leeks (with tops)

Heat all ingredients except leeks to boiling in Dutch oven; reduce heat. Cover and simmer 30 minutes. Add leeks. Heat to boiling; reduce heat. Cover and simmer until thickest pieces of chicken are done, about 15 minutes. Remove chicken from broth; cool slightly. Remove chicken from bones and skin; cut chicken into 1-inch pieces. Skim fat from broth; remove bay leaf. Add chicken to broth; heat until hot, about 5 minutes.

Mulligatawny Soup

*"Mulligatawny" is thought to have come from two words in the Tamil language—*milaku tanni, *meaning pepper water. The soup apparently originated in the Madras region of India and was probably a British inspiration prepared by Indian chefs with their traditional spices. Often Mulligatawny Soup is made with lamb rather than chicken.*

6 servings (about 1¼ cups each)

2½-	to 3-pound broiler-fryer chicken, cut up
4	cups water
1½	teaspoons salt
1	teaspoon curry powder
1	teaspoon lemon juice
⅛	teaspoon ground cloves
⅛	teaspoon ground mace
1	medium onion, chopped
2	tablespoons margarine or butter
2	tablespoons flour
1	medium carrot, thinly sliced
1	apple, chopped
1	green pepper, cut into ½-inch pieces
2	tomatoes, chopped
	Parsley

Heat chicken, water, salt, curry powder, lemon juice, cloves and mace to boiling in Dutch oven; reduce heat. Cover and simmer until thickest pieces of chicken are done, about 45 minutes. Remove chicken from broth; skim fat from broth if necessary. Add enough water to broth if necessary to measure 4 cups. Remove bones and skin from chicken; cut chicken into pieces.

Cook and stir onion in margarine in Dutch oven until tender. Remove from heat; stir in flour. Gradually stir in broth. Add chicken, carrot, apple, green pepper and tomatoes. Heat to boiling; reduce heat. Cover and simmer until carrot is tender, about 10 minutes. Serve in shallow soup bowls; garnish with parsley.

Chicken in Red Wine
(Coq au Vin Rouge)

Coq au vin *is another of France's favorite chicken dishes—and another version of* fricassée *(see Chicken Fricassée, page 82). This "brown" fricassée receives its robust flavor from bacon and red wine, which adds to the rich color. Parsleyed potatoes are the traditional accompaniment to* coq au vin rouge.

6 to 8 servings

6	slices bacon
½	cup all-purpose flour
1	teaspoon salt
¼	teaspoon pepper
3-	to 3½-pound broiler-fryer chicken, cut up
1	pound mushrooms
½	pound tiny pearl onions
8	baby carrots
2½	cups dry red wine
1½	cups chicken broth
2	cloves garlic, finely chopped
1	teaspoon salt
	Bouquet Garni (below)
	Snipped parsley

Fry bacon in Dutch oven until crisp; remove bacon. Mix flour, 1 teaspoon salt and the pepper. Coat chicken with flour mixture. Cook chicken in hot bacon fat over medium heat until light brown, 15 to 20 minutes. Remove chicken. Cook mushrooms, onions and carrots until light brown. Drain fat.

Return chicken to Dutch oven; crumble bacon over chicken and vegetables. Stir in wine, chicken broth, garlic, 1 teaspoon salt and the Bouquet Garni. Heat to boiling; reduce heat. Cover and simmer until thickest pieces of chicken are done, 35 to 40 minutes. Skim fat; remove Bouquet Garni. Sprinkle with parsley; serve in soup bowls.

Bouquet Garni
Tie 4 sprigs parsley, 2 bay leaves and 1 teaspoon dried thyme leaves in cheesecloth bag or place in tea ball.

Caribbean Chicken-and-Rice Stew

Caribbean Chicken-and-Rice Stew

(Asopao de Pollo)

The Caribbean is famous for elegant, imaginative stews using many combinations of vegetables, meat, fish and seasonings. This recipe from Puerto Rico owes its success to sofrito—a combination of tomatoes, onion, garlic, peppers and fresh herbs. Our adaptation can be made with ingredients easily found at your favorite market. Asopao, in Spanish, indicates a "soupy" rice dish.

8 servings

2½-	to 3-pound broiler-fryer chicken, cut up
2	teaspoons salt
1	teaspoon dried oregano leaves
½	teaspoon ground coriander
¼	teaspoon pepper
2	cups water
1	can (16 ounces) stewed tomatoes
1	onion, chopped
1	clove garlic, crushed
1	cup uncooked regular rice
1	package (10 ounces) frozen green peas
1	green pepper, chopped
½	cup cubed fully cooked smoked ham (about 2 ounces)
⅓	cup pitted small green olives
1	tablespoon capers
	Grated Parmesan cheese

Place chicken in 12-inch skillet or Dutch oven. Sprinkle with salt, oregano, coriander and pepper. Add water, tomatoes (with liquid), onion and garlic. Heat to boiling; reduce heat. Cover and simmer 30 minutes.

Stir rice into liquid. Cover and simmer until thickest pieces of chicken are done, about 20 minutes. Rinse frozen peas under running cold water to separate; drain. Add peas, green pepper, ham, olives, capers and 1 tablespoon caper liquid to chicken. Cover and simmer 5 minutes. Serve with cheese.

Chicken Soup with Tortellini

Chicken Soup with Tortellini

(Pollo in Brodo con Tortellini)

Tortellini—*little pasta turnovers filled with meat or cheese mixtures—are the specialty of the Piedmont area of northwestern Italy. North of Genoa this soup is traditionally served with the long, thin breadsticks called grissini, available at many supermarkets and Italian bakeries.*

8 servings (about 1¼ cups each)

3-	to 4-pound broiler-fryer chicken, cut up
6	cups water
1	stalk celery (with leaves), cut into 1-inch pieces
1	carrot, cut into 1-inch pieces
1	medium onion, cut into fourths
2	sprigs parsley
1	bay leaf
2½	teaspoons salt
1	teaspoon peppercorns
	Tortellini (page 99)
2	cups water
	Snipped parsley
	Grated Parmesan cheese

Heat chicken, 6 cups water, the celery, carrot, onion, 2 sprigs parsley, the bay leaf, salt and peppercorns to boiling in Dutch oven; reduce heat. Cover and simmer until thickest pieces of chicken are done, about 45 minutes. Remove chicken from broth; strain broth. Refrigerate chicken and broth separately until cool.

Remove chicken from bones and skin. Finely chop enough dark meat to measure ¾ cup; cover and refrigerate. Cut remaining chicken into bite-size pieces; add to broth. Cover and refrigerate. Prepare Tortellini.

Skim fat from broth. Heat broth and 2 cups water to boiling. Add Tortellini. Heat to boiling; reduce heat. Cover and simmer until Tortellini are tender, about 30 minutes. Sprinkle each serving with snipped parsley. Serve with cheese.

Tortellini

1½   cups all-purpose flour
1   egg
1   egg, separated
2   tablespoons water
1   tablespoon olive or vegetable oil
1   teaspoon salt
2   tablespoons grated Parmesan cheese
⅛   teaspoon grated lemon peel
⅛   teaspoon salt
       Dash of ground mace
       Dash of pepper

Make a well in center of flour; add 1 egg, 1 egg white, the water, oil and 1 teaspoon salt. Stir with fork until mixed; gather dough into a ball. (Sprinkle with a few drops water if dry.) Knead dough on lightly floured board until smooth and elastic, about 5 minutes. Cover and let rest 10 minutes.

Mix reserved ¾ cup chicken, the egg yolk, cheese, lemon peel, ⅛ teaspoon salt, the mace and pepper. Divide dough into halves. Roll one half on lightly floured board into 12-inch square. Cut into twenty 2-inch circles. Place ¼ teaspoon filling on center of each circle.

Moisten edge of each circle with water. Fold circle in half; press edge with fork to seal. Shape into rings by stretching tips of each half circle slightly; wrap ring around index finger. (See diagram.) Moisten one tip with water; gently press tips together. Repeat with remaining dough. Place on tray; cover and refrigerate no longer than 24 hours.

Do-Ahead Tip: Freeze broth and Tortellini separately no longer than 2 weeks. To serve, heat broth and 2 cups water to boiling; continue as directed except simmer 40 minutes.

Shape half circle into rings by stretching tips slightly; wrap ring around index finger.

Saving Chicken Parts

Did You Know?

When cutting up a chicken, save chicken necks, backs and giblets (except livers) to make a savory chicken broth, and store chicken livers for an elegant breakfast treat. The National Broiler Council suggests keeping two heavy plastic bags in your freezer—one for accumulating necks, backs and giblets, and the other for chicken livers. Cook the necks, backs and giblets in water to make Chicken Broth (Italian Vegetable Soup, page 100). When you have enough chicken livers, cut them into halves, fry in margarine, and serve on toast or cooked rice (page 253). Be sure to date the freezer packages and store the chicken parts no longer than 3 months.

Italian Vegetable Soup

Italian Vegetable Soup

(Minestrone)

Minestrone *literally means the big first course. In Italy there are as many recipes for* minestrone *as there are cooks—and there are strong regional preferences. In the South garlic, tomatoes and olive oil predominate and the soup is meatless; in central Italy beans play an important role; in the North rice is considered essential; and along the Italian Riviera fresh herbs are used in generous quantities. In the summer the Italians often serve* minestrone *cold or at room temperature.*

5 servings (about 1¼ cups each)

1	cup water
½	cup dried Great Northern, navy or kidney beans
4	cups Chicken Broth (page 101)
2	small tomatoes, chopped
2	medium carrots, sliced
1	stalk celery, sliced
1	medium onion, chopped
1	clove garlic, chopped
½	cup uncooked macaroni
1	tablespoon snipped parsley
1	teaspoon salt
½	teaspoon dried basil leaves
⅛	teaspoon pepper
1	bay leaf
4	ounces green beans, cut into 1-inch pieces (about ¾ cup)
2	small zucchini, cut into 1-inch slices
	Grated Parmesan cheese

Heat water and dried beans to boiling in Dutch oven; boil 2 minutes. Remove from heat. Cover and let stand 1 hour. Add enough water to cover beans if necessary. Heat to boiling; reduce heat. Cover and simmer until tender, 1 to 1½ hours (do not boil or beans will burst).

Add Chicken Broth, tomatoes, carrots, celery, onion, garlic, macaroni, parsley, salt, basil, pepper and bay leaf to beans. Heat to boiling; reduce heat. Cover and simmer 15 minutes. Add green beans and zucchini. Heat to boiling; reduce heat. Cover and simmer until macaroni and vegetables are tender, 10 to 15 minutes. Remove bay leaf. Serve with cheese.

Chicken Broth

2½ to 3 pounds chicken backs, necks and wings
4½ cups water
1 medium carrot, sliced
1 stalk celery, sliced
1 small onion, sliced
1 bay leaf
1½ teaspoons salt
4 peppercorns
2 sprigs parsley

Remove excess fat from chicken. Heat chicken and remaining ingredients to boiling in Dutch oven; reduce heat. Cover and simmer until chicken is done, about 45 minutes. Remove chicken from broth; strain broth. Cover and refrigerate broth until cool. (Broth can be frozen no longer than 6 months.) Makes 4 to 4½ cups broth.

Canned Chicken Broth Yields

Did You Know?

1 can (46 ounces) chicken broth yields about 6 cups chicken broth.

1 can (10¾ ounces) condensed chicken broth plus 1 soup can water yields about 2½ cups chicken broth.

1 cup water plus 1 teaspoon instant chicken bouillon or 1 cube chicken bouillon yields 1 cup chicken broth.

Chilled Chicken with Rice Sticks

(Bangbangji)

This is our easy version of one of China's most elaborate dishes—a spicy chicken-and-rice-stick "salad" that can be prepared well in advance. The recipe comes from the Szechwan region of China. Szechwan peppercorns and rice sticks can be purchased at oriental groceries and at many fancy food stores or gourmet sections of supermarkets.

6 servings

---

3 large whole chicken breasts
6 scallions, sliced
1 thin slice ginger root, chopped
1 teaspoon Szechwan peppercorns (optional)
½ teaspoon salt
2 ounces uncooked rice sticks *(mai fun)*
2 cucumbers
3 tablespoons vinegar
2 tablespoons sesame oil
2 tablespoons soy sauce
2 teaspoons sugar
½ teaspoon salt
2 tablespoons sesame seed, toasted

Heat chicken, half the scallions, the ginger root, peppercorns, ½ teaspoon salt and just enough water to cover to boiling in 2-quart saucepan; reduce heat. Cover and simmer until chicken is done, 30 to 40 minutes. Cool slightly. Remove chicken from bones and skin. Cut chicken into ¼-inch slices; cut slices into ¼-inch strips. Cover and refrigerate.

Prepare rice sticks as directed on package; drain. Pare cucumbers; cut lengthwise into halves. Scoop out seeds. Cut each half into 3 pieces; cut each piece lengthwise into thin slices.

Mix vinegar, sesame oil, soy sauce, sugar and ½ teaspoon salt. Toss with chicken, remaining scallions, the noodles and cucumber. Sprinkle with toasted sesame seed.

Chicken with Almonds
(Hsing Jen Chi Ting)

This quick and easy chicken dish is basic to stir-fry cookery and has long been one of the most popular items on Chinese restaurant menus in Britain and the United States. The final sprinkling of Deep-Fried Almonds provides the textural contrast characteristic of much of Chinese cooking.

6 servings

3	large whole chicken breasts
3	tablespoons peanut or vegetable oil
½	teaspoon salt
1	can (8½ ounces) water chestnuts, drained and sliced
1	can (8 ounces) bamboo shoots, drained and sliced, or 1 cup peeled, sliced bamboo shoots
¾	cup sliced celery
¾	cup sliced mushrooms
½	teaspoon monosodium glutamate (optional)
¾	cup chicken broth or bouillon
2	teaspoons soy sauce
2	tablespoons cornstarch
2	tablespoons cold water
	Deep-Fried Almonds (right)

Remove bones and skin from chicken breasts; cut chicken into 1-inch pieces. Heat oil in wok or electric skillet until hot; add salt. Stir-fry chicken over high heat until almost done, about 5 minutes.

Reduce heat to medium; add water chestnuts, bamboo shoots, celery, mushrooms and monosodium glutamate. Stir-fry over high heat until heated through, 3 to 5 minutes. Stir in chicken broth and soy sauce. Heat to boiling; reduce heat. Cover and simmer 6 minutes.

Mix cornstarch and water; stir into chicken mixture. Cook and stir until thickened, about 30 seconds. Serve on heated platter; garnish with Deep-Fried Almonds.

Deep-Fried Almonds
Heat 2 inches peanut or vegetable oil in 1-quart saucepan to 360°. Fry ½ cup whole blanched almonds, ¼ cup at a time, until golden brown, about 2 minutes. Remove with slotted spoon; drain on paper towels.

Stir-Frying
Did You Know?

Stir-frying (sometimes called toss-cooking) is a uniquely oriental technique of cooking food very quickly in a small amount of oil in a wok over high heat—higher than most Americans are accustomed to using. Uniform pieces of meat and vegetables are tossed in oil to seal in the meat juices and cook the vegetables just to the crisp-tender stage. All ingredients should be measured and arranged in order before heating the wok. The wok is the ideal utensil for stir-frying because of its sloping sides and rounded bottom. (If you don't have a wok, use a deep skillet with sloping sides.)

Vegetable or peanut oil, with a high smoking point, is the best choice for stir-frying. To stir-fry in a wok, place the adapter ring (wide side up on electric ranges, wide side down on gas ranges) over the largest burner. Place the wok on the ring; heat over high heat until one or two drops of water sizzle and evaporate. Then add a small amount of oil; when the oil is almost to the smoking point, add the food.

Use a wide, firm spatula or long-handled spoon to keep the food moving quickly and constantly. Bring the spatula down the side and across the bottom, lifting and turning the food. If the food sticks or moisture comes out of the meat and vegetables, it means the wok is not hot enough or you are adding too much food at a time. If any food should stick, wash and dry the wok completely between steps.

Boning a Chicken Breast

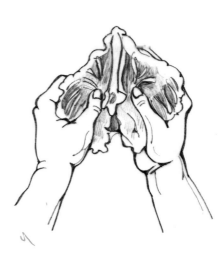

Place 12- to 16-ounce whole chicken breast skin side down on cutting board. Cut through just the white gristle at the end of the keel bone (the dark bone at the center of the breast).

Bend breast halves back to pop out the keel bone. Loosen keel bone by running the tip of the index finger around both sides. Remove in 1 or 2 pieces.

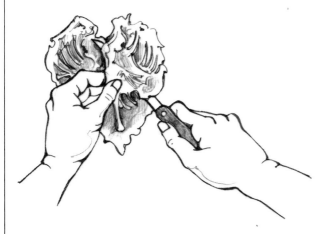

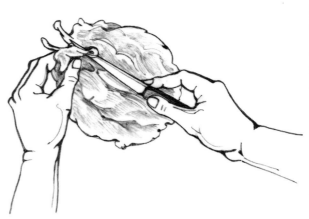

Working with one side of breast, cut rib cages away from breast, cutting through shoulder joint to remove entire rib cage. Repeat on other side.

Turn chicken breast over and cut away wishbone. Slip knife under white tendons on either side of breast; loosen and pull tendons out. Remove skin if desired.

Stir-Fried Chicken and Vegetables

Stir-Fried Chicken and Vegetables

Of the five main cooking regions of China—Szechwan, Hunan, Fukien, Shantung and Canton—this recipe perhaps most typifies the cooking of Canton. Yet the generous variety of vegetables included suggests other areas too. The recipe may be most representative of the cooking of China's capital city, Peking, where the cooking traditions of all China meet.

6 servings

2	large whole chicken breasts
1	egg white
1	teaspoon salt
1	teaspoon cornstarch
1	teaspoon soy sauce
6	ounces pea pods or 1 package (6 ounces) frozen pea pods, partially thawed

2	tablespoons vegetable oil
2	cloves garlic, finely chopped
1	teaspoon finely chopped ginger root
6	medium stalks celery, cut diagonally into ¼-inch slices (3 cups)
2	cups sliced mushrooms
1	can (8½ ounces) water chestnuts, drained and sliced
1	can (8½ ounces) sliced bamboo shoots, drained
2	tablespoons vegetable oil
¾	cup water
1	teaspoon instant chicken bouillon
½	teaspoon sugar
¼	cup cold water
2	tablespoons cornstarch
1	teaspoon soy sauce

Remove bones and skin from chicken breasts. Cut chicken across grain into strips, 1½ x ¼ inch. (For ease in cutting, partially freeze chicken about 1½ hours.) Toss chicken, egg white, salt, 1 teaspoon cornstarch and 1 teaspoon soy sauce in glass or plastic bowl. Cover and refrigerate 30 minutes.

Remove strings from pea pods. Heat 2 tablespoons oil in wok or 12-inch skillet until hot. Cook and stir garlic and ginger root in oil over medium heat until light brown. Add pea pods and celery; stir-fry 1 minute. Add mushrooms, water chestnuts and bamboo shoots; stir-fry 1 minute. Remove vegetables with slotted spoon.

Heat 2 tablespoons oil in wok until hot. Add chicken; stir-fry over high heat until chicken turns white, about 2 minutes. Stir in ¾ cup water, the bouillon and sugar. Heat to boiling; reduce heat. Cover and simmer 2 minutes, stirring occasionally.

Mix ¼ cup water and 2 tablespoons cornstarch; stir into chicken mixture. Heat to boiling, stirring constantly. Boil and stir 1 minute. Add vegetables and 1 teaspoon soy sauce. Cook and stir until hot, 1 to 2 minutes. Serve with additional soy sauce if desired.

Szechwan Chicken With Cashews

(Gai Ding)

Fresh ginger root and chili pepper paste bring the fiery flavors of the Szechwan region of southern China to this remarkable chicken dish. A side serving of steamed or boiled rice provides a soothing accompaniment. Hoisin sauce—one of the most important ingredients in many Szechwan dishes—is a thick dark paste made from grain. It is sold at oriental groceries and many large supermarkets.

6 servings

2 whole chicken breasts
1 egg white
1 teaspoon cornstarch
1 teaspoon salt
1 teaspoon finely chopped ginger root
1 teaspoon soy sauce
   Dash of pepper
1 tablespoon vegetable oil
1 cup raw cashews
½ teaspoon salt
¼ cup vegetable oil
6 green onions (with tops), chopped (reserve 2 tablespoons tops)
1 large green pepper, cut into ½-inch squares
1 can (4 ounces) button mushrooms, drained (reserve liquid)
1 tablespoon hoisin sauce
2 teaspoons chili pepper paste*
½ cup chicken broth
1 tablespoon cornstarch
1 tablespoon cold water
1 tablespoon soy sauce

Remove bones and skin from chicken breasts; cut chicken into ½-inch pieces. (For ease in cutting, partially freeze chicken about 1 hour.) Mix egg white, 1 teaspoon cornstarch, 1 teaspoon salt, the ginger root, 1 teaspoon soy sauce and the pepper in a 2-quart glass bowl; stir in chicken. Cover and refrigerate at least 30 minutes.

Heat 1 tablespoon oil in wok or 10-inch skillet until hot. Stir-fry cashews until light brown, about 1 minute; drain on paper towels. Sprinkle with ½ teaspoon salt. Heat 2 tablespoons of the oil until hot. Add chicken; stir-fry until chicken turns white, about 3 minutes. Remove chicken. Heat remaining 1 tablespoon oil until hot. Add green onions, green pepper, mushrooms, hoisin sauce and chili pepper paste. Stir-fry about 1 minute. Add chicken, chicken broth and reserved mushroom liquid; heat to boiling.

Mix 1 tablespoon cornstarch, the water and 1 tablespoon soy sauce; stir into chicken mixture. Cook and stir until thickened, about 1 minute. Stir in cashews; garnish with reserved green onion tops.

* 1 teaspoon chopped dried red pepper can be substituted for the chili pepper paste.

Tuscan Chicken Rolls with Pork Stuffing

(Rollatini di Pollo)

North of Rome is where you are most likely to encounter this little-known Italian dish—especially in Tuscany, in the vicinity of Florence. For a fine northern Italian dinner, serve the chicken rolls with buttered green noodles and a tossed green salad.

6 servings

3   large whole chicken breasts
½   pound ground pork
1   small onion, finely chopped
1   clove garlic, chopped
1   egg, beaten
½   cup soft bread crumbs
½   teaspoon salt
¼   teaspoon ground savory
¼   teaspoon pepper
2   tablespoons margarine or butter, melted
½   teaspoon salt
½   cup dry white wine
½   cup cold water
2   teaspoons cornstarch
½   teaspoon instant chicken bouillon
    Snipped parsley

Remove bones and skin from chicken breasts; cut chicken into halves. Place between 2 pieces plastic wrap; pound with mallet or side of saucer until ¼ inch thick, being careful not to tear the meat.

Cook and stir pork, onion and garlic over medium heat until pork is brown. Drain fat. Stir in egg, bread crumbs, ½ teaspoon salt, the savory and pepper. Place about ⅓ cup pork mixture on each chicken breast half. Roll up; secure with wooden picks. Place rolls in greased oblong baking dish, 11 x 7 x 1½ inches. Brush rolls with margarine; pour any remaining margarine over rolls. Sprinkle with ½ teaspoon salt. Add wine. Cook uncovered in 400° oven until chicken is done, 35 to 40 minutes.

Remove chicken to warm platter; remove wooden picks. Keep warm. Pour liquid from baking dish into 1-quart saucepan. Stir water into cornstarch; pour into liquid. Stir in bouillon. Heat to boiling over medium heat, stirring constantly. Boil and stir 1 minute. Pour gravy on chicken. Top with parsley.

Chicken Tacos with Avocado and Cheese

Mexico's enchanting taco dishes—long popular in our Southwestern states—are rapidly gaining national prominence. This quick, colorful dish is just the ticket for casual entertaining. The cheese-and-salad topping makes it a complete dinner on a plate. For a refreshing dessert, serve a tropical-fruit compote.

4 to 6 servings

1   small avocado
    Lemon juice
½   teaspoon salt
2   cups chopped cooked chicken
1   can (4 ounces) chopped green chilies, drained
1   small onion, sliced
¾   teaspoon salt
2   tablespoons vegetable oil
10   taco shells
2   cups shredded Monterey Jack cheese
⅓   cup sliced pimiento-stuffed olives
1   cup shredded lettuce
    Taco sauce
    Dairy sour cream

Cut avocado into halves; cut halves into slices. Sprinkle with lemon juice and ½ teaspoon salt. Cook and stir chicken, chilies, onion and ¾ teaspoon salt in oil in 10-inch skillet until chicken is hot. Heat taco shells as directed on package. Spoon about ¼ cup chicken mixture into each shell. Top with cheese, olives, lettuce and avocado. Serve with taco sauce and sour cream.

Chicken Cordon Bleu
(Poulet Cordon Bleu)

Both the Austrians and the Italians claim credit for inventing the delectable veal cordon bleu. In recent years the Swiss have taken such a fancy to it that cordon bleu has become virtually the national dish of Switzerland. In our blue-ribbon budget version, chicken breasts are substituted for veal.

4 servings

2	large whole chicken breasts
4	thin slices fully cooked smoked ham or prosciutto
4	thin slices Swiss cheese
¼	cup all-purpose flour
¾	teaspoon salt
¼	teaspoon pepper
1	egg, slightly beaten
½	cup dry bread crumbs
3	tablespoons vegetable oil
2	tablespoons water

Remove bones and skin from chicken breasts; cut chicken breasts into halves. Place chicken between 2 pieces plastic wrap. Pound with mallet or side of saucer until ¼ inch thick. Place 1 slice each ham and cheese on each piece chicken. Roll up carefully, beginning at narrow end; secure with wooden picks. (See diagram.) Mix flour, salt and pep- per; coat rolls with flour mixture. Dip rolls into egg; roll in bread crumbs.

Heat oil in 10-inch skillet over medium heat until hot. Cook rolls in oil until light brown, turning occasionally, 5 to 10 minutes. Add water. Cover and simmer until chicken is done, about 10 minutes. Remove picks.

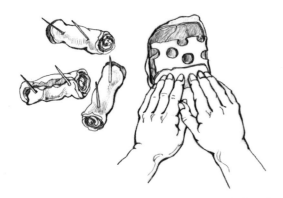

Roll chicken, ham and cheese carefully, beginning at narrow end; secure with wooden picks.

Chilled Chicken and Bean Sprouts

This easy low-calorie dish from the Orient can be made well in advance and is ideal for casual warm-weather entertaining. Mung beans are found at natural food stores and gardening centers. Instructions for sprouting beans appear on page 198.

3 or 4 servings

1	whole chicken breast
½	teaspoon salt
8	ounces mung bean sprouts*
1	tablespoon soy sauce
2	teaspoons vinegar
1	teaspoon sesame oil
½	teaspoon sugar
½	teaspoon salt
⅛	teaspoon monosodium glutamate (optional)

Heat chicken, salt and just enough water to cover to boiling; reduce heat. Cover and simmer until chicken is done, 25 to 30 minutes. Cool. Remove chicken from bones and skin; cut chicken into strips.

Pour boiling water over bean sprouts. Rinse in cold water; drain. Place chicken and bean sprouts in shallow glass or plastic dish. Mix remaining ingredients; pour over chicken and bean sprouts. Cover and refrigerate at least 1 hour. Garnish with chopped green onions if desired.

* 1 can (16 ounces) bean sprouts, drained, can be substituted for the mung bean sprouts. Chill bean sprouts in iced water 1 hour; drain.

Lemon Chicken, Hunan Style

Sweet-and-sour sauces predominate in the food of the Hunan province of China, where many of the dishes are extremely fiery. This Hunan specialty is zesty and soothing, designed to produce an intriguing contrast in textures. The chicken pieces are crisp on the outside, soft and tender inside. The smooth, pungent Lemon Sauce is sweetened with honey.

6 servings

3   large whole chicken breasts
    Vegetable oil
¼   cup all-purpose flour
¼   cup water
1   egg
2   tablespoons cornstarch
2   tablespoons vegetable oil
1   teaspoon salt
1   teaspoon soy sauce
¼   teaspoon baking soda
    Lemon Sauce (below)
½   lemon, thinly sliced

Remove bones and skin from chicken; cut chicken into halves. Heat oil (1 to 1½ inches) to 360°. Beat remaining ingredients except Lemon Sauce and lemon slices with hand beater until smooth. Dip chicken pieces one at a time into batter. Fry 2 pieces at a time until golden brown, turning once, about 7 minutes. Drain on paper towels. Repeat with remaining chicken.

Cut chicken crosswise into ½-inch slices; arrange in single layer on heated platter. Keep warm. Prepare Lemon Sauce; pour over chicken. Garnish with lemon slices.

Lemon Sauce

½   cup water
½   teaspoon grated lemon peel
¼   cup lemon juice
¼   cup honey
1   tablespoon catsup
½   teaspoon instant chicken bouillon
½   teaspoon salt
1   clove garlic, finely chopped
1   tablespoon cornstarch
1   tablespoon cold water

Heat ½ cup water, the lemon peel, lemon juice, honey, catsup, bouillon, salt and garlic to boiling. Mix cornstarch and 1 tablespoon water; stir into sauce. Cook and stir until thickened, about 30 seconds.

Do-Ahead Tip: After frying chicken, cover and refrigerate no longer than 24 hours. Heat chicken on ungreased cookie sheet in 400° oven until hot, 10 to 12 minutes. Cut crosswise into ½-inch slices.

Chicken Fried Rice

In China fried rice takes on a party appearance quite different from the "fried rice" served at many Chinese restaurants in America. Fresh mushrooms and water chestnuts provide an interesting textural contrast, and often snow peas are added for color. Chopped cooked seafood or meat can be substituted for chicken here.

4 or 5 servings

¾   cup diced cooked chicken
½   teaspoon cornstarch
¼   teaspoon salt
1   tablespoon vegetable oil
2   eggs, slightly beaten
2   tablespoons vegetable oil
1   can (8 ounces) water chestnuts, drained and sliced
1   cup sliced mushrooms
½   teaspoon salt
2   tablespoons vegetable oil
3   cups cooked rice (page 253)
1   tablespoon soy sauce
1   tablespoon chopped green onion (with tops)
    Dash of white pepper

Mix chicken, cornstarch and ¼ teaspoon salt. Heat wok until hot. Add 1 tablespoon oil; rotate wok to coat side. Add eggs; cook and stir until eggs are thickened throughout but still moist. Remove eggs from wok.

Add 2 tablespoons oil; rotate wok to coat side. Add chicken, water chestnuts, mushrooms and ½ teaspoon salt; stir-fry 1 minute. Remove from wok.

Add 2 tablespoons oil; rotate wok to coat side. Add rice; stir-fry 1 minute. Stir in soy sauce. Add chicken mixture, eggs, green onion and white pepper; stir-fry 30 seconds.

Chicken Kiev

Kiev is one of the oldest and most historic cities in the Soviet Union. Although Chicken Kiev may have been invented by French chefs employed by the Russian nobility who went sightseeing in Kiev in czarist days, today the dish is generally regarded as being authentically Russian throughout the world—even in the Soviet Union.

Take care when eating Chicken Kiev—the margarine or butter spurts out when the chicken breast is pierced with knife and fork.

12 servings

1	cup margarine or butter, softened
2	tablespoons snipped parsley
1½	teaspoons dried tarragon leaves
1	teaspoon snipped chives
½	to 1 clove garlic, crushed
½	teaspoon salt
⅛	teaspoon pepper
6	whole chicken breasts
¾	cup all-purpose flour
4	eggs, well beaten
2	cups dry bread crumbs
	Vegetable oil

Mix margarine, parsley, tarragon, chives, garlic, salt and pepper. Shape into 4-inch square on aluminum foil. Wrap and freeze until firm. Remove bones and skin from chicken breasts; cut chicken into halves. Place between 2 pieces plastic wrap. Pound chicken with mallet or side of saucer until ¼-inch thick, being careful not to tear the meat. Cut frozen margarine square into 12 pieces. Place 1 piece margarine on center of each chicken breast.

Fold chicken over margarine, making sure the margarine is enclosed. (See diagram.) Fasten with wooden picks. (It is important to seal margarine completely.) Roll chicken in flour; dip into egg. Coat completely with bread crumbs. Repeat. Shape chicken into triangular pieces. Cover and refrigerate at least 1 hour.

Heat oil (3 to 4 inches) in deep fat fryer or Dutch oven to 360°. Fry 3 pieces at a time until deep golden brown, turning if necessary, about 8 minutes. Drain on paper towels.

Do-Ahead Tip: After shaping into triangular pieces, chicken can be wrapped in aluminum foil and frozen no longer than 1 month. Thaw wrapped chicken 20 to 24 hours in refrigerator. Fry as directed. After frying, chicken can be covered and refrigerated no longer than 6 hours. Heat chicken in 350° oven 30 minutes. Uncover and heat 5 minutes.

Pound chicken between pieces of plastic wrap.

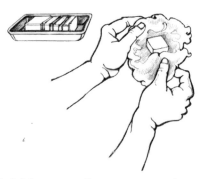

Fold chicken over frozen margarine, making sure the margarine is enclosed.

Clockwise from top: Marinated Pot Roast with Potato Dumplings (page 116), Skewered Lamb and Vegetables (page 164) and Canadian Pork Pie (page 157).

Meats

Chefs who like hearty traditional meals are always on the lookout for meat bargains. Despite soaring prices, meat continues to be an all-time favorite among country folk and city dwellers alike. If you're looking for meat stretchers and meat bargains, the wonderful world of international cooking is the place to go.

In this chapter we have collected low-cost country-style meat dishes from all over the world . . . and some grand "gourmet-style" recipes, too!

In the following pages you will find a number of hearty boiled dinners from Europe (slow simmering tenderizes those tough cuts of meat so rich in flavor). We've included basic pasta penny-pinchers from Italy (Lasagne, Ravioli and Cannelloni) plus recipes for homemade pasta dough, including the green pasta of northern Italy.

There are the Japanese favorites (Teriyaki and Sukiyaki) and their less well known Korean counterparts . . . spicy Chinese specialties . . . Hungarian goulashes . . . Mexican masterpieces . . . country cooking at its very best!

And that is only part of the picture. Although we have avoided the luxury cuts of beef, such as filet mignon, we have included delectable meat dishes suitable for the most auspicious occasion— our Braised Beef with Aspic and Marinated Vegetables . . . Osso Buco (braised veal shanks from Milan) . . . a Chinese Hot Pot . . . easy ground-meat recipes such as Sri Lanka Ground-Beef Curry . . . meaty, mouth-watering dishes you can serve to world travelers and armchair adventurers alike.

French Boiled Dinner
(Pot-au-Feu)

Pot-au-feu—literally "pot in the fire"—has long been a treasured family dish throughout France. Today it is considered excellent party fare too. Usually this gala dinner is presented as two courses: First the broth is strained and served as a light soup; then the beef, chicken and vegetables are served as the main course.

10 to 12 servings

1½-	pound beef boneless chuck roast*
1	marrow bone (optional)
8	peppercorns
1	teaspoon salt
¼	teaspoon dried thyme leaves
1	bay leaf
4	cups water
1½	pounds chicken drumsticks
10	to 12 small carrots
10	to 12 small onions or 3 large onions, cut into fourths
3	medium turnips, cut into fourths
4	stalks celery, cut into 1-inch pieces
¾	teaspoon salt
⅛	teaspoon pepper

Place beef, marrow bone, peppercorns, 1 teaspoon salt, the thyme and bay leaf in Dutch oven. Add water. Heat to boiling; reduce heat. Cover and simmer 1 hour. Add chicken; cover and simmer 1 hour longer.

Add carrots, onions, turnips and celery; sprinkle with ¾ teaspoon salt and the pepper. Cover and simmer until beef and vegetables are tender, about 45 minutes. Remove chicken and vegetables to warm platter; slice beef. Strain broth; serve in soup bowls as a first course.

* A 3-pound beef boneless chuck roast can be substituted for the 1½-pound roast and the chicken.

Braised Beef with Aspic and Marinated Vegetables
(Boeuf à la Mode en Gelée)

This streamlined version of a popular French entrée is splendid for warm-weather entertaining. It can be made a day in advance of the party and brought to table with a minimum of last-minute work.

10 to 12 servings

2	tablespoons vegetable oil
3-	pound beef rolled rump roast
½	cup water
1	teaspoon salt
¼	teaspoon pepper
1	envelope unflavored gelatin
2	tablespoons cold water
1	teaspoon instant beef bouillon
1	cup dry red wine
	Marinated Vegetables (page 113)

Heat oil in Dutch oven until hot. Cook beef over medium heat until brown on all sides; drain. Add ½ cup water; sprinkle beef with salt and pepper. Cover and cook in 325° oven until tender, about 1½ hours. Cool slightly. Cover and refrigerate beef and broth separately at least 8 hours.

Sprinkle gelatin over 2 tablespoons water in saucepan; stir in bouillon and wine. Cook over medium heat, stirring constantly, until gelatin is dissolved. Remove from heat. Skim fat from broth; add enough cold water to broth to measure 1 cup. Stir into gelatin mixture. Place pan with gelatin mixture in bowl of ice and water; stir until mixture begins to thicken, 5 to 10 minutes.

Remove string from beef; trim fat. Cut beef into very thin slices; arrange on large platter. Coat entire surface of beef with small amount of gelatin mixture. Pour any remaining mixture into loaf dish, 9 x 5 x 3 inches. Cover and

Braised Beef with Aspic and Marinated Vegetables

refrigerate beef and gelatin mixture no longer than 24 hours. Prepare Marinated Vegetables.

Arrange vegetables around beef. Cut aspic in loaf dish into small diamonds or squares; arrange around beef or serve separately.

Marinated Vegetables

8   medium carrots (about 1¼ pounds)
1   pound green beans
1   can (16 ounces) whole onions, drained
⅔   cup olive or vegetable oil
⅓   cup red wine vinegar
2   cloves garlic, finely chopped
2   teaspoons salt
⅛   teaspoon pepper

Cut carrots into 2-inch pieces, rounding the edges to resemble baby carrots if desired. Cover and cook carrots and beans in 1 inch boiling salted water (½ teaspoon salt to 1 cup water) in separate saucepans until tender, beans 15 to 20 minutes, carrots 20 to 25 minutes. Drain.

Arrange cooked vegetables and the onions in separate sections in shallow glass dish. Shake remaining ingredients in tightly covered jar; pour over vegetables. Cover and refrigerate, spooning marinade over vegetables occasionally, at least 2 hours.

Roast Beef and Yorkshire Pudding

Yorkshire pudding is a batter bread similar to a popover but baked in roast beef drippings in a baking pan rather than in custard cups. When puffed and golden, the pudding is cut into squares and served with the roast beef. In England a sirloin roast is often used rather than a standing rib roast.

8 servings

Place 5-pound beef rib roast fat side up on rack in shallow roasting pan. Sprinkle with salt and pepper. Insert meat thermometer so tip is in center of thickest part of beef and does not rest in fat. Do not add water.

Roast uncovered in 325° oven to desired degree of doneness: 125° to 130° for rare, about 1¾ hours; 145° to 150° for medium, about 2¼ hours. About 30 minutes before roast reaches desired temperature above, prepare Yorkshire Pudding Batter (below). Heat square pan, 9 x 9 x 2 inches, or oblong baking dish, 11 x 7 x 1½ inches, in oven.

When roast reaches desired temperature, remove from oven; increase oven temperature to 425°. Transfer roast to platter; cover lightly with aluminum foil. Pour off ¼ cup drippings from roasting pan; place drippings in heated square pan. Pour in pudding batter. Bake until puffed and golden brown, about 25 minutes. Cut into squares; serve with beef.

Yorkshire Pudding Batter

1   cup all-purpose flour
1   cup milk
2   eggs
½   teaspoon salt

Mix all ingredients with hand beater just until smooth.

Note: For easier carving, roast should be allowed to set about 20 minutes when removed from oven. Meat continues to cook as it stands, and to allow

for this, the internal temperatures above are 5 to 10 degrees below the recommended temperatures for rare and medium beef.

Dutch Boiled Dinner
(Hutspot met Klapstuk)

According to tradition, hutspot became a national celebration dish in Holland in 1574, when the lovely city of Leiden was besieged by the Spaniards from May until October. The city was saved only when the enterprising Dutch cut their famous dykes, flooding the city and permitting ships to carry food and supplies to the famished townsfolk. In honor of the victory the dish is still served (often with bread and herring) during Holland's annual liberation festival, held each October 3.

6 to 8 servings

2-   pound beef brisket
1½   cups water
1   teaspoon salt
4   medium potatoes, pared and cut into fourths
4   medium carrots, sliced
3   medium onions, chopped
1½   teaspoons salt
¼   teaspoon pepper
     Snipped parsley
     Prepared mustard or horseradish

Heat beef, water and 1 teaspoon salt to boiling in Dutch oven; reduce heat. Cover and simmer 1½ hours. Add potatoes, carrots and onions; sprinkle with 1½ teaspoons salt and the pepper. Cover and simmer until beef and vegetables are tender, about 45 minutes.

Drain meat and vegetables, reserving broth. Mash vegetables or purée in food mill; mound on heated platter. Cut beef across grain into thin slices; arrange around vegetables. Garnish with parsley; serve with reserved broth and the mustard.

Spanish Boiled Dinner

Spanish Boiled Dinner

Cocido—sometimes called olla podrida *or* pu-chero—*spells stew in Spain and Latin America. Recipes vary from region to region and country to country, but beef, sausage and garbanzo beans are generally considered essential to a true* cocido. *Like* Pot-au-Feu *(page 112), this Spanish stew is usually served as two courses: First the broth is presented, then the meat and vegetables.*

8 servings

1½-	pound beef boneless brisket or beef boneless chuck, tip or round
8	cups water
1	beef soup bone (about 1 pound)
1	medium onion, chopped
2	cloves garlic, chopped
1	bay leaf
2½	teaspoons salt
¼	teaspoon pepper
1	pound chorizo sausage, cut into ½-inch pieces
3	medium carrots, sliced
3	medium stalks celery, sliced
1	can (about 16 ounces) garbanzo beans (chickpeas)
1	small head cabbage, cut into 8 wedges

Trim excess fat from beef. Heat beef, water, soup bone, onion, garlic, bay leaf, salt and pepper to boiling in Dutch oven; reduce heat. Cover and simmer 1½ hours.

Cook sausage over medium heat, turning carefully, about 5 minutes; drain. Remove soup bone from broth. Add sausage, carrots, celery, garbanzo beans (with liquid) and cabbage to broth. Heat to boiling; reduce heat. Cover and simmer until beef and vegetables are tender, 30 to 40 minutes.

Remove beef from broth; cut into slices. Remove sausage and vegetables with slotted spoon. Arrange meat and vegetables on heated platter. Serve broth as first course, or if you prefer, serve vegetable mixture and broth in soup bowls.

Marinated Pot Roast with Potato Dumplings

(Sauerbraten mit Kartoffelklössen)

Perhaps the most famous of all German specialties, Sauerbraten *derives its tantalizing sweet-sour flavor from a tangy marinade and a sauce flavored with gingersnaps. The recipe originated in medieval days, when pickling was a basic method of meat preservation and ginger was an exotic spice imported at great expense from the Orient.*

12 servings

3- to 4-pound beef rolled rump roast, boneless chuck eye roast or bottom round roast
2 cups water
1 cup red wine vinegar
1 medium onion, sliced
6 whole cloves
4 peppercorns, crushed
1½ teaspoons salt
1 bay leaf
3 tablespoons vegetable oil
½ cup water
Potato Dumplings (right)
8 gingersnaps, crushed (about ⅓ cup)
2 tablespoons packed brown sugar
⅓ cup water
3 tablespoons flour

Prick beef roast thoroughly with fork. Place beef in 4-quart glass bowl or earthenware crock. Mix 2 cups water, the vinegar, onion, cloves, peppercorns, salt and bay leaf; pour over beef. Cover and refrigerate, turning several times each day, 2 to 3 days.

Remove beef from marinade; pat dry. Strain marinade; reserve. Heat oil in Dutch oven until hot. Cook beef in hot oil, turning occasionally, until brown, about 10 minutes. Remove beef; pour off fat. Heat 2 cups of the reserved marinade and ½ cup water to boiling

in Dutch oven (reserve remaining marinade). Return beef to Dutch oven; reduce heat. Cover and simmer until beef is tender, about 2 hours.

Prepare Potato Dumplings. Remove beef to heated platter; keep warm. Pour liquid from Dutch oven into large measuring cup; skim fat from liquid. Add enough reserved marinade to measure 2½ cups if necessary. Return to Dutch oven. (If liquid measures more than 2½ cups, boil rapidly to reduce to 2½ cups.)

Stir in gingersnap crumbs and brown sugar. Mix ⅓ cup water and the flour; stir gradually into liquid. Heat to boiling, stirring constantly. Boil and stir 1 minute. Strain gravy; serve with beef and Potato Dumplings.

Potato Dumplings

2 tablespoons margarine or butter
2 slices white bread (crusts removed), cubed
3½ cups riced cooked potatoes (5 medium)
1 cup all-purpose flour
1½ teaspoons salt
⅛ teaspoon ground nutmeg
⅛ teaspoon white pepper
2 eggs, beaten
4 quarts water
2 teaspoons salt
2 teaspoons margarine or butter
2 tablespoons dry bread crumbs

Heat 2 tablespoons margarine in 8-inch skillet until melted. Cook bread cubes in margarine over medium heat, stirring frequently, until golden brown.

Mix potatoes, flour, 1½ teaspoons salt, the nutmeg and white pepper. Stir in eggs; beat until dough holds its shape. Flour hands lightly. Shape about 2 tablespoons dough into ball. Press hole in center with fingertip; drop 4 bread cubes into hole. Seal by shaping into ball again. Repeat with remaining dough and bread cubes.

Heat water and 2 teaspoons salt to boiling in 6- to 8-quart Dutch oven. Heat 2 teaspoons margarine in skillet until melted. Cook and stir bread crumbs in margarine until margarine is absorbed; reserve.

Drop dumplings into boiling water; stir once or twice. Reduce heat. Simmer uncovered until dumplings are done, 12 to 15 minutes. Remove with slotted spoon. Sprinkle dumplings with reserved bread crumbs.

Braised Stuffed Beef Rolls (Rinderrouladen)

In Germany Rinderrouladen *is nearly as popular as* Sauerbraten. *The flavor is not quite so unique, but the intriguing pickle-and-bacon filling excites the taste buds.*

6 servings

2-   pound beef boneless round steak, ½ inch thick
     Salt and pepper
2   tablespoons prepared mustard
3   slices bacon, cut into halves
1   medium onion, chopped
¼   cup snipped parsley
3   dill pickles, cut into halves
2   tablespoons vegetable oil
1¼   cups water
½   teaspoon salt
¼   teaspoon pepper
2   tablespoons cold water
1   tablespoon flour
     Parsley sprigs

Pound beef until ¼ inch thick. Cut into pieces, about 7 x 4 inches. Lightly sprinkle with salt and pepper. Spread each piece with 1 teaspoon mustard. Place ½ strip bacon down center of each piece. Sprinkle with onion and snipped parsley. Place pickle half on narrow end of each; roll up. Fasten with wooden picks.

Heat oil in 10-inch skillet until hot. Cook rolls over medium heat until brown on all sides.

Add 1¼ cups water, ½ teaspoon salt and ¼ teaspoon pepper. Heat to boiling; reduce heat. Cover and simmer until beef is tender, about 1 hour.

Remove rolls to warm platter; keep warm. Add enough water to liquid in skillet if necessary to measure 1 cup. Shake 2 tablespoons water and the flour in tightly covered container; stir gradually into broth. Heat to boiling, stirring constantly. Boil and stir 1 minute. (Add water if necessary.) Serve gravy with rolls. Garnish with parsley sprigs. Serve with Red Cabbage with Apples (page 223) and boiled potatoes if desired.

Korean Barbecued Beef (Bul-Ko-Kee)

Bul-ko-kee is Korea's national dish and may have been the inspiration for Japan's teriyaki, which it resembles. In Korea the dish is usually sprinkled with sesame seeds before serving.

4 servings

1-   pound beef boneless top loin or sirloin steak
¼   cup soy sauce
3   tablespoons sugar
2   tablespoons sesame or vegetable oil
¼   teaspoon pepper
3   green onions, finely chopped
2   cloves garlic, chopped

Trim fat from beef; cut beef diagonally across grain into ⅛-inch slices. (For ease in cutting, partially freeze beef about 1½ hours.) Mix remaining ingredients; stir in beef until well coated. Cover and refrigerate 30 minutes.

Drain beef; stir-fry in 10-inch skillet or wok over medium heat until light brown, 2 to 3 minutes. Serve beef with hot cooked rice if desired.

Stuffed Rolled Steak
(Carne Rellena)

A thin, flat cut of beef spread with a savory stuffing, then rolled, skewered and braised, produces an applause-winning main dish that is particularly easy to serve—it can be sliced jelly roll fashion and eaten hot or cold. The dish is popular throughout Latin America. In Argentina it is called matambre, *or "hunger killer." The beef roll was originally prepared for travelers setting out on long journeys.*

8 servings

1½-	pound beef boneless round steak, ½ inch thick
1½	teaspoons salt
½	teaspoon dried oregano leaves
¼	teaspoon pepper
4	ounces thinly sliced fully cooked smoked ham
2	medium tomatoes, chopped
1	can (4 ounces) mild green chilies, drained and chopped
1	medium onion, chopped
1	clove garlic, finely chopped
¼	cup dry bread crumbs
1	medium carrot
1	hard-cooked egg, cut lengthwise into fourths
½	teaspoon salt
2	tablespoons vegetable oil
¾	cup water
1	teaspoon vinegar
1	teaspoon Worcestershire sauce
1	bay leaf

Trim fat from beef. Pound with mallet or edge of saucer until about ¼ inch thick. Sprinkle beef with 1½ teaspoons salt, the oregano and pepper. Arrange ham evenly on beef. Sprinkle tomatoes, chilies, onion, garlic and bread crumbs on ham. (See photograph.)

Cut carrot lengthwise into halves; cut halves lengthwise into 3 strips. Arrange on ham. Place egg pieces down center of ham. Sprinkle with ½ teaspoon salt. Carefully roll up beef. (See photograph.) Fasten with metal skewers or tie with string. (If beef separates when rolled, fasten with wooden picks.)

Heat oil in Dutch oven until hot. Carefully transfer beef roll to Dutch oven; cook over medium heat until brown on all sides. Drain fat. Add water, vinegar, Worcestershire sauce and bay leaf. Cover and cook in 325° oven until beef is tender, about 1½ hours. Remove skewers. Cut beef into 1-inch slices; serve with broth. Serve with Red Beans and Rice (page 199) if desired.

Sprinkle tomatoes, chilies, onion, garlic and bread crumbs evenly on ham.

Place egg pieces down center of ham; carefully roll up beef.

Stuffed Rolled Steak

Braised Beef Esterhazy

(Rostélyos Ezterhézy)

This tempting three-star classic—braised steak served with a perky sour cream sauce—was named in honor of a scion of the noble Esterhazy family of Hungary, whose origins are rooted in the early thirteenth century, when the Esterhazy name first became synonymous with wealth and luxurious living.

6 servings

1½	pounds beef boneless round steak, ½ inch thick
3	tablespoons flour
2	tablespoons vegetable oil
1	can (10½ ounces) condensed beef broth
½	cup water
3	carrots, cut into strips, 3 x ½ inch
3	medium parsnips, cut into strips, 3 x ½ inch
2	medium onions, sliced
1	teaspoon salt
¼	teaspoon pepper
¼	teaspoon dried thyme leaves
3	sweet gherkin pickles, cut lengthwise into ¼-inch strips
1	cup dairy sour cream

Sprinkle one side of beef with half the flour; pound in. Turn beef; pound in remaining flour. Cut into 6 serving pieces. Heat oil in 12-inch skillet until hot. Cook 3 or 4 pieces of beef at a time in oil over medium heat until brown on both sides, about 15 minutes; drain.

Add beef broth and water. Heat to boiling; reduce heat. Cover and simmer 15 minutes. Add carrots, parsnips and onions. Sprinkle with salt, pepper and thyme. Cover and simmer until beef and vegetables are tender, 40 to 60 minutes. Add gherkins during last 5 minutes.

Remove beef and vegetables to heated platter. Skim fat from broth if necessary; stir in sour cream. Heat just until hot. Serve gravy with beef and vegetables.

Korean Braised Short Ribs

The Korean cuisine reflects the influence of both Chinese and Japanese culinary traditions. In this recipe the Chinese flavors of ginger and sesame seed blend with Japanese soy sauce and take on a characteristic Korean flavor through slow cooking—a Korean luxury made possible by an abundant supply of fuel from rich forests. Try the ribs with boiled Chinese noodles.

4 to 6 servings

4	pounds beef short ribs, cut into pieces
2	cloves garlic, chopped
½	cup soy sauce
¼	cup chopped onion
2	tablespoons sugar
2	tablespoons ground sesame seed (see Note)
2	teaspoons chopped ginger root or ½ teaspoon ground ginger
½	teaspoon pepper

Trim fat from beef ribs; place beef in shallow glass or plastic dish. Mix remaining ingredients; pour over beef. Cover and refrigerate, turning occasionally, 24 hours.

Drain beef, reserving marinade. Cook beef in 4-quart Dutch oven over medium heat until brown; drain. Pour marinade over beef. Cover and cook in 350° oven until tender, about 2 hours.

Note: Ground sesame seed is available in oriental food specialty stores and some supermarkets. Whole sesame seed can be ground in the blender; one tablespoon whole sesame seed yields 2 tablespoons ground.

Deviled Short Ribs

Slow cooking sends pleasant aromas through the home and sharpens the appetite for these succulent deviled ribs from Britain. For an unusual side dish, try them with French Vegetable Ragout (page 238).

4 servings

2	tablespoons vegetable oil
4	pounds beef short ribs
2	medium onions, sliced
1	tablespoon dry mustard
1	tablespoon Worcestershire sauce
1	teaspoon salt
1	teaspoon curry powder
¼	teaspoon ground red pepper
¾	cup water

Heat oil in Dutch oven until hot. Cook beef over medium heat until brown on all sides; drain. Add onions. Mix remaining ingredients except water; stir in water. Pour over beef. Cover and cook in 350° oven until tender, about 2 hours.

Steak-and-Kidney Pie

Some British food historians maintain that their thrifty, nourishing Steak-and-Kidney Pie was brought to British shores in ancient times by the Romans.

6 servings

1	pound beef boneless round steak
1	beef kidney (about ¾ pound)
⅓	cup all-purpose flour
¼	cup vegetable oil
1	cup water
2	medium onions, chopped
4	ounces mushrooms, sliced
1½	teaspoons salt
1	teaspoon Worcestershire sauce
½	teaspoon dried thyme leaves
¼	teaspoon pepper
	Pastry Topping (right)

¼	cup cold water
2	tablespoons flour

Cut beef into ¾-inch cubes. Remove skin and membrane from kidney; cut kidney into halves. Remove white veins and fat with kitchen scissors. Cut kidney into ¾-inch cubes. Coat beef and kidney with ⅓ cup flour. Heat oil in 10-inch skillet over medium heat until hot. Cook meat in hot oil until brown on all sides. Add 1 cup water, the onions, mushrooms, salt, Worcestershire sauce, thyme and pepper. Heat to boiling; reduce heat. Cover and simmer 1 hour. Prepare Pastry Topping.

Mix ¼ cup water and 2 tablespoons flour; stir into meat mixture. Heat to boiling, stirring constantly. Boil and stir 1 minute. Pour mixture into ungreased 1½-quart casserole. Place baked crust on meat mixture in casserole.

Pastry Topping

⅓	cup plus 1 tablespoon shortening
1	cup all-purpose flour
½	teaspoon salt
2	to 3 tablespoons cold water

Cut shortening into flour and salt until particles are size of small peas. Sprinkle in water, 1 tablespoon at a time, tossing with fork until all flour is moistened and pastry almost cleans sides of bowl (1 to 2 teaspoons water can be added if necessary).

Gather pastry into a ball; shape into flattened round on lightly floured cloth-covered board (see Note). Roll out to fit top of casserole. Cut slits in pastry. Bake on ungreased cookie sheet in 400° oven until crust is golden brown, 25 to 30 minutes.

Note: For individual casseroles, divide pastry into 6 equal parts; pat each to fit top of 8-ounce casserole. Cut slits in pastry. Bake on ungreased cookie sheet in 400° oven 25 to 30 minutes. Divide cooked meat mixture among six 8-ounce casseroles; place baked crusts on meat mixture in casseroles.

Cornish Pasties

These tasty little pies were developed in Cornwall as a convenient way for miners and schoolchildren to take lunch to work. The local name for the pasties was "oggies." When the tin mines of Cornwall were depleted, low-cost potatoes were substituted for the beef stuffing, and "oggies" became "tiddy oggies" ("tiddy" is Cornwall slang for potatoes). When prosperity returned, beef reappeared, but potatoes remained in the recipe—and Cornish Pasties are still called tiddy oggies in Cornwall.

6 to 8 pasties

1-	pound beef top round or chuck steak
	Pastry (below)
2	medium onions, chopped
2	cups cubed potatoes (2 large)
1	cup diced rutabaga or carrots
2	teaspoons salt
¼	teaspoon pepper
	Margarine or butter
	Milk or half-and-half
	Hot mustard

Cut beef into ½-inch pieces. (For ease in cutting, partially freeze beef about 1 hour.) Prepare pastry; divide into 6 equal parts. Roll each part into 9-inch circle. Place on two ungreased cookie sheets. Toss beef, onions, potatoes, rutabaga, salt and pepper. Heat oven to 375°.

Place about 1 cup filling on half of each circle. Dot each with about 1 teaspoon margarine and sprinkle with 2 teaspoons water. Moisten edge of each circle with water; fold over. Press edges with fork to seal. Cut slits or design in top of each; brush with milk. Bake until crust is golden brown, 50 to 55 minutes. Serve hot or cold with hot mustard.

Pastry

1	cup lard
3	cups all-purpose flour
1½	teaspoons salt
5	to 6 tablespoons cold water

Cut lard into flour and salt until particles are size of small peas. Sprinkle in water, 1 tablespoon at a time, tossing with fork until all flour is moistened and pastry almost cleans side of bowl (1 to 2 teaspoons water can be added if necessary). Gather pastry into a ball.

African Beef and Rice
(Moui Nagden)

This mildly spiced recipe from North Africa makes an easy one-dish dinner for the family. When company is coming and a more elaborate menu is desired, serve the casserole with our Corn-Okra-Tomato Medley (page 227).

6 servings

1-	pound beef round steak, ½ inch thick
2	tablespoons vegetable oil
1	cup water
1	bay leaf
1	teaspoon salt
⅛	to ¼ teaspoon crushed red peppers
1	can (16 ounces) red kidney beans, drained
1	cup uncooked regular rice
2	medium green peppers, cut into 1-inch pieces
1	medium onion, chopped
1½	teaspoons salt
½	to 1 teaspoon curry powder
¼	teaspoon pepper

Cut beef into 1-inch pieces. Heat oil in 10-inch skillet until hot. Cook and stir beef in oil over medium heat until brown, about 15 minutes. Add water, bay leaf, 1 teaspoon salt and the red peppers. Heat to boiling; reduce heat. Cover and simmer 45 minutes.

Drain beef, reserving broth. Add enough water to reserved broth to measure 2 cups. Mix beef, broth and remaining ingredients. Pour into ungreased 2-quart casserole. Cover and cook in 350° oven until liquid is absorbed, 45 to 50 minutes. Serve with sliced tomatoes if desired.

Brazilian Black Bean Stew (Feijoada)

In its most extravagant form, Brazil's festive feijoada is called feijoada completa *and traditionally uses fifteen meats. Modern Brazilians rarely prepare so complete a* feijoada *except on very special occasions. You'll find our streamlined version of Brazil's national dish an imaginative addition to your favorite crowd-size party menus.*

12 to 14 servings

1   smoked beef tongue (3- to 4-pound)
8   cups cold water
2   packages (12 ounces each) dried black beans (4 cups)
½   pound dried beef
4   smoked chorizos or highly seasoned smoked Italian sausages (reserve 1 chorizo for Sauce)
½   pound sliced bacon, cut into 1-inch pieces
    Sauce (right)
1   large orange, thinly sliced
    Hot cooked rice (page 253)

Place beef tongue in Dutch oven; add enough water to cover beef. Heat to boiling; reduce heat. Cover and simmer until tender, about 3 hours.

Heat water and beans to boiling in Dutch oven or large kettle; boil gently 2 minutes. Remove from heat; cover and let stand 1 hour. Heat to boiling; reduce heat. Cover and simmer 1 hour. Remove and mash 2 cups beans and liquid; reserve mashed beans for Sauce.

Plunge beef tongue into cold water. Cut lengthwise slashes in skin; peel off skin. Remove any fat and cartilage. Cut beef tongue into ¼-inch slices; stir into unmashed beans. Cut dried beef into bite-size pieces; prick chorizos thoroughly with fork. Stir dried beef, chorizos and bacon into beans and tongue.

Add just enough water to cover. Heat to boiling; reduce heat. Cover and simmer 1 hour.

Prepare Sauce. Stir half the Sauce into meat-bean mixture. Cover and cook until beans are mushy, about 1 hour. (Add ½ to 1 cup water if necessary.) Heat remaining Sauce over low heat. Arrange beef tongue slices in center of platter; arrange sausages around tongue slices. Pour Sauce over meats. Cut orange slices into halves; arrange around meats. Pour remaining beans into tureen; serve with rice.

Sauce
4   jalapeño chilies, finely chopped
2   large tomatoes, chopped
1   large onion, chopped
2   cloves garlic, finely chopped
¼   teaspoon salt
⅛   teaspoon ground red pepper

Cut reserved chorizo into 1-inch pieces. Cook and stir chorizo, chilies and remaining ingredients in 10-inch skillet over medium heat 3 minutes. Stir 2 cups reserved beans into chorizo mixture; heat until hot.

Chorizo Sausages
Did You Know?

Chorizo is highly seasoned smoked pork sausage with ground red pepper, pimiento, garlic and paprika added. Link chorizo sausages are reddish brown, about 3½ inches long and similar to Italian sausages in flavor and spiciness. Spanish chorizos are widely available, and Mexican chorizos can be found in stores where Latin American foods are a specialty.

Sukiyaki

Sukiyaki

In Japan's early history, when peasants were forbidden to eat meat, savvy farmers quickly cooked on the spot what game they could find. Suki means hoe—the trademark of the Japanese peasant; yaki means to broil. According to legend, the farmers used their metal hoes as skillets!

4 servings

1   teaspoon instant beef bouillon
½   cup hot water
⅓   cup soy sauce
2   tablespoons sugar
1- pound beef tenderloin or boneless sirloin,*
        1 inch thick
2   tablespoons vegetable oil
3   stalks celery, cut diagonally into ¼-inch slices
2   medium carrots, cut diagonally into ⅛-inch slices
1   bunch green onions, cut diagonally into 2-inch pieces
8   ounces mushrooms, thinly sliced (about 4 cups)
1   can (about 8½ ounces) bamboo shoots, drained
4   ounces spinach, stems removed (4 cups)
        Hot cooked rice (page 253)

Dissolve bouillon in hot water; stir in soy sauce and sugar. Reserve. Cut beef into ⅛-inch slices. (For ease in cutting, partially freeze beef about 1 hour.) Heat oil in 12-inch skillet until hot. Place half each of the celery, carrots, green onions, mushrooms and bamboo shoots in separate areas in skillet. Pour half the reserved soy sauce mixture into skillet.

Simmer uncovered until vegetables are crisp-tender, turning vegetables carefully, 8 to 10 minutes. Push vegetables to side of skillet; add half each of the beef and spinach. Cook beef to desired doneness about 3 minutes. Repeat with remaining vegetables and beef. Serve from skillet with rice and additional soy sauce.

* 1 large whole chicken breast (1 pound), boned and skinned, can be substituted for the beef. (For ease in cutting, partially freeze chicken about 1½ hours.)

Beef Teriyaki
(Gyuniku no Teriyaki)

In Japan the word "teriyaki" refers to the technique of marinating foods in a mixture of soy sauce, wine and spices and then glazing them with the sauce, either in a skillet or on a grill. The word comes from teri *(shiny or glazed) and* yaki *(baked or broiled). In America, Beef Teriyaki is the most popular version—often done on a hibachi.*

4 or 5 servings

1   pound beef boneless sirloin steak, cut into ¾-inch cubes
¼   cup soy sauce
¼   cup sake or dry sherry
1   tablespoon vegetable oil
2   teaspoons chopped ginger root or ½ teaspoon ground ginger
1   teaspoon sugar
1   clove garlic, chopped

Place beef in glass or plastic bowl. Mix soy sauce, sake, oil, ginger root, sugar, and garlic; pour over beef. Cover and refrigerate, stirring occasionally, at least 1 hour.

Thread 6 beef cubes on each of 5 skewers; brush with marinade. Set oven control to broil and/or 550°. Broil kabobs with tops about 4 inches from heat 5 to 6 minutes; turn. Brush with marinade; broil 5 to 6 minutes. Place on heated platter; brush with marinade. Serve with hot cooked rice if desired.

Chinese Hot Pot

This Chinese "fondue" should be served at an intimate party for four and at a small table that gives each person easy access to the hot pot.

4 servings

½- pound pork tenderloin, top sirloin of beef or boneless lamb
1   whole chicken breast, skinned and boned, or ½ pound chicken livers, cut into halves
½   pound cleaned raw shrimp, cut lengthwise into halves, or ½ pound scallops, cut into ¾-inch pieces
8   ounces bean curd, cut into ½-inch cubes
8   ounces broccoli, separated into flowerets and sliced
1   package (10 ounces) frozen Chinese pea pods or 4 ounces spinach, stems trimmed
8   ounces mushrooms, sliced
¼   head cauliflower, separated into flowerets and sliced
2   medium carrots, cut diagonally into ⅛-inch slices
1   bunch green onions (about 8), trimmed and cut into 1½-inch pieces
3   ounces cellophane noodles
3   cups warm water
8   cups chicken broth
     Dipping Sauces (right)

Choose 2 meats or combination of meat and seafood and 3 vegetables from selections above. Cut pork, beef or lamb across grain into ⅛-inch slices; cut chicken breast across grain into ¼-inch slices. (For ease in cutting, partially freeze meat or chicken breast about 1 hour.) Divide meat, seafood and vegetables among serving trays or plates; arrange attractively in overlapping layers. Garnish each with parsley if desired. Cover and refrigerate until serving time.

Place cellophane noodles in oblong baking dish; cover with water. Let stand 30 minutes. Drain; cut noodles into 6-inch pieces.

Pour chicken broth into 12-inch electric skillet until half full; heat to boiling. Pass trays of meat, seafood and vegetables. Guests choose an assortment and, with chopsticks or fondue forks, place the food in hot broth to cook until done, 1 to 4 minutes. (Add hot chicken broth as needed.) Serve with 2 or 3 Dipping Sauces.

When the meat and seafood have been eaten, the cellophane noodles and any remaining vegetables are placed in remaining broth in the skillet. Cook until tender, 1 to 2 minutes. Ladle noodles and broth into soup bowls; serve as the last course.

Dipping Sauces: Soy sauce, teriyaki sauce, Chinese plum sauce, hoisin sauce or mustard sauce.

Beef-and-Liver Kabobs (Kyinkyinga)

These traditional West African kabobs are usually served quite spicy and hot, with boiled or steamed rice to cool the palate.

6 servings

1   pound high-quality beef chuck, tip or round, 1 inch thick
½   pound beef liver, 1 inch thick
¼   cup lemon juice
3   tablespoons vegetable oil
1   clove garlic, chopped
1½   teaspoons onion salt
¼   teaspoon ground ginger
⅛   teaspoon crushed red peppers

Cut beef and liver into 1-inch cubes. (For ease in cutting, partially freeze meat about 1½ hours.) Place meat in glass bowl. Mix remaining ingredients; pour over meat. Cover and refrigerate, stirring occasionally, at least 6 hours.

Thread beef and liver cubes on each of 6 skewers. Brush with marinade. Set oven control to broil and/or 550°. Broil kabobs with tops 4 inches from heat 5 to 6 minutes; turn. Brush with marinade; broil 5 to 6 minutes.

Venetian Liver with Onions

(Fegato alla Veneziana)

This quick and savory method of cooking liver with onions has been called "as Venetian as a gondolier." In Venice the liver is usually cut into thin strips about 1½ inches long and served with Polenta with Cheese (page 251) or boiled potatoes.

6 servings

2	medium onions, sliced
¼	cup olive or vegetable oil
1	pound calf or beef liver, ¼ to ½ inch thick
1	teaspoon salt
¼	teaspoon pepper
¼	teaspoon ground sage
1	tablespoon lemon juice
	Snipped parsley

Cover and cook onions in 2 tablespoons of the oil in 10-inch skillet over low heat until tender, about 15 minutes. Remove onions from skillet; keep warm. Heat remaining oil in skillet until hot. Cut liver into serving pieces; cook over medium heat until brown, about 4 minutes on each side. Sprinkle with salt, pepper and sage; remove liver from skillet.

Add lemon juice to skillet. Heat to boiling, stirring constantly to loosen browned particles; pour over liver. Top with onions; sprinkle with parsley.

Red Cooked Beef

(Hung Shao Niu Jo)

Hung shao, or red cooking, is a Chinese technique often unknown to Westerners familiar only with stir-fried Chinese foods. In red cooking, the meat is browned, then slowly simmered in a spicy broth. The "red" color comes from a liberal portion of soy sauce added to the braising liquid. Unlike the stir-fried dishes of China, red cooked foods require little last-minute work in the kitchen and can be made well in advance.

8 servings

2	pounds beef boneless chuck, tip or round
3	tablespoons peanut or vegetable oil
1½	cups water
¼	cup soy sauce
2	tablespoons dry white wine or sherry
1	thin slice peeled fresh or canned ginger root or 1 teaspoon ground ginger
1	green onion, cut lengthwise into halves
1	clove garlic, cut into halves
1	tablespoon sugar
⅛	teaspoon pepper
	Coriander leaves (optional)
	Toasted sesame seed

Trim fat from beef; cut beef into 1½-inch cubes. Heat 2 tablespoons of the oil in wok or 12-inch skillet until hot. Stir-fry half the beef cubes until brown on all sides, about 2 minutes. Remove beef to 3-quart saucepan. Repeat with remaining oil and beef.

Mix water, soy sauce, wine, ginger root, green onion, garlic, sugar and pepper; add to beef. Heat to boiling; reduce heat. Cover and simmer, stirring occasionally, until beef is tender, about 1 hour. Garnish with small sprigs of coriander; sprinkle with sesame seed. Serve with hot cooked Chinese noodles if desired.

Beef Stroganov

A French chef is credited with creating Beef Stroganov (or Stroganoff) in the late nineteenth century to tempt the palate of a Russian aristocrat named Count Paul Stroganov. In the early twentieth century when the Russian nobility fled from the Soviet Union, Beef Stroganov began to appear on fashionable menus.

4 servings

1- pound beef boneless sirloin or top loin steak, ½ inch thick
2 tablespoons margarine or butter
8 ounces mushrooms, sliced
2 medium onions, sliced
1 clove garlic, finely chopped
2 tablespoons margarine or butter
½ cup water
1 teaspoon instant beef bouillon
1 teaspoon salt
¼ teaspoon pepper
1 cup dairy sour cream
½ teaspoon prepared mustard
   Snipped parsley
   Hot cooked noodles or rice (page 253)

Cut beef across grain into strips, 1½ x ½ inch. (For ease in cutting, partially freeze beef about 1½ hours.) Heat 2 tablespoons margarine in 10-inch skillet until melted. Add mushrooms, onions and garlic. Cover and simmer, stirring occasionally, until onions are tender, 5 to 10 minutes. Remove vegetables and any liquid from skillet.

Cook and stir beef in 2 tablespoons margarine over medium heat until brown, about 10 minutes. Add water, bouillon, salt and pepper. Heat to boiling; reduce heat. Cover and simmer until beef is desired doneness, 10 to 15 minutes. Add vegetable mixture. Heat to boiling; reduce heat. Stir in sour cream and mustard. Heat just until hot. Garnish with parsley; serve with noodles.

Hungarian Beef Goulash

(Bogrács Gulyás)

Bogrács *means cauldron;* gulyás *means herdsman's meat. Hungarian goulash was originally cooked in an iron kettle over an open fire, probably by farmers and shepherds who contributed what they could. Since Hungary's earliest history there have been many versions of goulash. Paprika—introduced by invading Turks in the sixteenth century—is considered indispensable to a proper goulash.*

6 servings

2 tablespoons vegetable oil or bacon fat
1½ pounds beef boneless chuck, tip or round, cut into ¾-inch cubes
2 cups water
1 can (8 ounces) tomatoes
3 medium onions, chopped
1 clove garlic, chopped
2 teaspoons paprika
2 teaspoons salt
1 teaspoon instant beef bouillon
½ teaspoon caraway seed
¼ teaspoon pepper
2 medium potatoes, cut into 1½-inch pieces
2 green peppers, cut into 1-inch pieces
   French bread or rolls

Heat oil in Dutch oven or 12-inch skillet until hot. Cook and stir beef in hot oil until brown, about 15 minutes; drain. Add water, tomatoes (with liquid), onions, garlic, paprika, salt, bouillon, caraway seed and pepper. Break up tomatoes with fork. Heat to boiling; reduce heat. Cover and simmer 1 hour.

Add potatoes; cover and simmer until beef and potatoes are tender, about 30 minutes. Add green peppers; cover and simmer until tender, 8 to 10 minutes. Serve in soup bowls with chunks of French bread for dipping into hot broth.

Squash-and-Bean Soup

Squash-and-Bean Soup (Nkrakra)

In Ghana, every bride is expected to know how to prepare a fine nkrakra—*although there is no definitive recipe for the hearty soup. Our version uses ingredients easily found at the supermarket. In Ghana, pig's feet, lamb shanks, crabs and smoked fish are among the ingredients that may find their way into* nkrakra.

6 servings

1½	pounds beef for stew, cut into ¾-inch cubes
2	cups water
2	teaspoons salt
¼	teaspoon ground ginger
⅛	to ¼ teaspoon ground red pepper
1½	pounds Hubbard squash, pared and cut into 1-inch cubes*
2	medium tomatoes, chopped
1	package (10 ounces) frozen baby lima beans

Heat beef, water, salt, ginger and red pepper to boiling in Dutch oven; reduce heat. Cover and simmer 1½ hours. Add squash; cover and cook until beef and squash are tender, 30 to 45 minutes.

Remove squash; mash or purée in blender. Return squash to Dutch oven. Add tomatoes and beans. Heat to boiling; reduce heat. Cover and simmer until beans are tender, about 15 minutes. Top each serving with hot cooked rice if desired.

* 1 package (12 ounces) frozen cooked squash, thawed, can be substituted for the fresh squash; add with tomatoes.

Russian Beet Soup (Borscht)

As with most country-style soups, recipes for Russia's famed borscht *vary widely, from a light meatless broth to a meaty stewlike soup such as the one below. Beets are always the ingredient common to* borscht.

6 servings

6	cups water
4	ounces dried navy beans (about ½ cup)
1	pound beef boneless chuck, tip or round, cut into ½-inch cubes
1	smoked pork hock
1	can (10½ ounces) condensed beef broth
2½	teaspoons salt
¼	teaspoon pepper
6	cooked medium beets
2	medium onions, sliced
2	cloves garlic, chopped
2	medium potatoes, cut into ½-inch cubes
3	cups shredded cabbage
2	teaspoons dill seed or 1 sprig dill
1	tablespoon pickling spice
¼	cup red wine vinegar
1	cup dairy sour cream

Heat water and beans to boiling in Dutch oven; boil 2 minutes. Remove from heat; cover and let stand 1 hour. Add beef, pork, beef broth, salt and pepper to beans. Heat to boiling; reduce heat. Cover and simmer until beef is tender, 1 to 1½ hours. Shred beets or cut into ¼-inch strips.

Remove pork from Dutch oven; cool slightly. Remove pork from bone; cut into bite-size pieces. Add pork, beets, onions, garlic, potatoes and cabbage to beef mixture. Tie dill and pickling spice in cheesecloth bag or place in tea ball; add to beef mixture. Cover and simmer 2 hours. Stir in vinegar; simmer 10 minutes. Remove spice bag. Serve with sour cream; sprinkle with snipped dill if desired.

Beef Stew Provençale (Daube de Boeuf à la Provençale)

In France, a daube *is a meat stew braised in an aromatic stock in a tightly covered casserole called a* daubière. *A French* daubière *is oval-shaped and made of glazed earthenware or tin-lined copper. In our recipe the traditional flavors of Provence—garlic and rosemary—enrich the stew's flavor.*

6 servings

¼	pound salt pork
1½	pounds beef boneless chuck, tip or round
1	cup dry red wine
½	cup water
2	cloves garlic, chopped
½	teaspoon salt
½	teaspoon dried thyme leaves
¼	teaspoon dried rosemary leaves
¼	teaspoon pepper
1	bay leaf
6	carrots, cut into 1-inch pieces
2	medium onions, cut into fourths
½	cup pitted ripe olives
	Snipped parsley
	French bread

Remove rind from salt pork; cut pork into ¼-inch slices. Cut beef into 1-inch cubes. (For ease in cutting, partially freeze beef about 1 hour.) Fry salt pork in Dutch oven over medium heat until crisp; remove with slotted spoon. Drain on paper towels. Cook and stir beef in hot fat until brown, about 15 minutes. Drain fat. Add wine, water, garlic, salt, thyme, rosemary, pepper and bay leaf. Heat to boiling; reduce heat. Cover and simmer 1 hour.

Stir in salt pork, carrots, onions and olives. Cover and simmer until beef and vegetables are tender, about 40 minutes. Remove bay leaf. Sprinkle with parsley. Serve in bowls with French bread for dipping.

Beef Stew Provençale

Flemish Beef-and-Beer Stew

(Carbonnades à la Flamande)

In French, carbonnade *means carbonated, but* carbonnades *means stewed meat. Although this stew probably originated in France, the Belgians adapted it so successfully to their famous dark beers that soon even the French gave them credit and dubbed the dish Flemish.*

6 servings

1½-	pounds beef boneless chuck or round steak, 1 inch thick
¼	pound bacon
4	medium onions, sliced
1	clove garlic, chopped
3	tablespoons flour
1	cup water
1	can (12 or 16 ounces) light or dark beer
1	bay leaf
1	tablespoon packed brown sugar
2	teaspoons salt
½	teaspoon dried thyme leaves
¼	teaspoon pepper
1	tablespoon vinegar
	Snipped parsley
	Hot cooked noodles

Cut beef into ½-inch slices; cut slices into 2-inch strips. (For ease in cutting, partially freeze beef about 1½ hours.) Cut bacon into ¼-inch pieces; fry in Dutch oven until crisp. Remove bacon with slotted spoon; drain on paper towels. Pour off fat and reserve. Cook and stir onions and garlic in 2 tablespoons of the reserved bacon fat until tender, about 10 minutes. Remove onions. Cook and stir beef in remaining bacon fat until brown, about 15 minutes.

Stir in flour to coat beef; gradually stir in water. Add onions, beer, bay leaf, brown sugar, salt, thyme and pepper. Add just enough water to cover beef if necessary. Heat to boiling; reduce heat. Cover and simmer until beef is tender, 1 to 1½ hours. Remove bay leaf. Stir in vinegar; sprinkle with bacon and parsley. Serve with noodles.

Burgundy Beef Stew

(Boeuf Bourguignon)

The full French name for this stew is boeuf à la mode du Bourguignon, *which means beef prepared in the manner of the Burgundy district of France. To make a faithful Burgundy Beef Stew it is more important to follow our instructions for cooking and seasoning the stew than to use one of the many wines imported from Burgundy.*

8 servings

6	slices bacon, cut into 1-inch pieces
2-	pound beef boneless chuck eye, rolled rump roast or bottom round roast, cut into 1-inch cubes
½	cup all-purpose flour
1½	cups red Burgundy or other dry red wine
1	clove garlic, chopped
1	bay leaf
1¼	teaspoons salt
1	teaspoon instant beef bouillon
½	teaspoon dried thyme leaves
¼	teaspoon pepper
8	ounces mushrooms, sliced
4	medium onions, sliced
2	tablespoons margarine or butter
	Snipped parsley
	French bread

Fry bacon in Dutch oven over medium heat until crisp; remove bacon and reserve. Coat beef with flour; cook and stir beef in hot bacon fat until brown. Drain excess fat from Dutch oven. Add wine and just enough water to cover beef. Stir in garlic, bay leaf, salt, bouillon, thyme and pepper. Heat to boiling; reduce heat. Cover and simmer until beef is tender, about 1½ hours.

Cook and stir mushrooms and onions in margarine over medium heat until onions are tender. Stir mushrooms, onions and reserved bacon into stew. Cover and simmer 10 minutes. Remove bay leaf. Garnish with parsley. Serve with French bread.

Oxtail Stew

This British favorite is said to have been invented by the French Huguenots who fled to England in the mid-seventeenth century to avoid religious persecution.

6 servings

2½	pounds oxtails, cut into 2-inch pieces
1	tablespoon vegetable oil
3	cups water
2	teaspoons instant beef bouillon
1½	teaspoons salt
¼	teaspoon dried thyme leaves
¼	teaspoon pepper
1	bay leaf
4	medium carrots, cut into 1-inch pieces
4	medium stalks celery, cut into 1-inch pieces
2	medium turnips, cut into 1-inch pieces
1	large onion, coarsely chopped
½	cup cold water
2	tablespoons flour

Cook and stir oxtails in oil in Dutch oven until brown, about 15 minutes. Add 3 cups water, the bouillon, salt, thyme, pepper and bay leaf. Heat to boiling; reduce heat. Cover and simmer 3 hours.

Add carrots, celery, turnips and onion. Heat to boiling; reduce heat. Cover and simmer until oxtails and vegetables are tender, about 30 minutes. Skim fat from broth. Mix ½ cup water and the flour; stir gradually into stew. Heat to boiling, stirring constantly. Boil and stir 1 minute.

Spanish Shredded Beef Stew

(Ropa Vieja)

Ropa vieja means "old clothes" in Spanish—a humorous name for a stew popular in Spain and Latin America. The name comes from the shredded beef, which witty Hispanic chefs compare to old clothes in rags.

6 servings

1½	pounds beef boneless chuck, tip or round
½	cup water
2	teaspoons salt
¼	teaspoon pepper
1	bay leaf
2	medium onions, sliced
2	cloves garlic, chopped
2	tablespoons olive or vegetable oil
1	can (4 ounces) green chilies, drained, seeded and chopped (reserve liquid)
3	medium tomatoes, chopped
2	green peppers, cut into ½-inch squares
1	tablespoon vinegar
⅛	teaspoon ground cinnamon
⅛	teaspoon ground cloves
	Cuban Black Beans (page 197)

Cut beef into 1½-inch pieces. Heat beef, water, salt, pepper and bay leaf to boiling in Dutch oven; reduce heat. Cover and simmer until beef is tender, about 2 hours. (Add water if necessary.)

Remove beef from broth. Cook and stir onions and garlic in oil until onions are tender. Pull beef apart and into shreds. Stir beef, onions, garlic, chilies, reserved liquid and the remaining ingredients except beans into broth. Heat to boiling; reduce heat. Simmer uncovered 30 minutes. Serve with beans.

Ravioli

Familiar Italian ravioli becomes fancy party fare when you make it at home following our easy recipes for a delicious beef-and-spinach filling and homemade pasta.

8 servings (48 ravioli)

    Tomato Sauce* (right)
    Ravioli Dough (right)
¾   pound ground beef
1   small onion, finely chopped
1   package (10 ounces) frozen chopped spinach,
        thawed and well drained
1   egg
½   cup grated Parmesan cheese
1   teaspoon salt
¼   teaspoon pepper
6   quarts water
2   tablespoons salt

Prepare Tomato Sauce. Prepare Ravioli Dough. While dough is resting, cook and stir beef and onion over medium heat until beef is light brown and finely crumbled; drain. Squeeze any remaining moisture from spinach. Stir spinach, egg, cheese, 1 teaspoon salt and the pepper into beef and onion.

Divide dough into 6 equal parts. (Cover dough with plastic wrap to prevent drying.) Roll one part of the dough as thin as possible on lightly floured surface into about 13-inch square. Trim edges to make 12-inch square; fold in half. (Cover with plastic wrap.) Repeat with a second part of dough, but do not fold.

Mound about 1 teaspoon beef filling about 1½ inches apart in checkerboard pattern on sheet of dough. (See photograph.) Dip pastry brush into water; brush in straight lines between filling mounds and around edge of dough. (See photograph.) Unfold folded sheet of dough over filled half. Starting at center, press with fingertips and side of hand around filling and edges to seal. (See photograph.) Cut pasta between mounds into squares with pastry wheel or knife. (See photograph.) Sep-

arate squares; place on waxed paper. Repeat twice with remaining dough to make 48 squares.

Heat water and 2 tablespoons salt to boiling in large kettle. Add ravioli; stir to prevent sticking. Cook uncovered until tender, about 12 minutes; remove to colander with slotted spoon. Serve with Tomato Sauce.

* 1 cup margarine or butter, melted, and ½ cup grated Parmesan cheese can be substituted for the Tomato Sauce; toss with ravioli.

Tomato Sauce

2   cans (16 ounces each) tomatoes
1   can (15 ounces) tomato sauce
1   large onion, chopped
2   cloves garlic, chopped
2   teaspoons sugar
1   teaspoon dried basil leaves
½   teaspoon salt
¼   teaspoon pepper

Break up tomatoes with fork. Heat tomatoes (with liquid) and remaining ingredients to boiling; reduce heat. Simmer uncovered until thickened, about 30 minutes.

Ravioli Dough

3   cups all-purpose flour
3   egg yolks
3   eggs
1   tablespoon salt
¼   to ½ cup water

Make a well in center of flour. Add egg yolks, eggs and salt; mix thoroughly with fork. Mix in water, 1 tablespoon at a time, until dough forms a ball. Turn dough onto well-floured cloth-covered board; knead until smooth and elastic, about 5 minutes. Cover; let rest 10 minutes.

Do-Ahead Tip: After cutting ravioli into squares, place in single layer on cookie sheets; freeze. Place frozen ravioli in freezer containers; freeze no longer than 2 weeks. Cook frozen ravioli as directed above, about 15 minutes.

Mound filling by teaspoonfuls on pasta, about 1½ inches apart.

Draw straight lines between mounds with pastry brush dipped in water.

Press down between mounds with side of hand to form ravioli squares; moistened areas of pasta will seal fillings into squares.

Separate squares with pastry wheel, ravioli cutter or sharp knife.

Homemade Ravioli topped with Tomato Sauce (page 134) makes fine family or party fare.

Cannelloni

These meat-stuffed pasta rolls are ideally suited for freezing. Be prepared for a casual party with an Italian flavor: Make an extra batch to keep in the freezer for impromptu entertaining. Freezing instructions are included in the recipe below.

8 servings

	Pasta (right)
	Tomato-Wine Sauce (right)
1	small onion, finely chopped
1	clove garlic, finely chopped
1	tablespoon olive or vegetable oil
6	ounces fresh spinach,* cooked, drained and finely chopped
¾	pound ground beef
¼	cup grated Parmesan cheese
1	egg, slightly beaten
¾	teaspoon salt
½	teaspoon dried oregano leaves
¼	teaspoon dried basil leaves
	Freshly ground pepper
	White Sauce (page 137)
¼	cup grated Parmesan cheese

Prepare Pasta and Tomato-Wine Sauce. Cook and stir onion and garlic in oil in 10-inch skillet over medium heat until onion is tender. Add spinach; cook, stirring constantly, until moisture has evaporated. Remove spinach, onion and garlic to large bowl with slotted spoon. Cook and stir beef in skillet until light brown.

Remove beef with slotted spoon; add to spinach. Add ¼ cup cheese, the egg, salt, oregano, basil and pepper to beef mixture; mix thoroughly.

Place about 1 tablespoon beef mixture on bottom third of each pasta square; roll up. Pour thin layer of Tomato-Wine Sauce into 2 ungreased baking dishes, 11 x 7 x 1½ and 8 x 8 x 2 inches. Arrange cannelloni seam sides down in single layer in Tomato-Wine Sauce. Prepare White Sauce; pour over cannelloni.

Top with remaining Tomato-Wine Sauce. Sprinkle each baking dish with about 2 tablespoons cheese. Cook uncovered in 375° oven until cheese is bubbly, about 20 minutes.

* ½ package (10 ounces) frozen chopped spinach, thawed and drained, can be substituted for the fresh spinach.

Pasta

1	cup all-purpose flour
1	egg yolk
1	egg
1	teaspoon salt
2	to 4 tablespoons water

Make a well in center of flour. Add egg yolk, egg and salt; mix thoroughly. Mix in water, 1 tablespoon at a time, until dough is stiff but easy to roll. Turn dough onto well-floured cloth-covered board; knead until smooth and elastic, about 5 minutes. Cover; let rest 10 minutes. Divide dough into 2 equal parts. Roll dough, one part at a time (keeping remaining dough covered), into paper-thin 13-inch square. Trim edges to make 12-inch square.

Cut dough into 4-inch squares. Repeat with remaining dough. Cook pasta in 3 quarts boiling salted water (1 tablespoon salt) until done, about 8 minutes; drain. Rinse in cold water. Spread on racks or waxed paper to cool. (After cooling, pasta can be spread between sheets of waxed paper, covered and refrigerated no longer than 24 hours.)

Tomato-Wine Sauce

1	medium onion, chopped
1	tablespoon olive or vegetable oil
1	can (16 ounces) tomatoes
½	can (6-ounce size) tomato paste
½	cup dry red wine
2	tablespoons snipped parsley
1	teaspoon dried basil leaves
1	teaspoon sugar
¼	teaspoon salt
	Freshly ground pepper

Cook and stir onion in oil in 3-quart saucepan over medium heat until tender. Add tomatoes (with liquid) and remaining ingredients. Heat to boiling; reduce heat. Simmer with cover slightly ajar 1 hour. Press sauce through sieve or food mill.

White Sauce

2   tablespoons margarine or butter
2   tablespoons flour
½   teaspoon salt
     Dash of white pepper
1   cup half-and-half

Heat margarine over low heat until melted. Blend in flour, salt and white pepper. Cook over low heat, stirring constantly, until smooth and bubbly; remove from heat. Stir in half-and-half. Heat to boiling, stirring constantly. Boil and stir 1 minute.

Do-Ahead Tip: Before baking, cannelloni can be wrapped and frozen no longer than 2 weeks. Thaw in refrigerator about 8 hours. Bake as directed.

Beef-and-Cabbage Turnovers

(Beirocks)

These tasty German pastries, similar to the Russian Pirozhki *(page 5), are dandy do-ahead snacks to prepare for large groups or for outdoor entertaining.*

16 turnovers

1   package active dry yeast
1   cup warm water (105 to 115°)
2   tablespoons sugar
2   tablespoons vegetable oil
1   teaspoon salt
1   egg
3   to 3½ cups all-purpose flour
     Beef-and-Cabbage Filling (right)
     Margarine or butter, softened

Dissolve yeast in warm water. Stir in sugar, oil, salt, egg and 1 cup of the flour. Beat until

smooth. Mix in enough remaining flour to make dough soft but easy to handle. Turn onto well-floured surface; knead until smooth and elastic, about 5 minutes. Place in greased bowl; turn greased side up. Cover; let rise in warm place until double, about 1 hour. (Dough is ready if indentation remains when touched.) Prepare Beef-and-Cabbage Filling; cool.

Punch down dough. Roll into 16-inch square on well-floured cloth-covered board; cut into sixteen 4-inch squares. Place about ¼ cup filling on center of each square. Bring corners up and together; pinch to seal. Place seam sides down on greased cookie sheets. Shape into rounds. Let rise until double, about 1 hour. Heat oven to 375°. Bake until light brown, 20 to 25 minutes. Brush tops with margarine.

Beef-and-Cabbage Filling

1   pound ground beef
4   cups shredded cabbage
1   small onion, chopped
¼   cup water
1½   teaspoons salt
½   teaspoon caraway seed (optional)
⅛   teaspoon pepper

Cook and stir beef in 10-inch skillet until light brown; drain. Stir in cabbage, onion, water, salt, caraway seed and pepper. Heat to boiling; reduce heat. Cover and simmer until cabbage is tender, 10 to 15 minutes.

Do-Ahead Tip: Turnovers can be baked, wrapped and refrigerated no longer than 24 hours or frozen no longer than 2 weeks. Cover and heat refrigerated or frozen turnovers in 350° oven until hot, 20 to 30 minutes.

Swedish Meatballs
(Köttbullar)

The creative Swedes have many ways with meatballs—but cream is nearly always included, either in the meatballs or in an accompanying sauce. Our version goes well with hot boiled potatoes and Pickled Beets (page 220).

6 to 8 servings (about 48 meatballs)

1	pound ground beef
½	pound ground pork
¾	cup dry bread crumbs
¼	cup milk
1	egg
1	small onion, finely chopped
1½	teaspoons salt
¼	teaspoon ground nutmeg
¼	teaspoon pepper
3	tablespoons flour
¾	cup water
1	cup half-and-half
1	teaspoon instant beef bouillon
½	teaspoon salt
	Snipped parsley

Mix beef, pork, bread crumbs, milk, egg, onion, 1½ teaspoons salt, the nutmeg and pepper. Shape mixture into 1-inch balls. (For easy shaping, dip hands into cold water from time to time.) Place meatballs on ungreased jelly roll pan, 15½ x 10½ x 1 inch, or 2 oblong pans, 13 x 9 x 2 inches. Cook uncovered in 350° oven until light brown, about 20 minutes.

Remove meatballs to serving dish; keep warm. Place 3 tablespoons pan drippings in saucepan; stir in flour. Cook over low heat, stirring constantly, until mixture is smooth and bubbly. Remove from heat. Stir in water, half-and-half, bouillon and ½ teaspoon salt. Heat to boiling, stirring constantly. Boil and stir 1 minute. Pour gravy over meatballs; sprinkle with parsley.

Spaghetti and Meatballs
(Spaghetti con le Polpettone)

Spaghetti and Meatballs—nearly everyone's favorite "Italian" dish—is truly international fare. Spaghetti originated in the Orient; meatballs in the Middle East; tomato sauce in Spain; and the essential Parmesan cheese really does come from Italy—it has been produced in the city of Parma for more than eight hundred years!

6 servings

	Meatballs (page 139)
1	medium onion, chopped
1	clove garlic, finely chopped
1	tablespoon olive or vegetable oil
1	can (28 ounces) whole tomatoes
1	can (6 ounces) tomato paste
¼	cup water
¼	cup snipped parsley
1	teaspoon sugar
1	teaspoon salt
½	teaspoon dried basil leaves
¼	teaspoon pepper
1	package (16 ounces) spaghetti
	Grated Parmesan cheese

Prepare Meatballs. Cook and stir onion and garlic in oil in Dutch oven over medium heat until onion is tender. Add tomatoes (with liquid), tomato paste, water, parsley, sugar, salt, basil and pepper; break up tomatoes with fork. Heat to boiling; reduce heat. Cover and simmer, stirring occasionally, 30 minutes.

Add meatballs; cover and simmer 15 minutes. Cook spaghetti as directed on package. Drain; do not rinse. Place spaghetti on large platter. Top with meatballs and sauce. Sprinkle with cheese. Serve with hot French bread and tossed green salad if desired.

Meatballs

1½	pounds ground beef
¾	cup dry bread crumbs
1	medium onion, finely chopped
½	cup milk
1	egg
2	tablespoons grated Parmesan cheese
1	tablespoon snipped parsley
1½	teaspoons salt
½	teaspoon dried oregano leaves
¼	teaspoon pepper

Mix all ingredients. Shape mixture into 1½-inch balls. (For easier shaping, dip hands into cold water from time to time.) Place in ungreased jelly roll pan, 15½ x 10½ x 1 inch. Cook uncovered in 350° oven until light brown, 15 to 20 minutes.

Mint-Flavored Greek Meatballs

(Keftedakia)

A hint of mint is the secret of much of Greek cooking. The Greeks often serve meatballs with tomato sauce and hot cooked rice.

4 servings (about 36 meatballs)

1	pound ground beef or lamb
½	cup dry bread crumbs
¼	cup snipped parsley
¼	cup milk
1	egg
1	medium onion, finely chopped
1	clove garlic, finely chopped
1	tablespoon snipped fresh mint leaves or ½ teaspoon crushed dried mint
1	teaspoon salt
½	teaspoon crushed dried oregano leaves
¼	teaspoon pepper

Mix all ingredients. Shape mixture into 1-inch balls. (For easy shaping, dip hands into cold water from time to time.) Place meat-balls in ungreased jelly roll pan, 15½ x 10½ x 1 inch, or oblong pan, 13 x 9 x 2 inches. Cook uncovered in 350° oven until light brown, about 25 minutes.

Beef-Cabbage Loaf

(Lihakaalilaatikko)

Try this quick Finnish casserole when time is limited. It has the same delicious flavors as individual cabbage rolls but can be prepared for baking in twenty minutes or less.

6 servings

1	medium head cabbage, coarsely shredded (8 cups)
¼	cup water
¼	teaspoon salt
1	pound ground beef
1	cup soft bread crumbs (about 1½ slices)
½	cup milk
1	small onion, chopped
1	egg
1½	teaspoons salt
¼	teaspoon pepper
¼	teaspoon dried marjoram leaves

Heat cabbage, water and ¼ teaspoon salt to boiling; reduce heat. Cover and simmer until cabbage is wilted, about 5 minutes; drain. Mix remaining ingredients.

Place half the cabbage in ungreased 2-quart casserole. Spread beef mixture over cabbage; top with remaining cabbage. Cover and cook in 350° oven until done, 55 to 60 minutes. Serve with cranberry sauce and creamed potatoes if desired.

Stuffed Cabbage Rolls
(Kåldolmar)

Stuffed cabbage rolls are family favorites from Finland to the Balkans—and there are many recipes. Our Scandinavian recipe presents the rolls in a creamy white sauce. Boiled potatoes and lingonberry preserves are traditional Scandinavian accompaniments.

6 servings (2 rolls each)

1	large head cabbage (about 2 pounds)
1½	pounds ground beef
⅓	cup uncooked regular rice
½	cup milk
1	medium onion, chopped
1	egg
2	teaspoons salt
¼	teaspoon pepper
¼	teaspoon ground allspice
½	cup water
½	cup half-and-half or water
1	tablespoon flour
½	teaspoon instant beef bouillon

Remove core from cabbage. Cover cabbage with cold water; let stand about 10 minutes. Remove 12 cabbage leaves. Cover leaves with boiling water. Cover and let stand until leaves are limp, about 10 minutes; drain.

Mix beef, rice, milk, onion, egg, salt, pepper and allspice. Place about ⅓ cup beef mixture at stem end of each leaf. Roll leaf around beef mixture, tucking in sides. Place cabbage rolls seam sides down in ungreased oblong baking dish, 13½ x 9 x 2 inches. Pour water over rolls. Cover and cook in 350° oven until beef is done, about 1 hour. Remove cabbage rolls with slotted spoon; keep warm. Drain liquid from baking dish, reserving ½ cup liquid; skim fat.

Gradually stir half-and-half into flour in saucepan until smooth. Stir in reserved liquid and the bouillon. Heat to boiling, stirring constantly. Boil and stir 1 minute. Serve sauce with cabbage rolls.

Baked Macaroni with Beef and Cheese
(Pasticcio)

A touch of cinnamon and a tomato-beef sauce layer add new dimensions to this Greek version of the versatile macaroni casserole, so popular with American budget-watchers. In Greece, ziti (a pasta similar to elbow macaroni) is most often used in pasticcio.

6 servings

7	ounces uncooked ziti or elbow macaroni (about 2 cups)
¾	pound ground beef
1	small onion, chopped
1	can (15 ounces) tomato sauce
1	teaspoon salt
1½	cups grated Kasseri, Parmesan or Romano cheese (6 ounces)
⅛	teaspoon ground cinnamon
1¼	cups milk
3	tablespoons margarine or butter
2	eggs, beaten
⅛	teaspoon ground nutmeg

Cook macaroni as directed on package; drain. Cook and stir beef and onion in 10-inch skillet until beef is light brown; drain. Stir in tomato sauce and salt. Spread half the macaroni in greased square baking dish, 8 x 8 x 2 inches; cover with beef mixture. Mix ½ cup of the cheese and the cinnamon; sprinkle over beef mixture. Cover with remaining macaroni.

Cook and stir milk and margarine in 2-quart saucepan until margarine is melted. Remove from heat. Stir at least half the milk mixture gradually into beaten eggs. Blend into milk mixture in saucepan; pour over macaroni. Sprinkle with remaining 1 cup cheese. Cook uncovered in 325° oven until brown and center is set, about 50 minutes. Sprinkle with nutmeg. Garnish with parsley if desired.

Beef with Olives and Almonds

Beef with Olives and Almonds

(Picadillo)

Sometimes called Mexican hash, picadillo is found in many parts of Latin America and always includes ground or finely chopped meat (the Spanish picado means minced meat). In Mexico picadillo is often served with rice or used as a filling for tortillas, meat pies and peppers.

4 servings

1	pound ground beef
1	medium onion, chopped
1	clove garlic, chopped
2	tomatoes, chopped
1	green pepper, chopped
¼	cup raisins
1½	teaspoons salt
⅛	teaspoon ground cinnamon
⅛	teaspoon ground cloves
¼	cup slivered almonds
¼	cup sliced pimiento-stuffed olives
	Hot cooked rice (page 253)

Cook and stir beef, onion and garlic in 10-inch skillet until beef is light brown; drain. Add tomatoes, green pepper, raisins, salt, cinnamon and cloves. Cover and simmer 10 minutes.

Cook and stir almonds over medium heat until golden, 2 to 3 minutes. Stir almonds and olives into beef mixture. Serve with rice.

German Breakfast Sausage

(Knapwurst)

Knapwurst, *traditional fare in many German homes, is similar to the scrapple prized by our Pennsylvania Dutch, but oats rather than cornmeal are used to bind the meat loaf. Try this tasty sausage for breakfast as recommended in the recipe; or serve it as sandwich meat or on crackers for appetizers or snacks.*

8 servings

1	pound ground beef
½	pound ground pork
3	cups water
1	medium onion, chopped
3	cups rolled oats
1	tablespoon salt
1¼	teaspoons ground cloves
1	teaspoon ground allspice
1	teaspoon ground nutmeg
¾	teaspoon pepper

Crumble beef and pork in Dutch oven; stir in water and onion. Heat to boiling; reduce heat. Simmer uncovered, stirring occasionally, 30 minutes. Stir in remaining ingredients. Simmer uncovered, stirring frequently, 30 minutes.

Spoon mixture into ungreased loaf pan, 9 x 5 x 3 inches. Cover and refrigerate until firm, about 8 hours. Unmold and cut into ½-inch slices. Fry in ungreased skillet over medium-high heat until brown and crisp on both sides, about 10 minutes. Serve as breakfast sausage with eggs or on rye bread with sliced raw onion if desired.

Do-Ahead Tip: Loaf can be cut into 4 equal parts, wrapped and frozen no longer than 1 month.

Corn Soufflé Casserole

(Pastel de Choclo)

Although this popular Latin American dish is called pastel *(or pie) from Mexico to Argentina, it more closely resembles a hearty ground-beef casserole with a soufflé-like Corn Topping rather than a pastry crust. With this "dinner in a dish," you need only fresh tropical fruit to provide a typical Latin American finale to the meal.*

6 to 8 servings

1½	pounds ground beef
2	medium onions, chopped
1	green pepper, chopped
1	clove garlic, chopped
2	tomatoes, chopped
¼	cup raisins
1½	teaspoons salt
1	teaspoon sugar
½	teaspoon ground cumin
½	teaspoon dried marjoram leaves
¼	teaspoon pepper
	Corn Topping (below)

Cook and stir beef, onions, green pepper and garlic in skillet until beef is light brown; drain. Stir in remaining ingredients except Corn Topping. Pour into ungreased 2-quart casserole. Prepare Corn Topping; pour over beef mixture. Cook uncovered in 350° oven until knife inserted halfway between center and edge comes out clean, about 30 minutes.

Corn Topping

½	cup milk
2	tablespoons flour
¼	teaspoon salt
1	can (16 ounces) whole-kernel corn, drained
3	egg yolks, slightly beaten
3	egg whites
6	pimiento-stuffed olives, sliced

Stir milk gradually into flour and salt in saucepan; add corn. Cook over medium heat, stirring constantly, until mixture thickens and boils. Boil and stir 1 minute. Stir at least half of the hot mixture gradually into egg yolks. Blend into hot mixture in saucepan. Boil and stir 1 minute. Cool slightly. Beat egg whites until stiff but not dry. Fold corn mixture and olives into egg whites.

Beef Enchiladas

Enchiladas are tortillas rolled around a filling, usually made with meat or chicken, and then baked in a spicy sauce. Commercially prepared tortillas can be found in most supermarkets; our recipe includes an easy way to make tortillas from scratch.

8 servings (2 enchiladas each)

	Tortillas (right)
1½	pounds ground beef
2	cups shredded Monterey Jack cheese
¾	cup sliced green onion
¾	cup dairy sour cream
3	tablespoons snipped parsley
1½	teaspoons salt
¼	teaspoon pepper
3	cans (8 ounces each) tomato sauce
½	cup chopped green pepper
3	tablespoons chopped green chilies
1	tablespoon chili powder
¼	teaspoon ground cumin
⅓	cup sliced pitted ripe olives

Prepare Tortillas. Cook and stir beef in 12-inch skillet until light brown; drain. Remove from heat. Stir in 1½ cups of the cheese, the green onion, sour cream, parsley, salt and pepper. Cover and reserve. Heat remaining ingredients except olives to boiling; reduce heat. Simmer uncovered 5 minutes.

Spoon about ¼ cup beef mixture onto each tortilla; roll tortilla around filling. Arrange in 2 ungreased oblong baking dishes, 12 x 7 ½ x 2 inches. Pour sauce over enchiladas; sprinkle with remaining cheese. Cook uncovered in 350° oven until bubbly, about 20 minutes. Garnish with olives.

Tortillas

⅓	cup shortening or lard
3	cups all-purpose flour
1½	teaspoons salt
¾	cup water

Cut shortening into flour and salt thoroughly. Add water; stir with fork until dough almost cleans side of bowl. (Add 1 to 2 teaspoons water if necessary.) Turn dough onto lightly floured board. Knead until smooth, 15 to 20 times. Divide into 16 equal parts. Shape each part into ball; roll into 9-inch circle. (Cover remaining balls of dough with damp towel to prevent drying.) Cook on ungreased hot griddle or in ungreased hot skillet until golden brown, turning once, 1 to 2 minutes.

Ground Beef

Did You Know?

The classification of ground beef is determined by federal laws specifying the amount of fat permitted in the various types. Any ground beef labeled *hamburger* can contain up to 30 percent fat. Although *ground beef* can also contain 30 percent fat, only the fat attached to the beef can be used; no other fat can be added. *Lean ground beef* (ground chuck) contains 20 percent or less fat, while *extra-lean ground beef* (ground beef) contains 15 percent or less fat.

Ground beef is very perishable and should be stored in the coldest part of the refrigerator. Store prepackaged ground beef unopened in its package. If it is not to be used within 24 hours, it should be frozen.

Prepackaged ground beef can be frozen in its wrapper up to 2 weeks. For longer storage, overwrap tightly in moisture-proof, vapor-proof wrap. For optimum quality, ground beef should be frozen at 0°F no longer than 4 months.

Tostadas

Tostadas

A tostada is a tortilla topped with a variety of foods. Our Tostadas include Refried Beans, ground beef, cheese, lettuce, tomatoes and avocados. Tostadas are great fun to prepare—and easy on the chef—when served as a "make-your-own" dish.

8 servings

	Refried Beans* (page 145)
	Vegetable oil
8	six-inch corn tortillas
1	pound ground beef
1	medium onion, chopped
1	clove garlic, chopped
1	can (15 ounces) tomato sauce
2	teaspoons chili powder
1	teaspoon dried oregano leaves
1	teaspoon salt
¼	teaspoon ground cumin
¼	teaspoon crushed red peppers
1	package (8 ounces) shredded Monterey Jack or Cheddar cheese (2 cups)
4	cups shredded lettuce
3	medium tomatoes, sliced
1	avocado, sliced
	Dairy sour cream
1	jar (8 ounces) hot chili salsa

Prepare Refried Beans. Heat oil (¼ inch) to 360°. Fry 1 tortilla at a time until slightly brown and crisp, about 30 seconds on each side. Drain on paper towels. Keep warm in 200° oven no longer than 20 minutes.

Cook and stir beef, onion and garlic until beef is light brown; drain. Stir in tomato sauce, chili powder, oregano, salt, cumin and red peppers. Heat to boiling; reduce heat. Simmer uncovered 15 minutes.

Place ¼ to ⅓ cup beans on each tortilla; spread with about ⅓ cup meat mixture. Sprinkle each tostada with cheese and lettuce. Arrange tomato and avocado slices on top. Top with sour cream; serve with chili salsa.

Refried Beans

2 cups water
8 ounces dried pinto beans (about 1¼ cups)
1 medium onion, chopped
1 clove garlic, chopped
1 teaspoon salt
3 tablespoons melted bacon fat, melted lard or vegetable oil

Heat water, beans, onion and garlic to boiling in 2-quart saucepan; boil 2 minutes. Remove from heat; cover and let stand 1 hour.

Add just enough water to cover beans; add salt. Heat to boiling; reduce heat. Cover and simmer, stirring occasionally, until tender, about 1½ hours. (Add water during cooking if necessary.) Mash beans; stir in bacon fat until completely absorbed.

* 1 can (about 16 ounces) refried beans can be substituted for the Refried Beans.

Tortillas

Did You Know?

The tortilla, Mexico's most famous bread, is an unleavened corn or flour cake, thin enough to butter, roll up and eat hot. Rolled around a savory filling, it becomes an Enchilada (pages 143 and 176) or a Burrito (page 159); deep-fried, a crisp flat base for a Tostada (page 144); pressed into a half-moon shape around a filling and deep-fried, a Quesadilla (page 176). Cut into strips and fried, it becomes a garnish for Tortilla Soup (page 28). Corn and flour tortillas are available canned, frozen or refrigerated at grocery stores.

Baked Beef Curry with Custard Topping (Bobotie)

In the seventeenth century, when Holland maintained a virtual monopoly on the spice trade, the Dutch East India Company decided to establish a permanent refreshment station at Cape Town for ships sailing from the Netherlands to the Indian Ocean on the sea route blazed by Vasco da Gama. The Dutch settlement of South Africa quickly followed, and the flavor of curry made with Indian spices attracted many South African fans. Today bobotie is as characteristic of the food of South Africa as the tortilla is of Mexico.

8 servings

1½ pounds ground beef or lamb
1 cup soft bread crumbs (about 1½ slices)
1 cup milk
1 egg
1 medium onion, chopped
¼ cup slivered almonds, chopped
¼ cup raisins
1 tablespoon lemon juice
2 to 3 teaspoons curry powder
1½ teaspoons salt
¼ teaspoon pepper
2 eggs, beaten
1 cup milk
Paprika

Mix beef, bread crumbs, 1 cup milk, 1 egg, the onion, almonds, raisins, lemon juice, curry powder, salt and pepper. Spread mixture in ungreased 2-quart casserole. Cook uncovered in 325° oven 45 minutes; drain excess fat. Mix beaten eggs and 1 cup milk; pour over beef mixture. Sprinkle with paprika. Place casserole in oblong pan, 13 x 9 x 2 inches, on oven rack. Pour very hot water (1 inch) into pan. Cook uncovered until beef is done and custard is set, about 30 minutes. Garnish with lemon slices and pimiento if desired. Cut into wedges to serve.

Sri Lanka Ground-Beef Curry

Cinnamon and coconut are the ingredients that so often make the curries of Sri Lanka (formerly Ceylon) so memorable. In this recipe, diced potatoes help to stretch the meat. Dal (page 197) is a traditional Sri Lanka accompaniment to curry.

6 servings

1	pound ground beef
2	medium onions, chopped
2	medium potatoes, diced
1	green pepper, chopped
2	tablespoons vegetable oil
2½	cups water
¼	cup shredded coconut
2	tablespoons tomato paste
2	thin slices ginger root
1	stick cinnamon
1	whole clove
1½	teaspoons salt
1	teaspoon curry powder
1	teaspoon chili powder
½	teaspoon ground turmeric
½	teaspoon ground cardamom
3	cups hot cooked rice (page 253)
	Chutney or fresh pineapple chunks

Cook and stir beef, onions, potatoes and green pepper in oil in 12-inch skillet over medium heat until beef is brown; drain. Stir in remaining ingredients except rice and chutney. Heat to boiling; reduce heat. Simmer uncovered until vegetables are tender and mixture is desired consistency, 20 to 30 minutes. Remove ginger root, cinnamon and clove. Serve with rice and chutney.

Pasta with Prosciutto Sauce

Prosciutto—a smoked salty Italian ham—adds the characteristic flavor to this unusual adaptation of a classic Italian meat sauce. Prosciutto can be purchased at most delicatessens.

8 servings

1	pound ground beef
2	medium onions, sliced
2	cloves garlic, finely chopped
1	can (28 ounces) tomatoes
¼	pound prosciutto,* cut into thin strips
¾	cup dry red wine
1	teaspoon sugar
½	teaspoon salt
½	teaspoon dried rosemary leaves, crushed
¼	teaspoon ground nutmeg
¼	teaspoon pepper
1	pound uncooked mostaccioli or ziti
	Grated Parmesan cheese

Cook and stir beef, onions and garlic in 10-inch skillet until beef is light brown; drain. Stir in tomatoes (with liquid) and remaining ingredients except pasta and cheese; break up tomatoes with fork. Cover and simmer 15 minutes, stirring occasionally. Uncover and simmer, stirring occasionally, about 1 hour. Cook pasta as directed on package; drain. Serve sauce on hot cooked pasta; sprinkle with cheese.

* Dried beef can be substituted for the prosciutto.

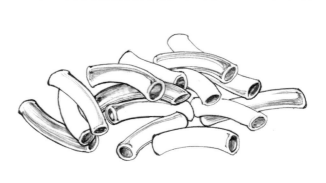

Danish Pork Tenderloins
(Fyldt Svinemørbrad)

Denmark has long been famous for the fine quality of its pork, and the Danes have long been fond of pork in many imaginative forms. Prunes are a traditional Danish accompaniment. In our recipe both prunes and apples are stuffed into the pork tenderloins—a show-stopping party dish! Serve with Sugar-Browned Potatoes (page 245) and our lucious Thousand Leaves Torte (page 314).

6 to 8 servings

12	dried prunes
2	pork tenderloins (¾ to 1 pound each)
	Salt and pepper
1	tart apple, chopped
¾	cup water
¼	cup cold water
2	tablespoons flour
¼	teaspoon salt
⅛	teaspoon pepper

Cook prunes in boiling water 5 minutes; drain. Remove pits. Cut tenderloins lengthwise almost in half. Sprinkle cut sides with salt and pepper. Place half each of the prunes and apple down center of one side of each tenderloin; cover with the other side. Fasten with metal skewers; lace with string. Place on rack in shallow roasting pan. Insert meat thermometer horizontally so tip is in center of thickest part of pork and does not rest in stuffing. Roast in 325° oven until thermometer registers 170°, 1¼ to 1½ hours.

Remove pork to warm platter; keep warm. Add ¾ cup water to roasting pan; stir to loosen brown particles. Pour into 1-quart saucepan; heat to boiling. Shake ¼ cup water and the flour in tightly covered container; stir gradually into drippings. Heat to boiling, stirring constantly. Add ¼ teaspoon salt and ⅛ teaspoon pepper. Boil and stir 1 minute. Cut pork into slices; serve with gravy.

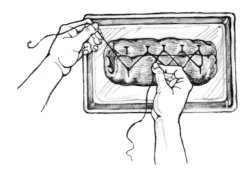

Fasten stuffed tenderloin with metal skewers; lace with string.

Roast Fresh Ham with Onion Stuffing

Slow cooking of this Welsh dish gently wafts the fragrant aromas of roasting pork and sage-onion stuffing all through the home, whetting the appetite of the most finicky diner.

8 to 10 servings

4-	pound pork boneless leg (fresh ham)
	Salt
3	cups water
6	medium onions, chopped
1	tablespoon dried sage leaves, crushed
2	cups soft bread cubes
1	egg, beaten
2	tablespoons margarine or butter
1	tablespoon dried sage leaves, crushed
1	teaspoon salt
¼	teaspoon pepper

Spread pork flat; sprinkle lightly with salt. Heat water to boiling; add onions. Cook 5 minutes; drain. Mix onions and remaining ingredients. Spread onion mixture on pork; roll up. Fasten with metal skewers.

Place pork fat side down on rack in shallow roasting pan. Spoon any remaining stuffing over top of pork. Insert meat thermometer so tip is in center of thickest part of pork and does not rest in stuffing. Roast uncovered in 325° oven until thermometer registers 170°, 3 to 3½ hours.

Alsatian Pork with Sauerkraut

Alsatian Pork with Sauerkraut

(Choucroute Garnie à l'Alsacienne)

When the French put their creative genius to work on the essentially humble ingredients of pork and sauerkraut, you can be certain that the result will be memorable. This combination is served in varied forms not only in the farm homes of the Alsace but also in many glamorous Parisian restaurants.

4 servings

4	slices bacon, cut into 1-inch pieces
1	medium onion, chopped
1	can (16 ounces) sauerkraut, drained
1	to 2 tablespoons packed brown sugar
2	medium potatoes, cut into fourths
2	tart apples, sliced
12	juniper berries (optional)
6	whole peppercorns
2	whole cloves
1	sprig parsley
1	bay leaf
4	smoked pork chops, ½ inch thick
4	frankfurters, slashed diagonally
2	cups chicken broth

Cook and stir bacon and onion in Dutch oven or 12-inch skillet until bacon is crisp; drain. Stir in sauerkraut and brown sugar. Add potatoes and apples.

Tie juniper berries, peppercorns, cloves, parsley and bay leaf in cheesecloth bag or place in tea ball; add to sauerkraut. Add pork chops and frankfurters. Pour chicken broth over meat. Heat to boiling; reduce heat. Cover and simmer until meat is done and potatoes are tender, about 30 minutes. Remove spice bag. Remove sauerkraut, potatoes and apples to large platter with slotted spoon. Arrange meat around edge.

Pork Chops with Barley and Sauerkraut

In this hearty recipe from Poland, barley is introduced as an economical meat-stretcher, and the flavor is enhanced with caraway seed, a traditional European seasoning for many centuries.

6 servings

2	cans (16 ounces each) sauerkraut, drained
1½	cups water
2	medium onions, chopped
½	cup barley
2	tablespoons packed brown sugar
2	teaspoons instant chicken bouillon
1	teaspoon caraway seed (optional)
¼	teaspoon pepper
6	pork chops, about ¾ inch thick
1	teaspoon salt
½	cup catsup
2	teaspoons Worcestershire sauce

Mix sauerkraut, water, onions, barley, brown sugar, bouillon, caraway seed and pepper. Place in oblong baking dish, 13½ x 9 x 2 inches. Trim excess fat from pork chops. Arrange pork chops on sauerkraut mixture; sprinkle with salt. Mix catsup and Worcestershire sauce; spread on pork chops. Cover and cook in 350° oven until pork is done, 1¼ to 1½ hours. Garnish with parsley sprigs if desired.

Soy-Honey Spareribs

A simple sweet-and-sour marinade is all you need to transform spareribs into a legendary Chinese delicacy. In China the ribs are usually served with hot boiled Chinese noodles.

6 servings

4	pounds fresh pork spareribs, cut into serving pieces
1½	cups beef broth or bouillon
⅓	cup soy sauce
⅓	cup honey
3	tablespoons cider vinegar
2	tablespoons sherry
1	tablespoon sugar
1	teaspoon salt
1	teaspoon finely chopped ginger root or 2 teaspoons ground ginger
2	medium cloves garlic, finely chopped, or ¼ teaspoon garlic powder
	Green onion tassels*

Place spareribs in shallow glass or plastic dish. Mix beef broth, soy sauce, honey, vinegar, sherry, sugar, salt, ginger root and garlic; pour over ribs. Cover and refrigerate, turning ribs 2 or 3 times, at least 6 hours.

Remove ribs from marinade; reserve marinade. Arrange ribs meaty sides up in single layer on rack in foil-lined broiler pan. Cover and cook in 350° oven 45 minutes. Brush ribs with marinade. Cook uncovered, brushing occasionally with marinade, until tender, about 50 minutes. Garnish with green onion tassels.

* Trim root end and green top from green onions, leaving white and some of the green, to about 4 inches. Slit ends 5 or 6 times almost to center. Chill in iced water; drain.

Mou Shu Pork with Mandarin Pancakes

As more and more Americans discover the joys of authentic Chinese cooking, more of us are trying our hand at exotic Mou Shu Pork, one of the gastronomical glories of China. Our Mandarin Pancakes are essential to the dish—and are fun to make at home with our easy-to-follow recipe. In China, each guest fills and rolls his or her own pancakes.

6 servings (3 pancakes each)

  Mandarin Pancakes (right)
1 pound pork boneless loin*
2 teaspoons soy sauce
1 teaspoon cornstarch
6 large dried mushrooms
1 tablespoon sesame or vegetable oil
2 eggs, slightly beaten
¼ teaspoon salt
2 tablespoons sesame or vegetable oil
1 can (8 ounces) bamboo shoots, drained and cut into ¼-inch strips
¼ cup water
3 tablespoons soy sauce
1 clove garlic, finely chopped
1 teaspoon sugar
1 tablespoon cold water
1 teaspoon cornstarch
2 green onions (with tops), cut diagonally in ¼-inch pieces

Prepare Mandarin Pancakes. Cut pork into slices, 2 x ⅛ inch. (For ease in cutting, partially freeze pork about 1 hour.) Stack slices; cut lengthwise into strips. Mix 2 teaspoons soy sauce and 1 teaspoon cornstarch in glass bowl; stir in pork. Cover and refrigerate 30 minutes. Soak mushrooms in warm water until soft, about 30 minutes.

Drain mushrooms. Remove and discard stems; cut caps into thin slices. Heat 1 tablespoon oil in 10-inch skillet or wok until hot. Mix eggs and salt. Cook eggs until firm, turning once. Remove eggs; cut into thin strips.

Heat 2 tablespoons oil in skillet until hot. Cook and stir pork in oil until no longer pink. Add mushrooms, bamboo shoots, ¼ cup water, 3 tablespoons soy sauce, the garlic and sugar. Heat to boiling. Mix 1 tablespoon water and 1 teaspoon cornstarch; stir into pork mixture. Cook and stir until thickened, about 1 minute. Add egg strips and green onions; cook and stir 30 seconds.

Pour pork filling into serving bowl; arrange hot pancakes on platter. To serve, unfold pancake and spoon about ¼ cup filling down center of each pancake. Roll up; fold one end over to contain filling.

* 1½ pounds pork chops can be substituted for the boneless pork.

Mandarin Pancakes
2 cups all-purpose flour
¾ cup boiling water
¼ teaspoon salt
  Sesame or vegetable oil

Mix flour, water and salt until dough holds together (add 2 tablespoons water if necessary); shape into a ball. Knead on lightly floured board until smooth, about 8 minutes. Shape dough into 9-inch roll; cut into 1-inch slices. Cut each slice into halves. (Cover pieces of dough with plastic wrap to prevent drying.)

Shape each piece of dough into a ball; flatten slightly. Roll each ball into 3-inch circle on lightly floured surface. Brush top of one circle with oil; top with another circle. (See diagram.) Roll each double circle into 6- or 7-inch circle on lightly floured surface. (See diagram.) Stack circles between pieces of waxed paper to prevent drying. Repeat with remaining pieces of dough.

Heat skillet over medium heat until warm. Cook one circle at a time in ungreased skillet, turning frequently, until pancake is blistered by air pockets and turns slightly translucent, about 2 minutes. (Do not brown or overcook or pancake will become brittle.) Carefully separate into 2 pancakes. (See diagram.) Fold each pancake into fourths. (Keep covered.) Repeat with remaining pancakes.

Reheat pancakes by placing on heatproof plate or rack in steamer. Cover and steam over boiling water 10 minutes. (A steamer can be improvised by using a large skillet or wok. A plate can be supported above water on trivet or canning jar rings.)

Do-Ahead Tip: Prepare Mandarin Pancakes, stack and cover until completely cool. Wrap in aluminum foil, label and freeze no longer than 2 weeks. Heat frozen wrapped pancakes in 325° oven 30 minutes.

Brush 1 circle with sesame oil; cover with remaining circle.

Roll 2 circles together into 6-inch circle.

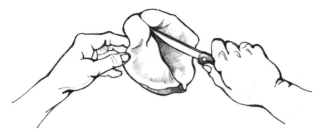

Separate cooked pancake with tip of knife into 2 pancakes.

Pork with Rice and Olives

(Arroz con Carne de Cerdo)

This classic Caribbean casserole from the Dominican Republic bears a close resemblance to certain of the rice Jollofs (page 78) of West Africa. The food of both countries has been strongly influenced by early Spanish settlers and African chefs.

4 servings

1½	pounds pork boneless shoulder
¼	cup vinegar
1	medium onion, chopped
2	cloves garlic, chopped
⅛	to ¼ teaspoon crushed red peppers
3	slices bacon
2	cups boiling water
1	cup uncooked regular rice
¼	cup sliced pimiento-stuffed olives
2	tablespoons snipped parsley
1½	teaspoons salt

Trim fat from pork; cut pork into ¾-inch cubes. Mix pork, vinegar, onion, garlic and red peppers in glass or plastic bowl. Cover and refrigerate, stirring occasionally, at least 6 hours.

Fry bacon until crisp; drain on paper towels. Remove pork from marinade, reserving marinade. Cook and stir pork in bacon fat until all liquid has evaporated and pork is brown on all sides; drain. Mix pork, reserved marinade, the bacon and remaining ingredients in ungreased 2-quart casserole. Cover and cook in 350° oven until liquid is absorbed, 25 to 30 minutes.

Pork and Chicken, Filipino Style

(Adobo)

The food of the Philippines reflects the influence of the Chinese, the Southeast Asians and the Spanish. Adobo is considered the national dish of the Philippines. There are many versions, but both pork and chicken are nearly always included and are first simmered, then fried. Our recipe has the tart flavor favored by many Filipinos; some families sweeten adobo *with coconut milk.*

8 servings

1½	pounds pork boneless shoulder
1½	pounds chicken legs or thighs
¾	cup water
⅓	cup white wine vinegar
3	cloves garlic, chopped
2	tablespoons soy sauce
1	teaspoon salt
¼	teaspoon pepper
2	tablespoons vegetable oil
	Hot cooked rice (page 253)

Trim fat from pork; cut pork into 1-inch cubes. Heat pork, chicken, water, vinegar, garlic, soy sauce, salt and pepper to boiling in Dutch oven; reduce heat. Cover and simmer until pork and chicken are done, 45 to 55 minutes.

Remove pork and chicken from Dutch oven. Skim fat from broth if necessary. Cook broth uncovered until reduced to about 1 cup. Heat oil in 10-inch skillet until hot. Cook chicken in oil over medium heat until brown on all sides. Add pork; cook and stir until brown. Serve pork, chicken and broth over rice. Garnish with snipped parsley and tomato wedges if desired.

Jellied Pork-and-Veal Loaf

(Sylta)

This jellied meat loaf from Sweden is often served at festive smorgasbords. It is equally at home on an American-style buffet table, and makes an unusual and welcome contribution to a pot-luck party.

6 servings

2	pounds pork boneless shoulder
1	pound veal or beef shanks
4	cups water
1	medium onion, cut into ½-inch slices
6	whole allspice
4	whole cloves
1	bay leaf
1	tablespoon salt
¼	teaspoon pepper
1	envelope unflavored gelatin
¼	cup cold water
1	tablespoon vinegar
1	teaspoon salt

Trim fat from pork. Heat pork, veal, 4 cups water, the onion, allspice, cloves, bay leaf, 1 tablespoon salt and the pepper to boiling in Dutch oven; reduce heat. Cover and simmer until meat is tender, about 1½ hours.

Remove meat from broth; cool meat slightly. Remove meat from bones. Finely chop meat or put through fine blade of food chopper.

Strain broth. Sprinkle gelatin over ¼ cup water in saucepan. Heat over low heat, stirring constantly, until gelatin is dissolved, about 3 minutes.

Mix meat, 2½ cups of the broth, the gelatin, vinegar and 1 teaspoon salt; pour into ungreased loaf pan, 9 x 5 x 3 inches. Cover and refrigerate until firm, at least 6 hours. Unmold onto platter; cut into slices. Garnish with celery leaves and pickled beets if desired.

Portuguese Pork with Lemon

Portugal's rugged terrain cannot support large herds of cattle, but pork is in abundance throughout the country. In this popular Portuguese stew the meat is flavored with lemon juice and garlic—often a half cup or so of a dry Portuguese wine is added too. For colorful service, garnish the finished dish with sliced oranges and lemon wedges.

6 servings

2	pounds pork boneless shoulder
2	cloves garlic, chopped
2	tablespoons lemon juice
1	tablespoon olive or vegetable oil
1	teaspoon salt
¼	teaspoon ground cumin
¼	to ½ teaspoon crushed red peppers
1	tablespoon olive or vegetable oil
¼	cup water
½	cup pitted ripe olives

Trim fat from pork; cut pork into ¾-inch cubes. Toss pork, garlic, lemon juice, 1 tablespoon oil, the salt, cumin and red peppers in glass or plastic bowl. Cover and refrigerate, stirring occasionally, at least 8 hours.

Remove pork from marinade; reserve any remaining marinade. Heat 1 tablespoon oil in skillet until hot. Cook and stir pork in oil over medium heat until liquid has evaporated and pork is brown; drain. Add water and reserved marinade. Cover and simmer until pork is tender, about 30 minutes. (Add water if necessary.) Stir in olives. Serve with Green Beans in Tomato Sauce (page 218) and hot cooked rice if desired.

Hungarian Pork Goulash

(Székely Gulyás)

The Székely people, who originated this interpretation of Hungarian goulash, come from the northern part of Hungary, once known as Transylvania and now a part of Rumania. The Székely people still live on in their ancient homeland and claim to be direct descendants of Atilla's Huns!

6 to 8 servings

2	pounds pork boneless shoulder
1	tablespoon vegetable oil or bacon fat
2	medium onions, chopped
1	clove garlic, chopped
3	cups water
2	tablespoons paprika
2	teaspoons instant chicken bouillon
1	teaspoon caraway seed
1	teaspoon salt
⅛	teaspoon pepper
2	cans (16 ounces each) sauerkraut, drained
¼	cup cold water
2	tablespoons flour
1	cup dairy sour cream
	Snipped parsley

Trim fat from pork; cut pork into 1-inch pieces. Heat oil in Dutch oven or 12-inch skillet until hot. Cook and stir pork in hot oil until brown; drain on paper towels. Cook and stir onions and garlic in Dutch oven until onions are tender. Drain fat from Dutch oven. Stir in pork, 3 cups water, the paprika, bouillon, caraway seed, salt and pepper. Heat to boiling; reduce heat. Cover and simmer 1 hour.

Stir sauerkraut into pork mixture. Heat to boiling; reduce heat. Cover and simmer until pork is tender, about 30 minutes. Shake ¼ cup water and the flour in covered container; stir into pork mixture. Heat to boiling, stirring constantly. Boil and stir 1 minute; reduce heat. Stir in sour cream; heat just until hot. Sprinkle with parsley. Serve with boiled potatoes if desired.

Austrian Ham-and-Noodle Casserole

Austrian Ham-and-Noodle Casserole

(Schinkenfleckerln)

An inexpensive and easy family casserole from Austria. Schinkenfleckerln is traditionally served with buttered broad beans or sliced fresh tomatoes, and followed with a rich Austrian dessert, such as Apple Strudel (page 316).

4 servings

8   ounces uncooked wide egg noodles
¼   cup margarine or butter
1   medium onion, chopped
2   eggs, beaten
½   cup dairy sour cream

2   cups diced fully cooked smoked ham (about ½ pound)
½   teaspoon caraway seed (optional)
¼   teaspoon pepper
¼   cup dry bread crumbs
    Paprika

Drop noodles into 6 cups rapidly boiling salted water (4 teaspoons salt). Heat to rapid boiling. Cook, stirring constantly, 3 minutes. Cover and remove from heat; let stand 10 minutes. Drain.

Stir margarine and onion into noodles. Stir eggs into sour cream. Stir egg mixture, ham, caraway seed and pepper into noodles. Sprinkle bread crumbs evenly in greased 2-quart casserole. Pour noodle mixture into casserole.

Sprinkle with paprika. Cook uncovered in 350° oven until mixture is set, 40 to 45 minutes.

Serve from casserole or unmold onto heated platter. To unmold, loosen edge of noodles around inside rim with knife. Place inverted platter over caserole; invert noodles onto platter. Garnish with parsley if desired.

French Bean Casserole with Pork

(Cassoulet)

Cassoulet *is the most highly regarded of all French country casseroles. The name comes from* cassole d'Issel, *an earthenware pot in which the bean-and-meat casserole was originally made. In France there are many versions of* cassoulet—*some include lamb, preserved goose and even partridge! Our version most closely resembles the original* cassoulet of Castelnaudary, *in the Languedoc region of France.*

8 servings

4	cups water
1	pound dried Great Northern or navy beans (about 2½ cups)
1½	pounds pork boneless shoulder
1	pound link sausage, cut into 1-inch pieces
6	slices bacon, cut into 2-inch pieces
4	medium carrots, sliced
2	medium onions, sliced
2	cloves garlic, chopped
2	bay leaves
1	can (6 ounces) tomato paste
2	teaspoons salt
½	teaspoon dried thyme leaves
½	teaspoon dry mustard
¼	teaspoon pepper
	Snipped parsley

Heat water and beans to boiling in Dutch oven; boil 2 minutes. Remove from heat; cover and let stand 1 hour. Add enough water to cover beans if necessary. Heat to boiling;

reduce heat. Cover and simmer until almost tender, about 1½ hours (do not boil or beans will burst). Drain, reserving liquid.

Trim fat from pork; cut pork into ¾-inch cubes. Cook and stir pork, sausage and bacon over medium heat until brown; drain. Place beans, meat mixture, carrots, onions, garlic and bay leaves in ungreased 4-quart bean pot, casserole or Dutch oven.

Add enough water to reserved bean liquid to measure 2 cups. Mix reserved liquid, the tomato paste, salt, thyme, mustard and pepper; pour over beans. Add water to almost cover mixture. Cover and cook in 325° oven, stirring occasionally, 1 hour. Uncover and cook until beans are desired consistency, about 30 minutes. Remove bay leaves. Garnish with parsley.

Energy-Saving Tips

Did You Know?

1. To save energy, thaw frozen meats and poultry in the refrigerator.

2. Portable electric appliances, such as skillets, coffee makers and toasters, use less energy than an electric range unit doing the same cooking job.

3. For efficient range-top cooking, use flat-bottomed pans with tight-fitting covers. Pan should be the same size or slightly larger than the surface unit.

4. Use minimum amount of water in range-top cooking to shorten the cooking time, and use lowest temperature possible for cooking.

5. When cooking with electricity, turn surface unit off a few minutes before food has completely cooked.

6. Do not preheat oven unless necessary. Most casseroles, all roasts and many baked desserts can be started in a cold oven.

Sweet-and-Sour Pork

Few Chinese dishes have endeared themselves to Westerners more than Sweet-and-Sour Pork. Although we usually serve Chinese food with rice, why not surprise your guests and serve this dish with bean thread (cellophane) noodles, available in many large supermarkets and at oriental groceries.

6 servings

2	pounds pork boneless loin
	Vegetable oil
½	cup all-purpose flour
¼	cup cornstarch
½	cup cold water
1	egg
1	teaspoon salt
1	can (about 20 ounces) pineapple chunks, drained (reserve syrup)
½	cup packed brown sugar
½	cup vinegar
2	carrots, cut diagonally into thin slices
2	teaspoons soy sauce
1	teaspoon salt
1	clove garlic, finely chopped
2	tablespoons cornstarch
2	tablespoons cold water
1	green pepper, cut into ¾-inch pieces
	Hot cooked rice (page 253)

Trim fat from pork; cut pork into ¾-inch pieces. Heat oil (1 inch) to 360°. Beat flour, ¼ cup cornstarch, ½ cup cold water, the egg and 1 teaspoon salt with hand beater until smooth. Stir pork into batter until well coated. Add pork pieces, 1 at a time, to oil. Fry about 20 pieces at a time until golden brown, turning 2 or 3 times, about 5 minutes. Drain on paper towels; keep warm.

Add enough water to reserved pineapple syrup to measure 1 cup. Heat syrup-water mixture, brown sugar, vinegar, carrots, soy sauce, 1 teaspoon salt and the garlic to boiling in Dutch oven; reduce heat. Cover and simmer until carrots are crisp-tender, about 6 minutes. Mix 2 tablespoons cornstarch and 2 tablespoons water; stir into sauce. Add pork, pineapple and green pepper. Heat to boiling, stirring constantly. Boil and stir 1 minute. Serve with rice.

Do-Ahead Tip: After frying, pork can be covered and refrigerated no longer than 24 hours. Heat uncovered in 400° oven until hot, about 7 minutes.

Serbian Skillet Pork with Feta Cheese

(Muckalica)

The Yugoslavs developed this unassuming, inexpensive pork-and-onion stew and distinguished it with a surprising garnish of feta cheese.

4 servings

1½	pounds pork boneless shoulder
2	tablespoons vegetable oil
¼	cup water
3	medium onions, sliced
1	tomato, chopped
1½	teaspoons salt
½	teaspoon paprika
¼	teaspoon pepper
⅛	to ¼ teaspoon crushed red peppers
1	green pepper, cut into strips
2	ounces feta cheese, cut into ¾-inch cubes
	Hot cooked rice (page 253)

Trim fat from pork. Cut pork into ½-inch slices; cut slices into ½-inch strips. (For ease in cutting, partially freeze pork about 1 hour.) Heat oil in 10-inch skillet until hot. Cook and stir pork in oil over medium heat until brown, about 15 minutes; drain. Add water, onions, tomato, salt, paprika, pepper and red peppers. Cover and simmer until pork is tender, about 30 minutes. (Add water if necessary.)

Add green pepper. Cover and simmer until green pepper is crisp-tender, 5 to 10 minutes. Top with cheese; serve with rice.

Canadian Pork Pie
(Tourtière)

Tourtière is the traditional holiday pie served by French Canadians at réveillon, the Christmas feast following Midnight Mass on Christmas Eve. In recent years tourtière has gained so many fans that it is served throughout the year, often preceded by a cup of yellow pea soup and followed with Canadian Blueberry Dessert (page 299).

8 servings

1	pound ground pork
½	pound ground beef
1	medium onion, chopped
1	clove garlic, chopped
½	cup water
1½	teaspoons salt
½	teaspoon dried thyme leaves
¼	teaspoon ground sage
¼	teaspoon pepper
⅛	teaspoon ground cloves
	Egg Pastry for 9-inch two-crust pie (below)

Heat all ingredients except Egg Pastry to boiling, stirring constantly; reduce heat. Cook, stirring constantly, until meat is light brown but still moist, about 5 minutes. Prepare Egg Pastry.

Heat oven to 425°. Pour meat mixture into pastry-lined pie plate. Cover with top crust that has slits cut in it; seal and press firmly around edge with fork. (Dip fork into flour occasionally to prevent sticking.) Cover edge with 3-inch strip of aluminum foil; remove foil during last 15 minutes of baking. Bake until crust is brown, 35 to 40 minutes. Let stand 10 minutes before cutting.

Egg Pastry
⅔	cup plus 2 tablespoons shortening
2	cups all-purpose flour
1	teaspoon salt
1	egg, slightly beaten
2	to 3 tablespoons cold water

Cut shortening into flour and salt until particles are size of small peas. Mix egg and water; stir into flour mixture until all flour is moistened. Gather pastry into a ball; divide into halves and shape into 2 flattened rounds. Place one round on lightly floured cloth-covered board. Roll pastry 2 inches larger than inverted pie plate with floured stockinet-covered rolling pin. Fold pastry into quarters; unfold and ease into plate.

Turn filling into pastry-lined pie plate. Trim overhanging edge of pastry ½ inch from rim of plate. Roll other round of pastry. Fold into quarters; cut slits so steam can escape. Place over filling and unfold. Trim overhanging edge of pastry 1 inch from rim of plate. Fold and roll top edge under lower edge, pressing on rim to seal securely.

Sausages Baked in Batter
(Toad-in-the-Hole)

Toad-in-the-hole is the whimsical name (like our pigs-in-a-blanket) the British give this sausage-and-pastry casserole. It is often prepared for children when the parents are dining out, and is a dish children enjoy making themselves with a little guidance from Dad or Mom. More elaborate versions of toad-in-the-hole include steak and kidneys.

4 to 6 servings

1	pound pork sausage links
1	cup all-purpose flour
1	cup milk
2	eggs
½	teaspoon salt

Cook sausages as directed on package; reserve drippings. Heat oven to 400°. Brush oblong baking dish, 11 x 7 x 1½ inches, with sausage drippings. Place sausages in single layer in baking dish. Beat flour, milk, eggs and salt with hand beater until smooth; pour over sausages. Bake uncovered until puffed and golden brown, about 30 minutes. Cut into squares.

Scotch Eggs

Scotch Eggs

These hard-cooked eggs coated with a sausage-and-bread-crumb mixture may have originated in Scotland as a food for breakfast, but have been served as snacking fare throughout Britain for many years and are as popular in English pubs as pretzels are in some American cafés. One theory holds that the recipe is an English invention and is dubbed Scotch because the thrifty Scots are famous for finding ways to stretch the meat bill.

8 servings

8 hard-cooked eggs, peeled
¼ cup all-purpose flour
1 pound bulk pork sausage
¾ cup dry bread crumbs
½ teaspoon ground sage
¼ teaspoon salt
2 eggs, beaten
   Vegetable oil

Coat each hard-cooked egg with flour. Divide sausage into 8 equal parts. Pat one part sausage onto each egg. Mix bread crumbs, sage and salt. Dip sausage-coated eggs into beaten eggs; roll in bread crumb mixture.

Heat oil (1½ to 2 inches) in 3-quart saucepan to 360°. Fry eggs, 4 at a time, turning occasionally, 5 to 6 minutes. Drain on paper towels. Serve hot or cold.

Spicy Sausage Burritos

Burritos— "little donkeys" to Mexicans—are soft tortillas wrapped around refried beans and chili-flavored ground meat. They can be eaten out-of-hand or served on shredded lettuce as a main dish. Serve with red pepper sauce for those who favor fiery Mexican food.

8 burritos

Refried Beans (page 145)
1 pound bulk pork sausage
1 medium tomato, coarsely chopped
1 tablespoon chili powder
1 tablespoon vinegar
1 clove garlic, finely chopped
½ teaspoon salt
¼ teaspoon ground cinnamon
8 ten-inch flour tortillas
1 cup shredded Monterey Jack cheese

Prepare Refried Beans. Cook and stir pork sausage in 10-inch skillet until light brown; drain. Stir in tomato, chili powder, vinegar, garlic, salt and cinnamon. Heat to boiling; reduce heat. Simmer uncovered, stirring occasionally, until thickened, about 10 minutes.

Soften tortillas one at a time in ungreased hot skillet, about 30 seconds on each side. Spread about 1/3 cup refried beans over each hot tortilla. Spoon about ¼ cup sausage mixture onto center of tortilla; sprinkle with cheese. Fold up bottom of tortilla. Fold sides over and roll from bottom. Place seam sides down in ungreased jelly roll pan, 15½ x 10½ x 1 inch. Cook uncovered in 350° oven until hot, about 20 minutes.

Lasagne

The fanciful names the Italians give their many kinds of pastas are often derived from the shapes of the pastas: Cannelloni *means big pipes,* farfalle *means butterflies. But* lasagne *is believed to come from the old Latin* lasanum, *meaning cooking pot, and may be one of the first kinds of pasta made on the Italian peninsula. This recipe is typical of southern Italian cooking.*

6 to 8 servings

1 pound Italian sausage
1 medium onion, chopped
1 clove garlic, finely chopped
3 cans (8 ounces each) tomato sauce*
2 tablespoons snipped parsley
1 teaspoon sugar
½ teaspoon salt
½ teaspoon dried basil leaves
½ teaspoon dried oregano leaves
¼ teaspoon pepper
1 package (8 ounces) lasagne noodles
1 carton (about 15 ounces) ricotta cheese
2 cups shredded mozzarella cheese (8 ounces)
¼ cup grated Parmesan cheese

Cut sausage into small chunks. Cook and stir sausage, onion and garlic in 10-inch skillet until sausage is light brown; drain. Stir in tomato sauce, parsley, sugar, salt, basil, oregano and pepper. Cover and simmer 20 minutes. Cook noodles as directed on package; drain.

Spread about 1 cup meat sauce in bottom of ungreased oblong baking dish, 13½ x 9 x 2 inches. Layer ½ each of the noodles, remaining meat sauce, the ricotta and mozzarella cheese on meat sauce; repeat. Sprinkle with Parmesan cheese. Cook uncovered in 350° oven until hot and bubbly, about 45 minutes. Let stand 15 minutes before cutting.

* 1 can (16 ounces) tomatoes (with liquid) and 1 can (6 ounces) tomato paste can be substituted for the tomato sauce.

Green Lasagne with Two Sauces

(Lasagne Verdi al Forno)

In northern Italy, lasagne is always made from homemade pasta—usually green pasta, flavored and colored with spinach. This recipe, suitable for the most discriminating Italian food buff, is typical of the Emilia-Romagna area of northern Italy.

12 servings

Meat Sauce (below)

Green Noodles (right) or 12 spinach lasagne noodles, cooked and drained

Cheese Filling (page 161)

Creamy Sauce (page 161)

Prepare Meat Sauce, Green Noodles, Cheese Filling and Creamy Sauce. Reserve ½ cup of the Cheese Filling. Spread 1 cup of the Meat Sauce in ungreased oblong baking dish, 13½ x 9 x 2 inches. Layer 3 lasagne noodles, ½ of the Creamy Sauce, ½ of the remaining Cheese Filling, 3 lasagne noodles and ½ of the remaining Meat Sauce; repeat. (See photograph.) Sprinkle with reserved Cheese Filling. Cook uncovered in 350° oven until hot and bubbly, about 35 minutes. Let stand 10 minutes before cutting.

Meat Sauce

8	ounces bulk Italian sausage, crumbled
1	package (4 ounces) smoked sliced chicken or turkey, finely chopped
1	large onion, finely chopped
1	medium stalk celery, finely chopped
1	medium carrot, finely shredded
2	cloves garlic, finely chopped
1¾	cups water
¾	cup dry red wine
⅓	cup tomato paste
½	teaspoon Italian herb seasoning
⅛	teaspoon pepper
	Dash of ground nutmeg

Green Lasagne with Two Sauces

Cook and stir sausage until light brown; drain. Stir in remaining ingredients. Heat to boiling; reduce heat. Simmer uncovered, stirring occasionally, 1 hour.

Green Noodles

8	ounces spinach*
2	eggs
1	tablespoon olive or vegetable oil
1	teaspoon salt
2	cups all-purpose flour
4½	quarts water
1	tablespoon salt
1	tablespoon olive or vegetable oil

Remove root ends and imperfect leaves from spinach. Wash several times in water, lifting out each time; drain. Cover and cook with just the water that clings to leaves until tender, 3 to 10 minutes.

Rinse spinach with cold water; drain. Place spinach, eggs, 1 tablespoon oil and 1 teaspoon salt in blender container. Cover and blend until puréed, about 20 seconds.

Add spinach mixture to flour; stir with fork until well mixed.

Roll dough into rectangle; cut into 6 strips, 13 x 2 inches each.

Layer 3 lasagne noodles over Cheese Filling in baking dish.

Make a well in center of flour. Add spinach mixture; stir with fork until mixed. (See photograph.) Sprinkle with a few drops water if dry; mix in small amount of flour if sticky. Gather dough into a ball. Knead on lightly floured cloth-covered board until smooth and elastic, about 5 minutes. Let stand 10 minutes.

Divide dough into halves. Roll one half into rectangle, 13 x 12 inches; cut rectangle into 6 strips, 13 x 2 inches each. (See photograph.) Repeat with remaining dough. Spread strips on rack; let stand 30 minutes.

Heat water to rapid boiling; stir in 1 tablespoon salt, 1 tablespoon oil and the noodles. Cook uncovered over medium heat until nearly tender, 15 to 20 minutes. Drain; rinse with cold water. Place in single layer between sheets of waxed paper.

* 1 package (10 ounces) frozen spinach can be substituted for the fresh spinach. Cook as directed on package.

Do-Ahead Tip: Before cooking, Green Noodles can be stored between sheets of waxed paper or paper towels no longer than 24 hours. Continue as directed.

Cheese Filling
Toss 2 cups shredded mozzarella cheese, 1½ cups grated Parmesan cheese and ¼ cup snipped parsley.

Creamy Sauce
⅓   cup margarine or butter
⅓   cup all-purpose flour
1   teaspoon salt
    Dash of ground nutmeg
3   cups milk

Heat margarine over low heat until melted. Blend in flour, salt and nutmeg. Cook over low heat, stirring constantly, until smooth and bubbly; remove from heat. Stir in milk. Heat to boiling, stirring constantly. Boil and stir 1 minute; cover and keep warm. (If sauce thickens, beat in small amount of milk. Sauce should be the consistency of heavy cream.)

Pizza

In Italy, pizza *simply means pie and takes many forms, from a humble meatless appetizer or country main dish to a holiday dessert.*

2 pizzas

½   pound Italian sausage*
1   can (8 ounces) tomato sauce
1   medium onion, chopped
1   clove garlic, finely chopped
½   teaspoon dried basil leaves
½   teaspoon dried oregano leaves
¼   teaspoon pepper
    Pizza Dough (below)
1   small green pepper, chopped
2   cups shredded mozzarella cheese (8 ounces)
¼   cup grated Parmesan cheese

Cut sausage into chunks. Cook and stir sausage until light brown; drain. Mix tomato sauce, onion, garlic, basil, oregano and pepper. Prepare Pizza Dough.

Divide dough into halves. Pat each half into 10-inch circle on lightly greased cookie sheet with floured fingers. Spread with sauce. Sprinkle with sausage, green pepper and cheeses. Bake in 425° oven until cheese is bubbly and crust is brown, 15 to 20 minutes.

* 1 can (about 2 ounces) anchovy fillets, drained and chopped, can be substituted for the cooked sausage.

Pizza Dough

1   package active dry yeast
¾   cup warm water (105 to 115°)
½   teaspoon sugar
½   teaspoon salt
2   tablespoons olive or vegetable oil
2   cups all-purpose flour

Dissolve yeast in warm water. Stir in sugar, salt, oil and 1¾ cups of the flour. Turn onto well-floured surface; knead until smooth and elastic, about 5 minutes. (Knead in enough of the remaining flour to prevent sticking.)

Irish Stew

The Scots favor barley, but in Ireland potatoes are the prominent meat-stretcher in lamb stew. A visit to Ireland will reveal that there are nearly as many ways to make Irish Stew as there are Irish chefs.

6 servings

2   pounds lamb boneless neck or shoulder
6   medium potatoes (about 2 pounds)
3   medium onions, sliced
2   teaspoons salt
¼   teaspoon pepper
2   cups water
    Snipped parsley

Trim fat from lamb; cut lamb into 1-inch cubes. Cut potatoes into ½-inch slices. Layer half each of the lamb, potatoes and onions in Dutch oven; sprinkle with half each of the salt and pepper. Repeat. Add water.

Heat to boiling; reduce heat. Cover and simmer until lamb is tender, 1½ to 2 hours. Skim fat from broth (see Note). Sprinkle with parsley. Serve in bowls with pickled red cabbage if desired.

Note: To remove fat easily, prepare stew the day before, cover and refrigerate. Remove fat before reheating.

Tips about Lamb
Did You Know?

Lamb is the meat from young sheep. In order for it to be labeled "lamb," the United States Department of Agriculture has specified that the meat must come from sheep that are less than 1 year old. Sheep between 1 and 2 years old are sold as yearling mutton. Lamb for stewing is usually cut from the neck and shoulders. Ground lamb is very perishable and should be stored at 35 to 40°F no longer than 2 days. For optimum quality, freeze ground lamb no longer than 2 to 3 months, stew lamb no longer than 3 months.

Moussaka

Although "moussaka" is an Arabic word and a popular dish in many Middle Eastern countries, the immortal eggplant-and-lamb casserole is generally credited to the Greeks, who claim it as a national treasure. Moussaka is an ideal dish to prepare for a buffet party.

8 servings

1   large eggplant (about 2 pounds)
2   tablespoons margarine or butter
1½   pounds ground lamb or beef
1   medium onion, chopped
1   can (15 ounces) tomato sauce
¾   cup red wine or beef broth
1   tablespoon snipped parsley
2   teaspoons salt
¼   teaspoon pepper
¼   teaspoon ground nutmeg
     White Sauce (right)
1   cup grated Parmesan cheese
⅔   cup dry bread crumbs
1   egg, beaten
     Tomato Sauce (right)

Cut unpared eggplant crosswise into ½-inch slices. Cook slices in small amount boiling, salted water (½ teaspoon salt to 1 cup water) until tender, 5 to 8 minutes. Drain. Heat margarine in 12-inch skillet until melted. Cook and stir lamb and onion until lamb is light brown; drain. Stir in tomato sauce, wine, parsley, salt, pepper and nutmeg. Cook uncovered over medium heat until half the liquid is absorbed, about 20 minutes. Prepare White Sauce.

Stir ⅔ cup of the cheese, ⅓ cup of the bread crumbs and the egg into meat mixture; remove from heat. Sprinkle remaining bread crumbs evenly in greased oblong baking dish, 13½ x 9 x 2 inches. Arrange half the eggplant slices in baking dish; cover with meat mixture. Sprinkle 2 tablespoons of the remaining cheese over meat mixture; top with remaining eggplant slices. Pour White Sauce over mixture; sprinkle with remaining cheese.

Cook uncovered in 375° oven 45 minutes. Prepare Tomato Sauce. Let moussaka stand 20 minutes before serving. Cut into squares; serve with Tomato Sauce.

White Sauce
¼   cup margarine or butter
¼   cup all-purpose flour
¾   teaspoon salt
¼   teaspoon ground nutmeg
2   cups milk
2   eggs, slightly beaten

Heat margarine over low heat until melted. Blend in flour, salt and nutmeg. Cook over low heat, stirring constantly, until smooth and bubbly; remove from heat. Stir in milk. Heat to boiling, stirring constantly. Boil and stir 1 minute. Gradually stir at least ¼ of the hot mixture into eggs. Blend into hot mixture in pan.

Tomato Sauce
1   medium onion, finely chopped
1   clove garlic, finely chopped
1   tablespoon olive or vegetable oil
2   cups chopped ripe tomatoes
½   cup water
1½   teaspoons salt
1   teaspoon dried basil leaves
½   teaspoon sugar
¼   teaspoon pepper
1   bay leaf, crushed
1   can (6 ounces) tomato paste

Cook and stir onion and garlic in oil in 3-quart saucepan over medium heat until onion is tender. Add remaining ingredients except tomato paste. Heat to boiling, stirring constantly; reduce heat. Simmer uncovered until thickened, about 30 minutes. Stir in tomato paste. (Add 2 to 3 tablespoons water if necessary for desired consistency.)

Lamb-and-Green Bean Stew

(Green Bean Bredie)

There are many versions of "bredie" in South Africa. This green bean-and-lamb stew is often served with hot cooked rice. Banana-Coconut Bake (page 297) makes a superlative South African dessert.

4 servings

1½   pounds lamb boneless shoulder
1   tablespoon vegetable oil
½   cup water
1   clove garlic, chopped
1   teaspoon salt
1   pound green beans, cut diagonally into 1-inch pieces (about 4 cups)
2   potatoes, cut into 1-inch pieces
1   medium onion, sliced
½   teaspoon salt
¼   teaspoon dried thyme leaves
⅛   to ¼ teaspoon crushed red peppers

Trim fat from lamb; cut lamb into ¾-inch cubes. Heat oil in Dutch oven or 12-inch skillet until hot. Cook and stir lamb in oil over medium heat until brown, about 10 minutes. Add water, garlic and 1 teaspoon salt. Cover and simmer over low heat 40 minutes.

Stir in beans, potatoes, onion, ½ teaspoon salt, the thyme and red peppers. (Add small amount of water if necessary. There should be just enough liquid to steam the vegetables and prevent scorching.) Heat to boiling; reduce heat. Cover and simmer, stirring occasionally, until lamb and vegetables are tender, about 30 minutes. Serve with hot cooked rice if desired.

Skewered Lamb and Vegetables

(Shish Kabob)

In Arabic, shish *means skewered,* kabob *means meat—but today the word "kabob" has come to be synonymous with skewered food whether it be meat, vegetables or fruit! This "authentic"* shish kabob *from Turkey makes a truly memorable main dish when served with our Cracked-Wheat Pilaf (page 250).*

4 servings

1   pound lamb boneless shoulder, cut into 1-inch cubes
¼   cup lemon juice
2   tablespoons olive or vegetable oil
2   teaspoons salt
½   teaspoon dried oregano leaves
¼   teaspoon pepper
1   green pepper, cut into 1-inch pieces
1   medium onion, cut into eighths
1   cup cubed eggplant

Place lamb in glass or plastic bowl. Mix lemon juice, oil, salt, oregano and pepper; pour over lamb. Cover and refrigerate, stirring occasionally, at least 6 hours.

Remove lamb; reserve marinade. Thread lamb on four 11-inch metal skewers, leaving space between each. Set oven control to broil and/or 550°. Broil lamb with tops about 3 inches from heat 5 minutes. Turn; brush with reserved marinade. Broil 5 minutes.

Alternate green pepper, onion and eggplant on four 11-inch metal skewers, leaving space between. Place vegetables on rack in broiler pan with lamb. Turn lamb; brush lamb and vegetables with reserved marinade. Broil kabobs, turning and brushing twice with marinade, until brown, 4 to 5 minutes. Serve with Minted Cucumber-and-Yogurt Salad (page 206) and fresh fruit if desired.

Stuffed Grapevine Leaves (Dolmades)

Dolmades *are found in every country in the Middle East and are often served cold as appetizers. The warm egg-and-lemon sauce in our recipe is most typical of a Greek main dish. Canned vine leaves can be purchased in large supermarkets.*

8 servings

1	jar (9 ounces) grapevine leaves
4	medium onions, finely chopped
1	teaspoon salt
3	tablespoons olive or vegetable oil
1½	pounds ground lamb or beef
⅔	cup uncooked regular rice
1	teaspoon salt
¼	teaspoon pepper
1	teaspoon snipped mint leaves or ½ teaspoon dried mint flakes
1½	cups water
3	eggs
3	tablespoons lemon juice
	Lemon slices

Wash and drain grape leaves. Cook and stir onions and 1 teaspoon salt in oil until tender, about 5 minutes. Mix half the cooked onions, lamb, rice, 1 teaspoon salt, the pepper and mint. Place rounded measuring tablespoon meat mixture on center of double layer of grape leaves. Fold stem ends over filling; fold in sides (see diagram).

Roll up tightly; place seam side down in 12-inch skillet or two 10-inch skillets. Repeat with remaining meat mixture and grape leaves. Add water and remaining cooked onions. Heat to boiling; reduce heat. Cover and simmer until tender, 50 to 55 minutes.

Beat eggs until thick and lemon colored, about 3 minutes. Slowly beat in lemon juice. Add enough water to broth from Dutch oven to measure 1 cup if necessary; gradually stir into egg mixture. Pour over grape leaves.

Simmer uncovered 10 to 15 minutes. Garnish with lemon slices.

Do-Ahead Tip: Grape leaves can be stuffed, covered and refrigerated no longer than 24 hours before cooking.

Place meat mixture on center of double layer of grape leaves; fold stem end over filling.

Scotch Broth

Barley is the identifying ingredient in this lamb stew prized by the penny-wise Scots. It makes an excellent winter soup supper.

6 servings

1½	pounds lamb boneless shoulder
6	cups water
½	cup barley
1	tablespoon salt
½	teaspoon pepper
3	carrots, sliced
2	stalks celery, sliced
2	medium onions, chopped
1	cup diced rutabaga or turnips
	Snipped parsley

Trim fat from lamb; cut lamb into ¾-inch cubes. Heat lamb, water, barley, salt and pepper to boiling in Dutch oven; reduce heat. Cover and simmer 1 hour.

Add vegetables to lamb mixture. Cover and simmer until lamb and vegetables are tender, about 30 minutes. Skim fat if necessary. Sprinkle with parsley.

Stuffed Meat Loaf
(Kibby bil Sanieh)

Kibby has been regarded as the national dish of Syria and Lebanon for many centuries—some say since Phoenician times. It differs from Western meat loaves in that bulgur wheat is used as the binding agent and the loaf is stuffed with a meat-and-nut mixture flavored with the spices loved in the Middle East.

6 to 8 servings

½	pound bulgur wheat (1¼ cups)
1	pound ground lamb or beef
1	medium onion, finely chopped
1¾	teaspoons salt
⅛	teaspoon pepper
	Stuffing (below)
2	tablespoons margarine or butter, melted

Cover bulgur with cold water; let stand 10 minutes. Drain; press bulgur to remove excess water. Mix lamb, onion, salt and pepper; add bulgur. Knead until well mixed. (Dip hands in cold water occasionally while kneading to moisten and soften mixture.) Prepare Stuffing.

Press half the lamb-bulgur mixture evenly in ungreased square pan, 8 x 8 x 2 inches. Cover with stuffing; spread remaining lamb-bulgur mixture evenly over stuffing. Cut diagonal lines across top to make diamond pattern. Pour margarine over meat loaf. Cook uncovered in 350° oven until brown, about 40 minutes. Cut into diamond shapes; serve hot or cold.

Stuffing
¼	pound ground lamb or beef
1	small onion, finely chopped
2	tablespoons pine nuts (pignolia)
⅛	teaspoon ground cinnamon
	Dash of ground nutmeg

Cook and stir all ingredients until lamb is light brown, about 5 minutes.

Veal with Tuna Sauce
(Vitello Tonnato)

This luxurious cold veal platter from northern Italy consists of thinly sliced braised veal flavored with anchovies in a creamy tuna sauce—an elegant and carefree dish.

10 to 12 servings

4-	pound leg of veal, boned, rolled and tied
1	can (2 ounces) anchovy fillets, drained
3	cloves garlic, sliced
2	cups dry white wine
3	stalks celery (with leaves), cut up
2	medium onions, cut into fourths
2	carrots, cut up
4	teaspoons instant chicken bouillon
8	peppercorns
4	sprigs parsley
2	bay leaves
2	teaspoons salt
½	teaspoon dried thyme leaves
	Tuna Sauce (right)
	Snipped parsley

Make 10 to 12 deep cuts in length of meat with small knife. Cut 3 anchovy fillets into ¾-inch pieces. Cover and refrigerate remaining anchovies for Tuna Sauce. Stuff a piece of anchovy and a slice of garlic into each cut. Place meat, wine, celery, onions, carrots, bouillon, peppercorns, 4 sprigs parsley, the bay leaves, salt, thyme and enough water to cover in 6-quart Dutch oven. Heat to boiling; reduce heat. Cover and simmer until meat is tender, 1½ to 2 hours. (Remove foam if necessary.) Remove from heat; cool.

Remove meat from broth; strain and reserve ¼ cup broth for Tuna Sauce. Prepare Tuna Sauce. Pat meat dry; cut into thin slices. Spoon a thin layer of Tuna Sauce into oblong baking dish, 13½ x 9 x 2 inches. Arrange meat slices in sauce. Spoon remaining sauce over meat slices. Cover and refrigerate at least 3 hours. Arrange meat slices on platter; spoon Tuna Sauce over meat.

Tuna Sauce

1 can (3½ ounces) white tuna, drained
1 jar (3¼ ounces) capers, drained
½ cup olive or vegetable oil
¼ cup lemon juice
1 egg yolk
1 clove garlic
   Salt and white pepper
¼ cup whipping cream

Place tuna, capers, oil, lemon juice, egg yolk, garlic and remaining anchovies in blender container. Cover and blend on low speed just until well blended, about 45 seconds. Season with salt and white pepper. Add whipping cream and reserved broth; blend on low speed just until well blended, about 30 seconds.

Veal in Lemon Sauce

(Piccata di Vitello al Limone)

This light, zesty dish from northern Italy appeals both to the most conscientious calorie counter and to the discriminating gourmet.

4 servings

¾- pound veal round steak, about ½ inch thick
¼ cup all-purpose flour
¼ cup margarine or butter
2 tablespoons vegetable oil
2 tablespoons lemon juice
   Salt and pepper

Cut veal steak into 4 serving pieces; pound until ¼ inch thick. Coat with flour; shake off excess. Heat 2 tablespoons of the margarine and the oil in 12-inch skillet over medium heat until hot. Cook veal until tender and brown, about 4 minutes on each side.

Remove veal to heated platter. Heat remaining 2 tablespoons margarine in skillet until melted; stir in lemon juice. Pour over veal; sprinkle with salt and pepper. Garnish with parsley and lemon slices if desired.

Veal Rolls, Roman Style

(Saltimbocca alla Romana)

Saltimbocca *means jump into the mouth, and these little ham-and-veal rolls—the pride of Rome—do just that when served to friends who appreciate fine classic Italian food.*

6 servings

1½- pound veal boneless round steak, ½ inch thick
¼ teaspoon dried sage leaves, crushed
¼ teaspoon pepper
6 thin slices prosciutto or fully cooked smoked or boiled ham
2 tablespoons margarine or butter
1 tablespoon olive or vegetable oil
2 tablespoons flour
½ cup Marsala or other dry white wine
¾ cup water
¼ teaspoon salt

Trim excess fat from veal; pound veal until ⅛ inch thick. Sprinkle one side of veal with sage and pepper; cut into 6 pieces, 4 or 5 inches square. Place ham slice on seasoned side of each veal piece. Roll up; secure with picks.

Heat margarine and oil in 10-inch skillet until hot. Cook veal rolls over high heat until brown, 5 to 10 minutes. Remove from heat. Place rolls in single layer in ungreased oblong baking dish, 10 x 6 x 2 inches.

Stir flour into drippings in skillet; stir in wine, water and salt. (The saltiness of the ham will determine the necessity of the salt addition.) Heat to boiling; pour over rolls. Cover and cook in 325° oven until tender, 35 minutes. Garnish with parsley if desired.

Do-Ahead Tip: After securing with wooden picks, cover and refrigerate meat rolls no longer than 24 hours.

Veal Sauté with Duchess Potatoes

Veal Sauté with Duchess Potatoes

In classic French cooking, a sauté *is a dish in which food is first cooked in a skillet or* sautoir, *then sauced with the pan drippings and simmered with aromatic vegetables. A* sautoir *is a deep skillet with straight sides and a tightly fitting cover. Our* sauté de veau *is a simple country stew given an elegant city touch with a decorative border of Duchess Potatoes.*

8 servings

2-	pound veal round steak, ½ inch thick
½	cup all-purpose flour
2	teaspoons salt
1	teaspoon paprika
¼	teaspoon pepper
¼	cup olive or vegetable oil
1	cup dry white wine
½	cup water
8	ounces tiny pearl onions, peeled (1½ cups)
8	to 10 tiny carrots or 4 medium carrots, cut into strips
½	teaspoon dried rosemary or thyme leaves
½	teaspoon salt
	Duchess Potatoes (page 169)
	Snipped parsley

Cut veal into serving pieces. Mix flour, 2 teaspoons salt, the paprika and pepper. Coat veal with flour mixture; pound until ¼ inch thick.

Cook veal in hot oil in 12-inch skillet until brown; drain. Add wine, water, onions, carrots and rosemary. Sprinkle with ½ teaspoon salt. Heat to boiling; reduce heat. Cover and simmer until veal and vegetables are tender, about 45 minutes. (Add water if necessary.)

Prepare Duchess Potatoes. Place veal and vegetables on platter; pour pan juices on top. Arrange Duchess Potatoes around edge. Sprinkle with parsley.

Duchess Potatoes

6 medium potatoes (about 2 pounds)
¼ cup milk
¼ cup margarine or butter, softened
½ teaspoon salt
  Dash of pepper
1 egg, beaten
2 tablespoons margarine or butter, melted

Pare potatoes; cut into large pieces. Heat 1 inch salted water (½ teaspoon salt to 1 cup water) to boiling. Add potatoes. Heat to boiling; reduce heat. Cover and cook until tender, 20 to 25 minutes; drain.

Shake pan gently over low heat to dry potatoes. Mash potatoes until no lumps remain. Beat in milk in small amounts. Add ¼ cup margarine, the salt and pepper; beat until potatoes are light and fluffy. Add egg; beat until blended. (Add more milk if necessary; potatoes should be smooth and fluffy.)

Drop mixture by spoonfuls or form rosettes with decorator's tube on ungreased cookie sheet. (Potatoes can be prepared several hours ahead and refrigerated.) Brush lightly with melted margarine. Heat in 425° oven until light brown, about 15 minutes.

Food Safety for Buffets
Did You Know?

Foods to be served hot should be prepared just before serving if possible. If necessary to hold foods, such as for a buffet, hot or cold foods should not remain at room temperature for more than 2 hours, as bacteria grow quickly in lukewarm food. A standard rule recommended by the Department of Agriculture is that hot foods should be kept hot (above 140°) and cold foods cold (below 40°).

For buffets or dinner parties, food can be kept hot in electric frypans, chafing dishes or hot trays. Or serve food in dishes that can be refilled frequently from stove or refrigerator. Refrigerate leftovers as soon as possible.

Braised Veal Shanks, Milan Style
(Osso Buco)

Osso buco *or* oss bus *is Milanese slang for "a hollowed bone." On restaurant menus this Milan masterpiece may be spelled* ossobuco *or* ossibuchi. *The dish is often served with a spicy condiment called* gremolada. *If you like, serve the condiment separately and invite guests to sprinkle* gremolada *onto their servings according to taste.*

6 servings

4 pounds veal or beef shanks
¼ cup all-purpose flour
3 tablespoons olive or vegetable oil
1 medium onion, chopped
1 medium carrot, chopped
1 stalk celery, chopped
1 clove garlic, chopped
1 bay leaf
1 cup water
½ cup dry white wine
1 teaspoon instant beef bouillon
½ teaspoon dried basil leaves
½ teaspoon salt
¼ teaspoon pepper
  Gremolada (below)

Trim excess fat from veal shanks if necessary. Coat veal with flour. Cook veal in oil in Dutch oven over medium heat until brown on all sides, about 20 minutes. Drain excess fat. Add remaining ingredients except Gremolada. Heat to boiling; reduce heat. Cover and simmer until veal is tender, 1½ to 2 hours.

Arrange veal and vegetables on platter. Skim fat from broth; pour broth over veal. Sprinkle with Gremolada if desired. Serve with Rice Milan Style (page 253), or hot cooked spaghetti if desired.

Gremolada
Mix 2 tablespoons snipped parsley, 1 clove garlic, finely chopped, and 1 teaspoon grated lemon peel.

Clockwise from top: Garbanzo Bean Soup (page 193), Swiss Cheese Pie (page 177) and Enchiladas with Green Sauce (page 176).

Cheese, Eggs and Dried Beans

Necessity is the mother of invention, and the urgent need to keep grocery costs low while providing tasty, nutritious meals for the family—and splendid party fare for guests—has confronted homemakers around the world for years.

The result: an inventive world-wide array of delectable dishes using protein-rich cheese and eggs, plus hearty soups and side dishes made from dried beans, peas and lentils. These are dishes that delight the family and win highest praise from guests.

In this chapter we have collected some of our favorite meatless main dishes, low in cost, high in flavor, rich in protein. You'll find a classic cheese soufflé from France, a creamy quiche from Switzerland, a pasta-and-cheese casserole from Italy, a spinach-and-cheese pie from Greece.

There are Mexican main dishes, such as Enchiladas with Green Sauce and the ever-popular *Huevos Rancheros* . . . quick-as-a-wink omelets and scrambled-egg dishes that bring the flavors of the Mediterranean into your kitchen. . . . Indian, Chinese, Scandinavian and Caribbean recipes and much more.

For those times when you want the rich flavor of meat without the expense, we have included main-dish soups and unusual dishes made with dried legumes (for high protein) and flavored with just a touch of meat—from salt pork, soup bones or bouillon.

Whether you are planning a Sunday morning brunch or an after-theater supper . . . a hearty family meal or an intimate candlelight dinner for two . . . the low-cost, quick and easy recipes you need can be found in this chapter. Special tips for selecting and keeping cheeses will ease your marketing problems.

Swiss Cheese Fondue (Fondue Neufchâteloise)

The Swiss have many recipes for cheese fondue, but the perennial prize-winner is fondue Neufchâteloise, *which takes its name from the sprightly dry white wine made in the Neufchâtel canton of Switzerland. White wine and a touch of kirsch provide the distinctive flavor to this fondue.*

4 to 6 servings

2   cups shredded Swiss cheese* (8 ounces)
2   cups shredded Gruyère cheese† (8 ounces)
1   tablespoon cornstarch
1   clove garlic, cut into halves
1   cup dry white wine
1   tablespoon lemon juice
3   tablespoons kirsch or dry sherry
½   teaspoon salt
⅛   teaspoon white pepper
     French bread, cut into 1-inch cubes

Toss cheeses with cornstarch until coated. Rub garlic on bottom and side of heavy saucepan or skillet; add wine. Heat over low heat just until bubbles rise to surface (wine should not boil). Stir in lemon juice.

Gradually add cheeses, about ½ cup at a time, stirring constantly with wooden spoon over low heat until cheeses are melted. Stir in kirsch, salt and white pepper. Remove to earthenware fondue dish; keep warm over low heat. Spear bread cubes with fondue forks; dip and swirl in fondue with stirring motion. If fondue becomes too thick, stir in ¼ to ½ cup heated wine.

* Swiss cheese should be natural (not processed) and aged at least six months.

† 2 cups shredded Swiss cheese can be substituted for the Gruyère cheese.

Alpine Cheese Supper (Raclette)

The word raclette *comes from the French* racler, *meaning to scrape. In Switzerland,* raclette *is both a kind of cheese and a favorite winter dish. A wheel of* raclette *cheese is placed near the fireplace. When it begins to melt, portions are scraped off and served on warm plates with boiled potatoes, midget dill pickles or gherkins, and sometimes with cocktail onions.* Raclette *is a popular pick-me-up after winter outings when a quick, no-fuss refreshment is wanted.*

4 servings

2   pounds new potatoes (12 to 14)
1   pound imported Swiss raclette cheese*
     Freshly ground pepper
1   jar (8 ounces) midget dill pickles or gherkins
1   jar (8 ounces) pickled cocktail onions

Heat 1 inch salted water (1 teaspoon salt to 1 cup water) to boiling. Add potatoes. Heat to boiling; reduce heat. Cover and cook until tender, 20 to 25 minutes; drain. Keep warm.

Cut cheese into 4 pieces; divide among 4 individual ovenproof casseroles. Heat in 400° oven until cheese is melted, about 10 minutes.

Place each hot casserole on a dinner plate. Guests sprinkle potatoes with pepper, then swirl in melted cheese. Potatoes are eaten alternately with pickles and onions.

* Other cheeses that melt smoothly and easily, such as Gruyère, muenster, Fontina, Swiss or Monterey Jack cheese, can be substituted for the raclette cheese.

Welsh Rarebit

This versatile budget dish from Britain is also called Welsh rabbit. One theory holds that it was substituted for rabbit when none had been caught in the hunt; another that Welsh kitchen help were fed the tasty cheese-and-beer ragout while the English gentry dined on rabbit and wine!

4 servings

¼	cup margarine or butter
¼	cup all-purpose flour
½	teaspoon salt
½	teaspoon dry mustard
½	teaspoon Worcestershire sauce
¾	cup milk
¾	cup beer
2	cups shredded Cheddar cheese (8 ounces)
8	slices toast

Heat margarine in 2-quart saucepan over low heat until melted. Stir in flour, salt, mustard and Worcestershire sauce. Cook over low heat, stirring constantly, until smooth and bubbly; remove from heat.

Stir in milk and beer. Heat to boiling, stirring constantly. Boil and stir 1 minute. Stir in cheese. Heat over low heat, stirring constantly, until cheese is melted.

Arrange toast slices on ungreased cookie sheet. Spoon about ⅓ cup sauce onto each slice. Set oven control to broil and/or 550°. Broil with tops 6 inches from heat until cheese is bubbly and light brown, about 3 minutes.

Cheddar Cheese Soup

The village of Cheddar, in southwest England, is one of the most charming spots in Britain, famed for its spectacular ravine and wonderful caves. Cheddar cheese was first made in Cheddar in the sixteenth century. Early English settlers brought the formula to the United States and Canada. Cheddar Cheese Soup is a great favorite in Britain, Canada, New Zealand and Australia.

4 servings

1	small onion, chopped
1	medium stalk celery, thinly sliced
2	tablespoons margarine or butter
2	tablespoons flour
¼	teaspoon pepper
¼	teaspoon dry mustard
1	can (10¾ ounces) condensed chicken broth
1	cup milk
2	cups shredded Cheddar cheese (8 ounces)
	Paprika

Cover and simmer onion and celery in margarine in 2-quart saucepan until onion is tender, about 5 minutes. Stir in flour, pepper and mustard. Add chicken broth and milk. Heat to boiling over medium heat, stirring constantly. Boil and stir 1 minute. Stir in cheese; heat over low heat, stirring occasionally, just until cheese is melted. Sprinkle with paprika.

Freezing Cheese

Did You Know?

To freeze cheese, wrap half-pound or smaller pieces tightly with freezer wrap. Slices and loaves of natural cheeses can be frozen as long as three months. Thaw them slowly in the refrigerator to minimize crumbling.

Pasta with Three Cheeses
(Pasta al Tre Formaggi)

This Italian version of that fine old American stand-by—baked macaroni and cheese—has many variations using different combinations of cheese and different kinds of pasta. It makes a memorable meatless main dish when served with Broccoli with Oil and Lemon (page 222).

8 servings

2   tablespoons margarine or butter
2   tablespoons flour
½   teaspoon salt
⅛   teaspoon pepper
2   cups milk
1   cup shredded Fontina or mozzarella cheese
      (4 ounces)
1   cup shredded Gruyère or Swiss cheese
      (4 ounces)
½   cup grated Parmesan cheese
10   ounces (6 cups) uncooked egg noodles
3   tablespoons dry bread crumbs
1   tablespoon margarine or butter

Heat 2 tablespoons margarine in 2-quart saucepan over low heat until melted. Blend in flour, salt and pepper. Cook over low heat, stirring constantly, until smooth and bubbly; remove from heat. Gradually stir in milk. Heat to boiling, stirring constantly. Boil and stir 1 minute. Stir in cheeses; keep warm over low heat.

Cook noodles as directed on package; drain. Alternate layers of noodles and sauce mixture in ungreased 2-quart casserole. Stir bread crumbs and 1 tablespoon margarine over medium heat until crumbs are toasted; sprinkle over noodles. Cook uncovered in 350° oven until bubbly, about 20 minutes.

Eggplant with Two Cheeses

(Melanzane con Due Formaggi)

This meatless version of the much-admired eggplant Parmesan uses mozzarella (for added protein) as well as Parmesan cheese. Tomato sauce and oregano add the characteristic Italian flavor contrasts that make the dish so popular with Italian food buffs.

4 servings

¼   cup olive or vegetable oil
⅓   cup all-purpose flour
¼   teaspoon garlic salt
1   medium eggplant (about 1½ pounds), cut into
      ½-inch slices
1   can (15 ounces) tomato sauce
⅓   cup grated Parmesan cheese
½   teaspoon dried oregano leaves
2   cups shredded mozzarella cheese (8 ounces)

Heat oil in 12-inch skillet until hot. Mix flour and garlic salt; coat eggplant with flour mixture. Cook over medium heat, turning once, until golden brown. (Add more oil if necessary.)

Pour half the tomato sauce into ungreased oblong baking dish, 13½ x 9 x 2 inches. Add eggplant; sprinkle with Parmesan cheese. Pour remaining tomato sauce over eggplant; sprinkle with oregano and mozzarella cheese. Cook uncovered in 325° oven until hot and bubbly, about 25 minutes.

Cheese-Stuffed Eggplant

Cheese-Stuffed Eggplant

In Jordan, peanuts are included in cheese-and-eggplant combinations; they provide a crisp, crunchy texture and distinctive flavor—and incorporate more protein into the dish.

4 servings

2	small eggplants (about 1 pound each)
1	medium onion, chopped
2	cloves garlic, finely chopped
¼	cup olive or vegetable oil
8	ounces mushrooms, thinly sliced
2	tomatoes, cut into wedges
1	cup salted peanuts
1½	cups soft bread crumbs
2	tablespoons snipped parsley
½	teaspoon salt
½	teaspoon ground marjoram
½	teaspoon ground oregano
⅔	cup grated Parmesan cheese

Cut eggplants lengthwise into halves. Cut and cube enough eggplant from shells to measure about 4 cups, leaving a ½-inch wall on side and bottom of each shell; reserve shells. (See diagram.) Cook and stir eggplant cubes, onion and garlic in oil in 10-inch skillet over medium heat 5 minutes. Add remaining ingredients, except cheese. Cover and cook over low heat 10 minutes.

Place eggplant shells in ungreased shallow pan; spoon peanut mixture into shells. Sprinkle cheese over filled shells. Cook uncovered in 350° oven until eggplant is tender, 30 to 40 minutes.

To remove eggplant from shell easily, cut around side with a grapefruit knife. Then scoop and cube enough eggplant from shells to measure 4 cups.

Serving Cheese

Did You Know?

To serve cheese as a snack, for sandwiches or for dessert, remove cheese from refrigerator about one hour before serving and let it warm to room temperature. For best results, unwrap the cheese, place it on a board or plate, and cover with a glass bowl or cheese bell. Very strong cheese, such as Limburger, is usually served cold; the powerful aroma released as it warms to room temperature can be displeasing, especially when the cheese is served with other foods.

Enchiladas with Green Sauce

The classic Mexican green sauce is made from a special variety of green Mexican tomatoes, difficult to find in the United States. Our Green Sauce—a Mexico City specialty—is made with spinach. The Cheese Filling makes this a fine Mexican party dish when you want to serve enchiladas but prefer a meatless main dish.

4 servings

Prepare Cheese Filling (below) and Green Sauce (below). Heat 8 six-inch tortillas, one at a time, in ungreased hot skillet until softened, about 30 seconds. (Cover hot tortillas to prevent drying.) Dip each tortilla into Green Sauce to coat both sides. Spoon about ¼ cup Cheese Filling onto each tortilla; roll tortilla around filling.

Arrange enchiladas seam sides down in ungreased oblong baking dish, 12 x 7½ x 2 inches. Pour remaining sauce over enchiladas. Cook uncovered in 350° oven until bubbly, about 20 minutes. Garnish with shredded Cheddar or Monterey Jack cheese and lime wedges if desired.

Cheese Filling

2	cups shredded Monterey Jack cheese (8 ounces)
1	cup shredded Cheddar cheese (4 ounces)
1	medium onion, chopped
½	cup dairy sour cream
2	tablespoons snipped parsley
1	teaspoon salt
¼	teaspoon pepper

Mix all ingredients.

Green Sauce

10	ounces spinach*
2	tablespoons margarine or butter
2	tablespoons flour
¼	teaspoon salt
½	cup milk
1½	cups chicken broth
1	to 2 tablespoons chopped canned chilies
1	small onion, chopped
1	clove garlic, finely chopped
¾	teaspoon ground cumin
⅔	cup dairy sour cream

Wash spinach; cover and cook with just the water that clings to leaves until tender, 3 to 5 minutes. Drain and pat dry with paper towels; chop coarsely.

Heat margarine over low heat until melted. Blend in flour and salt. Cook over low heat, stirring constantly, until smooth and bubbly; remove from heat. Stir in milk and ½ cup of the chicken broth; heat to boiling, stirring constantly. Boil and stir 1 minute. Stir in remaining chicken broth. Cook and stir over low heat until hot; remove from heat. Stir in spinach and remaining ingredients.

* 1 package (10 ounces) frozen chopped spinach, cooked and well drained, can be substituted for the fresh spinach.

Chili-Cheese Foldovers (Quesadillas)

Quesadillas *are fine fare for a light Mexican-style lunch or supper, but may be a trifle fiery for some tastes. For ease in serving, prepare the* quesadillas *ahead of time and fry just before serving.*

4 servings

8	six-inch flour tortillas
1	cup shredded Cheddar cheese (4 ounces)
1	cup shredded Monterey Jack cheese (4 ounces)
8	cilantro leaves*
1	medium tomato, chopped
¼	cup chopped green onion
¼	to ⅓ cup chopped green chilies
	Dash of salt
	Red or green taco sauce (optional)
	Lard or shortening

Heat tortillas, one at a time, in ungreased hot skillet until softened, about 30 seconds. (Cover hot tortillas to prevent drying.) Sprinkle 2 tablespoons each Cheddar and Monterey Jack cheese over half of each tortilla. Top each with a cilantro leaf; sprinkle with tomato, green onion, chilies and salt and top with ½ to 1 teaspoon taco sauce.

Moisten edge of each tortilla with water; fold tortilla over filling. Pinch to seal; secure with wooden picks. (Keep covered.) Heat lard (¼ inch) until hot. Fry tortillas until golden brown, about 4 minutes. Drain on paper towels. Remove wooden picks.

* Italian parsley or ⅛ teaspoon ground coriander can be substituted for each cilantro leaf (also known as coriander leaf and Chinese parsley)—but the flavor will be somewhat different. Fresh cilantro can be grown at home from coriander seeds purchased in the spice section of supermarkets.

Swiss Cheese Pie
(Quiche à la Suisse)

This Swiss version of the much-admired quiche makes an ideal brunch dish, accompanied by bacon, a citrus-fruit compote and steaming coffee. For lunch or supper, serve the quiche with a tossed green salad. The quiche differs from the famed French quiche Lorraine in that cheese rather than bacon is used.

6 servings

	Pastry (right)
2	tablespoons finely chopped onion
1½	cups shredded Swiss or Gruyère cheese (6 ounces)
1	cup milk
½	cup whipping cream
3	tablespoons cornstarch
3	tablespoons milk
3	eggs
¾	teaspoon salt
⅛	teaspoon ground nutmeg
	Dash of white pepper

Prepare pastry. Sprinkle onion and cheese in pastry-lined baking dish.

Heat oven to 425°. Pour 1 cup milk and the whipping cream into saucepan. Mix cornstarch and 3 tablespoons milk; stir into milk-cream mixture. Heat to boiling over medium heat, stirring constantly; boil and stir 1 minute. Remove from heat; cool slightly.

Beat eggs slightly with hand beater; gradually beat in cream sauce and remaining ingredients. Pour egg mixture into baking dish. Cook uncovered in oven 15 minutes. Reduce oven temperature to 300°. Cook uncovered until knife inserted halfway between center and edge comes out clean, about 30 minutes. Let stand 10 minutes before cutting.

Pastry

⅓	cup plus 1 tablespoon shortening or ⅓ cup lard
1	cup all-purpose flour
½	teaspoon salt
2	to 3 tablespoons cold water
1	teaspoon margarine or butter

Cut shortening into flour and salt until particles are size of small peas. Sprinkle in water, 1 tablespoon at a time, tossing with fork until all flour is moistened and pastry almost cleans side of bowl (1 to 2 teaspoons water can be added if necessary).

Gather pastry into a ball; shape into flattened round on lightly floured cloth-covered board. With floured stockinet-covered rolling pin, roll pastry 2 inches larger than inverted round baking dish, 8 x 1½ inches, or 9-inch pie plate.

Lightly brush baking dish with margarine. Fold pastry into quarters; unfold and ease into baking dish, pressing firmly against bottom and side. Flatten pastry evenly on rim of baking dish. Press firmly around edge with fork. (Dip fork into flour to prevent sticking.)

Spinach-Cheese Pie

Spinach-Cheese Pie

(Spanokopita)

The Greeks use filo leaves (page 7) in every course from appetizers to dessert. This meatless main dish requires care in preparation but is well worth the effort, for the end result is a superlative party dish suitable for the most gala occasion. To serve as appetizers, cut the pie into small pieces.

6 servings

10	ounces spinach (about 6 cups)
6	ounces feta cheese, crumbled (about 1 cup)
1	cup small-curd cottage cheese
1	small onion, chopped
2	tablespoons snipped parsley
2	teaspoons dried dillweed
½	teaspoon salt
3	eggs, beaten
1	tablespoon margarine or butter, softened
½	cup margarine or butter, melted
½	package (16-ounce size) frozen filo leaves, thawed

Wash spinach; drain and chop. Cover and cook with just the water that clings to the leaves until tender, about 3 minutes; drain. Mix spinach, feta cheese, cottage cheese, onion, parsley, dillweed and salt; stir into eggs. (To assemble, see photographs, right.)

Brush bottom and sides of oblong baking dish, 12 x 7½ x 2 inches, with softened margarine. Unfold filo leaves. Remove 10 leaves; cut crosswise into halves. (Cover completely with damp towel to prevent drying. Wrap and refreeze remaining filo leaves.) Gently separate 1 leaf; place in baking dish, folding edges over to fit bottom of dish. Brush lightly with melted margarine. (See photograph.) Repeat 9 times.

Heat oven to 350°. Spread spinach-egg mixture evenly over filo leaves. (See photograph.) Layer 10 more filo leaves over filling, spreading each leaf with margarine and tucking in sides around edges to cover filling. Cut pastry through top layer of filo leaves with sharp knife into 6 squares. (See photograph.) Cook uncovered in oven until golden, about 35 minutes. Let stand 10 minutes. Cut through scored lines to serve.

Place 1 filo leaf at a time in baking dish; brush with melted margarine.

Spread spinach-egg mixture over filo leaves; layer 10 more leaves over filling.

Cut through top layer of filo leaves with sharp knife into 6 squares.

Spaghetti with Garden-Vegetable Sauce

(Spaghetti al Giardino)

The Italians have many recipes for meatless sauces to serve with pasta. This tarragon-flavored sauce, made from a variety of fresh garden vegetables, captures the flavors of summer in a very special way.

6 servings

3	or 4 ripe medium tomatoes (1½ pounds), cut into wedges
1	small eggplant (about ¾ pound), diced
1	medium carrot, diced
1	medium onion, diced
1	stalk celery, thinly sliced
2	tablespoons snipped parsley
1	teaspoon chopped fresh basil or ½ teaspoon dried basil leaves
½	teaspoon chopped fresh tarragon or ¼ teaspoon dried tarragon leaves
½	clove garlic, chopped
1	teaspoon salt
¼	teaspoon pepper
8	ounces uncooked spaghetti
⅔	cup grated Parmesan cheese

Cover and cook all ingredients except spaghetti and cheese in 3-quart saucepan over low heat until vegetables are soft, 1 to 1½ hours, uncovering during last 30 minutes of cooking to thicken sauce. Cook spaghetti as directed on package. Serve sauce over spaghetti, allowing about ½ cup per serving. Sprinkle each serving with about 2 tablespoons cheese.

Note: Tomatoes vary in moisture content, depending on the season. If the tomatoes are firm rather than juicy, cover the sauce and cook until vegetables are soft, about 30 minutes.

Spaghetti with Eggs and Cheese

(Spaghetti alla Carbonara)

The Italians have several theories regarding the origin of the expression alla carbonara. *One maintains that this "blue-collar" dish was a favorite of laborers working near Rome; another claims that the dish was originally prepared outdoors over a coal fire. Whatever the truth,* spaghetti alla carbonara *has long been a Roman favorite—easy to make and easy on the budget.*

6 to 8 servings

6   slices bacon, cut into ½-inch squares
16 ounces thin spaghetti
3   eggs, beaten
1   cup grated Parmesan cheese
    Freshly ground pepper

Fry bacon over medium heat until almost crisp. Cook spaghetti as directed on package. Drain; do not rinse. Return to pan. Immediately add bacon, bacon fat, eggs and ½ cup of the cheese to spaghetti; toss over low heat until egg coats spaghetti and appears cooked. Serve with remaining cheese; sprinkle with pepper.

Gouda Cheese-and-Egg Casserole

Gouda cheese, from the Netherlands, gives a distinctively Dutch flavor to this casserole, which has a texture reminiscent of old-fashioned bread pudding. Using slightly aged cheese will lend a stronger cheese flavor to the casserole.

4 servings

4   eggs, slightly beaten
1¼   cups half-and-half
1¼   cups soft bread crumbs
1   cup shredded Gouda cheese (4 ounces)

¾   teaspoon salt
¼   teaspoon pepper
     Paprika

Mix all ingredients except paprika; pour into greased 1-quart casserole. Sprinkle with paprika. Cook uncovered in 325° oven until center is set, 45 to 50 minutes.

Dutch Cheese-and-Egg Ramekins

When planning a party breakfast or brunch, these refreshing little ramekins remove much of the last-minute worry and fuss of poaching, boiling or scrambling eggs. Let them bake in the oven while you make the coffee and toast bread or cook smoked sausages—especially good with the ramekins.

6 servings

2   tablespoons margarine or butter, softened
2   green onions (with tops), sliced
1   cup shredded Cheddar or mozzarella cheese (4 ounces)
6   eggs
6   tablespoons half-and-half
    Salt and pepper
    Paprika

Brush six 6-ounce custard cups or individual baking dishes with margarine. Divide green onions and half the cheese evenly among custard cups. Carefully break eggs onto cheese. Pour 1 tablespoon half-and-half over each egg.

Sprinkle eggs with salt, pepper, remaining cheese and the paprika. Cook uncovered in 325° oven until desired doneness, 20 to 22 minutes. (Whites should be set but yolks soft.)

Eggs Florentine

Eggs Florentine
(Oeufs à la Florentine)

Although named after Italy's lovely city of Florence, this recipe is really of French origin, and is usually served for lunch or a light supper, accompanied by French bread and a dry white wine or champagne.

4 servings

1   package (10 ounces) frozen chopped spinach
    Mornay Sauce (right)
4   Poached Eggs (right)
2   tablespoons grated Parmesan cheese
1   tablespoon dry bread crumbs

Cook spinach as directed on package; drain. Place spinach in ungreased shallow 1-quart baking dish; keep warm. Prepare Mornay Sauce and Poached Eggs. Place eggs on spinach. Cover with Mornay Sauce; sprinkle with cheese and bread crumbs. Set oven control to broil and/or 550°. Broil with top about 5 inches from heat until light brown, about 1 minute.

Mornay Sauce

2   teaspoons margarine or butter
2   teaspoons flour
½   teaspoon instant chicken bouillon
    Dash of ground nutmeg
    Dash of ground red pepper
¾   cup half-and-half
¼   cup shredded Swiss cheese

Heat margarine in 1-quart saucepan until melted. Blend in flour, bouillon, nutmeg and red pepper. Cook over low heat, stirring constantly, until mixture is smooth and bubbly. Stir in half-and-half. Heat to boiling, stirring constantly. Boil and stir 1 minute. Add cheese; stir until cheese is melted.

Poached Eggs

Heat water (1½ to 2 inches) to boiling; reduce to simmer. Break each egg into saucer; holding saucer close to water's surface, slip 1 egg at a time into water. Cook until desired doneness, 3 to 5 minutes. Remove eggs from water with slotted spoon.

Individual Eggs Florentine: Divide cooked spinach among four 8-ounce ramekins; top each with egg, Mornay Sauce, cheese and bread crumbs. Broil as directed above.

Ranch-Style Eggs

Ranch-Style Eggs
(Huevos Rancheros)

Mexico's all-time favorite—huevos rancheros—appears on nearly every restaurant menu in Mexico, and on every Mexican restaurant menu in the United States. It is not surprising, for the colorful dish is both easy and economical. Serve with chorizo sausages, rice and fruit if desired.

4 servings

	Mexican Sauce (right)
	Vegetable oil
8	four-inch tortillas
	Vegetable oil
8	eggs
	Salt and pepper
1	cup shredded Monterey Jack cheese (4 ounces)

Prepare Mexican Sauce. Heat oil (⅛ inch) in 6- or 8-inch skillet until hot. Cook tortillas until crisp and light brown, about 1 minute on each side. Drain on paper towels; keep warm.

Heat oil (⅛ inch) in 12-inch skillet until hot. Break each egg into measuring cup or saucer; carefully slip 4 eggs, 1 at a time, into skillet. Immediately reduce heat. Cook slowly, spooning oil onto eggs until whites are set and a film forms over the yolks. Or turn eggs over gently when whites are set and cook to desired doneness. Sprinkle with salt and pepper. Repeat with remaining eggs.

Spoon 1 tablespoon sauce over each tortilla; place 1 egg on each. Spoon sauce over white of egg; sprinkle yolk with cheese.

Mexican Sauce

1	medium onion, chopped
½	green pepper, chopped
1	clove garlic, finely chopped
1	tablespoon vegetable oil
2	cups chopped ripe tomatoes*
¼	to ½ cup chopped green chilies

5   drops red pepper sauce
½   teaspoon sugar
⅛   teaspoon salt

Cook and stir onion, green pepper and garlic in oil in 2-quart saucepan until green pepper is tender, about 5 minutes. Stir in remaining ingredients. Heat to boiling; reduce heat. Simmer uncovered until slightly thickened, about 15 minutes.

* 1 can (16 ounces) tomatoes (with liquid) can be substituted for the ripe tomatoes. Break up tomatoes with fork.

Chili Eggs with Cheese Sauce

A delicately flavored Cheese Sauce laced with wine and the familiar presence of fried eggs provide an unusual and nourishing texture contrast with the crunchy tortillas. Good for luncheon or brunch with a Mexican accent.

4 servings

Cheese Sauce (right)
Vegetable oil
4   nine-inch flour tortillas
8   eggs
Salt and pepper
4   teaspoons chopped green chilies

Prepare Cheese Sauce; cover and keep warm over very low heat. Heat oil (⅛ inch) in 12-inch skillet until hot. Cook tortillas until light brown. Drain on paper towels; keep warm.

Break each egg into measuring cup or saucer; carefully slip 1 egg at a time into same skillet. Immediately reduce heat. Cook slowly, spooning oil over eggs until whites are set and a film forms over the yolks (add small amount of oil if necessary). Or turn eggs over gently when whites are set and cook to desired doneness.

Place 2 eggs on each tortilla; sprinkle with salt and pepper. Pour Cheese Sauce over eggs; sprinkle with chilies.

Cheese Sauce

2   tablespoons margarine or butter
2   tablespoons flour
¼   teaspoon salt
⅛   teaspoon paprika
¾   cup milk
¼   cup dry white wine
1   cup shredded Monterey Jack cheese (4 ounces)

Heat margarine over low heat until melted. Blend in flour, salt and paprika. Cook over low heat, stirring constantly, until mixture is smooth and bubbly; remove from heat. Stir in milk and wine. Heat to boiling, stirring constantly. Boil and stir 1 minute. Stir in cheese. Cook and stir over low heat until cheese is melted.

Rice-and-Green-Chili Casserole

This easy Mexican casserole is a good do-ahead dish for entertaining. It can be assembled in the morning and baked shortly before serving.

6 servings

1   cup dairy sour cream
1   can (4 ounces) peeled, chopped green chilies, drained
3   cups cooked rice (page 253)
¾   pound Monterey Jack cheese, cut into strips
½   cup shredded Cheddar cheese (2 ounces)

Mix sour cream and chilies. Layer 1 cup of the rice, half the sour cream mixture and half the cheese strips in greased 1½-quart casserole; repeat. Cover with remaining rice. Cook uncovered in 325° oven until bubbly, about 30 minutes. Sprinkle with Cheddar cheese. Return to oven until cheese melts.

Cheese-and-Rice Casserole

Cheese-and-Rice Casserole

(Riso e Formaggio)

The much-praised rice of northern Italy (often found in American gourmet shops in small canvas bags at premium prices) is shorter and thicker than most American rice, and was so admired by Thomas Jefferson that he smuggled grains of it out of northern Italy in the eighteenth century and planted it in American soil! This excellent do-ahead recipe would be nice served with Italian Green Bean Salad (page 204).

8 servings

2	cups water
1	cup uncooked regular rice
1	teaspoon salt
½	teaspoon dry mustard
½	teaspoon red pepper sauce
¼	teaspoon pepper
1	medium onion, chopped
1	medium green pepper, chopped
2	cups shredded mozzarella or Cheddar cheese (8 ounces)
4	eggs, slightly beaten
2½	cups milk
½	cup grated Parmesan cheese

Heat water, rice, salt, mustard, red pepper sauce and pepper to boiling, stirring once or twice; reduce heat. Cover and simmer 14 minutes. (Do not lift cover or stir.) Remove from heat. Fluff rice lightly with fork; cover and let steam 5 to 10 minutes.

Layer half the rice, onion, green pepper and mozzarella cheese in greased oblong baking dish, 11 x 7 x 1½ inches; repeat. Mix eggs and milk; pour over rice mixture. Sprinkle with Parmesan cheese. (Casserole can be covered and refrigerated up to 24 hours at this point.) Cook uncovered in 325° oven until set, 45 to 50 minutes. Let stand 10 minutes. Cut into squares.

Guide to Cheeses

Cheese	Country of Origin	Flavor	Use
		SOFT	
Bel Paese	Italy	Mild, sweet, creamy	Snack, dessert, cooking
Brie	France	Mild to pungent	Snack, dessert
Camembert	France	Edible crust, mild to pungent	Snack, sandwich, dessert
		SEMISOFT	
Feta	Greece	Sharp, salty, crumbly	Salads, cooking
Mozzarella	Italy	Mild	Cooking, snack
Muenster	Germany	Mild to mellow	Sandwich, snack, dessert
Port du Salut	France	Edible crust, mellow to robust	Snack, sandwich, dessert
		FIRM	
Cheddar	England	Mild to very sharp	Sandwich, snack, cooking, dessert
Cheshire	England	Crumbly, ripe	Cooking, snack
Edam, Gouda	Holland	Mild, nutlike	Snack, dessert, sandwich, cooking
Fontina	Italy	Mellow, nutty	Snack, dessert, cooking
Gjetost	Norway	Sweet, caramel	Sandwich, snack
Gruyère	Switzerland	Nutty, slightly sharp	Cooking, dessert, snack
Provolone	Italy	Mild to sharp, smoky	Cooking, snack
Swiss (Emmenthaler)	Switzerland	Mild, nutty	Cooking, sandwich, dessert, snack
		HARD	
Kashkaval	Yugoslavia	Salty	Snack, dessert
Parmesan	Italy	Sharp, piquant	Cooking
Romano	Italy	Sharp, piquant	Cooking
		MOLD-RIPENED	
Bleu	Denmark	Tangy, sharp	Salads, snack, dessert
Gorgonzola	Italy	Piquant, creamy, crumbly	Salads, dessert
Roquefort	France	Sharp, piquant, spicy	Salads, snack, dessert
Stilton	England	Piquant, milder than Gorgonzola or Roquefort	Snack, salads, dessert

Austrian Egg Cake

(Eierkuchen)

Austria's irresistible Eierkuchen *goes well with fried ham or sausage, and makes a care-free entrée for a party brunch or breakfast. Let the cake bake and puff in the oven while you greet guests or relax with a cup of fresh juice or coffee.*

4 servings

6   eggs, beaten
1½   cups milk
1   teaspoon salt
    Dash of pepper
2½   cups soft bread crumbs (see Note)
2   green onions (with tops), chopped

Mix eggs, milk, salt and pepper; stir in bread crumbs and green onions. Pour into greased square baking dish, 8 x 8 x 2 inches. Cook uncovered in 325° oven until set and top is light brown, about 40 minutes.

Note: For soft bread crumbs, tear 3½ slices bread into pieces. Place in blender container, one slice at a time. Cover and blend until crumbed, about 3 seconds.

Storing Cheese

Did You Know?

All cheeses must be stored in the refrigerator. Hard cheeses, such as Swiss, Edam and Parmesan, can be refrigerated as long as two months; soft cheeses, such as Brie and Gourmandise, will keep for two weeks. Store cheese unopened until you use it, unless serving it as a snack (see page 185); then wrap leftovers tightly with aluminum foil or plastic wrap. Except for mold-ripened cheeses, such as Roquefort or Gorgonzola, which get their distinctive flavor from the mold, you should cut off any mold you discover on cheese. If the mold has penetrated the cheese, discard the cheese.

Cheese Soufflé

The inimitable French Cheese Soufflé always wins applause, whether presented at a light luncheon or a candlelight supper. Served with crusty bread, French Lettuce Salad (page 203) and a light red wine, it represents simple but classic French cuisine at its finest.

4 servings

¼   cup margarine or butter
¼   cup all-purpose flour
½   teaspoon salt
    Dash of ground red pepper
1   cup milk
1   cup shredded Swiss or Gruyère cheese
    (4 ounces)
4   eggs, separated
¼   teaspoon cream of tartar

Heat margarine in 2-quart saucepan over low heat until melted. Blend in flour, salt and red pepper. Cook over low heat, stirring constantly, until mixture is smooth and bubbly; remove from heat. Stir in milk. Heat to boiling, stirring constantly. Boil and stir 1 minute. Stir in cheese until melted; remove from heat.

Heat oven to 325°. Beat egg whites and cream of tartar in large mixer bowl until stiff but not dry. Beat egg yolks in small mixer bowl until very thick and lemon-colored, about 5 minutes; stir into cheese mixture. Stir about ¼ of the egg whites into cheese mixture. Fold cheese mixture into remaining egg whites.

Carefully pour into greased 1½-quart soufflé dish or casserole. Cook uncovered in oven until knife inserted halfway between center and edge comes out clean, 50 to 60 minutes. Serve immediately.

Scrambled Eggs with Peppers and Tomatoes

Scrambled Eggs with Peppers and Tomatoes

(Pipérade Basquaise)

Pipérade *is a combination of tomatoes, sweet peppers and onions, to which eggs are added. The dish probably originated in the Basque area of France. There are many variations. In our version—favored along the French Riviera—the eggs are cooked separately and mounded on top of the pepper mixture.*

4 to 6 servings

2	medium green peppers, sliced
1	medium onion, sliced
1	clove garlic, chopped
½	teaspoon salt
½	teaspoon dried thyme leaves
3	tablespoons olive oil or margarine
2	medium tomatoes, coarsely chopped
8	eggs
½	cup milk
½	cup ¼-inch strips fully cooked smoked ham
1½	teaspoons salt
¼	teaspoon pepper

Cook and stir green peppers, onion, garlic, ½ teaspoon salt and the thyme in 1 tablespoon of the oil in 10-inch skillet over medium heat until green peppers are crisp-tender, about 8 minutes. Add tomatoes; heat until hot, about 2 minutes. Drain excess liquid from vegetables; place vegetables on platter. Keep warm.

Heat remaining oil in same skillet over medium heat until hot. Mix remaining ingredients; pour into skillet. Cook uncovered over low heat, stirring frequently, until eggs are thickened throughout but still moist, 3 to 5 minutes. Mound scrambled eggs in center of vegetables. Sprinkle with snipped parsley if desired.

Scrambled Eggs with Rice

The Greeks developed this humble "egg-stretcher" recipe, which can be made in less than twenty minutes. For a colorful accompaniment, serve Fried Tomatoes (page 238) or Athenian Salad (page 203).

3 servings

1   medium onion, chopped
2   tablespoons margarine or butter
6   eggs
½   cup cooked rice (page 253)
¾   teaspoon salt
     Dash of pepper

Cook and stir onion in margarine in 10-inch skillet until tender. Mix eggs, rice, salt and pepper; pour into skillet. As mixture begins to set at bottom and sides, gently lift cooked portions with spatula so that thin, uncooked portion can flow to bottom. Avoid constant stirring. Cook until eggs are thickened throughout but still moist, 3 to 5 minutes.

Eggs Fu Yong

The Chinese have many ways to prepare and serve Eggs Fu Yong; often pea sprouts are used rather than bean sprouts, and some Chinese chefs prefer to cook the vegetables first, then ladle the eggs over them in the wok or skillet. Our recipe is easy and quick; if you like, serve with hot mustard and Chinese duck sauce.

2 servings (6 patties)

3   eggs
1   cup frozen green peas, thawed
½   cup drained bean sprouts
4   water chestnuts, sliced
1   tablespoon chopped green onion (with tops)
1   tablespoon soy sauce
2   tablespoons vegetable oil

Beat eggs; stir in remaining ingredients except oil. Heat oil in 10-inch skillet until hot. Pour ¼ cup egg mixture at a time into skillet.

Cook until set; turn. Cook over medium heat until other side is brown.

Shrimp Eggs Fu Yong: Omit bean sprouts. Stir in ½ cup cooked shrimp and 2 teaspoons dry white wine.

Italian Zucchini Omelet
(Frittata di Zucchine)

The Italian omelet, called frittata, *is one of the easiest omelets to make. When placed under the broiler for a few minutes, it doesn't need to be turned. Our recipe calls for zucchini, but the Italians also use many other vegetables in their frittate.*

3 servings

6   eggs
¼   cup water
3   tablespoons snipped parsley
3   tablespoons soft bread crumbs
1   teaspoon salt
1   clove garlic, finely chopped
2   tablespoons olive or vegetable oil
1   cup ¼-inch slices zucchini (1 medium)
     Flour
     Grated Parmesan cheese

Beat eggs, water, parsley, bread crumbs, salt and garlic. Heat oil in 8-inch skillet over medium heat until hot. Coat zucchini with flour; cook until golden, about 2 minutes on each side. Pour egg mixture over zucchini.

Cook until eggs are thickened throughout but still moist, 3 to 5 minutes. Gently lift edge with fork so that uncooked portion can flow to bottom. Sprinkle with cheese. Set oven control to broil and/or 550°. Broil omelet with top 5 inches from heat until golden brown, 3 to 4 minutes. Loosen edge with spatula; slip cheese side up onto serving plate.

Spanish Potato Omelet

Spanish Potato Omelet
(Tortilla de Patatas)

The Spanish word for omelet is tortilla—*but in Spain, the tortilla bears no resemblance at all to the Mexican tortilla. It is more like a fried "egg pie," cut into wedges before serving. Try it with Tomatoes, Peppers and Onions (page 237).*

4 servings

6	or 7 slices bacon, cut into 1-inch pieces
1	medium potato, cut into ½-inch cubes
1	medium onion, chopped
6	eggs
¾	teaspoon salt
⅛	teaspoon pepper
	Parsley

Fry bacon in 10-inch skillet over medium heat until crisp. Remove bacon and drain, reserving 4 tablespoons bacon fat in skillet. Cook and stir potato and onion until potato is golden brown and tender, about 10 minutes.

Beat eggs with salt and pepper. Stir bacon into potato mixture; add eggs. Cover and cook over low heat until eggs are set and light brown on bottom, about 10 minutes. Cut into wedges to serve; garnish with parsley.

French Omelet with Cheese

Once you have mastered the art of making a French omelet, you can improvise on the basic recipe with any number of stuffings. Omelets are perfect for spur-of-the-moment occasions.

2 servings

3	eggs
¼	teaspoon salt
	Dash of pepper
1	tablespoon margarine or butter
⅓	cup shredded Gruyère or Cheddar cheese

Mix eggs, salt and pepper just until whites and yolks are blended. Heat margarine in 7- or 8-inch omelet pan or skillet over medium-high heat. As margarine melts, tilt pan in all directions to coat sides thoroughly. When margarine just begins to brown, pan is hot enough to use.

Quickly pour eggs all at once into pan. Start sliding pan back and forth rapidly over heat. At the same time, stir quickly with fork to spread eggs continuously over bottom of pan as they thicken. Let stand over heat a few seconds to lightly brown bottom of omelet. (Do not overcook—omelet will continue to cook after folding.)

Tilt pan; run fork under edge of omelet, then jerk pan sharply to loosen eggs from bottom of pan. Sprinkle with cheese. Fold portion of omelet nearest to you just to center. (Allow for portion of omelet to slide up side of pan.) Grasp pan handle; turn omelet onto warm plate, flipping folded portion of omelet over so far side is on bottom.

Curry Powder

Did You Know?

Curry powder has long been one of the world's most popular commercial spice blends, sold in spice shops and groceries from Southeast Asia to Latin America. Yet curry powder is rarely used in India, although it is manufactured there and exported throughout the world.

Curry powder is a blend of many spices and herbs: The bright yellow color comes from turmeric, the distinctive flavor from fenugreek, ginger, red and green chilies, cumin, cardamom, nutmeg, cinnamon, cloves—and little-known herbs such as lemon grass and curry leaves (similar to bay leaves but of a different flavor).

In India, curry powder is usually made from scratch—each family blends its own spice mixture according to personal taste or tradition, often varying proportions and ingredients to suit particular dishes.

Today, specialty food shops carry many kinds of curry powder or curry spice blends, often subtitled according to the kind of blend.

Selecting the kind or brand of curry powder most to your liking is a matter of personal taste. In our recipes, the small jars of curry powder found on supermarket shelves will produce the appropriate Indian flavor needed for any of our curry recipes.

If you want a stronger curry flavor, add extra curry powder to the recipe; if you like fiery Indian foods and want a hotter curry, add additional red pepper.

Curried Eggs with Mushrooms

Curried Eggs with Mushrooms

(Ka Salun)

Many Indians are vegetarians; eggs and rice are principal sources of protein in India. This colorful low-cost dish has a party look. Serve with mango chutney and a warm Indian bread, such as Fried Bread Puffs (page 266) or Indian Flat Bread (page 267).

3 or 4 servings

6	hard-cooked eggs
8	ounces mushrooms
1	large onion, finely chopped
2	tablespoons margarine or butter
1	teaspoon ground coriander
1	teaspoon salt
½	teaspoon ground turmeric
½	teaspoon ground ginger
½	teaspoon ground cumin
3	medium tomatoes, cut into wedges
¼	cup chicken broth
1	teaspoon lemon juice
3	cups hot cooked rice (page 253)

Cut eggs lengthwise into halves. Cook and stir mushrooms and onion in margarine in 10-inch skillet until onion is tender, about 5 minutes. Stir in coriander, salt, turmeric, ginger and cumin; cook and stir 1 minute.

Stir in tomatoes and chicken broth. Heat to boiling; reduce heat. Simmer uncovered 5 minutes, stirring occasionally. Carefully place eggs in skillet; spoon sauce over eggs. Simmer uncovered without stirring until eggs are hot, 3 to 5 minutes. Stir in lemon juice just before serving. Serve over rice.

Dried Beans

Did You Know?

Dried beans, nutrient-packed basic foods in many countries of the world, can be smoky black, red, pink, tan, white or speckled, with sizes that vary from the large oval of limas to the small round of navy or pea beans. If you can't find the kind of dried bean called for in the recipe, use another variety; they are interchangeable.

All dried beans—and dried peas, too—are high in vegetable protein; combine them with meats and dairy foods for optimum use of the protein in each food. To prevent foaming during the first cooking, add a tablespoon of margarine to the beans, and if the water in your area is hard, it's a good idea to add ¼ teaspoon of baking soda to the cooking water for every cup of beans. You can expect the beans to double or triple in volume as they cook.

Bean Chart

Kidney Beans

Garbanzo Beans

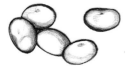

Navy or Pea Beans

Great Northern Beans

Pinto Beans

Black Beans

Lentils

Split Peas

Bean Soup with Pasta (Pasta e Fagioli)

This is the legendary pasta e fagioli—a hearty bean-and-pasta soup that every farm family in southern Italy cherishes. There are many recipes—some meatless—but pasta and beans (fagioli) are always the key ingredients. Served with Italian bread and fresh fruit, pasta e fagioli makes a nourishing soup supper for late autumn or winter meals.

5 servings (about 1⅓ cups each)

5   cups water
8   ounces dried Great Northern or navy beans (about 1¼ cups)
1   large onion, chopped
1   large tomato, chopped, or 1 can (8 ounces) tomato sauce
2   medium stalks celery, sliced
2   cloves garlic, chopped
¼   pound salt pork, chopped (see Note)
2   teaspoons instant beef bouillon
½   teaspoon salt
¼   teaspoon pepper
½   cup uncooked macaroni (shells, bows, or elbow macaroni)
     Grated Parmesan cheese

Heat water and beans to boiling in Dutch oven; boil 2 minutes. Remove from heat; cover and let stand 1 hour.

Add onion, tomato, celery, garlic, salt pork, bouillon, salt and pepper to beans. Heat to boiling; reduce heat. Cover and simmer until beans are tender, about 2 hours (do not boil or beans will burst). Skim fat if necessary.

Stir macaroni into soup. Cover and simmer until macaroni is tender, 10 to 15 minutes. Sprinkle with cheese.

Note: ¼ to ½ pound fully cooked smoked ham, chopped (1 to 2 cups), can be added with the salt pork.

Garbanzo Bean Soup

This robust soup from Spain is traditionally served as a soup supper in the winter, along with warm crusty bread or hard rolls and perhaps a classic Caramel Custard (page 307) for dessert.

8 servings (about 1½ cups each)

8   cups water
1   pound dried garbanzo beans (about 2½ cups)
1½- to 2-pounds smoked ham shank or 1 ham bone
1   large onion, chopped
2   cloves garlic, chopped
1   tablespoon instant beef bouillon
1   teaspoon salt
¼   teaspoon pepper
⅛   teaspoon ground red pepper
3   medium potatoes, cut into ½-inch cubes
1   small head cabbage (about 1 pound), coarsely chopped (about 6 cups)

Heat water and beans to boiling in Dutch oven; boil 2 minutes. Remove from heat; cover and let stand 1 hour. Add ham shank, onion, garlic, bouillon, salt, pepper and red pepper to beans. Heat to boiling; reduce heat. Cover and simmer until beans are almost tender, 1½ to 2 hours (do not boil or beans will burst). Skim fat if necessary.

Remove ham shank; cool slightly. Trim fat and bones from ham. Cut ham into ½-inch pieces. Stir ham, potatoes and cabbage into soup. Heat to boiling; reduce heat. Cover and simmer until beans and potatoes are tender, about 30 minutes.

Dutch Split-Pea Soup

Dutch Split-Pea Soup (Erwtensoep)

Smoked pork hocks and sausage provide the intriguing flavor that has made this soup a national dish in the Netherlands. It is especially good with pumpernickel bread. According to Dutch tradition, the soup should be so thick that a spoon will stand upright in it.

8 servings (about 1½ cups each)

9	cups water
1	pound dried green split peas (about 2¼ cups)
2	pounds smoked pork hocks
6	leeks, sliced
4	stalks celery (with leaves), sliced
2	cloves garlic, chopped
1½	teaspoons crushed dried savory leaves
1½	teaspoons salt
½	teaspoon pepper
½	pound cooked smoked sausage*

Heat water and peas to boiling in Dutch oven; boil 2 minutes. Remove from heat; cover and let stand 1 hour. Add remaining ingredients except sausage to peas. Heat to boiling; reduce heat. Cover and simmer until pork is tender, about 2 hours. Skim fat if necessary.

Remove pork hocks; cool slightly. Trim fat and bone from pork. Cut pork into ½-inch pieces. Stir pork and sausage into soup. Heat to boiling; reduce heat. Cover and simmer until sausage is hot, 10 to 15 minutes. Remove sausage and slice. Serve sausage with pumpernickel bread and prepared mustard if desired or return to soup.

*Dutch-type smoked sausage, Polish kielbasa, knackwurst or frankfurters.

Yellow Split-Pea Soup (Gul Ärtsoppa)

The Swedes, like the French Canadians, favor yellow split peas over green when planning a hearty soup supper for a cold winter night. Canada's habitant pea soup is made very much like this Swedish recipe, but uses smoked pork and generally includes a pinch of allspice for added flavor.

8 servings (about 1½ cups each)

8	cups water
1	pound dried yellow split peas (about 2½ cups)
1	pound lean salt pork, rind removed
2	medium onions, chopped
½	teaspoon dried marjoram leaves
¼	teaspoon pepper
4	medium carrots, sliced
4	medium stalks celery, sliced

Heat water and peas to boiling in Dutch oven; boil 2 minutes. Remove from heat; cover and let stand 1 hour. Add salt pork, onions, marjoram and pepper. Heat to boiling; reduce heat. Cover and simmer 1 hour. Skim fat if necessary.

Add carrots and celery. Heat to boiling; reduce heat. Cover and simmer until vegetables are tender, about 45 minutes. Remove salt pork; cut into ¼-inch slices. Add pork to soup or serve separately with mustard if desired.

Lentils

Did You Know?

Lentils, among the most ancient of foods, are disk-shaped and about the size of peas. There is no need to soak them before cooking, and unlike dried beans, lentils become tender in about half an hour. They are good sources of vegetable protein, A and B vitamins, and calcium. Available year-round, packaged (dried) lentils can be stored at room temperature, tightly covered, for six to eight months. In some areas, lentils are available canned. Red, brown, yellow or green lentils can be used interchangeably in cooking.

Lentil Soup with Spinach

The Middle East boasts many favorite lentil soups, all economical and nutritious. This recipe is especially colorful and tasty—brightened by the last-minute addition of fresh spinach, lemon peel and lemon juice.

4 servings (about 1¼ cups each)

2	medium onions, sliced
1	clove garlic, finely chopped
2	tablespoons olive or vegetable oil
3	cups water
8	ounces dried lentils (about 1¼ cups)
1	teaspoon salt
10	ounces spinach,* chopped (4 cups)
1	teaspoon grated lemon peel
2	teaspoons lemon juice

Cook and stir onions and garlic in oil in 3-quart saucepan over medium heat until onions are tender. Stir in water, lentils and salt. Heat to boiling; reduce heat. Cover and simmer 1 hour. Stir in spinach, lemon peel and lemon juice. Cover and simmer until spinach is tender, about 5 minutes.

* 1 package (10 ounces) frozen chopped spinach, thawed, can be substituted for the fresh spinach.

Lentil-and-Vegetable Stew ('Mjeddrah)

This ancient Middle Eastern soup (sometimes identified with Esau's pottage of the Bible) may be made with red, yellow, green or brown lentils, and is traditionally served with fried onions and shredded lettuce dressed with oil and vinegar.

4 or 5 servings

3	cups water
8	ounces dried lentils (about 1¼ cups)
2	medium potatoes, cut into 1-inch cubes
1	medium onion, chopped
1	stalk celery, chopped
2	cloves garlic, finely chopped
1	tablespoon finely snipped parsley
1	tablespoon instant beef bouillon
1	teaspoon salt
1	teaspoon ground cumin
2	medium zucchini, cut into ½-inch slices
	Lemon wedges

Heat water and lentils to boiling in Dutch oven; reduce heat. Cover and cook until lentils are almost tender, about 30 minutes. Stir in potatoes, onion, celery, garlic, parsley, bouillon, salt and cumin. Cover and cook until potatoes are tender, about 20 minutes.

Stir in zucchini; cover and cook until zucchini is tender, 10 to 15 minutes. Serve with lemon wedges.

Savory Lentils
(Dal)

Dal *is a word used to describe a mildly spiced dish served in India and in many parts of Southeast Asia as a protein-rich supplement to meat and vegetable dishes.* Dal *can be made with farina, dried beans, split peas or lentils. Red, brown or yellow lentils are the most popular form of* dal. *The dish provides a gentle contrast to fiery curries. In Sri Lanka,* dal *is often spooned over rice; curried meat, poultry or fish are served separately.*

5 servings

3	cups water
1	cup dried lentils or split peas
1	teaspoon salt
1	teaspoon ground turmeric
1	medium onion, finely chopped
2	cloves garlic, finely chopped
1	teaspoon ground cumin
¼	teaspoon ground cardamom
2	tablespoons Ghee (page 218) or vegetable oil
	Lime wedges

Heat water and lentils to boiling in 2-quart saucepan. Stir in salt and turmeric. Cover and simmer until lentils are tender, about 45 minutes. Cook and stir onion, garlic, cumin and cardamom in Ghee until onion is tender; stir into lentils. Cook uncovered over low heat, stirring frequently, until consistency of refried beans, 20 to 30 minutes. Serve with lime wedges.

Cuban Black Beans

Braised black beans are a staple food in the country cooking of Cuba and other islands of the Caribbean. Often they are served over rice and accompanied by a tossed green salad for a simple meatless main dish. Try our recipe with Spanish Shredded Beef Stew (page 133) or roast pork.

4 servings

2	cups water
6	ounces black beans (about 1 cup)
1	small green pepper, chopped
1	small onion, sliced
1	clove garlic, finely chopped
1	tablespoon olive or vegetable oil
1	bay leaf
¾	teaspoon crushed dried oregano leaves
½	teaspoon ground cumin
½	teaspoon salt
	Dash of pepper
2	cups hot cooked rice (page 253)

Heat water and beans to boiling in 3-quart saucepan; boil 2 minutes. Remove from heat; cover and let stand 1 hour.

Cook and stir green pepper, onion and garlic in oil until onion is tender; stir into beans. Add enough water to cover beans if necessary. Heat to boiling; reduce heat. Stir in bay leaf, oregano, cumin, salt and pepper. Cover and simmer until beans are tender and most of the liquid is absorbed, 1½ to 2 hours. Remove bay leaf. Serve over rice.

Swedish Brown Beans
(Bruna Bönor)

These brown beans are similar to Mexican pink beans in appearance. You'll find them in large supermarkets and at Scandinavian specialty stores. Our recipe is prepared with a simple sweet-and-sour sauce. It goes especially well with Swedish Meatballs (page 138) and roast pork or pork chops.

4 servings

2½	cups water
½	pound Swedish brown beans (1 cup)
⅓	cup packed brown sugar
2	tablespoons vinegar
¾	teaspoon salt

Heat water and beans to boiling in Dutch oven; boil 2 minutes. Remove from heat; cover and let stand 1 hour.

Add enough water to cover beans if necessary. Heat to boiling; reduce heat. Cover and simmer 1 hour. Stir in remaining ingredients. Cover and simmer until beans are tender, 50 to 60 minutes. (Add a small amount water if necessary.)

Do-Ahead Tip: Soak beans in 5 cups water at least 8 hours. Heat to boiling in same water; cover and simmer 1 hour. Continue as directed above.

Mexican Beans with Cheese
(Frijoles)

The Mexicans have many varieties of beans and many versions of the popular "refried beans." Try our recipe when planning an unusual patio breakfast (serve the beans with tortillas and eggs)—or simply serve them as a side dish with a penny-wise family meal.

4 to 6 servings

2	cups water
8	ounces dried pinto beans (about 1¼ cups)
1	medium onion, chopped
2	tablespoons margarine, butter or lard
¾	teaspoon salt
¼	teaspoon pepper
½	cup shredded Monterey Jack cheese

Cover and heat water, beans and onion to boiling; boil 2 minutes. Remove from heat; let stand 1 hour.

Add just enough water to cover beans. Heat to boiling; reduce heat. Cover and boil gently, stirring occasionally, until beans are very tender, about 1½ hours. (Add water during cooking if necessary.) Mash beans. Stir in margarine, salt and pepper until margarine is completely absorbed. Stir in cheese.

How to Grow Your Own Bean Sprouts

Did You Know?

It's easy to sprout mung beans in your kitchen. Fold a piece of terry toweling or cheesecloth (about 16 x 8 inches) into fourths (8 x 4 inches). Place in loaf pan, 9½ x 5 x 3 inches. Pour water over the toweling until it is saturated, then sprinkle ¼ cup dried green mung beans on top in a single layer. Cover with aluminum foil; let stand 24 hours.

Uncover the planter and set it in a dark, draft-free place. Water it each day as the top layer dries out. Beans will sprout in two or three days, and will be ready to harvest in four to six days.

To harvest, snip the plants off at the base with scissors. Rinse to remove the husks and dry well. Place in a plastic bag; close tightly and refrigerate no longer than three days. The yield from ¼ cup dried mung beans is three cups.

Fava Bean Rounds
(Falafel)

Falafel *(also called ta' amia) is found in many parts of the Middle East, but is considered Egypt's national dish. In Egypt, the spicy deep-fried patties are often served with Pocket Bread (page 272) and Eggplant Dip (page 18). In Israel,* falafel *is sold by street vendors. The little patties are inserted into warm pocket bread along with salad greens and yogurt.*

4 to 6 servings

2   cups water
1   cup dried white fava or garbanzo beans*
       (chickpeas)
1   egg
1   small red onion, finely chopped
3   tablespoons snipped parsley
2   tablespoons flour
2   teaspoons finely chopped garlic
1   teaspoon salt
1   teaspoon ground coriander
¾   teaspoon ground cumin
¼   teaspoon baking powder
       Dash of ground red pepper
       Vegetable oil

Heat water and beans to boiling in 2-quart saucepan; boil 2 minutes. Remove from heat; cover and let stand 1 hour. Add enough water to cover beans if necessary. Heat to boiling; reduce heat. Cover and simmer until tender, 1 to 1½ hours. Drain, reserving liquid.

Mash beans; add 2 to 3 tablespoons reserved liquid if necessary. (Do not purée beans in blender or food processor.) Stir in remaining ingredients except oil. (Mixture should be thick.) Cover and let stand 1 hour.

Pinch off 1-inch pieces; shape into rounds and flatten. Let stand 30 minutes. Heat oil (2 inches) in 3-quart saucepan to 375°. Fry 4 or 5 rounds at a time in hot oil, turning once, until golden brown, 2 to 3 minutes; drain on paper towels.

* 2 cans (15 ounces each) garbanzo beans, drained (reserve liquid), can be substituted for the dried garbanzo beans.

Red Beans and Rice

This robust and colorful dish can be the answer to your party-planning questions when you expect a crowd. The dish is served throughout Latin America.

12 servings

2   cups water
8   ounces dried kidney beans* (about 1 cup)
2   ounces salt pork, diced, or 3 slices bacon, cut
       up
1   medium onion, chopped
1   medium green pepper, chopped
1   cup uncooked regular rice
1½   teaspoons salt

Heat water and beans to boiling in 3-quart saucepan; boil 2 minutes. Remove from heat; cover and let stand 1 hour. Add enough water to cover beans if necessary. Heat to boiling; reduce heat. Cover and simmer until tender, 1 to 1½ hours (do not boil or beans will burst). Drain; reserve liquid.

Fry salt pork in 10-inch skillet until crisp; add onion and green pepper. Cook and stir until onion is tender. Add enough water to reserved liquid to measure 2 cups if necessary. Add reserved liquid, the salt pork, onion, green pepper, rice and salt to beans in 3-quart saucepan. Heat to boiling, stirring once or twice; reduce heat. Cover and simmer 14 minutes. (Do not lift cover or stir.) Remove from heat. Fluff lightly with fork; cover and let steam 5 to 10 minutes.

* 1 can (16 ounces) red kidney beans, drained, can be substituted for the cooked dried kidney beans.

Clockwise from top: Athenian Salad (page 203), Corn-Okra-Tomato Medley (page 227) and Cauliflower-Avocado Salad (page 204).

Salads, Vegetables and Hearty Side Dishes

Crisp, cool salads and colorful vegetables bring excitement to the simplest family meals and round out your party menus in a truly memorable manner. They can do even more: provide flavor and texture contrasts to delight the discriminating palate . . . boost nutrition when planning budget main dishes . . . bring the fresh taste of the garden to do-ahead or freezer dinners.

This chapter opens with a worldwide collection of salads, ranging from the classic tossed green salads of Europe (suitable for every occasion) to show-stopping sensations such as Green Banana Salad from the Caribbean . . . Christmas Eve Salad from Mexico . . . Cracked-Wheat-and-Parsley Salad from the Middle East . . . and Indonesian Salad with Coconut-Peanut Dressing!

The vegetable side dishes include low-calorie zucchini recipes, low-cost celery and carrot concoctions, elegant ways with mushrooms and festive vegetable medleys to make your international menu planning a real joy. And you'll find hearty potato recipes from France, the Scandinavian countries, Hungary, Germany, the British Isles and even Mexico.

To provide tempting alternatives to potatoes, we've also included a selection of grain, rice and pasta side-dish recipes. Buckwheat and barley, cracked wheat and cornmeal, pasta and pilaf—these are the tasty treats that will bring international variety to your meals and open the door to a fascinating new world of menu planning.

Cracked-Wheat-and-Parsley Salad

Cracked-Wheat-and-Parsley Salad

(Tabooley)

The colorful appearance and rich, sun-kissed flavor of tabooley *make it a splendid party salad. In Syria and Lebanon, where* tabooley *takes many forms, the salad is traditionally served by Orthodox Christians as a meat substitute during Lent. Cracked wheat (bulgur) can be purchased at large supermarkets and specialty food stores.*

6 servings

¾	cup cracked wheat (bulgur)
1½	cups snipped parsley
3	medium tomatoes, chopped
⅓	cup chopped green onions (with tops)
2	tablespoons snipped fresh mint or 2 teaspoons crushed dried mint
¼	cup olive or vegetable oil
¼	cup lemon juice
1	teaspoon salt
¼	teaspoon pepper

Cover cracked wheat with cold water; let stand 30 minutes. Drain; press out as much water as possible. Place wheat, parsley, tomatoes, green onions and mint in glass or plastic bowl. Mix remaining ingredients; pour over wheat mixture. Toss. Cover and refrigerate at least 1 hour. Garnish with ripe olives if desired.

Note: For a softer texture, cover cracked wheat with boiling water; let stand 1 hour.

French Lettuce Salad
(Salade de Laitue)

Although the French have created many elaborate salads, the most frequently served salad is a mixture of tender greens tossed with a simple dressing of oil, vinegar, salt, mustard and pepper; sugar is never used. Three-star chefs often use walnut oil (available at gourmet shops), prized for its nutty flavor, and may include freshly snipped herbs, such as parsley, thyme or chives.

6 to 8 servings

⅓	cup olive or vegetable oil
2	tablespoons wine vinegar
¼	teaspoon salt
¼	teaspoon dry mustard
⅛	teaspoon pepper
10	cups mixed greens (half Boston, butter or leaf lettuce, half endive or romaine)

Shake all ingredients except greens in tightly covered jar; refrigerate. Shake before serving. Toss with greens.

Bulgur (Cracked Wheat)
Did You Know?

Bulgur wheat, also known as parboiled wheat or wheat pilaf, is one of the basic foods of the Middle East and is often cooked in broth as an accompaniment to chicken or lamb. It is also used in salads with black olives, mint and cumin or other spices, or as an alternate for rice. To produce bulgur, whole wheat is cooked and dried. Part of the bran is removed, and what remains is cracked into coarse, angular fragments. Bulgur kernels retain their shape and chewiness after cooking.

Athenian Salad
(Salata Athenas)

In Greece salad is often served as a first course or as an intermediate course after the soup and before the main dish. Athenian Salad is a fitting accompaniment to almost any Middle Eastern meal.

8 servings

1	medium head lettuce
1	bunch romaine
10	radishes, sliced
1	medium cucumber, sliced
6	green onions (with tops), cut into ½-inch pieces
½	cup olive or vegetable oil
⅓	cup wine vinegar
1	teaspoon salt
1	teaspoon dried oregano leaves
24	Greek or ripe green olives
¼	cup crumbled feta cheese (about 1 ounce)
1	can (2 ounces) rolled anchovies with capers, drained

Tear lettuce and romaine into bite-size pieces. Place lettuce, romaine, radishes, cucumber and green onions in large plastic bag. Close bag tightly and refrigerate. Shake oil, vinegar, salt and oregano in tightly covered jar; refrigerate.

Just before serving, shake dressing. Add dressing and olives to vegetables in bag. Close bag tightly and shake until ingredients are well coated. Pour salad into large bowl; top with cheese and anchovies.

Leaf Lettuce Salad

Few greens are more tender, more buttery or fresher than the sweet leaf lettuce that thrives most abundantly in cool weather. A touch of cream and sugar is typical of this Scandinavian favorite.

3 or 4 servings

1   bunch leaf lettuce
2   green onions (with tops), sliced
¼   cup whipping cream
2   tablespoons lemon juice or cider vinegar
1   tablespoon sugar
⅛   teaspoon salt

Tear lettuce into bite-size pieces (about 4 cups); add green onions. Just before serving, mix remaining ingredients. Pour over lettuce; toss.

Cauliflower-Avocado Salad

This show-stopping salad from Mexico is a conversation piece as well as a palate-pleaser—a whole head of cauliflower is cooked, chilled, spread with an avocado sauce and brought to table whole. To serve, cut cauliflower into wedges at table.

4 to 6 servings

1   medium head cauliflower (about 2 pounds)
    Avocado Dip (page 18)
    Leaf lettuce
½   to 1 cup shredded Monterey Jack cheese

Trim outer leaves from cauliflower; slice off stem end so cauliflower rests evenly when placed upright on a flat surface. Heat 1 inch salted water (½ teaspoon salt to 1 cup water) to boiling. Add cauliflower. Heat to boiling; reduce heat. Cover and cook until tender, 20 to 25 minutes; drain. Cover and refrigerate cauliflower at least 3 hours. Prepare Avocado Dip.

Place cauliflower on lettuce-lined platter. Spread avocado mixture over cauliflower; serve with cheese.

Italian Green Bean Salad

This crisp, fresh salad features snappy green beans—use yellow, too, when in season. Italian Green Bean Salad goes wonderfully well with Ravioli (page 134).

4 to 6 servings

1   pound green beans
    Vinaigrette Dressing (below)
    Lettuce (optional)
2   tomatoes, cut into wedges
1   small onion, sliced
¼   cup grated Parmesan cheese
    Ripe olives

Remove ends from beans. If beans are large, cut French style into lengthwise strips. Heat beans and 1 inch salted water (½ teaspoon salt to 1 cup water) to boiling. Cook uncovered 5 minutes. Cover and cook until tender, whole 10 to 15 minutes, French style 5 to 10 minutes; drain.

Prepare Vinaigrette Dressing. Pour over warm beans and toss. Cover and refrigerate at least 2 hours. Remove beans to lettuce-lined plate with slotted spoon. Add tomatoes and onion. Sprinkle with cheese; garnish with olives.

Vinaigrette Dressing

⅓   cup olive or vegetable oil
2   tablespoons wine vinegar
1   clove garlic, chopped
1   teaspoon salt
½   teaspoon prepared dark mustard
    Dash of pepper

Mix all ingredients.

Clockwise from top: Pickled Beets (page 220), Italian Green Bean Salad (page 204) and Zucchini-and-Avocado Salad (page 209).

Fresh Mushroom Salad
(Sienisalaatti)

This creamy mushroom salad from Finland goes well with roast beef or pork. When fresh dill is available, garnish the salad with several sprigs in the traditional Finnish manner.

4 servings

1	pound mushrooms, sliced
2	tablespoons snipped chives
¼	cup whipping cream or half-and-half
2	teaspoons sugar
½	teaspoon salt
	Dash of pepper

Heat 1 inch salted water (½ teaspoon salt to 1 cup water) to boiling. Add mushrooms. Heat to boiling; reduce heat. Cover and simmer 1 minute. Drain and chill.

Add chives. Mix remaining ingredients. Pour over mushrooms and chives; toss. Serve in lettuce cups if desired.

Cucumbers and Tomatoes in Yogurt
(Raita)

A cool, refreshing salad from northern India, raita is often served as a relish with curried meats. Try it with our Chicken Curry (page 84) or Chicken with Golden Pilaf (page 88).

6 servings

2	medium cucumbers
2	green onions (with tops), chopped
1	teaspoon salt
2	tomatoes, chopped
½	clove garlic, finely chopped
2	tablespoons snipped cilantro or parsley
½	teaspoon ground cumin
⅛	teaspoon pepper
1	cup unflavored yogurt

Cut cucumbers lengthwise into halves. Scoop out seeds; chop cucumbers. Mix cucumbers, green onions and salt; let stand 10 minutes. Add tomatoes. Mix remaining ingredients except yogurt; toss with cucumber mixture. Cover and refrigerate at least 1 hour. Drain thoroughly. Just before serving, fold in yogurt.

Minted Cucumber-and-Yogurt Salad
(Cacik)

During the hot summer months, the Turks often lunch on a light, nutritious salad, rounding out the meal with cheese and bread. At suppertime salads such as cacik *are served "American style" in Turkey—in separate salad plates along with the main dish.*

4 servings

1	cup unflavored yogurt
2	tablespoons finely snipped fresh mint or ½ teaspoon dried mint flakes
1	tablespoon lemon juice
1	clove garlic, finely chopped
	Dash of white pepper
1	medium cucumber, thinly sliced

Mix all ingredients except cucumber; cover and refrigerate. Just before serving, stir in cucumber. Place in serving dish; garnish with additional mint if desired.

Eggplant Salad

Eggplant Salad

(Caponata)

The eggplant is respected throughout Italy, but is considered the prince of vegetables in Sicily, which boasts the world's finest eggplants. This easy salad is often served as part of an antipasto platter or as a dip or spread.

4 to 6 servings

1	medium eggplant (about 1½ pounds)
1	small onion, chopped
2	tablespoons white wine vinegar
1	clove garlic, chopped
½	teaspoon dried oregano leaves
½	teaspoon salt
¼	teaspoon pepper
1	medium tomato, chopped
¼	cup snipped parsley
¼	cup olive or vegetable oil

Cut eggplant into ¾-inch cubes (about 5 cups). Heat small amount salted water (½ teaspoon salt to 1 cup water) to boiling. Add eggplant. Heat to boiling; reduce heat. Cover and cook until tender, about 10 minutes; drain.

Place eggplant and onion in glass or plastic bowl. Mix vinegar, garlic, oregano, salt and pepper; pour over eggplant and onion. Toss. Stir in tomato and parsley. Cover and refrigerate at least 6 hours. Just before serving, stir in oil.

French Potato Salad

The French regarded the potato with suspicion until the late eighteenth century, when the vegetable was praised by the French food scientist Antoine Auguste Parmentier as an excellent food to be used in times of poor harvests. The thrifty French quickly invented hundreds of exciting potato recipes. This salad is a favorite in southern France.

4 to 6 servings

6   medium potatoes (about 2 pounds)
1   clove garlic, cut into halves
¼   teaspoon beef or chicken bouillon
⅓   cup hot water
⅓   cup dry white wine
     Tarragon Dressing (below)
3   tablespoons snipped parsley

Heat 1 inch salted water (½ teaspoon salt to 1 cup water) to boiling. Add potatoes. Heat to boiling; reduce heat. Cover and cook until tender, 30 to 35 minutes. Drain and cool.

Rub 2-quart bowl with garlic; discard garlic. Cut potatoes into ¼-inch slices; place in bowl. Dissolve bouillon in hot water; add wine. Pour over potatoes. Cover and refrigerate, stirring once or twice; drain.

Prepare Tarragon Dressing; gently toss with potatoes. Sprinkle with parsley. Garnish with tomato wedges and sliced cooked luncheon meat if desired.

Tarragon Dressing

3   tablespoons olive or vegetable oil
2   tablespoons tarragon vinegar
2   teaspoons snipped chives
1   teaspoon salt
1   teaspoon dark prepared mustard
½   teaspoon dried tarragon leaves
⅛   teaspoon pepper

Shake all ingredients in tightly covered jar.

Quick Mexican Potato Salad

Because Mexicans like to sprinkle crisp, fresh vegetables over soups and stews, salads are rarely served south of the border. When they are, they often contain both cooked and raw vegetables. This salad makes a bright and nourishing summertime accompaniment to Mexican Fried Chicken (page 87).

6 to 8 servings

3   tablespoons vinegar
⅓   cup olive or vegetable oil
1   teaspoon salt
1   can (16 ounces) potatoes, drained and sliced
1   can (8 ounces) diced carrots, drained
1   can (8 ounces) cut green beans, drained
½   cup sliced pitted ripe olives
3   tablespoons snipped parsley
     Lettuce leaves
1   medium cucumber, sliced
1   small tomato, cut into wedges

Mix vinegar, oil and salt; stir in potatoes, carrots, beans and olives. Cover and refrigerate, stirring occasionally, at least 2 hours.

Just before serving, toss vegetable mixture with parsley; drain. Pour into lettuce-lined bowl. Top with cucumber and tomato.

Sweet Potatoes and Yams

Did You Know?

The true yam is the root of a tropical vine that is grown in Africa, South America and southern Asia, but yams and sweet potatoes native to this country are available most of the year. Sweet potatoes usually have dry yellow flesh; yams are deeper in color, sweeter and more moist than sweet potatoes. When choosing sweet potatoes or yams, color is not important; look for thick, medium-sized potatoes that taper at the ends. Avoid any with signs of decay.

African Sweet Potato Salad

In Africa the true yam is the vegetable of choice for this unusual salad. Sweet potatoes, native to the Western Hemisphere, are substituted for African yams in our recipe.

6 servings

4	medium sweet potatoes (about 1½ pounds)
¼	cup peanut or vegetable oil
2	tablespoons lemon juice
½	teaspoon salt
¼	teaspoon pepper
1	medium green pepper, chopped
1	small onion, chopped
1	stalk celery, chopped
	Parsley

Heat enough salted water to cover potatoes (½ teaspoon salt to 1 cup water) to boiling. Add potatoes. Heat to boiling; reduce heat. Cover and cook until tender, 30 to 35 minutes; drain.

Cool potatoes; slip off skins. Cube potatoes; place in glass or plastic bowl. Mix oil, lemon juice, salt and pepper; pour over potatoes. Cover and refrigerate at least 4 hours. Stir in green pepper, onion and celery. Garnish with parsley.

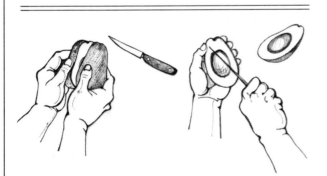

To cut up an avocado, cut it lengthwise around the pit; twist to separate the halves.

To remove the pit, strike it with a sharp knife, then twist gently with knife and lift out. Pare skin.

Zucchini-and-Avocado Salad

(Ensalada de Calabacitas y Aguacates)

Although zucchini as we know it today was developed by the Italians in modern times, the squash flourished in Mexico in prehistoric times and has long been one of Mexico's favorite green vegetables.

4 servings

4	small zucchini* (about 1 pound), cut into ¼-inch slices
8	green onions (with tops), sliced
1	tablespoon vegetable oil
1	medium avocado
1	tablespoon lemon juice
1	small green pepper, coarsely shredded
1	can (4 ounces) chopped green chilies, drained
	Oil-and-Vinegar Dressing (below)
	Salad greens

Cook and stir zucchini and green onions in oil until zucchini is crisp-tender, about 3 minutes. Cover and refrigerate at least 2 hours.

Cut avocado lengthwise into halves; cut halves into ¼-inch slices. Sprinkle with lemon juice. Toss zucchini mixture, avocado, green pepper, chilies and Oil-and-Vinegar Dressing. Serve on salad greens.

Oil-and-Vinegar Dressing

¼	cup vegetable oil
2	tablespoons vinegar
½	teaspoon salt
	Dash of pepper

Shake all ingredients in tightly covered jar; refrigerate. Shake before serving.

* Other summer squash, such as crookneck or straightneck, can be substituted for the zucchini.

Avocado-and-Tomato Salad

Avocado-and-Tomato Salad

(Ensalada de Guacamole)

In this Central American salad, the basic ingredients are the same as those found in the popular Mexican dip called Guacamole *(page 18)—but here the avocados and tomatoes retain their distinctive shapes, and the flavor is enhanced with a smoky hint of bacon!*

4 to 6 servings

6   slices bacon
3   tablespoons vegetable oil
1   tablespoon vinegar
½   teaspoon salt
⅛   teaspoon pepper
3   drops red pepper sauce
2   medium avocados, cubed
2   medium tomatoes, cut into ½-inch pieces
1   small onion, chopped
    Salad greens

Fry bacon until crisp; drain and crumble. Mix oil, vinegar, salt, pepper and red pepper sauce; pour over avocados. Toss. Stir in bacon, tomatoes and onion. Cover and refrigerate about 2 hours. Just before serving, place on salad greens with slotted spoon.

Fully ripened avocados taste the best; they should be soft and yield to gentle pressure. Hard avocados soften in several days at room temperature. To make avocado shells, cut avocado in half lengthwise, twisting gently to separate the halves. To take out the seed, strike a knife directly into the seed and twist to lift it out. To cut slices, place peeled halves cut side down to prevent breaking. Cut them lengthwise or crosswise; then, if you wish, cut the crescent-shaped slices into cubes.

Mexican Fruit Salad

Bright red apple skins provide a pleasing color contrast to the avocados and salad greens in a favorite party salad from Mexico. Raisins, nuts and a chili-flavored dressing provide the memorable texture and flavor.

8 servings

Fruit Dressing (below)
2 avocados, cut into 1-inch pieces
2 stalks celery, thinly sliced
2 apples, cut up
1 banana, sliced
¼ cup raisins
¼ cup chopped walnuts
Lettuce

Prepare Fruit Dressing. Toss with remaining ingredients except lettuce. Spoon onto lettuce-lined plates or into salad bowls.

Fruit Dressing
½ cup vegetable oil
¼ cup lemon juice
2 teaspoons sugar
½ teaspoon salt
⅛ teaspoon dry mustard
Dash of chili powder

Shake all ingredients in tightly covered jar.

Orange Salad with Onion and Olives

Oranges and ripe olives play an important role in North African and Middle Eastern cooking from Casablanca to Istanbul. But this unique Mediterranean salad goes well with European and Latin American foods, too.

4 servings

2 large oranges, pared and thinly sliced
2 cups shredded lettuce
1 large onion, thinly sliced
8 pitted ripe olives, sliced
2 tablespoons olive or vegetable oil
2 tablespoons lemon juice
⅛ teaspoon salt
Dash of ground red pepper

Arrange orange slices on lettuce; top with onion and olive slices. Shake remaining ingredients in tightly covered container; drizzle over salad.

Indonesian Salad with Coconut-Peanut Dressing (Gado-Gado)

The cuisine of Indonesia has been influenced by the culinary traditions of other countries since ancient times—the Chinese, Indians and Arabians all sailed to Indonesia's spice islands in search of new seasonings centuries ago. This traditional salad from Java reflects both foreign influences and native cooking customs.

6 to 8 servings

Coconut-Peanut Dressing (below)
1   cup bean sprouts
1   cup shredded cabbage
4   ounces bean curd, cut into 1-inch pieces
2   tablespoons peanut or vegetable oil
1   cup sliced cooked potatoes
1   cup cooked cut green beans
1   cup cooked sliced carrots
1   medium cucumber, sliced
2   hard-cooked eggs, sliced

Prepare Coconut-Peanut Dressing. Pour enough boiling water over bean sprouts and cabbage to cover; let stand 2 minutes. Drain.

Cook and gently turn bean curd in oil in 10-inch skillet over medium heat until light brown; remove with slotted spoon and drain on paper towels. Cook potatoes in same skillet until light brown; drain.

Arrange bean sprouts, cabbage, bean curd, potatoes and remaining ingredients on platter. Pour dressing over salad.

Coconut-Peanut Dressing

½   cup flaked coconut
1   cup hot water
1   small onion, chopped
1   clove garlic, finely chopped
1½   teaspoons peanut oil or Ghee (page 218)
⅔   cup peanut butter
½   cup water
1   tablespoon sugar
½   teaspoon salt
¼   to ½ teaspoon chili powder
⅛   teaspoon ground ginger

Place coconut in blender container; add 1 cup water. Cover and blend on high speed about 30 seconds.

Cook and stir onion and garlic in oil in 2-quart saucepan until onion is tender, about 5 minutes. Stir in coconut and remaining ingredients. Heat to boiling, stirring constantly; reduce heat. Simmer uncovered, stirring occasionally, until slightly thickened, about 3 minutes. Serve warm.

Green Banana Salad

Green bananas are used as vegetables throughout Latin America. In this Caribbean recipe, they are cooked and tossed with vegetables to make a truly unique salad—and a unique way to use green bananas. Plantains (members of the banana family) are often used interchangeably with green bananas. Both may be difficult to peel. If necessary, make shallow lengthwise cuts along the natural ridges of the fruit, and pull off the skin in sections.

8 servings

3   green (unripe) bananas, peeled
2   cups water
1   teaspoon salt
2   medium carrots, shredded
1   small cucumber, sliced
1   medium tomato, chopped
1   avocado, cubed
1   stalk celery, sliced
    Vinaigrette Dressing (page 204)

Heat bananas, water and salt to boiling; reduce heat. Cover and simmer until bananas are tender, about 5 minutes. Drain and cool.

Cut bananas crosswise into ½-inch slices. Toss bananas and remaining ingredients with Vinaigrette Dressing.

Green Banana Salad

Christmas Eve Salad

Christmas Eve Salad

(Ensalada de Noche Buena)

Mexico's lavish Christmas Eve Salad is traditionally served as a beginning course at midnight supper on Christmas Eve—often as a prelude to a roast turkey or Turkey Mole (page 75). It can also serve as a delightful party salad or be served with the main course.

8 to 10 servings

2   medium oranges, pared and sectioned
2   bananas, sliced

1   can (8¼ ounces) sliced beets, drained (reserve liquid)
1   can (8 ounces) chunk pineapple in juice, drained (reserve juice)
½   jicama, pared and sliced, or 1 can (8 ounces) water chestnuts, drained and sliced
2   tablespoons lemon juice
2   tablespoons sugar
½   teaspoon salt
3   cups shredded lettuce
1   lime, cut into wedges
¼   cup chopped peanuts
⅓   cup pomegranate seeds or sliced radishes
1   tablespoon anise seed
1   tablespoon sugar

Place oranges, bananas, beets, pineapple and jimaca in bowl. Mix reserved beet liquid and pineapple juice, the lemon juice, 2 tablespoons sugar and the salt; pour over fruit. Let stand 10 minutes; drain.

Arrange fruit on shredded lettuce. Garnish with lime, peanuts and pomegranate seeds. Mix anise seed and 1 tablespoon sugar; sprinkle over salad.

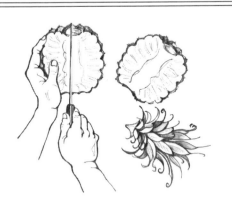

Twist top from pineapple; cut pineapple into quarters.

Holding pineapple securely, cut fruit from rind.

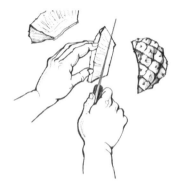

Cut off pineapple core and remove "eyes." Slice lengthwise; cut into chunks.

Jicama

Did You Know?

Jicama is the sweet, watery root of a tall-climbing Mexican vine, and is used by Mexican families as the potato is in the United States. This tuber looks somewhat like a turnip but has a flavor like a water chestnut—delicious cooked or eaten raw in salads. Choose as you would a potato, but keep in mind the smaller ones are more tender.

Pineapple Salad

The cooking of Thailand began to gain many fans in both France and the United States in the early 1970's; today Thai restaurants and food buffs can be found from Los Angeles to Monte Carlo. This unusual fruit salad, tossed with a soy sauce dressing, provides a pleasing accent to hearty oriental foods.

6 servings

⅓ cup olive or vegetable oil
2 tablespoons lemon juice
1 tablespoon soy sauce
1 to 2 teaspoons packed brown sugar
1 small pineapple
1 tart red apple, diced
3 green onions (with tops), sliced
1 small bunch romaine, shredded

Shake oil, lemon juice, soy sauce and brown sugar in tightly covered jar. Twist top from pineapple; cut pineapple into fourths. Cut fruit from rind; remove core and any "eyes." Slice each fourth lengthwise; cut crosswise into chunks.

Toss pineapple chunks, apple and green onions with dressing. Place romaine in shallow bowl; mound fruit mixture in center.

Fruit-and-Cabbage Salad

Fruit-and-Cabbage Salad

(Kål- och Äppelsallad)

Coleslaw will never seem the same after you have tried this delicious Scandinavian cabbage salad graced with delectable fruits and a creamy dressing.

6 servings

2   oranges, pared and sectioned
2   apples, chopped
2   cups shredded cabbage (about ¼ medium head)
1   cup seedless green grapes
½   cup whipping cream
1   tablespoon sugar
1   tablespon lemon juice
¼   teaspoon salt
½   cup mayonnaise or salad dressing

Place oranges, apples, cabbage and grapes in bowl. Beat whipping cream in chilled bowl until stiff. Fold whipped cream, sugar, lemon juice and salt into mayonnaise. Stir into fruit mixture.

Prosciutto-Stuffed Artichokes

(Carciofi Ripieni con Prosciutto)

Fresh whole artichokes make a sumptuous lower-calorie side dish with nearly any entrée, but are more easily managed when served as a separate course. Artichokes take time to eat and require plates or bowls for disposing of leaves. In this recipe from Italy the artichokes are stuffed with a ham-and-bread-crumb mixture and braised in wine and oil. The pan juices can be used as a dip for the artichoke leaves.

To eat stuffed artichokes, pluck leaves off one at a time. Dip stem end of leaf into sauce; draw between the teeth, scraping off the meaty portion. Discard leaf on plate. Eat the stuffing and the artichoke bottom with fork and knife when you get to them; there is no need to remove choke in this recipe—this is done before cooking.

4 servings

4	artichokes
1	quart water
1	tablespoon lemon juice
¼	pound prosciutto or fully cooked smoked ham, finely chopped
¼	cup dry bread crumbs
1	small onion, finely chopped
1	clove garlic, finely chopped
2	tablespoons snipped parsley
¼	teaspoon pepper
2	cups dry white wine
2	tablespoons olive or vegetable oil

Remove any discolored leaves and the small leaves at base of artichoke; trim stem even with base of artichoke. Cutting straight across, slice 1 inch off top; discard top. Snip off points of remaining leaves with scissors. Rinse artichokes under cold water. Mix 1 quart water and the lemon juice; invert artichoke in mixture to prevent discoloration.

Mix prosciutto, bread crumbs, onion, garlic, parsley and pepper. Spread artichoke leaves open; dig out the fuzzy purple choke of each artichoke with the point of a knife or a pointed spoon. Discard choke. Spoon prosciutto mixture into center of each artichoke. Place artichokes upright in Dutch oven. Pour wine over artichokes; drizzle with oil. Heat to boiling; reduce heat. Cover and simmer until bottoms of artichokes are tender when pierced with a knife, about 1 hour. Spoon liquid over each artichoke before serving.

Asparagus with Gruyère

(Asperges à la Gruyère)

True Gruyère cheese is made only in the Gruyère Valley of Switzerland, but there are many imitators. The cheese is similar to Emmenthaler (the familiar supermarket "Swiss") but has smaller holes and is sharper in flavor. Remember this recipe when planning an energy-efficient meal—bake the asparagus in the oven along with the other foods; the full fresh garden flavor of the asparagus is retained.

6 servings

1½	pounds asparagus*
½	teaspoon salt
¼	cup margarine or butter
½	cup grated Gruyère or Parmesan cheese

Break off tough ends of asparagus as far down as stalks snap easily. Wash asparagus. Arrange in single layer in ungreased oblong baking dish, 11 x 7 x 1½ inches. Sprinkle with salt. Cover with aluminum foil and cook in 350° oven until tender, about 25 minutes.

Heat margarine over low heat until light brown. Drizzle over asparagus; sprinkle with cheese. Place in oven just until cheese softens, 5 to 8 minutes.

* 2 packages (10 ounces each) frozen asparagus spears can be substituted for the fresh asparagus. Rinse asparagus under running cold water to separate; drain. Cover and cook in oven about 35 minutes.

Savory Green Beans with Coconut

(Same ki Bhaji)

Crisp, quickly cooked green beans are favored in many parts of the world, but in India green beans—like many fresh vegetables—are slowly simmered with spices until tender. Coconut adds character to this spicy vegetable dish, often served with curries.

4 or 5 servings

¼	cup Ghee (below)
½	cup flaked coconut
½	cup water
1½	pounds green beans
1	medium onion, sliced
1	teaspoon ground coriander
½	teaspoon ground turmeric
½	teaspoon ground ginger
1½	teaspoons salt

Prepare Ghee. Place coconut and water in blender container. Cover and blend on high speed until coconut is finely chopped, about 10 seconds. Cut beans lengthwise into halves; cut halves lengthwise into halves.

Cook and stir onion, coriander, turmeric and ginger in Ghee in 10-inch skillet over medium heat until onion is coated. Stir coconut, beans and salt into onion. Cover and cook over medium heat, stirring occasionally, until beans are tender, 20 to 30 minutes.

Ghee

Cut 1 pound unsalted butter into pieces. Heat over low heat until melted. Increase heat to medium; heat to boiling. Immediately remove from heat and stir gently.

Return to heat; slowly heat to simmering. Simmer uncovered until butter separates into transparent substance on top and milk solids on bottom, 30 to 40 minutes. Remove from heat; let stand 5 minutes. Strain through cheesecloth into container. Cover and refrigerate no longer than 2 months.

Green Beans in Tomato Sauce

Green beans with tomatoes and herbs are a popular vegetable combination in Portugal and in the Basque region of northern Spain, where they are often served with fried eggs and country sausages.

6 servings

1	medium onion, chopped
1	clove garlic, chopped
2	tablespoons olive or vegetable oil
1½	pounds green beans, cut into 3-inch pieces (about 5 cups)
3	medium tomatoes, chopped
¼	cup snipped parsley
1	teaspoon sugar
1	teaspoon salt
½	teaspoon dried basil leaves
⅛	teaspoon pepper
	Grated Parmesan cheese

Cook and stir onion and garlic in oil in 3-quart saucepan until onion is tender. Add remaining ingredients except cheese. Cover and simmer over low heat until beans are tender, 15 to 20 minutes. Sprinkle with cheese.

Ghee

Did You Know?

Ghee, sometimes called Indian butter oil, results from cooking and straining or skimming butter, and is somewhat similar to clarified butter. In India, spices are sometimes cooked in ghee before other ingredients are added, and the skimmings from ghee can be used as well for flavoring vegetables. Ghee, which is often stored in India without refrigerating, is also used in some desserts.

Green Beans Oregano

Lemon juice and oregano, traditional Greek flavorings, perk up this straightforward recipe. Try it with our Baked Macaroni with Beef and Cheese (page 140).

4 servings

1   pound green beans
2   tablespoons olive or vegetable oil
1   tablespoon lemon juice
½   teaspoon salt
¼   teaspoon dried oregano leaves

Remove ends from beans. Leave beans whole or cut crosswise into 1-inch pieces. Heat beans and 1 inch salted water (½ teaspoon salt to 1 cup water) to boiling. Cook uncovered 5 minutes. Cover and cook until tender, 10 to 15 minutes; drain. Mix remaining ingredients; pour over beans.

Stir-Fried Bean Sprouts with Mushrooms

Dried black mushrooms imported from China are available at oriental groceries and large supermarkets; they have a firm texture and earthy flavor much prized by Chinese food buffs. It's easy to raise your own bean sprouts—instructions appear on page 198.

4 servings

6   to 8 medium dried black mushrooms
¾   pound bean sprouts (about 3½ cups)
2   tablespoons vegetable oil
1   clove garlic, finely chopped
1   teaspoon finely chopped ginger root
½   cup water
1   tablespoon cold water
1   tablespoon soy sauce
2   teaspoons cornstarch
2   green onions (with tops), cut into 1-inch pieces

Soak mushrooms in warm water until soft, about 30 minutes; drain. Remove and discard stems; slice caps. Rinse bean sprouts in cold water; drain.

Heat oil in wok or skillet until hot. Add mushrooms, bean sprouts, garlic and ginger root; stir-fry 2 minutes. Stir in ½ cup water; heat to boiling. Mix 1 tablespoon water, the soy sauce and cornstarch; stir into vegetable mixture. Cook and stir until thickened, about 20 seconds. Garnish with green onions.

Beets in Orange Sauce

Beets and oranges are used in combination in both Finland and the Soviet Union. In this Finnish recipe, the tangy orange sauce accents the flavor of the beets and highlights the rich beet color.

4 servings

5   medium beets (about 1¼ pounds)
6   cups water
1   teaspoon salt
1   tablespoon packed brown sugar
2   teaspoons cornstarch
½   teaspoon salt
     Dash of pepper
¾   cup orange juice
2   teaspoons vinegar

Cut off all but 2 inches of beet tops. Leave beets whole with root ends attached. Heat water and 1 teaspoon salt to boiling in 3-quart saucepan. Add beets. Heat to boiling; reduce heat. Cover and cook until tender, 35 to 45 minutes; drain. Run cold water over beets; slip off skins and remove root ends. Cut beets into slices.

Mix brown sugar, cornstarch, ½ teaspoon salt and the pepper in 2-quart saucepan. Stir orange juice gradually into cornstarch mixture; stir in vinegar. Cook, stirring constantly, until mixture thickens and boils. Boil and stir 1 minute. Stir in beets; heat until hot.

Pickled Beets
(Inkokta Rödbetor)

The brilliant color of sliced beets pickled in a spicy sweet-sour sauce lights up simple family meals and holiday smorgasbords throughout the Scandinavian countries. Be sure to cook beets in their skins for ease in peeling.

3½ cups
___

5   medium beets (about 1¼ pounds)
6   cups water
1   tablespoon vinegar
1   teaspoon salt
1   small onion, sliced
½   cup vinegar
⅓   cup sugar
⅓   cup water
1   teaspoon salt
¼   teaspoon ground cloves
⅛   teaspoon pepper

Cut off all but 2 inches of beet tops. Leave beets whole with root ends attached. Heat 6 cups water, 1 tablespoon vinegar and 1 teaspoon salt to boiling. Add beets. Heat to boiling; reduce heat. Cover and cook until tender, 35 to 45 minutes; drain.

Run cold water over beets; slip off skins and remove root ends. Cut beets into slices. Place beets and onion in glass or plastic bowl. Heat remaining ingredients to boiling; reduce heat. Simmer uncovered 2 minutes. Pour over beets and onion. Cover and refrigerate, spooning marinade over beets occasionally, at least 12 hours.

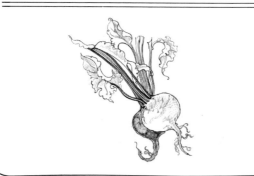

Bok Choy with Bean Curd

This unusual side dish from China serves as a good protein supplement to meatless main dishes as well as a conversation piece. Bean curd, bok choy and oyster sauce are available at oriental groceries, natural food stores and in the Chinese produce sections of many large supermarkets.

6 to 8 servings
___

1   pound bean curd
4   medium stalks bok choy
4   green onions (with tops)
¼   cup vegetable oil
1   can (4 ounces) button mushrooms, drained (reserve liquid)
3   tablespoons oyster sauce
½   teaspoon instant chicken bouillon
1   tablespoon cornstarch
1   tablespoon cold water

Cut bean curd into ¾-inch cubes; drain thoroughly. Cut bok choy (with leaves) diagonally into ¼-inch slices. Cut green onions into 2-inch pieces.

Heat 2 tablespoons of the oil in wok or 10-inch skillet over medium-high heat until hot. Cook bean curd, stirring carefully, 3 to 5 minutes. Remove bean curd. Add remaining oil and the bok choy to wok; stir-fry over medium-high heat 2 minutes. Add mushrooms.

Add enough water to reserved liquid to measure ½ cup. Stir reserved liquid, the oyster sauce and bouillon into vegetables; heat to boiling. Mix cornstarch and water; stir into vegetable mixture. Cook and stir until thickened, about 1 minute. Stir in bean curd and green onions; heat until hot.

Stir-Fried Broccoli and Carrots

Stir-Fried Broccoli and Carrots

Broccoli has been popular in Italy since the days of the Roman Empire, but was slow to catch on in other parts of the world. The Chinese, however, were quick to admire the bright green color, which is heightened when the flowerets are quickly stir-fried.

4 servings

2	tablespoons vegetable oil
2	thin slices ginger root, finely chopped
1	clove garlic, finely chopped
1½	cups small broccoli flowerets
1	cup thinly sliced carrots
1	small onion, sliced and separated into rings
¾	cup chicken broth
1	teaspoon salt
1	tablespoon cornstarch
1	tablespoon cold water
1	can (8½ ounces) water chestnuts, drained and thinly sliced
1	cup sliced mushrooms
2	tablespoons oyster sauce

Heat oil in wok or 12-inch skillet until hot. Add ginger root and garlic; stir-fry until light brown, 1 minute. Add broccoli, carrots and onion; stir-fry 1 minute. Add chicken broth and salt; cover and cook until carrots are crisp-tender, about 3 minutes.

Mix cornstarch and water; stir into vegetable mixture. Cook and stir until thickened, about 10 seconds. Add water chestnuts, mushrooms and oyster sauce; cook and stir 30 seconds.

Ginger Root

Did You Know?

Fresh ginger root, native to China and India and now grown throughout the world, can be sliced, shredded, grated, finely chopped or crushed. To crush ginger root, place a slice between two pieces of waxed paper and crush with a wooden mallet. In any form, ginger root adds zest to vegetables and salads, and is also an excellent tenderizer when added to meat marinades. The new sprouts on the sides of the ginger root are more delicately flavored than the root itself, and can be very finely grated and used in cooking.

Once purchased, ginger root can be grown at home: Just bury a fresh ginger root below the surface in moist all-purpose potting soil. Set it in a closet to sprout. Then place it in a sunny window, keeping the soil evenly moist. Soon it will develop tall, pointed greenery and the root itself will grow. In a few months you will have a pot of fresh ginger to use in cooking and in starting new pots of ginger!

Broccoli with Oil and Lemon

The Italians season many green vegetables with a simple dressing of oil and lemon juice— the lemon juice perks up the broccoli flavor.

6 servings

1½   pounds broccoli
3   tablespoons olive or vegetable oil
2   tablespoons lemon juice
¼   teaspoon salt
⅛   teaspoon pepper

If broccoli stems are thicker than 1 inch, make lengthwise gashes in each stem. Heat 1 inch salted water (½ teaspoon salt to 1 cup water) to boiling. Add broccoli. Heat to boiling; reduce heat. Cover and cook just until stems are tender, 12 to 15 minutes; drain. Mix remaining ingredients; pour over broccoli. Serve hot or cold.

Brussels Sprouts Parmigiana

Brussels sprouts were developed in Belgium in the sixteenth century, but did not gain a following in France or Italy until the nineteenth century. They remained a luxury item until frozen food processors discovered their adaptability to freezer packaging. Serve these Italian-style sprouts with robust Italian dishes—or delicate French ones.

6 servings

1½   pounds Brussels sprouts*
1   small onion, chopped
¼   cup margarine or butter
¼   cup grated Parmesan cheese

Heat 1 inch salted water (½ teaspoon salt to 1 cup water) to boiling. Add Brussels sprouts. Heat to boiling; reduce heat. Cover and cook until tender, 8 to 10 minutes; drain. Cook and stir onion in margarine until tender. Pour over Brussels sprouts; sprinkle with cheese.

* 2 packages (8 ounces each) frozen Brussels sprouts can be substituted for the fresh Brussels sprouts.

Mixed Vegetable Casserole

Mixed Vegetable Casserole

(Grönsaksgratin)

This delightful recipe from Scandinavia makes a colorful addition to a party menu and can be prepared several hours in advance. Add sauce and place under broiler just before serving.

6 servings

3	medium carrots, sliced (about 1½ cups)
8	ounces green beans, cut into 1-inch pieces
½	small head cauliflower, separated into flowerets (about 2 cups)
1	small onion, sliced
2	tablespoons margarine or butter
2	tablespoons flour
½	teaspoon salt
⅛	teaspoon pepper
½	cup whipping cream
¼	cup grated Parmesan cheese

Heat 1 inch salted water (½ teaspoon salt to 1 cup water) to boiling. Add carrots, beans, cauliflower and onion. Heat to boiling; reduce heat. Cover and simmer until tender, 12 to 15 minutes. Drain vegetables, reserving liquid. Place vegetables in ungreased oblong baking dish, 11 x 7 x 1½ inches, or square baking dish, 8 x 8 x 2 inches.

Heat margarine over low heat until melted. Blend in flour, salt and pepper. Cook over low heat, stirring constantly, until mixture is smooth and bubbly; remove from heat.

Stir in 1 cup of the reserved liquid and the whipping cream. Heat to boiling, stirring constantly. Boil and stir 1 minute; remove from heat. Pour sauce over vegetables; sprinkle with cheese.

Set oven control to broil and/or 550°. Broil until top is light brown and bubbly, 3 to 5 minutes.

Red Cabbage with Apples

Tart boiled red cabbage and apples provide a refreshing change of pace when served with rich dishes such as roast pork or duck. In Germany and Denmark, this side dish is often served with roast goose.

6 servings

2	tart red apples, sliced
3	tablespoons margarine or butter
1	medium head red cabbage, coarsely shredded (about 8 cups)
¼	cup water
¼	cup red wine vinegar
2	tablespoons sugar
1	teaspoon salt
¼	teaspoon pepper

Cook and stir apples in margarine in Dutch oven over medium heat 5 minutes. Stir in remaining ingredients. Heat to boiling; reduce heat. Cover and simmer until cabbage is tender, 35 to 40 minutes.

Korean Vegetable Pickle (Kimchee)

The Koreans serve kimchee *as a condiment with meals from sunrise to sunset—it is a "must" when presenting Korea's national dish,* Bul-Ko-Kee *(page 120).* Kimchee *also goes well with Japanese meat dishes such as teriyaki.*

3 or 4 servings

1	cup ¼-inch slices carrot
1	cup 1-inch pieces celery cabbage
1	cup cauliflowerets
2	teaspoons salt
3	green onions (with tops), finely chopped
1	thin slice ginger root, finely chopped
2	teaspoons salt
½	teaspoon garlic salt
¼	teaspoon crushed red peppers

Sprinkle carrot, celery cabbage and cauliflowerets with 2 teaspoons salt; toss. Let stand 20 minutes; rinse with cold water and drain. Toss drained vegetables with remaining ingredients. Cover tightly and refrigerate at least 48 hours but no longer than 4 days.

Honeyed Carrots

This recipe may have originated in ancient Egypt, where honey was the basic sweetener. Today Honeyed Carrots are served throughout the Middle East.

6 servings

12	medium carrots (about 1½ pounds), sliced
⅓	cup honey
2	tablespoons vegetable oil
1	teaspoon lemon juice
½	teaspoon salt

Heat 1 inch salted water (½ teaspoon salt to 1 cup water) to boiling. Add carrots. Heat to boiling; reduce heat. Cover and cook until tender, 12 to 15 minutes; drain.

Cook and stir remaining ingredients in 10-inch skillet until bubbly; add carrots. Cook uncovered over low heat, stirring occasionally, until carrots are glazed, 2 to 3 minutes.

Glazed Carrots (Carottes Glacées)

The French use Glazed Carrots liberally as an attractive accompaniment to roasts. When planning an important party, look for young bright orange carrots.

4 to 6 servings

8	medium carrots (about 1¼ pounds)
¾	cup water
2	tablespoons margarine or butter
1	tablespoon sugar
½	teaspoon instant beef bouillon
	Dash of pepper
	Snipped parsley

Cut carrots into 2-inch pieces. Heat carrots and remaining ingredients except parsley to boiling; reduce heat. Cover and simmer until carrots are tender, about 25 minutes. Remove carrots and boil rapidly to reduce liquid to glaze consistency. Add carrots; turn to coat evenly with glaze. Sprinkle with parsley.

Celery Cabbage

Did You Know?

Celery cabbage, also known as Chinese cabbage, is often used for salads but is also popular stir-fried or steamed. A distant relative of the cabbage family, it has some of the characteristics of both celery and romaine. Bok choy, also known as Chinese chard, resembles celery cabbage and chard. The leaves are sometimes prepared like spinach and the stems are often used in chow mein or chop suey. When purchasing celery cabbage or bok choy, look for crisp, green plants that are free from blemishes.

Deep-Fried Cauliflower

"French fries" are but one of many deep-fried vegetables in international cooking. These batter-dipped cauliflowerets from Portugal go especially well with baked fish dishes, such as Salt Cod in Tomato Sauce (page 47).

4 to 6 servings

1   medium head cauliflower (about 2 pounds), separated into flowerets
     Vegetable oil
2   eggs, beaten
½   teaspoon salt
⅛   teaspoon pepper
¾   cup dry bread crumbs
½   teaspoon paprika

Heat 1 inch salted water (½ teaspoon salt to 1 cup water) to boiling. Add cauliflower. Heat to boiling; reduce heat. Cover and cook 10 minutes. Drain and cool.

Heat oil (1 to 1½ inches) to 360°. Mix eggs, salt and pepper. Mix bread crumbs and paprika. Dip cauliflower into egg mixture; coat with bread crumb mixture.

Fry 8 to 10 flowerets at a time in hot oil, turning occasionally, until golden brown, about 2 minutes. Drain on paper towels. Keep warm in 200° oven 10 to 15 minutes.

Storing Vegetables

Did You Know?

Most vegetables will keep best if stored in the refrigerator either in the crisper or in plastic bags or plastic containers. The exceptions are potatoes, sweet potatoes, mature onions, hard-shelled squash and rutabagas. Potatoes should be stored in a cool, dry place with a temperature of 45 to 50°F. If stored at room temperature, they should be used within a week. Mature onions should be stored in a dry, well-ventilated place. Sweet potatoes, hard-shelled squash and rutabagas should be stored at room temperature. Unripe tomatoes should be kept at room temperature until ripe, then stored uncovered in the refrigerator.

Celery Milan Style

Crisp-tender celery sticks, braised in bouillon, make an elegant, low-cost and low-calorie side dish suitable for important dinners or casual get-togethers.

4 to 6 servings

6   large stalks celery
¾   cup water
½   teaspoon instant chicken bouillon
2   tablespoons margarine or butter
¼   cup grated Parmesan cheese
     Snipped parsley

Cut celery into 2-inch pieces (about 4 cups). Heat celery, water and bouillon to boiling; reduce heat. Cover and cook until crisp-tender, about 15 minutes; drain, Dot with margarine; cover and let stand until margarine is melted. Sprinkle with grated cheese and parsley.

Clockwise from top: Mexican Corn and Zucchini (page 227), Glazed Carrots (page 224) and Celery Milan Style (page 225).

Mexican Corn Pudding

Vanilla and raisins add a tempting, slightly sweet flavor to corn pudding, which the Mexicans often serve as a second course. You needn't wait for a Mexican evening to try this recipe—it goes well with chili con carne or an American-style meat loaf.

8 servings

1   can (14½ ounces) evaporated milk
¼   cup all-purpose flour
2   cans (about 16 ounces each) cream-style corn
4   eggs, slightly beaten
½   cup sugar
¼   cup raisins
1   teaspoon baking soda
1   teaspoon salt
1   teaspoon vanilla

Shake ½ cup of the milk and the flour in tightly covered container. Mix milk mixture, remaining milk and the remaining ingredients. Pour into greased square pan, 9 x 9 x 2 inches. Cook uncovered in 350° oven until knife inserted halfway between center and edge comes out clean, about 1 hour.

Mexican Corn and Zucchini

This hearty, colorful casserole is at its best when made with fresh sweet corn.

6 servings

3   ears corn*
1   medium onion, chopped
1   clove garlic, chopped
2   tablespoons bacon fat, margarine or butter
3   medium tomatoes, chopped
3   medium zucchini, cut into ¼-inch slices
1   teaspoon salt
1   teaspoon sugar
¼   teaspoon ground cumin
¼   teaspoon pepper

Cut corn from cobs (about 1½ cups). Cook and stir onion and garlic in bacon fat in 10-inch skillet until onion is tender. Stir in corn and remaining ingredients. Heat to boiling; reduce heat. Cover and simmer until vegetables are tender, 10 to 15 minutes.

* 1 can (about 16 ounces) whole-kernel corn, drained, can be substituted for the fresh corn.

Corn-Okra-Tomato Medley

Okra played a prominent role in the cooking of ancient Egypt and has continued to be a favorite African vegetable throughout the centuries. It was introduced to the American South and the Caribbean by African slaves, and quickly became a hallmark of the Creole cooking of both the Caribbean and Louisiana. Try this Caribbean medley with Jamaican Codfish Fritters (page 45).

8 servings

6   ears corn*
2   cups cut-up okra† (about 1 pound)
⅓   cup margarine or butter
2   tablespoons margarine or butter
3   medium tomatoes, chopped
1   tablespoon sugar
1½   teaspoons salt
¼   teaspoon pepper

Cut corn from cobs (about 4 cups). Cook and stir okra in ⅓ cup margarine in 12-inch skillet over medium heat until tender, about 7 minutes. Add corn and 2 tablespoons margarine. Cook uncovered until tender, 10 to 12 minutes.

Stir in remaining ingredients. Cook uncovered until tomatoes are hot, about 3 minutes.

* 2 cans (about 16 ounces each) whole-kernel corn, drained, can be substituted for the fresh corn.
† 1 package (10 ounces) frozen okra can be substituted for the fresh okra. Rinse under running cold water to separate; cut crosswise into slices. Cook as directed above.

Cucumber-and-Tomato Skillet

Cucumber-and-Tomato Skillet

When cucumbers are in season, try cooking them—as the Germans do. In our recipe the cucumbers are cooked a minimum of time to retain the crisp texture and fresh garden flavor.

6 to 8 servings

2	medium cucumbers, cut into 1-inch pieces
1	medium onion, sliced and separated into rings
2	tablespoons margarine or butter
4	medium tomatoes, cut into wedges
½	teaspoon salt
	Dash of pepper
1	tablespoon snipped fresh dill or 1 teaspoon dried dillweed

Cook and stir cucumbers and onion in margarine in 12-inch skillet until cucumbers are crisp-tender, about 5 minutes. Stir in tomatoes; sprinkle with salt and pepper. Cook, stirring occasionally, just until tomatoes are heated through. Sprinkle with dill.

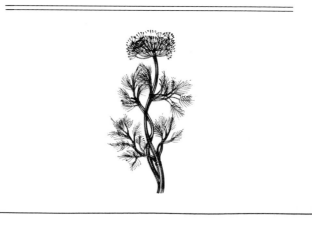

Danish Pickled Cucumbers

(Syltede Agurker)

Quick cucumber pickles, with their crisp texture and cool, pungent flavor, can be added to any menu featuring northern European food. In Denmark they are indispensable in making the famous Danish open-faced sandwiches. In Germany they are often served as snacks or appetizers, with buttered pumpernickel bread.

6 servings

2	medium cucumbers, thinly sliced
⅓	cup cider vinegar
⅓	cup water
2	tablespoons sugar
½	teaspoon salt
⅛	teaspoon pepper
	Snipped dill or parsley

Place cucumbers in glass or plastic bowl. Mix vinegar, water, sugar, salt and pepper; pour over cucumbers. Cover and refrigerate, stirring occasionally, at least 3 hours. Drain; sprinkle with dill.

Eggplant with Tomatoes

Eggplant has been a mainstay of Mediterranean cooking for many centuries. Cooked with tomatoes, it forms a dish that is a favorite in India, China, southern Europe and Latin America.

6 servings

6	slices bacon, cut into 1-inch pieces
1	medium onion, sliced
1	clove garlic, chopped
2	medium tomatoes, chopped
1	small eggplant (about 1 pound), cut into 1-inch cubes
½	teaspoon salt
⅛	teaspoon crushed red peppers

Fry bacon in 10-inch skillet until crisp; drain on paper towels. Cook and stir onion and garlic in bacon fat until onion is tender. Drain fat from skillet.

Add tomatoes, eggplant, salt and red peppers to onion. Cover and simmer until eggplant is tender, about 15 minutes. Top with bacon.

Eggplants

Did You Know?

The eggplant is believed to have been first used as a vegetable in India. The name is said to have originated from the first variety known to Europeans, which resembled an egg. Eggplants are grown in several shapes, sizes and colors. White eggplants are widely used in Europe, while the purple variety is common in this country. The eggplant skin is usually tender and flavorful, so it is not necessary to pare. Eggplant is available year round but is most plentiful in August and September. Look for eggplant that is firm, heavy, uniform in color and about 3 to 6 inches in diameter. Store in a cool place.

Eggplant with Yogurt Sauce

Eggplant with Yogurt Sauce

(Bonjan Borani)

In Afghanistan, bonjan borani *might be served hot or cold, with chicken or lamb—and sometimes as a vegetarian main dish accompanied by cheese and bread.*

6 servings

1	medium onion, sliced
¼	cup olive or vegetable oil
1	medium eggplant (about 1½ pounds), cut into ½-inch slices
1	cup unflavored yogurt
3	tablespoons snipped fresh mint or 1½ teaspoons crushed dried mint
2	cloves garlic, finely chopped
½	teaspoon salt
	Dash of pepper
	Paprika

Cook and stir onion in oil in 12-inch skillet until tender; remove onion. Cook half the eggplant over medium-high heat, turning once, until tender and golden brown, about 10 minutes. Repeat with remaining eggplant. (Add more oil if necessary.)

Arrange onion and eggplant slices on ovenproof platter or in ungreased oblong baking dish, 11 x 7 x 1½ inches. Mix remaining ingredients except paprika; pour over eggplant. Sprinkle with paprika. Heat in 350° oven until hot and bubbly, 10 to 15 minutes.

Deep-Fried Mushrooms

A crisp complement to a dinner party menu, these tasty tidbits from Germany and Austria can also be served as tempting hot appetizers at walkabout parties. Our recipe yields 8 to 10 appetizer servings.

4 servings

1	pound medium mushrooms
	Vegetable oil
½	cup all-purpose flour
⅓	cup milk
1	egg
1	teaspoon baking powder
½	teaspoon salt

Trim stem ends of mushrooms ¼ inch below caps. If mushrooms are large, cut into halves. Heat oil (1 inch) to 360°. Beat remaining ingredients with hand beater until smooth. (Add 1 to 3 tablespoons milk if necessary.)

Dip mushrooms into batter, letting excess batter drip into bowl. Fry mushrooms, a few at a time, until golden brown, turning once, about 2 minutes. Drain on paper towels.

Mushrooms

Did You Know?

Mushrooms do not "ripen" the way fruits or vegetables do, and size is no indication of maturity. They come in varied sizes, with creamy white to light brown caps, which are closed around the stems. If slightly open, the "gills" should be pink or tan. Gently wash them or rinse with cool water, and wipe with fingers or a damp paper towel. For best results, do not wash mushrooms until you are ready to use them. All mushrooms will darken eventually; they will stay fresh longer at refrigerator temperature.

Mushrooms with Sour Cream

Another mushroom specialty from Poland, this pleasant and easy dish can be served with the main course or presented on toast rounds or in miniature pastry shells as hot appetizers.

4 servings

8	ounces mushrooms, sliced
2	tablespoons margarine or butter
1	teaspoon flour
½	cup dairy sour cream
¼	teaspoon salt
	Dash of pepper
	Snipped dill or parsley

Cook and stir mushrooms in margarine 3 minutes. Stir in flour; cook and stir 1 minute. Stir in sour cream, salt and pepper. Heat, stirring occasionally, just until hot. Sprinkle with dill.

Golden Pan-Fried Mushrooms

Delicious crumb-coated mushrooms from Poland go well with roast chicken or beef. If the mushrooms are large, slice into halves or fourths.

4 servings

1	pound small mushrooms
1	egg, beaten
½	cup dry bread crumbs
1	medium onion, chopped
⅓	cup margarine or butter

Dip mushrooms into egg; coat with bread crumbs. Cook mushrooms and onion in margarine in 12-inch skillet, turning occasionally, until mushrooms are tender and golden brown, 7 to 8 minutes.

Mushrooms with Tomatoes and Peas

Mushrooms with Tomatoes and Peas

This spicy, colorful medley from India can be served as a side dish with many Western roasts and stews, and makes an especially compatible accompaniment to our Roast Chicken with Spiced Yogurt (page 76).

6 servings

1	medium onion, sliced
½	to 1 teaspoon ground turmeric
¼	teaspoon ground ginger
1	tablespoon Ghee (page 218) or vegetable oil
1	package (10 ounces) frozen green peas, thawed and drained
8	ounces whole mushrooms
2	teaspoons lemon juice
1¼	teaspoons salt
2	medium tomatoes, cut into wedges

Cook and stir onion, turmeric and ginger in Ghee in 10-inch skillet over medium heat until onion is tender, about 3 minutes. Stir in peas, mushrooms, lemon juice and salt. Cook uncovered, stirring occasionally, until peas are tender, about 8 minutes. Stir in tomatoes; heat just until hot.

French Garden Peas

The French way of cooking peas with lettuce and onions is admired throughout Europe and is often called petits pois, *which means young or immature peas. The French cook their* petits pois *in many ways. If you use young peas when preparing this recipe, its name would be* petits pois à la Française.

4 servings

1½	cups green peas* (1½ pounds in pods)
1	cup shredded lettuce
3	green onions, sliced
2	tablespoons water
2	tablespoons margarine or butter
½	teaspoon salt
¼	teaspoon sugar
	Dash of pepper

Heat all ingredients to boiling; reduce heat. Cover and simmer until peas are tender, about 8 minutes.

* 1 package (10 ounces) frozen green peas can be substituted for the fresh peas.

Indian Green Pepper and Zucchini

Indian Green Pepper and Zucchini

A touch of turmeric brings a golden glow and an exotic flavor to this quick zucchini recipe from India.

4 servings

4	small zucchini (about 1 pound)
2	tablespoons Ghee (page 218) or vegetable oil
2	green onions (with tops), sliced
1	small green pepper, chopped
1	teaspoon salt
½	teaspoon ground turmeric

Cut zucchini into ½-inch slices. Heat Ghee in 10-inch skillet until melted. Add zucchini and remaining ingredients. Cover and simmer until zucchini is tender, about 10 minutes.

Saffron and Turmeric

Did You Know?

Saffron and turmeric can be used interchangeably in most recipes. Both spices have been highly prized by chefs since ancient times for the rich golden color and suave flavor they add to stews, soups and rice dishes.

Saffron is harvested from the stigma of a crocus grown principally in southern Europe and Asia Minor; turmeric is derived from a rhizome native to southern Asia. Although connoisseurs generally prefer the subtler and more aromatic qualities of saffron, its rarity and very high cost often prompt budget-watchers to prefer using turmeric.

Stuffed Green Peppers and Tomatoes

Stuffed Green Peppers and Tomatoes

Stuffed vegetables are popular throughout the Middle East and the Mediterranean, and may be served hot or cold. This rice-and-raisin-stuffed variation is a particular favorite in Turkey.

8 servings

4	medium green peppers
4	large firm tomatoes
1	medium onion, chopped
2	tablespoons unsalted sunflower seeds (shelled)
2	tablespoons vegetable oil
1⅓	cups water
⅔	cup uncooked regular rice
¼	cup raisins
¼	cup snipped parsley
1	tablespoon finely snipped fresh mint or 1 teaspoon dried mint leaves
2	teaspoons salt
½	teaspoon ground cinnamon
¼	teaspoon pepper
1	cup water
¼	cup tomato paste

Cut thin slice from stem end of each green pepper and tomato; reserve. Remove seeds and membranes from green peppers; rinse peppers. Cook green peppers in enough boiling water to cover 5 minutes; drain. Cut thin slice from bottom of each tomato if necessary to prevent tipping. Remove pulp from tomatoes, leaving a ¼-inch wall. Chop pulp; reserve.

Cook onion and sunflower seeds in oil in 10-inch skillet over medium heat, stirring frequently, 5 minutes. Stir in reserved pulp, 1⅓ cups water, the rice, raisins, parsley, mint, salt, cinnamon and pepper. Heat to boiling; reduce heat. Cover and simmer 15 minutes. Uncover and simmer 3 to 5 minutes to reduce liquid if necessary.

Stuff each tomato and green pepper with rice mixture, filling each about ¾ full. Place stem tops on each. Arrange vegetables in ungreased oblong baking dish, 13½ x 9 x 2 inches. Mix 1 cup water and the tomato paste; pour around vegetables. Cover tightly with aluminum foil. Cook in 350° oven until vegetables are tender, about 45 minutes. Serve hot or cold.

Rumanian Mixed Vegetables

Rumanian Mixed Vegetables

(Ghiveci)

The national dish of Rumania (and popular in Bulgaria, too), ghiveci is traditionally made in a Turkish guvens, or earthenware casserole, and may include meat—a dinner in a dish. Recipes for ghiveci vary considerably from village to village and family to family, and fluctuate with availability of vegetables.

8 servings

2	medium potatoes, cut into ½-inch cubes
2	medium carrots, sliced
8	ounces green beans, cut into 1-inch pieces
2	medium onions, chopped
2	cloves garlic, chopped
2	tablespoons olive or vegetable oil
4	tomatoes, chopped
2	cups cauliflowerets
1	stalk celery, sliced
2	teaspoons salt
¼	teaspoon dried thyme leaves
¼	teaspoon ground marjoram
¼	teaspoon pepper
1	medium zucchini, sliced
1	medium green pepper, chopped

Heat 1 inch water to boiling in 3-quart saucepan. Add potatoes, carrots and beans Heat to boiling; reduce heat. Cover and simmer 10 minutes; drain. Cook and stir onions and garlic in oil in 10-inch skillet over medium heat until almost tender. Add tomatoes, cauliflowerets, celery, salt, thyme, marjoram and pepper. Cover and cook 5 minutes.

Place potato mixture in greased 3-quart casserole. Spread half the tomato mixture over top. Layer zucchini and green pepper over tomato mixture. Top with remaining tomato mixture. Cover and cook in 350° oven until vegetables are tender, 50 to 60 minutes.

African Green Pepper and Spinach

Peanut butter brings a rich nutty flavor to an unusual spinach dish from Africa. Nice with roast chicken.

4 servings

1	medium onion, chopped
1	medium green pepper, chopped
1	tablespoon vegetable oil
1	medium tomato, chopped
1	pound fresh spinach*
¾	teaspoon salt
⅛	teaspoon pepper
¼	cup peanut butter

Cook and stir onion and green pepper in oil in 3-quart saucepan until onion is tender. Add tomato and spinach. Cover and simmer until spinach is tender, about 5 minutes. Stir in salt, pepper and peanut butter; heat just until hot.

* 1 package (about 10 ounces) frozen chopped spinach, thawed and drained, can be substituted for the fresh spinach.

Finnish Rutabaga Casserole

(Lanttulaatikko)

The rutabaga, a member of the cabbage family, closely resembles a turnip and is often called a Swedish turnip or "Swede." This recipe from Finland is a traditional Christmas side dish.

6 to 8 servings

2   medium rutabagas* (about 2 pounds)
2   eggs, beaten
¼   cup dry bread crumbs
¼   cup half-and-half
2   teaspoons sugar or corn syrup
1   teaspoon salt
¼   teaspoon ground nutmeg
2   tablespoons margarine or butter

Slice and pare rutabagas (page 236); cut into ½-inch cubes. Heat 1 inch salted water (½ teaspoon salt to 1 cup water) to boiling. Add rutabagas. Heat to boiling; reduce heat. Cover and cook until tender, about 20 minutes.

Drain rutabagas, reserving ¼ cup cooking liquid. Mash rutabagas with reserved liquid or purée through food mill (see Note). Stir remaining ingredients except margarine into rutabagas. Pour into greased 1½-quart casserole; dot with margarine. Cook in 350° oven until top is light brown, 45 to 50 minutes.

* 6 medium turnips (about 2 pounds) can be substituted for the rutabagas.

Note: Rutabagas can be puréed in blender. Place half the cubes at a time in blender container; add 2 tablespoons reserved liquid. Cover and blend until of uniform consistency. Repeat.

Glazed Rutabagas

(Ruskistetut Lantut)

When cubed and glazed with brown sugar, low-cost rutabagas are popular substitutes for potatoes in Scandinavia and go well with most meat, fish or poultry dishes.

4 to 6 servings

2   medium rutabagas (about 2 pounds)
¼   cup margarine or butter
2   tablespoons packed brown sugar
1   tablespoon water
1   teaspoon salt

Slice and pare rutabagas (page 236); cut into ½-inch cubes. Heat margarine in 10-inch skillet until melted. Add rutabagas. Cook uncovered over medium heat, stirring frequently, until light brown on all sides, about 10 minutes. Sprinkle with brown sugar, water and salt. Cover and simmer over low heat, stirring occasionally, until tender, about 20 minutes.

Rutabagas

Did You Know?

Rutabagas are large yellow-fleshed cousins to turnips. They are sometimes coated with a thin layer of paraffin to prevent loss of moisture and shriveling. To slice a rutabaga, cut off the top to give a flat surface. With flat surface down, cut several slices from one side, making a second flat surface. Place the rutabaga on the second flat side and finish cutting the slices. Peel the waxed skin, then dice for cooking, cut into sticks for dipping or shred for salads.

Tomatoes, Peppers and Onions

Tomatoes, Peppers and Onions

(Peperonata)

This colorful Roman dish can be served hot or cold, and can accompany a simple meal of scrambled eggs or pasta or be served with an elegant party dish. In Rome, cold peperonata is often included on the antipasto platter.

4 servings

2	medium onions, sliced
2	tablespoons olive or vegetable oil
3	medium green peppers, cut into strips
1	teaspoon dried basil leaves
1	teaspoon red wine vinegar
½	teaspoon salt
¼	teaspoon pepper
2	medium tomatoes, coarsely chopped (about 2 cups)

Cook and stir onions in oil in 10-inch skillet until tender; add remaining ingredients except tomatoes. Cover and cook over low heat 10 minutes. Add tomatoes. Cover and simmer until green pepper is tender, about 5 minutes. Garnish with ripe olives if desired.

Fried Tomatoes

When your budget suggests a simple, low-cost supper, give it a fragrant Greek accent—serve these tomatoes with Scrambled Eggs with Rice (page 188).

4 servings

4	firm ripe medium tomatoes
½	cup fine cracker crumbs
1	teaspoon salt
¼	teaspoon pepper
¼	cup olive or vegetable oil

Cut tomatoes into ¾-inch slices. Mix cracker crumbs, salt and pepper. Coat tomato slices with crumb mixture. Heat oil in 12-inch skillet until hot. Cook tomato slices in oil, turning once, until golden brown on both sides.

French Vegetable Ragout (Ratatouille)

Ratatouille has long been a pet vegetable medley in southern France, especially during the summer harvest season.

8 servings

1	small eggplant (about 1 pound)
1	medium onion, sliced
1	clove garlic, chopped
2	tablespoons olive or vegetable oil
4	medium tomatoes, cut into fourths
1	medium zucchini, sliced
1	medium green pepper, cut into strips
¼	cup snipped parsley
1	teaspoon salt
½	teaspoon dried basil leaves
¼	teaspoon pepper

Cut eggplant into ½-inch cubes (about 5 cups). Cook and stir onion and garlic in oil in 12-inch skillet until onion is tender. Add eggplant and remaining ingredients. Heat to boiling; reduce heat. Cover and simmer, stirring occasionally, until vegetables are crisp-tender, about 10 minutes.

Dilled Zucchini

Yogurt and fresh dill bring country-fresh flavor to this Hungarian dish.

6 servings

6	small zucchini (about 1½ pounds), cut into ½-inch slices
1	clove garlic, finely chopped
2	tablespoons olive or vegetable oil
1	small onion, sliced and separated into rings
½	teaspoon salt
	Dash of pepper
½	cup unflavored yogurt
3	tablespoons snipped fresh dill or 1 teaspoon dried dillweed

Cook and stir zucchini and garlic in oil in 10-inch skillet over medium heat until zucchini is light brown, 5 to 8 minutes. Stir in onion; heat just until hot. Sprinkle with salt and pepper; remove from heat. Mix yogurt and dill; stir into zucchini mixture.

Broiled Parmesan Zucchini

A fine vegetable side dish to serve with an Italian specialty, such as Chicken Cacciatore (page 87) or lasagne.

8 servings

8	small zucchini (about 2 pounds)
1	tablespoon olive or vegetable oil
½	teaspoon garlic salt
	Dash of pepper
	Dash of ground marjoram
½	cup grated Parmesan cheese

Cut zucchini lengthwise into halves; place cut sides up on rack in broiler pan. Brush with oil; sprinkle with garlic salt, pepper and marjoram. Set oven control to broil and/or 550°. Broil with tops 4 inches from heat, 6 minutes. Sprinkle with cheese; broil until tender, 5 to 6 minutes.

French Vegetable Ragout

Hasselback Potatoes

These Swedish baked potatoes are easy to eat and to serve—and go especially well with roasts and baked fish dishes.

6 servings

6	medium baking potatoes
¼	cup margarine or butter, melted
	Salt
	Pepper
¼	cup grated Parmesan cheese
2	tablespoons dry bread crumbs
	Paprika

Cut potatoes crosswise into ⅛-inch slices, cutting only ¾ through. (See diagram.) Place cut side up in greased oblong baking dish, 11 x 7 x 1½ inches. Brush with margarine; sprinkle with salt and pepper.

Bake in 375° oven, brushing with margarine once or twice, 45 minutes (see Note). Mix cheese and bread crumbs; sprinkle on potatoes. Sprinkle with paprika. Bake until tender, 20 to 30 minutes.

Note: Potatoes can be baked with a roast at 325° 1 hour. Brush with meat drippings; sprinkle with cheese mixture. Bake until tender, about 30 minutes.

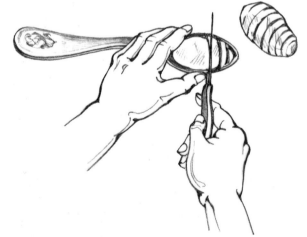

To avoid slicing potatoes too deeply, place each on a large spoon before slicing. The concave bowl of the spoon prevents the knife from cutting the potato too far.

Scalloped Potatoes with Cheese

(Gratin Dauphinois)

The pride of many a Parisian restaurant, this nutritious French scalloped-potato casserole fits comfortably into a grand party menu.

6 servings

4	medium potatoes (about 1½ pounds)
1	clove garlic, cut into halves
1	teaspoon margarine or butter
1	teaspoon salt
½	teaspoon ground nutmeg
¼	teaspoon pepper
1½	cups shredded Gruyère cheese (6 ounces)
2	eggs
1⅔	cups half-and-half
1	tablespoon margarine or butter

Cut potatoes into enough thin slices to measure about 4 cups. Rub oblong baking dish, 10 x 6 x 1½ inches, with cut garlic clove; brush with 1 teaspoon margarine. Arrange potatoes in 3 layers in casserole, sprinkling each layer with ⅓ each of the salt, nutmeg, pepper and cheese.

Beat eggs and half-and-half; pour over potato slices. Dot with 1 tablespoon margarine. Cook uncovered in 350° oven until potatoes are tender and top is golden brown, about 1 hour.

Parmesan Cheese

Did You Know?

Parmesan cheese, one of the most versatile and best-known Italian cheeses, was originally developed in Italy in the vicinity of Parma. It is made from a mixture of whole and skim milk and is characterized by its hard granular texture, making it ideal for grating. Parmesan is also a great delicacy when eaten as a cheese. Romano is similar to Parmesan but has a sharper, more piquant flavor.

Scalloped Potatoes with Cheese (page 240) and Crusty Potato Cake (page 242).

Crusty Potato Cake (Pommes de Terre Anna)

One of France's many inspired potato creations, "potatoes Anna" was created during the reign of Napoleon III and named after one of the fashionable ladies of the day.

6 servings

6	medium baking potatoes, thinly sliced
1	teaspoon salt
	Pepper
⅓	cup margarine or butter, melted

Arrange layer of potato slices in bottom of generously greased 9-inch pie plate. Sprinkle with small amount of salt and dash of pepper. Repeat until all potatoes have been layered, sprinkling each layer with small amount of salt and dash of pepper. Pour margarine over potatoes. Cook uncovered in 400° oven until potatoes are tender, about 50 minutes.

Loosen edge and bottom of potatoes with wide spatula. Place inverted platter over pie plate; invert potatoes onto platter. Cut into wedges to serve.

Hungarian Potato-and-Egg Casserole (Rakott Krumpli)

A hearty hot potato salad from Hungary—especially good with baked ham and tomatoes.

6 servings

6	medium potatoes (about 2 pounds)
1	medium onion, chopped
2	tablespoons vegetable oil
1	cup dairy sour cream
1½	teaspoons salt
¼	teaspoon pepper
2	hard-cooked eggs, sliced
2	tablespoons dry bread crumbs
	Paprika

Heat 1 inch salted water (½ teaspoon salt to 1 cup water) to boiling. Add potatoes. Heat to boiling; reduce heat. Cover and cook until tender, 30 to 35 minutes. Drain; cool slightly.

Cook onion in oil until tender. Mix onion, oil, sour cream, salt and pepper. Peel potatoes; cut into ¼-inch slices. Carefully mix potatoes and sour cream mixture.

Arrange half the potatoes in greased oblong baking dish, 10 x 6 x 1½ inches, or 1½-quart casserole. Arrange eggs on top; add remaining potatoes. Sprinkle with bread crumbs and paprika. Cook uncovered in 325° oven until light brown, 30 to 40 minutes. Garnish with snipped parsley if desired.

Swedish Creamed Potatoes

For a nice and easy Scandinavian dinner, serve this dish with baked or broiled fish fillets, rye bread and Pickled Beets (page 220).

4 to 6 servings

¼	cup margarine or butter
6	medium potatoes, cubed (about 6 cups)
1	medium onion, chopped
1	to 1¼ cups half-and-half
1	teaspoon salt
¼	teaspoon pepper

Heat margarine in 12-inch skillet until melted. Cook potatoes and onion uncovered in margarine over medium heat, turning frequently, until potatoes are light brown, 10 to 15 minutes. Add 1 cup half-and-half; sprinkle with salt and pepper.

Cover and simmer over low heat, stirring occasionally, until potatoes are tender, about 10 minutes. (Add 1 to 4 tablespoons half-and-half if necessary.)

Sweet Potatoes with Apples

Sweet Potatoes with Apples

In Mexico, sweet potato dishes such as this one may be served with meat or even as a dessert. We find they go especially well with roast pork or baked ham.

6 servings

6	medium sweet potatoes or yams (about 2 pounds)
2	tart apples, cored and cut into ¼-inch rings
½	cup orange juice
¼	cup packed brown sugar
¼	teaspoon ground ginger
¼	teaspoon ground cinnamon
2	tablespoons margarine or butter

Heat enough water to cover potatoes to boiling. Add potatoes. Heat to boiling; reduce heat. Cover and simmer until tender, 30 to 35 minutes. Cool slightly; slip off skins. Cut potatoes into ¼-inch slices.

Layer potatoes and apples in greased oblong baking dish, 10 x 6 x 1½ inches. Pour orange juice over potatoes and apples. Mix brown sugar, ginger and cinnamon; sprinkle over apples. Dot with margarine. Cook uncovered in 350° oven until apples are crisp-tender, about 30 minutes.

Potato-and-Anchovy Scallop

This is Sweden's famous version of scalloped potatoes, often called Jansson's temptation. As with the elusive Anna of our Crusty Potato Cake, the identity of the original Jansson remains obscure.

6 servings

6	medium potatoes, thinly sliced (about 4 cups)
1	can (1¾ ounces) anchovy fillets, drained and chopped
1	medium onion, chopped
⅛	teaspoon pepper
2	cups half-and-half
¼	cup dry bread crumbs
2	tablespoons margarine or butter, melted
2	tablespoons snipped parsley

Arrange half the potato slices in greased oblong baking dish, 12 x 7½ x 2 inches, or square baking dish, 9 x 9 x 2 inches. Layer anchovies and onion on potatoes; top with remaining potato slices. Sprinkle with pepper.

Heat half-and-half over medium heat just until hot; pour over potatoes. Mix bread crumbs and margarine; sprinkle over top. Cover and cook in 325° oven 40 minutes. Uncover and cook until potatoes are tender, 50 to 60 minutes. Sprinkle with parsley.

Scottish Skillet Potatoes

Scottish Skillet Potatoes (Stovies)

In the Highlands, "stovies" are often served with cold meats and a frosty pitcher of buttermilk—a traditional Scottish Sunday supper, using the roast remaining from the midday meal.

6 servings

2	tablespoons bacon fat, margarine or butter
6	medium potatoes, thinly sliced (about 4 cups)
2	medium onions, sliced
1½	teaspoons salt
¼	teaspoon pepper
¼	cup snipped parsley
¾	cup water

Heat bacon fat in 10-inch skillet until hot. Layer half each of the potato and onion slices in skillet. Sprinkle with half each of the salt, pepper and parsley. Repeat. Add water. Cover and simmer over low heat until potatoes are tender and liquid is absorbed, about 30 minutes. (Add water if necessary.)

Sugar-Browned Potatoes

The Danes like to serve this luscious potato dish with their much-loved pork. Try it with our unusual Danish Pork Tenderloins (page 147).

4 to 6 servings

2	pounds new potatoes
¼	cup margarine or butter
¼	cup sugar
½	teaspoon salt
3	tablespoons water

Heat 1 inch salted water (1 teaspoon salt to 1 cup water) to boiling. Add potatoes. Heat to boiling; reduce heat. Cover and cook until tender, 20 to 25 minutes; drain.

Cook and stir margarine, sugar and salt in 10-inch skillet over medium heat until mixture starts to turn golden brown. Remove from heat; cool slightly. Stir in water until blended. Add potatoes. Cook over low heat, turning potatoes to coat with sugar mixture.

Butter-Steamed New Potatoes

(Smørdampete Nypoteter)

In Norway, these steamed potatoes are usually served with the Norwegians' national dish—cod. We recommend our Lemon Baked Cod (page 45).

4 to 6 servings

⅓	cup margarine or butter
1½	pounds new potatoes (see Note)
½	teaspoon salt
⅛	teaspoon pepper
2	tablespoons snipped dill or parsley

Heat margarine in Dutch oven or 10-inch skillet until melted. Add potatoes; stir to coat with margarine. Sprinkle with salt and pepper. Cover and cook over low heat, shaking pan occasionally, until tender, about 30 minutes. Place in serving dish. Pour any remaining margarine over potatoes; sprinkle with dill.

Note: Potatoes should be 1 inch or less in diameter. If larger, cut into halves or 1-inch chunks.

Apples and Potatoes (Himmel und Erde)

Himmel und Erde—"heaven and earth"—comes from northern Germany, where it is traditionally served with blood sausage. It adds a festive touch to many economy meat dishes—ribs, frankfurters, ground-meat casseroles.

4 to 6 servings

4	medium potatoes, cut into 1-inch cubes (about 4 cups)
2	tart apples, sliced
1	tablespoon sugar
4	slices bacon, cut into 1-inch pieces
1	medium onion, sliced
1	tablespoon margarine or butter, softened
	Dash of ground nutmeg

Heat 1 inch salted water (1 teaspoon salt to 1 cup water) to boiling. Add potatoes, apples and sugar. Heat to boiling; reduce heat. Cover and cook until tender, 10 to 15 minutes; drain.

Fry bacon until crisp; drain on paper towels. Cook and stir onion in bacon fat until tender. Place potatoes and apples in serving bowl. Dot with margarine; sprinkle with nutmeg. Top with onion and bacon.

Swiss Fried Potatoes (Roesti)

Switzerland's much-praised fried potatoes are often served for breakfast (like our hash browns), accompanied by porridge or eggs, bacon and coffee liberally laced with warm milk.

4 to 6 servings

4	medium potatoes (about 1½ pounds)
¼	cup margarine or butter
1	small onion, chopped
½	cup diced Gruyère or Swiss cheese
½	teaspoon salt
¼	teaspoon pepper
2	tablespoons water

Heat 1 inch salted water (½ teaspoon salt to 1 cup water) to boiling. Add potatoes. Heat to boiling; reduce heat. Cover and cook until tender, 30 to 35 minutes. Peel and shred potatoes or cut into ¼-inch strips.

Heat margarine in 10-inch skillet until melted. Add potatoes, onion and cheese. Sprinkle with salt and pepper. Cook uncovered over medium heat, turning frequently, until potatoes start to brown, about 10 minutes. (Add 1 to 2 tablespoons margarine to prevent sticking if necessary.)

Press potatoes with spatula to form flat cake; sprinkle with water. Cover and cook over low heat, without stirring, until bottom is golden brown and crusty, about 10 minutes. Place inverted platter over skillet; invert potatoes onto platter.

Mashed Potatoes with Cabbage (Colcannon)

The Irish have many versions of colcannon, but throughout the Emerald Isle it is a favorite dish to serve on Hallowe'en, when a ring or coin may be added to the mixture, forecasting good luck for the guest who is served the portion containing the prize.

6 servings

6	medium potatoes (about 2 pounds)
½	small head cabbage, shredded (about 3 cups)
6	scallions (with tops), chopped
¼	cup water
⅛	teaspoon salt
⅓	to ½ cup milk
¼	cup margarine or butter, softened
1	teaspoon salt
	Dash of pepper
	Margarine or butter

Heat 1 inch salted water (½ teaspoon salt to 1 cup water) to boiling. Add potatoes. Heat to boiling; reduce heat. Cover and cook until tender, 30 to 35 minutes; drain. Heat cabbage, scallions, water and ⅛ teaspoon salt to boiling; reduce heat. Cover and simmer until crisp-tender, 5 to 10 minutes; drain.

Mash potatoes until no lumps remain. Beat in milk in small amounts. Add ¼ cup margarine, 1 teaspoon salt and the pepper; beat until potatoes are light and fluffy. Stir in cabbage and scallions; dot with margarine.

German Potato Pancakes (Kartoffelpuffer)

The Germans serve potato pancakes as a vegetable side dish with roasts, stews and sausages, often accompanied by applesauce. Kartoffelpuffer can also be served as a dessert—omit onions and serve with applesauce.

16 pancakes

4	medium potatoes (about 1½ pounds)
2	eggs, beaten
1	small onion, finely chopped (optional)
¼	cup all-purpose flour
1	teaspoon salt
¼	cup bacon fat, margarine or butter

Shred enough potatoes to measure 4 cups; drain. Mix potatoes, eggs, onion, flour and salt. Heat 2 tablespoons of the bacon fat in 12-inch skillet over medium heat until hot. Pour in about ¼ cup batter for each pancake. Flatten each with spatula into pancake about 4 inches in diameter.

Cook pancakes until golden brown, about 2 minutes on each side. Keep warm. Repeat with remaining batter. (Add remaining bacon fat as needed to prevent sticking.)

Scandinavian Potato Casserole

This substantial potato casserole is similar to a soufflé—made light and fluffy with beaten egg whites. But it is not nearly so temperamental as a soufflé; it's easy to make and doesn't collapse.

6 to 8 servings

6	medium potatoes (about 2 pounds), pared
¾	cup half-and-half
½	cup grated Parmesan cheese
1	teaspoon salt
¼	teaspoon ground nutmeg
	Dash of pepper
3	eggs, separated

Heat 1 inch salted water (½ teaspoon salt to 1 cup water) to boiling. Add potatoes. Heat to boiling; reduce heat. Cover and cook until tender, whole 30 to 35 minutes, pieces 20 to 25 minutes; drain.

Mash potatoes until no lumps remain. Beat in half-and-half in small amounts. Stir in cheese, salt, nutmeg, pepper and egg yolks. Beat egg whites until stiff; fold into potato mixture. Pour into ungreased 1½-quart soufflé or baking dish. Cook uncovered in 375° oven until golden brown, about 45 minutes.

Spaghetti with Amatriciana Sauce

The flavor of salt pork and a generous pinch of pepper define Amatriciana Sauce, which originated in Amatrice, a town in the Sabine Mountains northeast of Rome. The dish has long been a favorite among Romans and is often served with Pecorino cheese rather than Romano or Parmesan.

4 servings

¼	pound salt pork
1	medium onion, chopped
1	clove garlic, chopped
1	tablespoon olive or vegetable oil
1	can (28 ounces) tomatoes
1	teaspoon sugar
¼	to ½ teaspoon pepper
8	ounces uncooked spaghetti
2	tablespoons grated Romano cheese
2	tablespoons grated Parmesan cheese

Trim rind from salt pork; dice pork. Cook and stir salt pork, onion and garlic in oil in 10-inch skillet until onion is tender; drain. Add tomatoes (with liquid), sugar and pepper; break up tomatoes with fork. Simmer uncovered until mixture is desired consistency, 30 to 40 minutes.

Cook spaghetti as directed on package; drain. Mix cheeses. Serve tomato sauce over spaghetti; sprinkle with cheeses.

Pasta with Basil-and-Cheese Sauce

(Pasta con Pesto)

Pesto is a specialty of Genoa, whose citizens claim to grow the most fragrant basil in the world. The sauce is also popular along the French Riviera, where it is called pistou. *It can be served with all kinds of vegetable side dishes and spooned into individual bowls of Italian Vegetable Soup (page 100). The name comes from "pestle"—the cheese and basil were originally crushed with mortar and pestle.*

6 servings

⅔	cup packed coarsely chopped basil leaves*
⅓	cup grated Parmesan cheese
⅓	cup olive or vegetable oil
2	tablespoons pine nuts or walnuts
½	teaspoon salt
⅛	teaspoon pepper
1	clove garlic
10	ounces uncooked spaghetti or noodles
2	tablespoons margarine or butter

Place all ingredients except spaghetti and margarine in blender container. Cover and blend on high speed until mixture is uniform consistency. Cook spaghetti as directed on package; drain. Toss spaghetti with basil mixture and the margarine. Serve with additional Parmesan cheese if desired.

* 2 tablespoons crushed dried basil leaves can be substituted for the fresh basil.

Pine Nuts (Pignolias or Pinolias)

Did You Know?

Pine nuts, tasty, tender little seeds from several kinds of pine trees in southern Europe, have been widely used around the Mediterranean for years—added to pastries, vegetables, salads, sauces and pasta. They can be found in Italian or Spanish markets or in health food stores, shelled and ready to toast and munch or use in a variety of ways. About the size of small dried beans, pine nuts have light meat and a sweet, mild flavor. If you can't find pine nuts, substitute walnuts, almonds or sunflower nuts.

Armenian Noodles and Rice

(Pilav)

This enchanting combination of rice and noodles can add interest to the most routine family meal and serve as a smart party-brightener, too.

8 servings

1	cup uncooked fine egg noodles
¼	cup margarine or butter
2½	cups water
1	cup uncooked long grain rice
1¼	teaspoons salt
	Dash of pepper
	Snipped parsley

Break noodles into 1-inch pieces if necessary. Cook and stir noodles in margarine in 2-quart saucepan 5 minutes. Stir in remaining ingredients except parsley. Heat to boiling, stirring once or twice; reduce heat. Cover and simmer 14 minutes. (Do not lift cover or stir.) Remove from heat. Fluff mixture lightly with fork; cover and let steam 5 to 10 minutes. Sprinkle with parsley.

Fettuccine with Cheese and Cream

(Fettuccine alla Panna)

In Italian cooking, alla panna *indicates a sauce made with butter, cream and cheese. It is served throughout the country but is often associated with the food of northern Italy. This recipe is best known to Americans as* fettuccine al Alfredo. *Alfredo was a dashing Roman restaurateur who tossed his noodles with a gold fork and spoon given to him by Mary Pickford and Douglas Fairbanks!*

6 servings

8	ounces uncooked wide egg noodles
½	cup margarine or butter
½	cup whipping cream
¾	cup grated Parmesan cheese
½	teaspoon salt
	Dash of pepper
2	teaspoons snipped parsley

Cook noodles as directed on package; drain. Heat margarine and whipping cream over low heat until margarine is melted. Stir in cheese, salt and pepper. Pour sauce over hot noodles, stirring until noodles are well coated. Sprinkle with parsley.

Spaghetti with Tomato-and-Anchovy Sauce

The pungent flavor of anchovies gives this country-style sauce its vibrant flavor and character; oregano and garlic help bring to mind the flavors of southern Italy.

6 servings

1	medium onion, chopped
1	clove garlic, chopped
2	tablespoons olive or vegetable oil
1	can (8 ounces) tomato sauce
1	can (1¾ ounces) anchovies, drained and chopped
¼	cup snipped parsley
½	teaspoon dried oregano leaves
¼	teaspoon salt
⅛	teaspoon pepper
¼	cup dry bread crumbs
1	tablespoon olive oil, margarine or butter
8	ounces uncooked spaghetti

Cook and stir onion and garlic in 2 tablespoons oil in 10-inch skillet until onion is tender. Stir in tomato sauce, anchovies, parsley, oregano, salt and pepper. Heat to boiling; reduce heat. Cover and simmer 15 minutes.

Cook and stir bread crumbs in 1 tablespoon oil until golden brown. Cook spaghetti as directed on package; drain. Toss spaghetti with sauce; sprinkle with bread crumbs.

Pasta

The many varieties of pasta on the market present a fascinating assortment of sizes and shapes. Some are known by more than one name. A few of these varieties are illustrated below:

Mostaccioli: *Medium-sized pasta tubes with diagonally cut ends.*

Ziti: *Large macaroni tubes in long or short lengths.*

Conchiglie: *Commonly called shells. Sold in several sizes.*

Farfalle: *Also called bows or butterflies.*

Tagliatelle: *Egg noodles about ¾ inch wide.*

Vermicelli: *Very thin spaghetti. Sold straight or folded.*

Cracked-Wheat Pilaf (Bulgur Pilav)

Try this Turkish specialty with meat or poultry. It goes especially well with lamb and is a traditional accompaniment to the popular Skewered Lamb and Vegetables (page 164).

6 servings

1	cup cracked wheat (bulgur)
1	medium onion, chopped
2	tablespoons margarine or butter
2¼	cups water
2	teaspoons instant beef or chicken bouillon
½	teaspoon salt

Cook and stir cracked wheat and onion in margarine until onion is tender, about 5 minutes. Stir in remaining ingredients. Heat to boiling; reduce heat. Cover and simmer until wheat is tender but firm, 20 to 25 minutes.

Barley with Mushrooms

This unusual vegetable casserole from Scotland is flavored with mushrooms, onions and chicken bouillon, and has the inimitable texture of barley—a fine dish to serve with roast lamb, beef or chicken.

6 servings

8	ounces mushrooms, sliced
2	medium onions, chopped
2	tablespoons margarine or butter
3¼	cups boiling water
1	cup barley
2	teaspoons instant chicken bouillon
½	teaspoon salt
	Dash of pepper

Cook and stir mushrooms and onions in margarine 5 minutes; place in ungreased 1½-quart casserole. Stir in remaining ingredients. Cover and cook in 375° oven, stirring once, until barley is tender, about 1¼ hours.

Polenta with Cheese

Polenta *is the famed cornmeal mush of northern Italy. In the area around Venice it is a staple grain for country cooks. Our recipe, which includes cheese, goes very well with Venetian Liver with Onions (page 127). In Rumania a similar dish is called* mamaliga.

6 servings

1	cup yellow cornmeal
¾	cup water
3¼	cups boiling water
2	teaspoons salt
1	tablespoon margarine or butter
1	cup grated Parmesan cheese
⅓	cup shredded Swiss or Kashkaval cheese (about 1½ ounces)

Mix cornmeal and ¾ cup water in 2-quart saucepan. Stir in 3¼ cups water and the salt. Cook, stirring constantly, until mixture thickens and boils; reduce heat. Cover and simmer, stirring occasionally, 10 minutes. Remove from heat; stir until smooth.

Spread ⅓ of the mixture in greased 1½-quart casserole. Dot with ⅓ of the margarine; sprinkle with ⅓ of the Parmesan cheese. Repeat twice. Sprinkle with Swiss cheese. Cook uncovered in 350° oven until hot and bubbly, 15 to 20 minutes.

Fried Cornmeal Mush: Omit 1 tablespoon margarine, the grated Parmesan and Swiss cheese. After cooking 10 minutes, spread in greased loaf pan, 9 x 5 x 3 inches. Cover and refrigerate until firm, at least 12 hours. Invert pan to unmold; cut into ½-inch slices.

Heat 2 tablespoons margarine in 10-inch skillet until melted. Coat slices with flour; cook uncovered in margarine over low heat until brown, about 5 minutes on each side. Serve with molasses, jam, maple syrup or sour cream if desired.

Braised Buckwheat Kernels
(Kasha)

Our quick method of cooking buckwheat kernels (or groats) makes this dish—popular in Russia and throughout Eastern Europe—a fine and hearty side dish to serve with hurry-up suppers.

6 servings

1	cup medium buckwheat kernels (kasha)
1	egg
2½	cups boiling water
2	tablespoons margarine or butter
2½	teaspoons instant beef bouillon
¼	teaspoon salt
¼	teaspoon pepper

Mix buckwheat kernels and egg; cook in ungreased skillet over medium-high heat, stirring constantly, until kernels separate and brown. Stir in water, margarine, bouillon, salt and pepper; reduce heat. Cover and simmer until liquid is absorbed and buckwheat kernels are tender, about 5 minutes.

Kasha

Did You Know?

Kasha is the Russian word for porridge made from buckwheat kernels or groats (oats with the hulls removed). An inexpensive, nutritious and versatile food, kasha can be served with honey and cream, used as a stuffing for poultry or fish, mixed with rice, or used as a side dish with *Borscht* (page 130), pork or goose. To most Westerners, kasha has come to mean the roasted buckwheat kernels themselves, which are packaged and sold as kernels, groats and kasha.

Roman Farina Dumplings

Roman Farina Dumplings
(Gnocchi alla Romana)

These easy baked dumplings—the pride of Rome—are thought to date back to the days of the Caesars. They make a truly exciting side dish and are guaranteed to win applause. If you like, serve them Roman style: Present the dumplings to guests as a separate course preceding the main course.

6 servings

3   cups milk
1   cup farina or semolina
2   eggs, well beaten
1   tablespoon margarine or butter
1   teaspoon salt
    Dash of pepper
¼   cup margarine or butter
1   cup grated Parmesan cheese

Heat milk to scalding in 2-quart saucepan; reduce heat. Sprinkle farina slowly into hot milk, stirring constantly. Cook, stirring constantly, until thick, about 5 minutes (spoon will stand upright in mixture); remove from heat.

Stir in eggs, 1 tablespoon margarine, the salt and pepper; beat until smooth. Spread in greased oblong pan, 13 x 9 x 2 inches; cool. Cover and refrigerate until firm, 2 to 3 hours.

Cut farina mixture into 1½-inch squares or circles. (Dip knife in cold water to prevent sticking.) Place cakes, overlapping, in ungreased baking dish. Dot with ¼ cup margarine; sprinkle with cheese. Bake uncovered in 350° oven until crisp and golden, about 30 minutes.

Note: For a browner top, set oven control to broil and/or 550°. Broil dumplings with tops 2 or 3 inches from heat until golden brown, about 3 minutes.

Rice Milan Style
(Risotto alla Milanese)

This rice recipe has become so famous throughout Italy that it is sometimes simply called ri-sotto—a word often used by non-Italian chefs for rice. The difference is this: Riso *is the Italian word for rice;* risotto *is an Italian method of cooking rice similar to a Pilaf (page 99). Ri-sotto alla Milanese is* Milan's elegant preparation—rice cooked "risotto style," but gilded in color and flavor with saffron, beef marrow and Parmesan cheese.

6 servings

1   cup uncooked regular rice
1   small onion, chopped
1   tablespoon chopped beef marrow (optional)
3   tablespoons margarine or butter
2   cups water
2   teaspoons instant chicken bouillon
¼   teaspoon salt
    Dash of ground saffron
¼   cup grated Parmesan cheese

Cook and stir rice, onion and beef marrow in margarine in 2-quart saucepan until rice is golden, 4 to 5 minutes. Stir in remaining ingredients except cheese. Heat to boiling, stirring once or twice; reduce heat. Cover and simmer 14 minutes. (Do not lift cover or stir.) Remove from heat. Stir in cheese lightly with fork; cover and let steam 5 to 10 minutes. Serve rice with additional Parmesan cheese if desired.

Italian Rice and Peas
(Risi e Bisi)

One of the best-known of Venetian dishes, risi e bisi *makes a fine party side dish. It has a festive appearance, and the combination of peas and rice provides both vegetable and grain in one dish, cutting down on cooking and serving time. In Venice, prosciutto is the ham of choice to use in making* risi e bisi.

10 servings

1   small onion, chopped
2   tablespoons margarine or butter
1   package (10 ounces) frozen green peas
2   cups water
1   cup uncooked regular rice
2   ounces fully cooked smoked ham, chopped
        (about ½ cup)
1   teaspoon instant chicken bouillon
¼   teaspoon salt
¼   cup grated Parmesan cheese

Cook and stir onion in margarine in 2-quart saucepan until tender. Stir in remaining ingredients except cheese. Heat to boiling, stirring once or twice; reduce heat. Cover and simmer 14 minutes. (Do not lift cover or stir.) Remove from heat. Fluff rice lightly with fork; cover and let steam 5 to 10 minutes. Stir in cheese lightly with fork.

Basic Directions for Cooking Regular White Rice

Uncooked Rice	Water	Salt	Yield, Cooked
½ cup	1 cup	½ teaspoon	1½ cups
⅔ cup	1⅓ cups	½ teaspoon	about 2 cups
1 cup	2 cups	1 teaspoon	about 3 cups
1⅓ cups	2⅔ cups	1 teaspoon	about 4 cups

Heat rice, water and salt to boiling, stirring once or twice; reduce heat. Cover and simmer 14 minutes. (Do not lift cover or stir.) Remove from heat. Fluff rice lightly with fork; cover and let steam 5 to 10 minutes.

Indian Fried Rice and Braised Buckwheat Kernels (page 251).

Indian Fried Rice

(Pulao)

Raisins, almonds and curry powder bring a sumptuous appearance, delectable flavor and interesting texture to India's pulao—*tradition-ally served on festive occasions and sometimes ornamented with gilt or silver leaf!*

6 servings

1	cup uncooked regular rice
1	medium onion, chopped
½	cup Ghee (page 218), margarine or butter
½	cup raisins (optional)

2	teaspoons instant chicken bouillon
1	teaspoon curry powder
½	teaspoon salt
2¼	cups boiling water
¼	cup toasted slivered almonds

Cook and stir rice and onion in Ghee until rice is yellow and onion is tender. Stir in raisins, bouillon, curry powder and salt. Pour into ungreased 1½-quart casserole. Stir in water. Cover and cook in 350° oven until liquid is absorbed, 25 to 30 minutes. Stir in almonds. Serve with chicken or lamb.

Rice with Mushrooms (Risotto con Funghi)

A few sliced mushrooms do much to enhance the flavor and appearance of this Italian specialty, which goes well with roast chicken or baked fish.

6 servings

4   ounces mushrooms, sliced
1   small onion, chopped
1   small clove garlic, finely chopped
¼   cup margarine or butter
2   cups water
1   cup uncooked regular rice
¼   cup snipped parsley
2   teaspoons instant chicken bouillon
½   teaspoon salt
¼   teaspoon dried basil leaves
    Grated Parmesan or Romano cheese

Cook and stir mushrooms, onion and garlic in margarine in 2-quart saucepan until mushrooms and onion are tender. Stir in remaining ingredients except cheese. Heat to boiling, stirring once or twice; reduce heat. Cover and simmer 14 minutes. (Do not lift cover or stir.) Remove from heat. Fluff rice lightly with fork; cover and let steam 5 to 10 minutes. Sprinkle with cheese.

Lemon-and-Celery Pilaf

The zest (or peel) of lemon, the crisp, refreshing texture and flavor of celery, and a touch of mustard and red pepper are the secret agents that startle the tastebuds into happy awakening. The recipe is Portuguese. Try it with roast pork or baked fish.

7 servings

1   small onion, chopped
1   small clove garlic, finely chopped
¼   cup margarine or butter
2   cups water

1   cup uncooked regular rice
2   stalks celery, sliced
2   teaspoons instant chicken bouillon
2   teaspoons finely shredded lemon peel
½   teaspoon salt
¼   teaspoon dry mustard
⅛   teaspoon red pepper sauce
2   tablespoons snipped parsley

Cook and stir onion and garlic in margarine in 3-quart saucepan until onion is tender. Stir in remaining ingredients except parsley. Heat to boiling, stirring once or twice; reduce heat. Cover and simmer 14 minutes. (Do not lift cover or stir.) Remove from heat. Stir in parsley lightly with fork; cover and let steam 5 to 10 minutes.

Greek Tomato Pilaf

Tomatoes add a bright touch of color and a mellow flavor to this recipe—found from the Balkans to Afghanistan, and particularly prized by the Greeks. Try it with Zesty Chicken Oregano (page 81).

8 servings

2   medium tomatoes, coarsely chopped
2   tablespoons chopped onion
2   tablespoons margarine or butter
2   cups water
1   cup uncooked regular rice
1   teaspoon instant beef bouillon
¾   teaspoon salt
⅛   teaspoon pepper

Cook and stir tomatoes and onion in margarine in 2-quart saucepan over medium heat 2 minutes. Stir in remaining ingredients. Heat to boiling, stirring once or twice; reduce heat. Cover and simmer 14 minutes. (Do not lift cover or stir.) Remove from heat. Fluff rice lightly with fork; cover and let steam 5 to 10 minutes. Serve with grated Parmesan cheese if desired.

Clockwise from top: French Bread (page 269), German Turban Cake (page 286), Indian Flat Bread (page 267), Finnish Rye Bread (page 267) and Individual Brioches (page 271).

Breads

Turning from a nomadic hunting existence to an agricultural society has marked the beginning of civilization since the dawn of history—the literal setting down of roots to grow the grains that could be stored and cooked to provide sustenance during the long winter months.

Breads are truly the staff of life. They accompany our simplest and most humble meals and are present at our most festive celebrations. In this chapter we have collected quick bread recipes than can be prepared in an hour or so to round out a meal or to serve with tea or coffee or as a snack . . . unleavened breads that are as old as civilization itself . . . yeast breads whose fragrant aromas fill the home with nostalgic childhood memories . . . coffee cakes and holiday breads that have delighted the young and old for centuries.

Many of these breads will be familiar to Americans who have preserved the baking traditions of their European ancestors. But there are exciting surprises in store for everyone!

Whether it be an easy, all-purpose French Bread that goes well with any meal . . . a hearty Middle Eastern Pocket Bread to add sparkle to appetizers or sandwiches . . . unusual Indian breads that add that special quality to curry parties . . . coffee cakes or teatime treats . . . these are the cherished breads that linger in the memory and make us think, "Mmm—home-cooked food!"

Banana Bread
(Paõ de Banano)

Cinnamon, allspice and the perky flavor of lime distinguish this quick Guatemalan Banana Bread from all others. Serve it as an unusual breakfast treat, as a snack or even as a dessert, accompanied by fresh fruit or ice cream.

1 loaf

2½	cups all-purpose flour
½	cup sugar
½	cup brown sugar
3½	teaspoons baking powder
1	teaspoon salt
½	teaspoon ground cinnamon
½	teaspoon ground allspice
1¼	cups mashed bananas (2 large bananas)
¼	cup milk
3	tablespoons vegetable oil
1	egg
1½	teaspoons grated lime peel
1	tablespoon lime juice

Heat oven to 350°. Grease bottom only of loaf pan, 9 x 5 x 3 inches, or 2 loaf pans, 8½ x 4½ x 2½ inches. Mix all ingredients; beat 30 seconds. Pour into pan. Bake until wooden pick inserted in center comes out clean, 9-inch loaf 70 to 80 minutes, 8-inch loaves 55 to 60 minutes. Cool slightly. Loosen sides of loaf from pan; remove from pan. Cool completely before slicing. To store, wrap and refrigerate no longer than 1 week.

Bananas
Did You Know?

Once bananas have reached the desired stage of ripeness, they can be stored in the refrigerator for several days. The skin will darken when refrigerated, but the edible portion will remain unchanged. Bananas that are to be mashed should remain at room temperature until they are fully ripe. To mash easily, slice the bananas and beat with mixer, rotary beater or fork.

Paraguayan Corn Bread
(Sopa Paraguaya)

Two kinds of cheese and perky Latin spices give this lively Paraguayan bread a special character of its own. In Paraguay the bread is traditionally served with a hearty beef soup. We find it goes well with nearly any main-dish soup or stew, and especially like it with chili corn carne.

9 to 12 servings

1½	cups boiling water
1	cup cornmeal
2	tablespoons margarine or butter, softened
3	eggs, separated
½	cup milk
½	cup (4 ounces) cottage cheese
1	teaspoon salt
1	teaspoon baking powder
¼	teaspoon ground cumin
⅛	teaspoon ground allspice
⅛	teaspoon ground red pepper
1	can (8 ounces) whole-kernel corn, drained
1	cup shredded Monterey Jack cheese (4 ounces)
1	small onion, chopped

Heat oven to 375°. Stir boiling water into cornmeal in 3-quart bowl; continue stirring until smooth. Blend in margarine and egg yolks. Stir in milk, cottage cheese, salt, baking powder, the spices, corn, cheese and onion. Beat egg whites just until soft peaks form; fold into batter. Pour into greased 2-quart casserole. Bake until knife inserted near the center comes out clean, 45 to 50 minutes.

Irish Soda Bread

Irish Soda Bread

This teatime favorite from Ireland was origi-nally baked in an iron pot over a peat fire—a primitive Irish oven. Today it remains one of Ireland's favorite breads, served hot or cold, with butter and jam. There are many varia-tions on the basic recipe, but the bread is nearly always identified by the cross on top of the loaf.

1 loaf

3	tablespoons margarine or butter, softened
2½	cups all-purpose flour
2	tablespoons sugar
1	teaspoon baking soda
1	teaspoon baking powder
½	teaspoon salt
⅓	cup raisins (optional)
¾	cup buttermilk

Cut margarine into flour, sugar, baking soda, baking powder and salt until mixture resem-bles fine crumbs. Stir in raisins and enough buttermilk to make a soft dough.

Turn onto lightly floured surface; knead until smooth, 1 to 2 minutes. Shape into round loaf, about 6½ inches in diameter. Place on greased cookie sheet. Cut an X about ¼ through loaf with floured knife. Bake in 375° oven until golden brown, 35 to 45 minutes. Brush with margarine if desired.

Currant-Cream Scones

The British have many recipes for scones. This rather rich version is a favorite at tea shops and inns throughout Britain. The scones are usually served with strawberry or currant jam and butter. At "cream teas" the scones are served with a generous dollop of Devonshire cream—a thick, clotted cream from England's county of Devonshire.

10 to 12 scones

⅓	cup margarine, butter or shortening
1¾	cups all-purpose flour
3	tablespoons sugar
2½	teaspoons baking powder
½	teaspoon salt
1	egg, beaten
½	cup currants or raisins
4	to 6 tablespoons half-and-half
1	egg, beaten

Heat oven to 400°. Cut margarine into flour, sugar, baking powder and salt until mixture resembles fine crumbs. Stir in 1 egg, the cur-rants and just enough half-and-half so dough leaves side of bowl. Turn dough onto lightly floured surface. Knead lightly 10 times. Roll ½ inch thick.

Cut dough into 2¼-inch circles with floured cutter. Place on ungreased cookie sheet. Brush with 1 egg. Bake until golden, 10 to 12 minutes. Immediately remove from cookie sheet.

Gruyère Cheese Ring (Gougère)

Gougère, a cheese-flecked ring, is thought to have originated in the Burgundy district of France, along the lush Loire River valley. Today it is a favorite throughout France, served cold, warm or hot—often as an appetizer or as a light main dish, accompanied by a tossed green salad and, in Burgundy, a glass of red wine.

8 to 10 servings

1   cup milk
½   cup margarine or butter
1   cup all-purpose flour
4   eggs, slightly beaten
1   cup shredded Gruyère cheese (about 3 ounces)

Heat oven to 400°. Heat milk and margarine to rolling boil in 2-quart saucepan. Stir in flour. Stir vigorously over low heat until mixture forms a ball, about 1 minute; remove from heat. Beat in 4 eggs all at once; continue beating until smooth.

Fold in ⅔ cup of the cheese. Drop dough by tablespoonfuls onto greased cookie sheet to form 8-inch ring; smooth with spatula. Sprinkle with remaining cheese. Bake until puffed and golden, 50 to 60 minutes.

Gruyère Cheese

Did You Know?

Gruyère cheese is of Swiss origin and is somewhat similar to Swiss cheese. They are often used interchangeably in recipes. Although Gruyère cheese also has a nutty flavor, it is sharper than Swiss. Gruyère is commonly used in Europe but has not been as popular in this country. The Gruyère cheese sold in the United States is a pasteurized process cheese, usually sold in small individually wrapped wedges or in half-round or round packages.

Oatmeal Pancakes

In Scandinavia, Oatmeal Pancakes are traditionally served with lingonberry preserves (available at large supermarkets and gourmet shops) and sour cream, or with applesauce. They go equally well with any fruit-flavored or maple syrup.

12 to 14 pancakes

1   egg
¾   cup buttermilk
½   cup quick-cooking oats
½   cup all-purpose flour
¼   cup milk
2   tablespoons vegetable oil
1   tablespoon sugar
1   teaspoon baking powder
½   teaspoon baking soda
½   teaspoon salt

Beat egg with hand beater until fluffy; stir in remaining ingredients. (For thinner pancakes, stir in additional 2 to 4 tablespoons milk.) Grease heated griddle if necessary. (To test griddle, sprinkle with a few drops water. If bubbles skitter around and quickly evaporate, heat is just right.)

Pour about 3 tablespoons batter from tip of large spoon or from pitcher onto hot griddle. Cook pancakes until puffed and dry around edges. Turn and cook other sides until golden brown.

German Apple Pancakes (Apfelpfannkuchen)

Giant apple pancakes are baked in the oven for twenty to twenty-five minutes, eliminating last-minute fuss when planning a party brunch. But be sure to serve them as soon as they're done, for they sink rapidly, like soufflés.

2 large pancakes (4 servings)

4	eggs
¾	cup all-purpose flour
¾	cup milk
½	teaspoon salt
¼	cup margarine or butter
2	medium apples, thinly sliced
¼	cup sugar
¼	teaspoon ground cinnamon

Heat oven to 400°. Place 2 round layer pans, 9 x 1½ inches, in oven. Beat eggs, flour, milk and salt in small mixer bowl on medium speed 1 minute. Remove pans from oven. Place 2 tablespoons margarine in each pan; rotate pans until margarine is melted and coats sides of pans.

Arrange half the apple slices in each pan; divide batter evenly between pans. Mix sugar and cinnamon; sprinkle 2 tablespoons sugar mixture over batter in each pan. Bake uncovered until puffed and golden brown, 20 to 25 minutes.

Bread Dumplings (Houskove Knedliky)

European dumplings come in all shapes and sizes, from the gnocchi of Italy to the spaetzle and fruit-filled dumplings of Germany and Austria. These easy Bread Dumplings are a Czechoslovakian specialty, usually formed into rolls and then cooked and sliced. Serve them as a side dish with any meat or poultry dish that includes a gravy.

30 dumplings

3	tablespoons finely chopped onion
3	tablespoons margarine or butter
4	slices bread or 2 rolls, cut into ½-inch cubes (about 3½ cups)
2	eggs, beaten
¾	cup milk
1	tablespoon snipped parsley
¾	teaspoon salt
2	to 2½ cups all-purpose flour
2	quarts water

Cook and stir onion in margarine in 10-inch skillet until tender. Add bread cubes; cook and stir until golden brown. Cool. Mix eggs, milk, parsley and salt in large bowl; add onion-bread mixture. Let stand until bread is thoroughly moistened, 5 to 10 minutes. Stir in enough flour to make a soft dough. (Dough will be slightly sticky.)

Heat water to boiling in Dutch oven. Shape mixture into 1½-inch balls. (For easy shaping, dip hands in cold water from time to time.) Carefully place dumplings in boiling water. Simmer uncovered until dumplings rise to surface, 2 to 4 minutes; stir occasionally to prevent sticking. Simmer uncovered until done, 5 to 8 minutes. Remove dumplings with slotted spoon.

Swedish Filled Dumplings
(Kroppkakor)

A savory filling made with fried onions and salt pork is the surprise touch that makes these tasty potato dumplings so popular in Sweden. Try them with lingonberry preserves and a favorite pot roast.

36 dumplings

4	medium potatoes (about 1½ pounds)
1	cup finely chopped salt pork (6 ounces)
1	medium onion, chopped
	Dash of ground allspice
1	cup all-purpose flour
1	teaspoon salt
1	egg, beaten
2½	quarts water
1	teaspoon salt
¼	cup margarine or butter, melted

Pare potatoes; cut into large pieces. Heat 1 inch salted water (½ teaspoon salt to 1 cup water) to boiling. Add potatoes. Heat to boiling; reduce heat. Cover and cook until tender, 20 to 25 minutes; drain. Shake pan gently over low heat to dry potatoes. Put enough potatoes through ricer or food mill to measure 3 cups; cool.

Cook and stir salt pork until brown; remove with slotted spoon. Cook and stir onion in pork fat until tender; remove onion. Mix salt pork, onion and allspice; cool.

Mix potatoes, flour and 1 teaspoon salt; beat in egg. (Knead in ¼ to ½ cup flour if necessary to make dough easy to handle.) Shape dough into 1-inch balls. Press hole in center of each; place ¼ teaspoon pork mixture in hole. Seal by reshaping into ball. Repeat with remaining dough and pork mixture.

Heat water and 1 teaspoon salt to boiling in Dutch oven. Place dumplings in boiling water; stir once or twice. Reduce heat. Simmer uncovered, turning once, until dumplings are done, 6 to 8 minutes; remove with slotted spoon. Heat margarine over low heat until golden brown; pour over dumplings.

Little German Noodle Dumplings
(Spaetzle)

Spaetzle more nearly resemble noodles than dumplings and are made in a number of ways in Germany. Our recipe is quick and easy and requires no special equipment. Use the spaetzle as a garnish for soups or as a side dish sprinkled with toasted bread crumbs or grated cheese.

4 to 6 servings

2	eggs, beaten
¼	cup milk or water
1	cup all-purpose flour
½	teaspoon salt
	Dash of pepper
2	quarts water (see Note)
1	teaspoon salt
2	tablespoons margarine or butter, melted

Mix eggs, milk, flour, ½ teaspoon salt and the pepper. (Batter will be thick.) Heat water and 1 teaspoon salt to boiling in Dutch oven. Press batter through colander (preferably one with large holes), a few tablespoons at a time, into boiling water. Stir once or twice to prevent sticking.

Cook until dumplings rise to surface and are tender, about 5 minutes; drain. Pour margarine over dumplings. Serve with *Sauerbraten* (page 116), meatballs, chicken or sauerkraut.

Note: Spaetzle can also be cooked in beef or chicken broth.

Potato Dumplings with Cheese Sauce

(Gnocchi di Patate)

The Italians have devised a number of tasty gnocchi (or dumpling) recipes, ranging from tiny cheese-and-spinach balls to the unusual Roman Farina Dumplings (page 252). Potatoes—something of a novelty in Italy—form the base for these dumplings, which are served with a tasty and unusual Gorgonzola Cheese Sauce.

8 or 9 servings

4   large baking potatoes (2 pounds)
1   egg
1   clove garlic, finely chopped
2   teaspoons salt
⅛   teaspoon ground nutmeg
1   to 1½ cups all-purpose flour
    Bread cubes
1   tablespoon salt
6   cups boiling water
    Cheese Sauce (right)

Pare potatoes; cut into large pieces. Heat 1 inch salted water (½ teaspoon salt to 1 cup water) to boiling. Add potatoes. Cover and heat to boiling. Cook until tender, 25 to 30 minutes; drain.

Mash or put through potato ricer. Beat in egg, garlic, 2 teaspoons salt and the nutmeg. Stir in enough flour, ½ cup at a time, to make dough easy to handle. Pinch off 1-inch pieces of dough; shape each around a bread cube into a ball.

Stir 1 tablespoon salt into boiling water in 3-quart saucepan. Place dumplings, 20 at a time, in water. Cook uncovered over medium heat until dumplings rise to surface, about 3 minutes. Remove with slotted spoon; keep warm. Prepare Cheese Sauce. Stir dumplings carefully into sauce; heat over low heat until hot.

Cheese Sauce

2   tablespoons margarine or butter
2   tablespoons flour
¼   teaspoon salt
⅛   teaspoon pepper
1   cup milk
1   cup crumbled Gorgonzola cheese (about 4 ounces)

Heat margarine over low heat in 3-quart saucepan until melted. Blend in flour, salt and pepper. Cook over low heat, stirring constantly, until smooth and bubbly; remove from heat. Stir in milk. Heat to boiling, stirring constantly. Boil and stir 1 minute. Stir in cheese. Heat over low heat, stirring constantly, until cheese is melted and sauce is smooth.

Scottish Oatcakes

These quick oatcakes can be served with butter and jam, honey or, for a more substantial teatime snack, cheese or herring. The sweetened cookie variation, below, resembles our oatmeal cookies.

18 oatcakes

½   cup shortening
1   cup oats or quick-cooking oats
1   cup all-purpose flour
½   teaspoon baking soda
¼   teaspoon salt
2   to 3 tablespoons cold water

Cut shortening into oats, flour, baking soda and salt until mixture resembles fine crumbs. Add water, 1 tablespoon at a time, until mixture forms a stiff dough.

Roll until ⅛ inch thick on lightly floured surface. Cut into 2½-inch rounds or squares. Place on ungreased cookie sheet. Bake in 375° oven until oatcakes just start to brown, 12 to 15 minutes. Cool on wire rack.

Oatcake Cookies: Prepare as directed above except add ⅓ cup sugar with flour.

Fried Potato Bread

Fried Potato Bread

(Lefse)

This thin, soft griddle-fried bread from Norway is served warm or cold, spread with butter and sometimes sprinkled with brown sugar—then rolled up or folded into small serving-size portions. It makes a fine complement to a Scandinavian smorgasbord and goes well with meatballs or fish. Lefse is a great Norwegian favorite during the holidays, when commercial versions can often be found at large supermarkets and shops that carry Scandinavian specialty foods. Norwegian chefs use special lefse bakers and corrugated rolling pins when making their favorite holiday bread—you'll find them at shops carrying Scandinavian housewares.

20 lefse

5	cups hot mashed potatoes (no milk, margarine or salt added)
¼	cup shortening
2	tablespoons milk
1½	teaspoons salt
2	cups all-purpose flour

Beat mashed potatoes, shortening, milk and salt until no lumps remain. Cover and refrigerate until completely chilled, at least 4 hours.

Turn potato mixture onto floured surface; knead in flour. (Dough will be soft.) Divide into 20 equal parts; shape each part into a ball. (For best results, work with 4 or 5 balls at a time; cover and refrigerate remaining balls until needed.)

Shape each ball into a flattened round on heavily floured board. Roll each round as thin as possible into 10- to 12-inch circle with floured stockinet-covered rolling pin or lefse rolling pin. (See photograph.) Lift dough occasionally with spatula to make sure it is not sticking, adding flour as needed.

Heat ungreased griddle or lefse baker to 400°. Cook until blisters form and brown spots appear on bottom, about 1 minute on each side. (Do not overcook. Lefse should be soft, not crisp.) Stack between 2 towels to prevent drying. Wrap in plastic wrap and refrigerate no longer than 3 days or freeze no longer than 1 month.

Roll each round as thin as possible with floured stockinet-covered rolling pin.

Roll circles around rolling pin; unroll on hot griddle to cook.

Whole-Wheat Flat Bread (Flatbröd)

The Norwegians originally baked this bread— one of their favorites—on top of wood burning stoves in the days before ovens became standard kitchen appliances. The flat bread can be served, spread with butter, as a simple snack, and is traditionally served with fish and cheese.

9 rounds

1	cup stone-ground whole-wheat flour
1	cup all-purpose flour
⅔	cup cornmeal
¼	cup vegetable oil
2	tablespoons sugar
1	teaspoon baking soda
½	teaspoon salt
¾	to 1 cup buttermilk

Mix flours, cornmeal, oil, sugar, baking soda and salt. Stir in just enough buttermilk to make a stiff dough. Knead 30 seconds. Shape dough, ¼ cup at a time, into a ball; shape into flattened round. (Cover remaining dough to prevent drying.) Roll as thin as possible into 10-inch circle with floured stockinet-covered rolling pin or lefse rolling pin (see Fried Potato Bread, page 264) on well-floured surface. (Lift dough occasionally with spatula to make sure it is not sticking, adding flour as needed.)

Heat oven to 350°. Place flat bread on ungreased cookie sheet. (See Note.) Bake until crisp and slightly brown around edges, 8 to 10 minutes. Cool on wire rack. Repeat with remaining dough. Break into irregular pieces; serve with margarine or butter if desired.

Note: Rounds can be cut or scored into wedges or squares with knife or pastry cutter before baking for more uniform shapes if desired. After baking, break along scored lines.

Fried Bread Puffs

Fried Bread Puffs

(Puris)

When planning a curry party, puffy, deep-fried bread from India provides a fine answer to the perennial question, "What shall we serve for bread?" The puffs are best when served warm (see Do-Ahead Tip, below).

About 24 puris

1	cup whole-wheat flour
1	cup all-purpose flour
½	teaspoon salt
3	tablespoons Ghee (page 218) or vegetable oil
½	to ¾ cup water
	Vegetable oil

Mix flours, salt and Ghee until mixture resembles fine crumbs. Stir in just enough water to make a very stiff dough. Turn dough onto lightly floured surface; knead until smooth and elastic, 5 to 8 minutes. Cover; let rest 20 minutes.

Shape dough by rounded teaspoonfuls into 1-inch balls. Roll into 3- to 4-inch circles ⅛ inch thick on lightly floured surface. (Cover to prevent drying.)

Heat oil (1½ to 2 inches) to 370°. Fry 1 to 3 puris at a time, turning once, until golden brown and evenly puffed, 1½ to 2 minutes. (Press flat portions into hot oil with spoon if necessary to insure even puffing.) Drain on paper towels.

Do-Ahead Tip: Puris can be covered with aluminum foil and kept warm in 300° oven no longer than 40 minutes. Or reheat by placing foil-covered puris in 300° oven 20 minutes.

Indian Flat Bread

(Naan)

Naan is popular in both India and Pakistan and is found throughout the central steppes of Asia. It goes especially well with barbecued meats and Roast Chicken with Spiced Yogurt (page 76). Often naan is served with yogurt or cheese and fresh fruit.

6 or 8 breads

2	cups all-purpose flour
¼	cup unflavored yogurt
1	egg, slightly beaten
1½	teaspoons baking powder
1	teaspoon sugar
¼	teaspoon salt
⅛	teaspoon baking soda
½	cup milk
	Ghee (page 218) or vegetable oil
	Poppy seed

Mix all ingredients except milk, Ghee and poppy seed. Stir in enough milk to make a soft dough. Turn dough onto lightly floured surface; knead until smooth, about 5 minutes. Place in greased bowl; turn greased side up. Cover; let rest in warm place 3 hours.

Divide dough into 6 or 8 equal parts. Flatten each part on lightly floured surface, rolling it into a 6- x 4-inch leaf shape about ¼ inch thick. Brush with Ghee; sprinkle with poppy seed.

Place 2 cookie sheets in oven; heat oven to 450°. Remove hot cookie sheets from oven; place breads on cookie sheets. Bake until firm, 6 to 8 minutes.

Finnish Rye Bread

(Suomalaisruisleipä)

The rich color and taste of Finland's memorable rye bread come from brown sugar and rye— one of the few grains that ripen in Finland's short growing season. The Finlanders usually cut the bread into wedges, which are then split and served warm with butter.

1 loaf

1	package active dry yeast
1¼	cups warm water* (105 to 115°)
1	tablespoon packed brown sugar
1	tablespoon vegetable oil
1½	teaspoons salt
1¼	cups medium rye flour
1½	to 2 cups all-purpose flour
	Margarine or butter, softened

Dissolve yeast in warm water in large bowl. Stir in brown sugar, oil, salt and 1 cup of the rye flour. Beat until smooth. Stir in enough all-purpose flour to make the dough easy to handle.

Turn dough onto surface that has been sprinkled with the remaining rye flour. Cover; let rest 10 to 15 minutes. Knead until smooth and elastic, about 5 minutes. Place in greased bowl; turn greased side up. Cover; let rise in warm place until double, about 1 hour. (Dough is ready if indentation remains when touched.)

Punch down dough; shape into a round, slightly flat loaf. Place in greased round layer pan, 9 x 1½ inches. Cover; let rise until double, about 1 hour.

Heat oven to 375°. Bake until loaf sounds hollow when tapped, 40 to 50 minutes. Immediately remove from pan. Brush top of loaf with margarine; cool on wire rack.

* Potato water (water in which potatoes have been cooked) can be substituted for the water. This is traditional in this recipe.

French Cheese Braid

French Cheese Braid (Natte)

The rich yellow dough used to make this braid (the French call it natte) *is similar to the Jewish holiday bread called* Challah *(page 272), but somewhat richer in flavor and flecked with bits of cheese. It is delicious as a luncheon or light supper bread served with soup and salad.*

1 braid

1	package active dry yeast
¾	cup warm water (105 to 115°)
1	tablespoon sugar
1	teaspoon salt
3	eggs
½	cup margarine or butter, softened
3½	to 4 cups all-purpose flour
6	ounces Swiss or Gruyère cheese, diced (about 1½ cups)
	Vegetable oil
1	egg yolk
2	tablespoons water

Dissolve yeast in warm water in large bowl. Stir in sugar, salt, eggs, margarine and 2 cups of the flour. Beat until smooth. Stir in enough remaining flour to make the dough easy to handle.

Turn dough onto lightly floured surface; knead until smooth and elastic, about 5 minutes. Place in greased bowl; turn greased side up. Cover; let rise in warm place until double, 1 to 2 hours. (Dough is ready if indentation remains when touched.)

Punch down dough; knead in cheese until well distributed. Divide into 3 equal parts. Roll each part into a rope, 15 inches long. Place ropes together on lightly greased cookie sheet. Braid ropes gently and loosely; do not stretch. (See diagram.) Pinch ends to fasten; tuck under securely. Brush lightly with oil. Let rise until double, 40 to 50 minutes.

Heat oven to 375°. Beat egg yolk and 2 tablespoons water slightly; brush over braid. Place on oven rack below center of oven. Bake until braid sounds hollow when tapped, 25 to 30 minutes. (If braid is browning too quickly, cover loosely with aluminum foil.)

Place ropes close together on cookie sheet; braid ropes gently and loosely.

Swiss Cheese

Did You Know?

The distinguishing characteristic of Swiss cheese is the "eyes"—holes that are formed during the ripening of the cheese. To some extent the size of the holes can be regulated by controlling the temperature and length of the ripening time. Swiss cheese is well liked for its mild, nutty, slightly sweet flavor and is one of the most popular varieties of cheese in this country. In Switzerland, its country of origin, Swiss cheese is known as Emmenthaler or Emmentaler.

French Bread

The French have been famous for their bread since the eighth century, when Charlemagne first policed the baking industry to insure an adequate supply and standard quality of bread throughout France. During the Crusades of the thirteenth century, King Louis IX exempted French bread bakers from going to war. Today French Bread continues to be the classic loaf that is a favorite with nearly any meal.

1 loaf

1	package active dry yeast
1¼	cups warm water (105 to 115°)
1	tablespoon sugar
1½	teaspoons salt
2¾	to 3 cups all-purpose flour
1	tablespoon cornmeal
1	egg white
2	tablespoons cold water

Dissolve yeast in warm water in large bowl. Stir in sugar, salt and 2 cups of the flour. Beat until smooth. Stir in enough remaining flour to make dough easy to handle.

Turn dough onto lightly floured surface; knead until smooth and elastic, about 5 minutes. Place in greased bowl; turn greased side up. Cover with damp cloth; let rise in warm place until double, 1½ to 2 hours. (Dough is ready if indentation remains when touched.)

Punch down dough; cover and let rest 15 minutes. Grease cookie sheet; sprinkle with cornmeal. Roll dough into rectangle, 15 x 10 inches. Roll up tightly; seal edge. Roll gently back and forth to taper ends. Place on cookie sheet. Make ¼-inch slashes in loaf at 2-inch intervals or make 1 lengthwise slash. Brush top of loaf with cold water. Let rise uncovered until double, 1½ hours.

Heat oven to 375°. Brush loaf with cold water. Bake 20 minutes. Mix egg white and 2 tablespoons water; brush over loaf. Bake until loaf is deep golden brown and sounds hollow when tapped, about 25 minutes.

Swedish Rye Bread (Limpa)

Americans have concocted many versions of limpa. *The original Swedish version—traditional holiday fare—is generally flavored with molasses, orange peel and anise or fennel.*

2 loaves

2	packages active dry yeast
1½	cups warm water (105 to 115°)
⅓	cup packed brown sugar
⅓	cup molasses
1	tablespoon salt
1	tablespoon anise seed or fennel seed, crushed
1	tablespoon finely shredded orange peel
2	tablespoons vegetable oil
2½	cups medium rye flour
2¼	to 2¾ cups all-purpose or unbleached flour

Dissolve yeast in warm water in large bowl. Stir in brown sugar, molasses, salt, anise seed, orange peel, oil and rye flour. Beat until smooth. Stir in enough all-purpose flour to make a soft dough.

Turn dough onto lightly floured surface. Cover; let rest 10 to 15 minutes. Knead until smooth and elastic, about 5 minutes. Place in greased bowl; turn greased side up. Cover; let rise in warm place until double, about 1 hour. (Dough is ready if indentation remains when touched.)

Punch down dough; divide into halves. Shape each half into a round, slightly flat loaf. Place loaves in opposite corners of greased cookie sheet. Cover; let rise until double, about 1 hour.

Heat oven to 375°. Bake until loaves sound hollow when tapped, 40 to 50 minutes. Brush with margarine or butter if desired. Cool on wire racks.

Dark Pumpernickel Bread

Cocoa is the mystery ingredient that helps bring the fragrance and flavor to our recipe for pumpernickel—an all-time German favorite that makes a fine accompaniment to hearty soups.

2 loaves

3	packages active dry yeast
1¾	cups warm water (105 to 115°)
½	cup dark molasses
2	tablespoons vegetable oil
1	tablespoon caraway seed
1	tablespoon salt
2½	cups dark rye flour
1	cup whole-bran cereal
¼	cup cocoa
2	to 2½ cups all-purpose flour
	Cornmeal
	Margarine or butter, softened

Dissolve yeast in warm water in large bowl. Stir in molasses, oil, caraway seed, salt, rye flour, bran cereal and cocoa. Beat until smooth. Stir in enough all-purpose flour to make dough easy to handle.

Turn dough onto lightly floured surface. Cover; let rest 10 to 15 minutes. Knead until smooth, about 5 minutes. Place in greased bowl; turn greased side up. Cover; let rise in warm place until double, about 1 hour. (Dough is ready if indentation remains when touched.)

Grease cookie sheet; sprinkle with cornmeal. Punch down dough; divide into halves. Shape each half into a round, slightly flat loaf. Place loaves in opposite corners of cookie sheet. Brush tops lightly with margarine; let rise until double, 40 to 50 minutes. Heat oven to 375°. Bake until loaves sound hollow when tapped, 30 to 35 minutes. Cool on wire racks.

Brioche

Brioche is one of the most sophisticated of breads. The word comes from the old French bris *(meaning to break) and* hacher *(to stir)—a reference to the butter being broken and stirred into the dough. Our easy electric-mixer recipe enables you to make two large brioches or two dozen individual ones. Individual brioches served with marmalade and coffee comprise a classic French breakfast.*

2 brioche loaves or 24 individual brioches

1	package active dry yeast
¼	cup warm water (105 to 115°)
2	tablespoons sugar
1	teaspoon salt
4	eggs
1	egg white
1	cup butter, softened
3½	cups all-purpose flour
1	egg yolk
1	tablespoon water

Dissolve yeast in warm water in large mixer bowl. Add sugar, salt, 4 eggs, egg white, butter and 2 cups of the flour. Beat on low speed, scraping bowl constantly, 30 seconds. Beat on medium speed, scraping bowl occasionally, 10 minutes. Stir in remaining flour until smooth. Scrape batter from side of bowl. Cover with plastic wrap; let rise in warm place until double, about 1 hour.

Stir down batter by beating about 25 strokes. Cover bowl tightly with plastic wrap; refrigerate at least 8 hours.

Stir down batter. (Batter will be soft and slightly sticky.) Divide batter into halves. Refrigerate one half until ready to use. Shape ¼ of the batter into a ball on lightly floured surface. Shape remaining ¾ batter into a 3½-inch flattened round. Repeat with refrigerated batter.

Grease two 5-cup brioche pans or two 1½-quart ovenproof bowls. Place large rounds in pans, patting to fit. Make indentation about 2 inches in diameter in center of each; place smaller balls in indentations. Let rise until double, about 1½ hours.

Heat oven to 375°. Beat egg yolk and 1 tablespoon water slightly; brush over tops. (Do not let egg-yolk mixture accumulate around edges of pans.) Bake until golden brown, 25 to 30 minutes. Immediately remove from pans.

Individual Brioches: Grease 24 brioche pans or muffin cups, 2½ x 1¼ inches. Divide chilled batter into halves; refrigerate one half. Shape remaining half into roll about 7½ inches long. Cut into 15 slices about ½ inch thick.

Working quickly with floured hands (batter will be soft and slightly sticky), shape 12 of the slices into balls; place in muffin cups. Flatten and make a deep indentation in center of each. Cut each of the remaining 3 slices into 4 equal parts. Shape each part into a small ball; place a ball in each indentation. Repeat with refrigerated batter. Let rise until double, about 40 minutes.

Heat oven to 375°. Beat egg yolk and 1 tablespoon water slightly; brush over tops. (Do not let egg yolk mixture run down into muffin cups.) Bake until golden brown, 15 to 20 minutes. Immediately remove from pans.

Jewish Egg Braid

(Challah)

Challah—a Sabbath and holiday bread for Jewish people throughout the world—is steeped in tradition and history. Challah actually refers to the act of preparing dough for baking in the Jewish kitchen.

1 braid

1   package active dry yeast
¾   cup warm water (105 to 115°)
2   tablespoons sugar
1   teaspoon salt
1   egg
1   tablespoon vegetable oil
2½   to 2¾ cups all-purpose flour
      Vegetable oil
1   egg yolk
2   tablespoons cold water
      Poppy seed

Dissolve yeast in warm water in large bowl. Stir in sugar, salt, 1 egg, 1 tablespoon oil and 1¼ cups of the flour. Beat until smooth. Stir in enough remaining flour to make dough easy to handle.

Turn dough onto lightly floured surface; knead until smooth and elastic, about 5 minutes. Place in greased bowl; turn greased side up. Cover; let rise in warm place until double, 1½ to 2 hours. (Dough is ready if indentation remains when touched.)

Punch down dough; divide into 3 equal parts. Roll each part into a rope, 14 inches long. Place ropes close together on lightly greased cookie sheet. Braid ropes gently and loosely; do not stretch. Fasten ends; tuck under braid securely. Brush with oil. Let rise until double, 40 to 50 minutes.

Heat oven to 375°. Mix egg yolk and 2 tablespoons water; brush braid with egg yolk mixture. Sprinkle with poppy seed. Bake until golden brown, 25 to 30 minutes.

Pocket Bread

A standard bread throughout the Middle East, Pocket Bread has many names—pita, Arab bread, Armenian bread, Israeli flat bread, khubz, and in some American supermarkets, "sandwich pockets." The recipes are all similar and the uses are many. The pockets can be filled with meats or salads; or the bread can be cut into wedges or strips to serve with dips.

6 pocket breads

1   package active dry yeast
1⅓   cups warm water (105 to 115°)
1   tablespoon vegetable oil
1   teaspoon sugar
1   teaspoon salt
3   to 4 cups all-purpose or unbleached flour

Dissolve yeast in warm water in large bowl. Stir in oil, sugar, salt and 2 cups of the flour. Beat until smooth. Stir in enough remaining flour to make dough easy to handle.

Turn dough onto lightly floured surface; knead until smooth and elastic, about 10 minutes. Place in greased bowl; turn greased side up. Cover; let rise in warm place until double, about 1 hour. (Dough is ready if indentation remains when touched.)

Punch down dough; divide into 6 equal parts. Shape into balls. Cover; let rise 30 minutes. Roll each ball into a 6- to 7-inch circle ⅛ inch thick on floured surface. Place 2 circles in opposite corners of each of 3 ungreased cookie sheets. Cover; let rise 30 minutes.

Heat oven to 450°. Bake until loaves are puffed and golden brown, about 10 minutes. Cut or tear crosswise into halves; fill with desired meat filling or salad.

Koláče

This popular Czechoslovakian sweet roll has many fans in our Midwestern states and can be made with a variety of fillings—but dried fruit fillings like those below are the most popular.

30 koláče

2   packages active dry yeast
½   cup warm water (105 to 115°)
¾   cup lukewarm milk (scalded, then cooled)
⅓   cup sugar
1   teaspoon salt
     Dash of ground nutmeg
2   egg yolks or 1 egg
½   cup margarine or butter, softened
4¼   to 4¾ cups all-purpose flour
     Prune, Poppy Seed or Apricot Filling (below)
     Margarine or butter, softened

Dissolve yeast in warm water in large bowl. Stir in milk, sugar, salt, nutmeg, egg yolks, ½ cup margarine and 3 cups of the flour. Beat until smooth. Stir in enough remaining flour to make dough easy to handle.

Turn dough onto lightly floured surface; knead until smooth and elastic, about 5 minutes. Place in greased bowl; turn greased side up. Cover; let rise in warm place until double, about 1½ hours. (Dough is ready if indentation remains when touched.) Prepare filling.

Punch down dough; divide into halves. Roll each half into 12-inch square ¼ inch thick on lightly floured surface. Cut into 3-inch squares. Place 1 tablespoon filling on each square. Moisten corners of squares; bring 2 opposite corners up over filling and pinch. Repeat with remaining corners. Place in greased muffin cups. Let rise until double, 30 to 45 minutes.

Heat oven to 350°. Bake until light brown, 10 to 15 minutes. Brush with margarine. Cool on wire racks.

Prune Filling

1½   cups (14 ounces) pitted prunes
⅓   cup sugar
1   teaspoon grated lemon peel
1   tablespoon lemon juice
½   teaspoon ground cinnamon

Simmer prunes in just enough water to cover until tender, about 30 minutes; drain. Finely chop prunes or purée in blender or press through food mill. Stir in remaining ingredients; cool.

Poppy Seed Filling

¾   cup (4 ounces) poppy seed
½   cup whipping cream
⅓   cup honey
1   tablespoon cornstarch
1   tablespoon margarine or butter

Heat all ingredients to boiling, stirring constantly. Boil and stir 1 minute; cool.

Apricot Filling

Simmer 1½ cups (10 ounces) dried apricots in just enough water to cover until tender, about 30 minutes; drain. Finely chop apricots or purée in blender or press through food mill. Stir in ⅓ cup sugar and ⅛ teaspoon ground mace (optional); cool.

Alternate Shaping Method: Divide dough into 4 equal parts; cut each part into 8 equal pieces. Shape each piece into a ball; place about 2 inches apart on greased cookie sheets. Make a depression in center of each. Fill with about 1 tablespoon filling. Let rise until double, about 30 minutes. Bake as directed.

Croissants

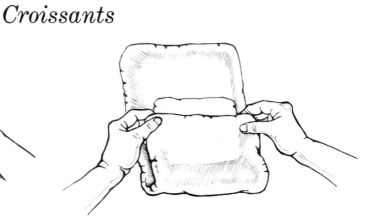

Flatten 2 pieces butter between waxed paper into 8-inch square. Repeat with remaining butter; refrigerate.

Place 1 square butter on center of 25 x 10-inch rectangle of dough; fold sides over butter to make 3 layers.

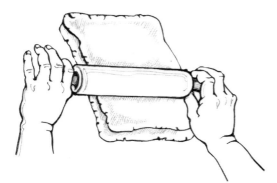

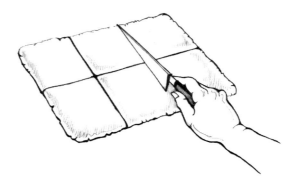

Turn dough; roll out. Repeat twice, placing butter square on center each time.

To shape, roll half of dough into 12 x 8-inch rectangle; cut into squares.

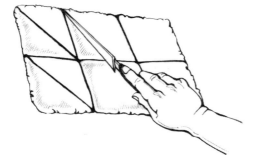

Cut each square diagonally into 2 triangles.

Roll up each triangle, beginning at long side.

Croissants

Although generally regarded as one of the triumphs of French gastronomy, Croissants are said to have been invented by Hungarians in Budapest in 1686. One night when the Ottoman Turks were about to besiege the city, the bakers, who worked through the wee hours, gave the alarm and the Turks were defeated. As a reward, the bakers were granted the privilege of creating a special pastry in the form of the crescent that decorated the Ottoman flag! Today, of course, Croissants are generally identified with France—but they are a cherished breakfast treat wherever food buffs gather.

24 croissants

2	sticks cold butter
2	packages active dry yeast
½	cup warm water (105 to 115°)
⅔	cup lukewarm milk (scalded, then cooled)
¼	cup butter, softened
2	tablespoons sugar
1½	teaspoons salt
2	eggs
4	to 4½ cups all-purpose flour
1	egg yolk
1	tablespoon milk

Cut each stick butter crosswise into 3 equal pieces. Place 2 pieces side by side on piece of waxed paper. Cover with second piece of waxed paper. Flatten butter into 8-inch square with rolling pin to form a solid sheet. (See diagram.) Repeat with remaining pieces of butter. Refrigerate squares of butter until firm, at least 1½ hours. (Butter must be very cold to prevent sticking when dough is rolled.)

Dissolve yeast in warm water in large bowl. Stir in ⅔ cup milk, ¼ cup butter, the sugar, salt, eggs and 2 cups of the flour. Beat until smooth. Stir in enough remaining flour to make dough easy to handle.

Turn dough onto lightly floured surface; knead until smooth and elastic, about 5 minutes. Place in greased bowl; turn greased side up. Cover; let rise in warm place until double, about 1 hour. (Dough is ready if indentation remains when touched.) Punch down dough. Cover; refrigerate 1 hour.

Punch down dough. Roll into rectangle, 25 x 10 inches, on lightly floured surface. Place 1 square firm butter on center of dough. Fold dough over butter to make 3 layers. (See diagram.) Turn dough one quarter turn; roll out. Repeat twice, placing butter square on center each time. (See diagram.) Work rapidly so butter does not become soft. Cut dough crosswise into halves; cover and refrigerate 1 hour.

Shape half of the dough at a time (keep other half refrigerated). Roll into rectangle, 12 x 8 inches. Cut lengthwise into halves; cut each half crosswise into 3 squares. (See diagrams.) Cut each square diagonally into 2 triangles. Roll up each triangle, beginning at long side. Place rolls with points underneath on ungreased cookie sheet; curve slightly to form crescents. Refrigerate 30 minutes.

Heat oven to 475°. Beat egg yolk and 1 tablespoon milk slightly; brush croissants with egg yolk mixture. Bake 5 minutes; decrease oven temperature to 400°. Bake until croissants are brown and crisp, 8 to 10 minutes.

Freezing Breads

Did You Know?

For tender, higher bread and rolls, bake before freezing. Cool completely, then slice if you wish for quick thawing later. Seal tightly, label, date and freeze breads no longer than one year, rolls and coffee cakes no longer than nine months. To thaw, let stand, wrapped, at room temperature, two or three hours. Frozen slices of bread can be popped into the toaster without thawing or used to make lunch-box sandwiches.

Danish Pastry

The basic puff pastry needed to make various Danish breads is called Wienerbröd *(Vienna bread) by the Danes, who adapted it from the Austrians long ago. The Austrians may have developed the pastry from the layered filo recipes they learned from the Turks. Our basic recipe is sufficient to make two of the variations given below. The dough takes time to make, but you will consider it well worth the effort when the compliments start coming!*

1½   sticks cold butter
1   package active dry yeast
¼   cup warm water (105 to 115°)
¼   cup lukewarm milk (scalded, then cooled)
2   tablespoons sugar
½   teaspoon salt
1   egg
2⅓   cups cake flour

Cut whole stick butter crosswise into halves. Place the 3 pieces side by side on piece of waxed paper. Cover with second piece of waxed paper. Flatten butter into 6-inch square with rolling pin to form a solid sheet. Refrigerate until firm, at least 1½ hours. (Butter must be very cold to prevent sticking when dough is rolled.)

Dissolve yeast in warm water in large bowl. Stir in milk, sugar, salt, egg and 1⅓ cups of the flour. Beat until smooth. Stir in enough remaining flour to make the dough easy to handle.

Turn dough onto lightly floured surface; knead until smooth and elastic, about 5 minutes. Place in lightly greased bowl; cover with damp cloth. Refrigerate 1½ hours (see Note).

Roll dough on lightly floured cloth-covered board into 12-inch circle with floured stockinet-covered rolling pin. Place 1 square firm butter on center of dough. (See diagrams.) Fold top and bottom edges of dough to center, covering butter. Fold right and left edges of dough to center; press to seal securely. (Dough should form a square envelope around butter.)

Roll dough into rectangle 20 x 6 inches. (Dough will be stiff in the beginning.) Fold rectangle crosswise into thirds to make 3 layers. (Use a pastry brush to remove excess flour from dough while folding.) Press edges of rectangle to secure dough and seal seam.

(Work rapidly so that butter does not become soft. Flour cloth generously as needed to prevent dough from sticking. If butter breaks through dough onto cloth, flour area heavily and continue rolling.)

Turn dough one quarter turn. Roll into rectangle, 20 x 6 inches. Fold rectangle into thirds, keeping sides and ends straight (uneven rolling results in less flakiness).

Turn dough one quarter turn; repeat rolling step a third time. Fold rectangle into thirds; place on tray. Cover with plastic wrap; refrigerate until dough is well chilled, 1½ to 2 hours.

Cut rectangle into halves. Use half the dough for any of the variations. Refrigerate remaining half until ready to use.

Danish Strip: Roll one half of dough into rectangle, 15 x 6 inches, on lightly floured cloth-covered board. Spread ½ cup Apricot Filling (below) or ⅓ cup preserves to within ½ inch of edges. Moisten edges of dough. Fold dough lengthwise into thirds; press seam and edges to seal securely. Place seam side down on ungreased cookie sheet. With sharp knife, make diagonal cuts ¼ inch deep at 2-inch intervals. Cover; let rise in warm place until double, about 30 minutes.

Heat oven to 400°. Bake until deep golden brown, about 25 minutes. Cool slightly on wire rack. Sprinkle with powdered sugar or drizzle with Powdered Sugar Frosting (page 278). 1 strip.

Jam Pastries: Roll one half of dough into 12-inch square on lightly floured cloth-covered board. Cut into nine 4-inch squares. Place ½ inch apart on ungreased cookie sheet. Place 1 tablespoon apricot, cherry or raspberry preserves on center of each pastry. Bring 2 opposite corners to center; press firmly to seal. Cover; let rise in warm place until double, about 30 minutes. Brush lightly with water or beaten egg.

Heat oven to 400°. Bake until deep golden brown, about 20 minutes. Drizzle with Powdered Sugar Frosting (page 278) if desired. 9 pastries.

Twists: Roll one half of dough into rectangle, 12 x 7 inches. Cut into twelve 1-inch strips. Shape into snails or figure 8's. For snails, hold one end of strip on ungreased cookie sheet; wind strip around to form snail shape. Tuck free end under roll. For figure 8's, hold one end of strip in each hand and twist in opposite directions, stretching strip slightly. Bring ends together; shape into figure 8's on ungreased cookie sheet. Cover; let rise in warm place until double, about 30 minutes.

Heat oven to 400°. Make a depression in center of each snail or in center of each loop of figure 8's. Fill with 1 teaspoon jam, jelly, preserves or Apricot Filling (below). Bake until golden brown, about 15 minutes. 12 twists.

Apricot Filling

Simmer 1 cup dried apricots in just enough water to cover until tender, about 30 minutes; drain and cut up. Mix apricots, ⅓ cup sugar and ¼ teaspoon ground allspice. About 1 cup.

Note: Dough can be refrigerated 8 hours before rolling with butter; cover with plastic wrap to prevent drying. Punch down dough; continue as directed.

Place 1 square firm butter on center of dough.

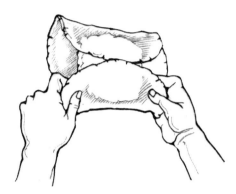

Fold top and bottom edges of dough to center.

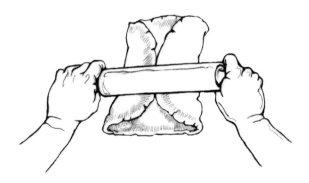

Fold right and left edges of dough to center; press to seal.

Hot Cross Buns

The nursery rhyme has made Hot Cross Buns familiar to children who have never tasted them—but most British children have. There are many legends in England about the origin of the Hot Cross Bun; some date back to pre-Roman times and all are linked to spring festivals. For many centuries Hot Cross Buns have been traditional Easter fare in Britain (when served on Good Friday they are said to have remarkable curative powers!).

24 buns

1	package active dry yeast
¼	cup warm water (105 to 115°)
1	cup lukewarm milk (scalded, then cooled)
⅓	cup sugar
⅓	cup shortening, margarine or butter, softened
1	teaspoon salt
1	teaspoon ground cinnamon
¼	teaspoon ground cloves
¼	teaspoon ground nutmeg
1	egg
1	egg yolk
3¾	to 4¼ cups all-purpose flour
½	cup currants or raisins
1	egg white, slightly beaten
1	tablespoon water
	Powdered Sugar Frosting (right)

Dissolve yeast in warm water in large bowl. Stir in milk, sugar, shortening, salt, cinnamon, cloves, nutmeg, egg, egg yolk and 2 cups of the flour. Beat until smooth. Stir in currants and enough remaining flour to make dough easy to handle.

Turn dough onto lightly floured surface; knead until smooth and elastic, about 5 minutes. Place in greased bowl; turn greased side up. Cover; let rise in warm place until double, about 1½ hours. (Dough is ready if indentation remains when touched.)

Punch down dough; divide into 4 equal parts. Cut each part into 6 equal pieces. Shape each piece into a ball; place about 2 inches apart on greased cookie sheets. Snip a cross on top of each ball with scissors. Cover; let rise until double, about 40 minutes.

Heat oven to 375°. Mix egg white and 1 tablespoon water; brush tops of buns with egg white mixture. Bake until golden brown, about 20 minutes. Cool slightly; frost crosses on buns with Powdered Sugar Frosting.

Powdered Sugar Frosting
Mix 1 cup powdered sugar, 1 tablespoon water or milk and ½ teaspoon vanilla until smooth. Stir in additional water if necessary, ½ teaspoon at a time.

Swedish Lucia Buns

These sweet, cardamom-scented buns are traditionally served in Sweden to family and guests by the young female members of the family on the dawn of the Queen of Light Festival (December 13), marking the beginning of the Christmas festivities. Often they are flavored with saffron, and can be shaped in a variety of ways. The S shape in our recipe is the most popular.

24 buns

2	packages active dry yeast
½	cup warm water (105 to 115°)
⅔	cup lukewarm milk (scalded, then cooled)
½	cup sugar
½	cup margarine or butter, softened
2	eggs
1	teaspoon ground cardamom
1	teaspoon salt
1	teaspoon grated orange peel
5	to 5½ cups all-purpose flour
½	cup raisins
	Margarine or butter, softened
1	egg, slightly beaten
1	tablespoon water
2	tablespoons sugar

Dissolve yeast in warm water in large bowl. Stir in milk, ½ cup sugar, ½ cup margarine, 2

Swedish Lucia Buns

eggs, the cardamom, salt, orange peel and 3 cups of the flour. Beat until smooth. Stir in enough remaining flour to make dough easy to handle.

Turn dough onto lightly floured surface; knead until smooth and elastic, about 5 minutes. Place in greased bowl; turn greased side up. Cover; let rise in warm place until double, 1½ to 2 hours. (Dough is ready if indentation remains when touched.)

Punch down dough; divide into 4 equal parts.

Cut each part into 6 equal pieces. Shape each piece into a smooth rope, 10 to 12 inches long. Shape each rope into an *S*; curve both ends into a coil. Place a raisin in center of each coil. Place on greased cookie sheets. Brush tops lightly with margarine; let rise until double, 35 to 45 minutes.

Heat oven to 350°. Mix 1 egg and 1 tablespoon water; brush buns lightly with egg mixture. Sprinkle with 2 tablespoons sugar. Bake until golden brown, 15 to 20 minutes.

Crumpets

Crumpets—sometimes called pikelets—are griddle-fried cakes served at breakfast and teatime in Britain. They emerged in seventeenth-century England and are similar to, but somewhat softer than, the familiar "English muffins" Americans have so long admired.

12 crumpets

1   package active dry yeast
¼   cup warm water (105 to 115°)
½   cup lukewarm milk (scalded, then cooled)
1   tablespoon margarine or butter
1   teaspoon sugar
¾   teaspoon salt
1   egg
1   cup all-purpose flour

Dissolve yeast in warm water in small bowl. Stir in remaining ingredients; beat until smooth. Cover; let rise in warm place until double, 40 to 60 minutes.

Grease griddle or heavy skillet and insides of four to six 3-inch flan rings.* Place rings on griddle over medium heat until hot. Pour about 2 tablespoons batter into each ring. Cook until tops form bubbles and bottoms are golden brown, 1 to 2 minutes. Remove rings; turn crumpets to brown other sides, 1 to 2 minutes. Repeat with remaining batter, greasing insides of rings each time. Serve with margarine or butter and jam or marmalade if desired.

* 6½-ounce tuna, minced clam or shrimp cans, tops and bottoms removed, can be substituted for the flan rings.

Sally Lunn

Homemakers in our Southeastern states have been exchanging recipes for Sally Lunn bread and buns for many generations, but the British claim the famous bread as their own. According to tradition, the bread was originally sold in the streets of the English city of Bath. There is even a theory that a real Sally Lunn once lived and sold her famous bread there!

12 to 16 servings

2   packages active dry yeast
½   cup warm water (105 to 115°)
1½   cups lukewarm milk (scalded, then cooled)
⅓   cup sugar
1½   teaspoons salt
3   eggs
½   cup shortening
5½   cups all-purpose flour

Dissolve yeast in warm water in large mixer bowl. Add milk, sugar, salt, eggs, shortening and 2½ cups of the flour. Beat on low speed, scraping bowl constantly, 30 seconds. Beat on medium speed, scraping bowl occasionally, 2 minutes. Stir in remaining flour until smooth. Scrape batter from side of bowl. Cover and let rise in warm place until double, 40 to 60 minutes.

Stir down batter by beating about 25 strokes. Spread in well-greased tube pan, 10 x 4 inches. Cover; let rise until double, 30 to 40 minutes. Heat oven to 350°. Bake until golden brown and crusty, 50 to 60 minutes. Cool in pan 10 minutes. Serve with margarine or butter if desired.

Portuguese Sweet Bread

Portuguese Sweet Bread
(Pão Dôce)

The Portuguese are famous for their Christmas bread and their Easter bread (which contains decorative Easter eggs baked into the loaf!). But pão dôce is Portugal's favorite bread for all seasons. Serve it as a coffee or teatime accompaniment or as a replacement for dinner rolls at a gala buffet party.

2 loaves

2	packages active dry yeast
¼	cup warm water (105 to 115°)
1	cup lukewarm milk (scalded, then cooled)
¾	cup sugar
1	teaspoon salt
3	eggs
½	cup margarine or butter, softened
5½	to 6 cups all-purpose flour
1	egg
1	teaspoon sugar

Dissolve yeast in warm water in large bowl. Stir in milk, ¾ cup sugar, the salt, 3 eggs, the margarine and 3 cups of the flour. Beat until smooth. Stir in enough remaining flour to make dough easy to handle.

Turn dough onto lightly floured surface; knead until smooth and elastic, about 5 minutes. Place in greased bowl; turn greased side up. Cover; let rise in warm place until double, 1½ to 2 hours. (Dough is ready if indentation remains when touched.)

Punch down dough; divide into halves. Shape each half into a round, slightly flat loaf. Place each loaf in greased round layer pan, 9 x 1½ inches. Cover; let rise until double, about 1 hour. Heat oven to 350°. Beat 1 egg slightly; brush over loaves. Sprinkle with 1 teaspoon sugar. Bake until loaves are golden brown, 35 to 45 minutes.

Snail Loaves (Caracois): After dividing dough into halves, roll each half into a rope about 25 x 1½ inches. Coil each to form a snail shape in greased round layer pan, 9 x 1½ inches. Continue as directed.

Swedish Coffee Ring

Swedish Coffee Ring

This proud party bread is as rewarding to look at as it is to taste. Serve it at informal kaffee klatsches or at family or holiday celebrations.

1 coffee cake

1	package active dry yeast
¼	cup warm water (105 to 115°)
¾	cup lukewarm milk (scalded, then cooled)
¼	cup sugar
¼	cup margarine or butter, softened
1	egg
½	teaspoon ground cardamom
½	teaspoon salt
3¼	to 3½ cups all-purpose flour
	Almond Filling (right)
	Glaze (page 287)

Dissolve yeast in warm water in large bowl. Stir in milk, sugar, margarine, egg, cardamom, salt and 2 cups of the flour. Beat until smooth. Stir in enough remaining flour to make dough easy to handle.

Turn dough onto lightly floured surface; knead until smooth and elastic, about 5 minutes. Place in greased bowl; turn greased side up. Cover; let rise in warm place until double, 1 to 1½ hours. (Dough is ready if indentation remains when touched.) Prepare Almond Filling.

Punch down dough. Roll into rectangle, 15 x 9 inches, on lightly floured surface. Spread with filling. Roll up tightly, beginning at 15-inch side. (See diagram.) Pinch edge of dough into roll to seal well. Stretch roll to make even. With sealed edge down, shape into ring on lightly greased cookie sheet. Pinch ends together. With scissors, make cuts ⅔ of the way through ring at 1-inch intervals. Turn each section on its side. (See diagram.) Let rise until double, 40 to 50 minutes.

Heat oven to 350°. Bake until golden brown, 25 to 30 minutes. (If coffee ring browns too quickly, cover loosely with aluminum foil.) Spread ring with Glaze; garnish with nuts and cherries if desired.

Almond Filling

Mix ½ cup almond paste, ¼ cup packed brown sugar and ¼ cup margarine or butter, softened, until smooth.

Roll up tightly, beginning at wide side.

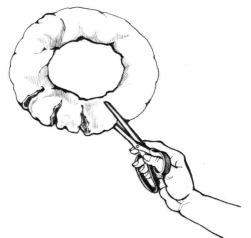

Cut into ring at intervals.

Turn sections on sides.

Yugoslavian Coffee Cake

Yugoslavian Coffee Cake (Potica)

These snail-shaped coffee cakes are easy to make and can be filled with a variety of tasty mixtures. The Walnut Filling included in our recipe is especially pleasing to the palate.

2 coffee cakes

1	package active dry yeast
¼	cup warm water (105 to 115°)
¾	cup lukewarm milk (scalded, then cooled)
½	cup margarine or butter, softened
3	eggs
¼	cup sugar
½	teaspoon salt
4½	to 5 cups all-purpose flour
	Walnut Filling (right)
	Glaze (page 287)

Dissolve yeast in warm water in large bowl. Stir in milk, margarine, eggs, sugar, salt and 3 cups of the flour. Beat until smooth. Stir in enough remaining flour to make dough easy to handle.

Turn dough onto lightly floured surface; knead until smooth and elastic, about 5 minutes. Place in greased bowl; turn greased side up. Cover; let rise in warm place until double, 1 to 1½ hours. (Dough is ready if indentation remains when touched.)

Punch down dough; divide into halves. Roll each half into rectangle, 15 x 12 inches, on lightly floured surface. Spread half the filling over each rectangle. Roll up tightly, beginning at 15-inch side. Pinch edge of dough into roll to seal well. Stretch roll to make even.

With sealed edges down, coil into snail shapes on lightly greased cookie sheets. Cover; let rise until double, about 1 hour. Heat oven to 350°. Bake until golden brown, 35 to 45 minutes. Brush with margarine if desired; spread with Glaze.

Walnut Filling

2½	cups finely chopped walnuts
1	cup packed brown sugar
⅓	cup margarine or butter, softened
1	egg
2	teaspoons ground cinnamon

Mix all ingredients.

Tips for Yeast Baking

Did You Know?

1. Milk should be scalded for the best yeast-bread results. (Heat it to just below the boiling point. Tiny bubbles will form at edges.) Cool the milk to lukewarm before adding it to the other ingredients.

2. Dissolve the yeast in warm water (105 to 115°). The water should feel warm—not lukewarm or hot. Water that is too cool will fail to activate the yeast; water that is too warm will kill the yeast.

3. Knead to develop the structure of the bread. Fold dough toward you. With heels of hands, push dough away with short rocking motions. Turn dough one-quarter turn and repeat until it feels elastic and the surface appears smooth and blistered.

4. Help dough to rise on cool days by making a "tent." Place the bowl of dough on a rack over another bowl filled with hot water. Cover both bowls with a towel to capture the warmth from the water.

5. Punch down risen dough with your fist to release the air bubbles and get a finer texture before you shape it.

6. Bake loaves with tops of pans in the middle of the oven. Pans should not touch each other or the side of the oven. If baking on a cookie sheet, place it in the center of the oven; the sides of the cookie sheet should not touch the sides of the oven.

German Turban Cake (Gugelhupf)

Seventeenth-century victories over the Turks are credited with giving us the Croissant (page 275) as well as this Austrian favorite (it has a number of spellings). The Viennese traditionally serve Gugelhupf *on Christmas morning, often toasted with butter and jam.*

1 loaf

1   package active dry yeast
¼   cup warm water (105 to 115°)
½   cup lukewarm milk (scalded, then cooled)
⅓   cup sugar
½   teaspoon salt
⅓   cup margarine or butter, softened
3   eggs
½   teaspoon vanilla
3   cups all-purpose flour
½   cup golden raisins
1   tablespoon finely shredded lemon peel
1   tablespoon sugar
½   teaspoon ground cinnamon
½   cup chopped blanched almonds

Dissolve yeast in warm water in large mixer bowl. Add milk, ⅓ cup sugar, the salt, margarine, eggs, vanilla and 1½ cups of the flour. Beat on low speed, scraping bowl constantly, 30 seconds. Beat on medium speed, scraping bowl occasionally, 4 minutes. Stir in raisins, lemon peel and remaining flour. Scrape batter from side of bowl. Cover; let rise in warm place until double, about 1½ hours. Stir down batter by beating 25 strokes. (Batter will be sticky.)

Grease side and bottom of 12-cup bundt cake pan or anodized aluminum ring mold. Mix 1 tablespoon sugar and the cinnamon; sprinkle half the sugar mixture in pan. Spread half the batter in pan; sprinkle with almonds. Spread remaining batter over almonds; sprinkle with remaining sugar mixture. Cover; let rise until double, about 1 hour. Heat oven to 350°. Bake until golden brown, about 50 minutes. Immediately remove from pan.

Danish Kringle

This coffee cake, made with rich, flaky pastry and a choice of fillings, is especially appropriate at Christmas (as the name implies). The Danes dote on kringle all year long.

2 coffee cakes

½   cup margarine or butter
2   cups all-purpose flour
1   tablespoon sugar
½   teaspoon salt
1   package active dry yeast
¼   cup warm water (105 to 115°)
1   egg
½   cup lukewarm milk (scalded, then cooled)
     Almond or Pecan Filling (below)
     Glaze (right)
¼   cup chopped nuts

Cut margarine into flour, sugar and salt in large bowl until mixture resembles fine crumbs. Dissolve yeast in warm water. Stir yeast mixture, egg and milk into flour mixture; beat until smooth (dough will be very soft). Cover and refrigerate at least 2 but no longer than 24 hours.

Prepare filling. Divide dough into halves; return half to refrigerator. Roll other half into rectangle, 15 x 6 inches, on floured cloth-covered board with floured stockinet-covered rolling pin. Spread half the filling lengthwise down center of rectangle in 3-inch strip. Fold sides of dough over filling with 1½-inch overlap; pinch edges to seal.

Carefully arrange kringle on greased cookie sheet in oval or horseshoe shape; pinch ends together for the latter. Repeat with remaining dough. Cover; let rise in warm place 30 minutes. Heat oven to 375°. Bake until golden brown, 20 to 25 minutes. Spread with Glaze; sprinkle with nuts.

Almond Filling

Mix 1 can (8 ounces) almond paste (1 cup), ½ cup packed brown sugar and ½ cup margarine or butter, softened, until smooth.

Pecan Filling
Mix 1½ cups chopped pecans, 1 cup packed brown sugar and ½ cup margarine or butter, softened.

Glaze
Mix 1 cup powdered sugar, 1 tablespoon water and ¼ teaspoon vanilla until smooth. Stir in additional water if necessary, ½ teaspoon at a time.

Scandinavian Christmas Fruit Bread

(Julekage)

Breads made with dried Middle Eastern fruits are thought to have been introduced to northern Europe during the Crusades and soon became Christmas favorites. Fresh fruits were scarce during medieval winters, and dried Mediterranean fruits were pretty, festive and exotic—and they came from the Holy Land.

1 loaf

1	package active dry yeast
¼	cup warm water (105 to 115°)
¾	cup lukewarm milk (scalded, then cooled)
¼	cup sugar
½	teaspoon salt
½	teaspoon ground cardamom
1	egg
¼	cup shortening
½	cup raisins
⅓	cup cut-up citron or mixed candied fruit
3¼	to 3½ cups all-purpose flour
	Margarine or butter, softened
	Glaze (right)

Dissolve yeast in warm water in large mixer bowl. Add milk, sugar, salt, cardamom, egg, shortening, raisins, citron and 2 cups of the flour. Beat on low speed, scraping bowl constantly, 30 seconds. Beat on medium speed, scraping bowl occasionally, 2 minutes. Stir in enough remaining flour to make dough easy to handle.

Turn dough onto lightly floured surface; knead until smooth and elastic, about 5 minutes. Place in greased bowl; turn greased side up. Cover; let rise in warm place until double, 1 to 1½ hours. (Dough is ready if indentation remains when touched.)

Punch down dough; shape into round loaf. Place in greased round layer pan, 9 x 1½ inches. Brush top lightly with margarine; let rise until double, about 45 minutes. Heat oven to 350°. Bake until loaf is golden brown, 35 to 45 minutes. Brush with margarine. Spread with Glaze. Cool on wire rack.

Glaze
Mix 1 cup powdered sugar and 1 to 2 tablespoons water until smooth and of desired consistency.

Cardamom

Did You Know?

Cardamom, native to south India and Sri Lanka, was prized by Indians, Persians and Egyptians in ancient times and was introduced to Europe by the Romans.

Today cardamom remains a prominent seasoning in Indian cooking, is highly valued in the Middle East, has literally taken root in Latin America and continues to be prized by the Scandinavians for the flavor it adds to pastries and breads.

Cardamom can be purchased as ground seed, as shelled seed and in the pod ("whole"). Each whole cardamom pod contains about fifteen small seeds. Some Indian chefs place whole cardamom pods into curries and rice and remove them after cooking. Western chefs generally remove seeds from the pod and grind them with mortar and pestle or in a spice mill before using.

German Christmas Bread and Italian Coffee Cake (page 289).

German Christmas Bread
(Stollen)

The Germans have many recipes for Stollen; *this one, from Dresden, contains fruit, nuts and rum or brandy, and is one of the best known of Germany's* Stollen *recipes.*

2 stollens

½   cup diced citron
½   cup raisins
¼   cup candied diced orange peel
¼   cup brandy or rum
1   package active dry yeast
¼   cup warm water (105 to 115°)
½   cup lukewarm milk (scalded, then cooled)
½   cup margarine or butter, softened
½   cup granulated sugar
½   teaspoon salt
¼   teaspoon ground nutmeg
3   eggs
4   to 4½ cups all-purpose flour
½   cup chopped blanched almonds
1   tablespoon finely shredded lemon peel
2   tablespoons margarine or butter, melted
    Powdered sugar

Mix citron, raisins, orange peel and brandy; let stand at least 1 hour. Drain; reserve brandy. Dissolve yeast in warm water in large bowl. Stir in reserved brandy, the milk, ½ cup margarine, the granulated sugar, salt, nutmeg, eggs and 2 cups of the flour. Beat until smooth. Stir in brandied fruit mixture, almonds, lemon peel and enough remaining flour to make dough easy to handle.

Turn dough onto lightly floured surface; knead until smooth and elastic, about 5 minutes. Place in greased bowl; turn greased side up. Cover; let rise in warm place until double, about 1½ hours. (Dough is ready if indentation remains when touched.)

Punch down dough; divide into halves. Press 1 half into an oval, about 10 x 7 inches. Brush with melted margarine. Fold lengthwise in half; press folded edge firmly. Place stollen on greased cookie sheet. Repeat with remaining dough. Cover; let rise until double, 45 to 60 minutes. Brush with melted margarine. Heat oven to 375°. Bake until golden brown, 20 to 25 minutes. Brush with melted margarine; sprinkle with powdered sugar.

Italian Coffee Cake
(Panettone)

Panettone *originated in Milan but is now popular throughout Italy, especially in the Lombardy region. It is served at family celebrations.*

2 loaves

2	packages active dry yeast
1	cup warm water (105 to 115°)
½	cup sugar
½	cup margarine or butter, softened
3	eggs
1	teaspoon salt
1	teaspoon grated lemon peel
1	teaspoon vanilla
5	to 5½ cups all-purpose flour
½	cup golden raisins
½	cup chopped citron
2	tablespoons pine nuts or walnuts (optional)
	Margarine or butter, softened

Dissolve yeast in warm water in large bowl. Stir in sugar, ½ cup margarine, the eggs, salt, lemon peel, vanilla and 2½ cups of the flour. Beat until smooth. Stir in raisins, citron, pine nuts and enough remaining flour to make dough easy to handle.

Turn dough onto lightly floured surface; knead until smooth and elastic, about 5 minutes. Place in greased bowl; turn greased side up. Cover; let rise in warm place until double, 1½ to 2 hours. (Dough is ready if indentation remains when touched.)

Punch down dough; divide into halves. Shape each half into round loaf, about 7 inches in diameter. Place loaves in 2 ungreased round layer pans, 8 x 1½ inches. Cut a cross ½ inch deep on top of each loaf. Generously grease one side of a strip of heavy brown paper, about 25 x 4 inches. Fit around inside of pan, forming a collar; fasten with paper clip. Repeat with second loaf. Cover; let rise until double, about 1 hour.

Heat oven to 350°. Bake loaves until golden brown, 35 to 45 minutes. Remove paper. Brush tops with margarine. Cool on rack.

Espresso
Did You Know?

Espresso, a strong, dark Italian coffee, is very popular as an after-dinner beverage both at home and in coffee shops. It is traditionally served in demitasse cups with sugar but never with cream. Espresso is made with a special dark roasted Italian coffee that has been roasted to a much deeper color and ground much more finely than regular American coffee. Espresso and instant espresso are available in specialty food stores and many supermarkets. Prepare the instant espresso according to package directions.

True espresso is made with steam pressure in special espresso coffee makers. Italian coffee can also be made in a *macchinetta,* an Italian drip coffee maker. If neither of these is available, you can prepare Italian coffee in a regular drip or percolator coffee maker, or use freshly brewed strong black coffee.

Irish Fruit Bread
(Barmbrack)

The Irish have differing opinions on the origin of their celebrated barmbrack. *One school holds that it is a literal translation from the Irish, meaning yeast bread; another that it is an adaptation of* aran breac, *meaning speckled bread. All agree that an Irish Hallowe'en wouldn't be complete without* barmbrack *and the ring or little treasure hidden in the bread for the lucky finder.*

2 loaves

2	packages active dry yeast
½	cup warm water (105 to 115°)
1	cup lukewarm milk (scalded, then cooled)
⅓	cup sugar
¼	cup margarine or butter, softened
2	eggs
1	teaspoon ground allspice
1	teaspoon ground cinnamon
1	teaspoon salt
5¼	to 5¾ cups all-purpose flour
¾	cup raisins or currants
½	cup candied orange or lemon peel
	Margarine or butter, softened
	Sugar

Dissolve yeast in warm water in large bowl. Stir in milk, ⅓ cup sugar, ¼ cup margarine, the eggs, allspice, cinnamon, salt and 3 cups of the flour. Beat until smooth. Stir in raisins, orange peel and enough remaining flour to make dough easy to handle.

Turn dough onto lightly floured surface; knead until smooth and elastic, about 5 minutes. Place in greased bowl; turn greased side up. Cover; let rise in warm place until double, 1½ to 2 hours. (Dough is ready if indentation remains when touched.)

Punch down dough; divide into halves. Shape each half into a round loaf, about 7 inches in diameter. Place loaves in 2 greased round layer pans, 8 x 1½ inches. Brush tops lightly with margarine; let rise until double, 50 to 60 minutes. Heat oven to 350°. Bake until loaves are golden brown, 40 to 45 minutes. Brush tops of loaves with margarine; sprinkle with sugar. Cool on wire racks.

Russian Easter Bread
(Kulich)

In czarist Russia, kulich *was considered so fragile a creation that bakers placed pillows around the pan of dough to prevent it from falling! Usually the initials XV (meaning Christ is risen) appear on top of the loaf—either sprinkled on the frosting with colored sugar or icing or shaped on top of the loaf with small strips of dough. The top slice traditionally is served to the guest of honor or the senior member of the family.*

2 loaves

2	packages active dry yeast
½	cup warm water (105 to 115°)
¾	cup lukewarm milk (scalded, then cooled)
⅓	cup sugar
1	teaspoon salt
2	eggs
½	cup shortening
½	cup raisins
½	cup cut-up mixed candied fruit
¼	cup chopped blanched almonds
1	teaspoon grated lemon peel
4½	to 5 cups all-purpose flour
	Lemon Icing (right)

Dissolve yeast in warm water in large bowl. Stir in milk, sugar, salt, eggs, shortening, raisins, candied fruit, almonds, lemon peel and 3 cups of the flour. Beat until smooth. Stir in enough remaining flour to make dough easy to handle.

Turn dough onto lightly floured surface; knead until smooth and elastic, about 5 minutes. Place in greased bowl; turn greased side up. Cover; let rise in warm place until double,

Russian Easter Cheese Dessert (page 336) and Russian Easter Bread (page 290).

1 to 1½ hours. (Dough is ready if indentation remains when touched.)

Punch down dough; divide into halves. Shape each half into round bun-shaped loaf. Place in two well-greased 3-pound shortening cans.* Let rise until double, 40 to 50 minutes.

Heat oven to 375°. Place cans on low rack so that midpoint of each can is in center of oven. Bake until tops are golden brown, 40 to 45 minutes. (If tops brown too quickly, cover loosely with aluminum foil.) Cool 10 minutes; remove from cans. Spoon Lemon Icing over tops of warm kulich, allowing some to drizzle down sides. Trim with tiny decorating candies if desired.

* Two 46-ounce juice cans can be substituted for the 3-pound shortening cans.

Lemon Icing
Mix 1 cup powdered sugar, 1 tablespoon warm water and 1 teaspoon lemon juice until smooth. (Icing should be glaze consistency. Add 1 to 2 teaspoons water if necessary.)

Clockwise from top: Brazil Nut Cake (page 325), Mocha Praline Torte (page 341), French Chocolate Custard (page 337) and Sliced Oranges in Syrup (page 301).

Desserts

In this chapter we have collected cherished recipes for many of the traditional pastries and puddings, cakes and tortes of Europe, and have rounded the collection out with a tempting array of Latin American, Middle Eastern, Indian and even oriental specialties.

You'll find sweets for all seasons and all occasions you may wish to celebrate—perhaps a crimson-sauced Danish Rice Pudding to serve to your valentine . . . snowy Russian *pashka* to crown a candle-lit Easter dinner . . . a flaming English Plum Pudding to bring warmth to your guests during the winter holidays.

Thrifty dishes like Mexican Bread Pudding or Persian Apple Dessert make family meals special; casual get-togethers can be enhanced with such simple combinations as Finnish Cranberry Whip, Almond Custard with Litchis or Caramel Bananas with Rum, an Australian favorite. For midday or midnight snacks, make a supply of crunchy Greek Crescent Cookies or melt-in-your-mouth Spanish Crullers. More formal after-dinner entertainments call for a tempting Italian Ricotta Cheesecake, a seven-layer Hungarian Dobos Torte, sparkling fruit-filled Savarin or a delicately flavored Vanilla Soufflé . . . encore desserts that linger in the memory like a song.

For the practical minded: Most of our desserts can be made well in advance. When party time comes, all you need to do is serve your selections forth and wait for your guests to exclaim, "Bravo!"

Apple Charlotte
(Charlotte aux Pommes)

In France, a charlotte *is a round metal baking dish similar to our soufflé molds. The* charlotte *comes in a variety of sizes and is equipped with handles for ease in unmolding the many mousses, casseroles and soufflés that grace the French cuisine.*

Apple Charlotte is a very old French recipe. Our simplified version, which uses bread crumbs and requires no unmolding, is inexpensive and makes a fine finish to a hearty winter soup supper.

8 servings

3   cups soft bread crumbs (see Note)
¼   cup margarine or butter
¾   cup sugar
1   teaspoon grated lemon peel
½   teaspoon ground cinnamon
4   cups thinly sliced tart apples (about 4 medium)
½   cup apricot jam
¾   cup chilled whipping cream
2   tablespoons sugar
½   teaspoon vanilla
1   tablespoon rum or brandy (optional)

Cook and stir bread crumbs in margarine over medium heat until crumbs are toasted and golden brown. Mix ¾ cup sugar, the lemon peel and cinnamon. Place 1 cup bread crumbs in greased 1½-quart soufflé dish or casserole; top with half the apples and sugar mixture. Spoon ¼ cup jam over top. Repeat, ending with 1 cup bread crumbs. Bake in 350° oven until apples are tender, 35 to 40 minutes.

Beat whipping cream, 2 tablespoons sugar and the vanilla in chilled bowl until stiff. Fold in rum. Serve with Apple Charlotte.

Note: Use firm bread, such as French bread; purée in blender.

Persian Apple Dessert

This light, quick dessert from the Middle East can be served at the end of an evening meal or as a midday snack. It is a fine refresher during hot weather. On formal occasions spoon the chilled apple mixture into frosted parfait glasses and garnish with fresh mint sprigs.

3 servings

3   medium apples, cut up
2   to 3 tablespoons sugar
2   tablespoons lemon juice
1   tablespoon rose or orange blossom
       water (optional)
    Dash of salt

Place half the apples and the remaining ingredients in blender container. Cover and blend until coarsely chopped, 20 to 30 seconds. Add remaining apples; repeat.

Whipped Avocado Dessert

The versatile avocado is spotlighted in this unusual and elegant recipe from Brazil. Served in parfait glasses and garnished with lime wedges, it makes a fine finale to any Latin American meal.

3 or 4 servings

2   ripe avocados
⅓   cup powdered sugar
¼   cup whipping cream
3   tablespoons lime juice

Cut avocado into pieces; place with remaining ingredients in blender container. Cover and blend until smooth and creamy.

Clockwise from top: Whipped Avocado Dessert (page 294), Finnish Cranberry Whip (page 300) and Russian Apricot Pudding.

Russian Apricot Pudding

(Kissel)

Kissel—*a fruit pudding thickened with cornstarch and served warm or cold with cream—is the national dessert of the Soviet Union. Many kinds of fruit can be used, but tart fruits, such as cranberries and currants, are favored by many* kissel *fans.*

4 servings

2   cups water
1   cup dried apricot halves (6 ounces)
¼   cup sugar
3   tablespoons cornstarch
    Dash of salt

Heat water and apricots to boiling; reduce heat. Cover and simmer until tender, about 20 minutes. Place apricots and ½ cup cooking liquid in blender container; cover and purée until uniform consistency. Press purée through sieve.

Mix sugar, cornstarch and salt in 1½-quart saucepan; gradually stir in apricot purée and remaining cooking liquid. Heat to boiling over medium heat, stirring constantly. Boil and stir 1 minute. Pour into dessert dishes. Serve with half-and-half or sweetened whipped cream if desired.

Caramel Bananas with Rum

This easy Australian version of the banana split features a satiny caramel sauce and a sprinkling of sliced almonds for texture. It's a light and satisfying dessert after a hearty main dish, such as Steak-and-Kidney Pie (page 121) or Oxtail Stew (page 133).

4 to 6 servings

⅔   cup packed brown sugar
2   tablespoons whipping cream
1   tablespoon margarine or butter
3   tablespoons rum
4   medium bananas
½   cup chilled whipping cream
1   tablespoon packed brown sugar
¼   cup sliced almonds

Cook and stir ⅔ cup brown sugar, 2 tablespoons whipping cream and the margarine over low heat until sugar is dissolved and mixture is smooth. Remove from heat; stir in rum. Cover and refrigerate at least 1 hour.

Cut bananas crosswise into halves; cut each half lengthwise into halves. Arrange in serving dishes; top with caramel sauce. Beat ½

cup whipping cream and 1 tablespoon brown sugar in chilled bowl until stiff. Spoon whipped cream over bananas and sauce; garnish with almonds.

Mexican Banana Bake

Rum and cinnamon bring the vibrant flavors of Mexico to this nice and easy recipe, and cream cheese adds its own rich character. Try the dessert after a traditional Mexican main dish, such as Ranch-Style Eggs (page 182) or Spicy Sausage Burritos (page 159).

4 to 6 servings

1   package (3 ounces) cream cheese, softened
¼   cup packed brown sugar
¼   cup rum
3   tablespoons half-and-half
⅛   teaspoon ground cinnamon
5   medium bananas
1   tablespoon margarine or butter

Place cream cheese, brown sugar, rum, half-and-half and cinnamon in blender container. Cover and blend on high speed until smooth, 30 seconds. Slice half the bananas into ungreased 1-quart casserole. Dot with margarine; spread with half the cheese mixture. Slice remaining bananas into casserole; spread with remaining cheese mixture. Bake uncovered in 325° oven until hot and bubbly, 20 to 25 minutes.

Whipping Cream
Did You Know?

Cream used for whipping should have at least 35 percent butterfat to insure success, and the cream, bowl and beaters should be thoroughly chilled. Whipping the cream will double its volume. It is important not to overbeat the cream, because this will cause it to separate. Leftover whipped cream can be frozen in small mounds, then packaged and stored in the freezer for dessert toppings.

Caribbean Bananas

Warm rum set aflame and poured over baked bananas adds a rosy glow to a Caribbean-style dinner party. Try this glamorous recipe with a dinner featuring a Latin classic, such as Ropa Vieja *(page 133), or with one of the Caribbean's famous chicken stews (see Index by Country or Region).*

4 to 6 servings

¼ cup margarine or butter, melted
4 medium bananas
⅓ cup packed brown sugar
1 tablespoon lemon juice
½ teaspoon ground allspice
¼ cup light rum

Place margarine in baking dish; rotate dish to coat bottom. Cut bananas crosswise into halves; cut each half lengthwise into halves. Place cut sides down in baking dish. Mix brown sugar, lemon juice and allspice; drizzle over bananas.

Bake uncovered in 350° oven 15 minutes. Heat rum until warm; ignite and pour over bananas.

Dates

Did You Know?

Dates have been called the "candy that grows on trees." They are the fruit of the date palm, originally imported from the Middle East and North Africa. Naturally sweet, dates have considerable nutritive value. It is said that some natives of the Near East live almost entirely on a diet of dates and milk.

Store dates in a covered container in a cool place or in the refrigerator. To cut dates easily, use kitchen scissors, dipping scissors in water occasionally to prevent sticking. A pound of pittted dates, cut up, will yield 2½ cups.

Banana-Coconut Bake
(Akwadu)

Bananas baked with brown sugar, fruit juices and coconut provide a welcome refreshment after a spicy African meal. This recipe from Ghana requires only a few minutes preparation time.

5 or 6 servings

5 medium bananas
1 tablespoon margarine or butter
⅓ cup orange juice
1 tablespoon lemon juice
3 tablespoons packed brown sugar
⅔ cup shredded coconut

Cut bananas crosswise into halves; cut each half lengthwise into halves. Arrange in greased 9-inch pie plate. Dot with margarine; drizzle with orange and lemon juice. Sprinkle with brown sugar and coconut. Bake in 375° oven until coconut is golden, 8 to 10 minutes.

Date-and-Banana Dessert

Sweets based on dried fruits are traditional throughout the Middle East. In this unusual recipe, dates are combined with fresh bananas and cream and prepared well in advance of serving—convenient for the chef, a pleasure for the guests.

3 or 4 servings

4 ounces pitted dates, cut up (1 cup)
2 bananas, thinly sliced
2 to 3 teaspoons finely shredded lemon peel
½ cup half-and-half
Sliced almonds (optional)

Alternate layers of dates and bananas in serving dish or dessert dishes. Sprinkle with lemon peel; pour half-and-half over top. Cover and refrigerate at least 4 hours. Just before serving, sprinkle with almonds.

Chinese Glazed Fruit

Chinese Glazed Fruit

Bringing a classic Chinese dinner to a close with a delectable sweet can pose a real difficulty, for although the Chinese share our Western fondness for sweets, the gala Chinese menu is more likely to conclude with a soup! Here is an exception. These remarkable deep-fried fruit tidbits are sure to please oriental and occidental guests.

6 servings

¾	cup cold water
⅓	cup all-purpose flour
¼	cup cornstarch
¾	teaspoon baking powder
½	teaspoon salt
	Peanut or vegetable oil

2	medium apples, pared and cut into eighths
2	firm medium bananas, cut diagonally into ½-inch slices
2	cups sugar
1	cup water
½	cup light corn syrup
¼	cup white or black sesame seed
	Iced water

Beat ¾ cup water, the flour, cornstarch, baking powder and salt with hand beater until smooth. Heat oil (1 to 1½ inches) to 360°. Stir apples into batter until coated. Remove 1 piece at a time with slotted spoon, letting excess batter drip into bowl. Fry 6 to 8 at a time, turning occasionally, until golden brown, about 5 minutes. Drain on paper towels. Repeat with bananas.

Thoroughly mix sugar, 1 cup water and the corn syrup in heavy 3-quart saucepan. Heat to boiling, without stirring, over high heat. Cook, without stirring, over high heat to 300° on candy thermometer or until small amount of mixture dropped into very cold water separates into threads that are hard and brittle (mixture will be light golden brown). Decrease heat to very low; stir in sesame seed.

Generously oil large flat serving plate. Stir 1 piece of fruit at a time into syrup until evenly coated. Immediately remove from syrup and place on oiled plate so pieces do not touch. At the table, dip each piece of fruit into iced water to harden coating.

Danish Berry Pudding

(Rødgrød)

Strawberries and raspberries give to this luscious do-ahead pudding its characteristic color and unforgettable flavor. The fragrant fruit purée goes well after a rich main dish, such as Danish Stuffed Duckling (page 74).

6 servings

1   package (10 ounces) frozen raspberries, thawed
1   package (10 ounces) frozen strawberries, thawed
¼   cup cornstarch
2   tablespoons sugar
½   cup cold water
1   tablespoon lemon juice
    Slivered almonds

Purée berries in blender or press through sieve. Mix cornstarch and sugar in 1½-quart saucepan. Gradually stir in water; add purée. Heat to boiling, stirring constantly. Boil and stir 1 minute. Remove from heat; stir in lemon juice. Pour into dessert dishes or serving bowl. Cover and refrigerate at least 2 hours. Sprinkle with almonds; serve with half-and-half if desired.

Canadian Blueberry Dessert

Blueberries, native to the Western Hemisphere, have not yet gained a wide following in Europe, but are every bit as popular in Canada as they are in the United States. This perky little pudding can be served in summer when blueberries are at their seasonal peak, or in the winter, when frozen berries can be used.

This dessert goes well after main-dish pies, such as Canadian Pork Pie (page 157) or Cornish Pasties (page 122).

5 or 6 servings

4   cups blueberries*
2   tablespoons lemon juice
⅓   cup packed brown sugar
2   teaspoons cornstarch
⅔   cup quick-cooking oats
½   cup all-purpose flour
⅓   cup packed brown sugar
    Dash of salt
⅓   cup margarine or butter
    Vanilla ice cream

Toss blueberries with lemon juice in ungreased 1½-quart casserole. Mix ⅓ cup brown sugar and the cornstarch; stir into blueberries. Mix oats, flour, ⅓ cup brown sugar and the salt; cut in margarine with fork. Sprinkle over blueberries. Bake uncovered in 350° oven until topping is light brown and blueberries are bubbly, about 40 minutes. Serve warm with ice cream.

* 1 package (16 ounces) frozen unsweetened blueberries can be substituted for the fresh blueberries.

Seasonal Guide to Fresh Fruits

Name of Fruit	Peak Season	Name of Fruit	Peak Season
Apples	September to April	Peaches	June to October
Apricots	June and July	Pears, Bartlett	July to December
Avocados	All year	D'Anjou	October to June
Bananas	All year	Pineapple	April to June
Blueberries	June to August	Plums	June to October
Sweet cherries	June and July	Pomegranates	September to November
Cranberries	September to February	Raspberries	June and July
Grapes	June to January	Rhubarb	January to August
Kiwi fruit	June to March	Strawberries	May to July
Oranges	November to July		

Baked French Cherry Dessert
(Clafouti)

Clafouti is a splendid example of the country cook's talent for producing superb desserts as well as robust soups and stews. This tasty, light cherry "pancake" is traditional country fare in the Limousin region of central France and is most popular there during the cherry-picking season.

6 servings

3   eggs
1   cup milk
½   cup all-purpose flour
¼   cup granulated sugar
1   teaspoon vanilla
2   cups pitted dark sweet cherries
    Powdered sugar

Heat oven to 350°. Beat eggs, milk, flour, granulated sugar and the vanilla with hand beater until smooth. Spread cherries in greased oblong baking dish, 10 x 6 x 1½ inches, or square baking dish, 8 x 8 x 2 inches. Pour batter over cherries. Bake uncovered until puffed and golden brown, 45 to 60 minutes. Sprinkle with powdered sugar. Serve warm.

Finnish Cranberry Whip
(Vatkattu Marjapuuro)

When fresh cranberries are in season, take a tip from Finland's inventive chefs and whip up this fine and easy dessert. Farina gives a pudding-like texture to the dessert. Try it as a tangy side dish with roast turkey or pork!

4 to 6 servings

2   cups cranberries (6 ounces)
1½ cups water
1   cup sugar
1   cup water
    Dash of salt
⅓   cup farina

Heat cranberries and 1½ cups water to boiling; reduce heat. Simmer uncovered until berries pop, about 8 minutes. Press cranberries through sieve to remove skins. Return juice to saucepan.

Add sugar, 1 cup water and the salt; heat to boiling. Add farina gradually, stirring constantly. Cook, stirring occasionally, until thickened, 3 to 5 minutes. Pour into small mixer bowl. Beat on high speed until pudding becomes fluffy and light pink, 3 to 5 minutes.

Dried-Fruit Compote
(Khoshaf)

Let your imagination be your guide in creating new versions of this classic from the Middle East. The suggestions below will guide you in tailoring your compote to your personal tastes and menus.

8 servings

1	package (8 ounces) mixed dried fruit*
¾	cup dried figs
3	cups water
½	cup raisins
2	tablespoons honey
2	teaspoons lemon juice

Cut dried fruit and figs into bite-size pieces. Heat dried fruit, figs, water and raisins to boiling; reduce heat. Cover and simmer until tender, about 20 minutes. Stir in honey and lemon juice. Top with sweetened whipped cream and sliced almonds if desired.

* 1½ cups dried apricots, apples, peaches, pears or prunes can be substituted for the mixed dried fruit.

Sliced Oranges in Syrup

This grand but economical dessert can be found throughout the Middle East and as far west as the French Riviera. Its true home may be Greece, where subtle ways with fruits have prevailed since ancient times. Try the orange compote after sampling Moussaka (page 163) or Zesty Chicken Oregano (page 81).

4 servings

3	seedless oranges
½	cup water
⅓	cup sugar

Cut thin slivers of peel from 1 orange with vegetable parer or sharp knife, being careful not to cut into white membrane. Cover peel with boiling water; let stand 5 minutes. Drain. Heat orange peel, water and sugar to boiling; simmer uncovered until slightly thickened, 10 to 15 minutes. Cool.

Pare oranges, cutting deep enough to remove all white membrane. Cut into slices. Pour syrup over slices; cover and refrigerate. Garnish with sprig of mint if desired.

Pears with Nut Stuffing

This Hungarian recipe goes well on a cold autumn or winter evening, when pears are in season and a steaming dessert is desired. The dish is especially appropriate after a robust goulash or our colorful Chicken Paprika with Dumplings (page 92).

8 servings

⅓	cup sugar
⅓	cup water
1	tablespoon lemon juice
4	pears, cut into halves
⅓	cup finely chopped nuts
2	tablespoons sugar
1	tablespoon brandy
1	tablespoon dairy sour cream
¼	teaspoon vanilla
½	cup dairy sour cream
1	tablespoon sugar

Mix ⅓ cup sugar, the water and lemon juice in ungreased square pan, 8 x 8 x 2 inches, until sugar is dissolved. Arrange pears in pan, turning to coat with sugar mixture. Cover and bake in 325° oven until pears are almost tender when pierced with fork, 25 minutes.

Place 1 pear half cut side up in each of 8 serving dishes. Mix nuts, 2 tablespoons sugar, the brandy, 1 tablespoon sour cream and the vanilla; fill centers of pear halves with nut mixture. Mix ½ cup sour cream and 1 tablespoon sugar. Top each pear half with dollop of sour cream mixture.

Fresh Pineapple Compote

Fresh Pineapple Compote

The food of Cambodia bears the hallmarks of the cooking of both China and India, and has been influenced by the foods of the South Pacific as well. Litchis are essential for the success of this recipe—you'll find them at oriental groceries, gourmet shops and in the oriental-foods section of large supermarkets.

4 to 6 servings

1   can (11 ounces) litchis
2   teaspoons lime juice
2   cups cut-up fresh pineapple
1   medium orange, pared and sectioned

Drain litchis, reserving ½ cup syrup. Mix reserved syrup and lime juice. Cut litchis into halves; toss with pineapple and orange sections. Pour syrup mixture over fruit; cover and refrigerate.

Litchi

Did You Know?

Litchi, the fruit of a tropical tree native to Southeastern Asia, has played an important role in Chinese cooking for more than two thousand years. Today, as Chinese food becomes more and more popular in the West, the litchi tree is being cultivated in many parts of North and South America.

Litchis can be eaten fresh, canned or dried. The mature, fresh litchi—most prized by Chinese gourmets—is about 1½ inches in diameter and has a thick red shell resembling a strawberry. Often the fresh pulp is seeded and canned. Canned litchis can be purchased at oriental groceries and are valued for their juicy texture and aromatic, sweet-tart flavor. Dried litchis have a color, texture and flavor very similar to raisins.

Plum Dumplings
(Zwetschgenknödel)

Both the Germans and the Hungarians are fond of these unique little potato dumplings, which are shaped around sugar-stuffed plums. Country folk traditionally serve them as a Sunday afternoon snack with tea or coffee.

6 servings (2 dumplings each)

3   medium potatoes (about 1 pound), pared and cut into pieces
12 cubes sugar
12 purple plums, pitted
    Almond extract (optional)
2   eggs
1   teaspoon salt
⅓   cup margarine or butter, softened
1½ cups all-purpose flour
8   cups water
1   teaspoon salt
½   cup dry bread crumbs
2   tablespoons margarine or butter
¼   cup sugar
¼   teaspoon ground cinnamon

Heat 1 inch salted water (½ teaspoon salt to 1 cup water) to boiling. Add potatoes. Heat to boiling; reduce heat. Cover and cook until tender, 20 to 25 minutes; drain. Put potatoes through ricer. Cover and refrigerate until cold.

Place sugar cube in each plum; sprinkle each cube with 1 drop almond extract. Mix 2 cups of the potatoes, the eggs and 1 teaspoon salt; stir in ⅓ cup margarine and the flour. Shape into flattened rectangle on lightly floured cloth-covered board.

Roll pastry into rectangle, 16 x 12 inches. Cut into 4-inch squares. Place plum on each square. Moisten edges of squares with water. Bring corners up and together; pinch to seal. Shape into smooth ball.

Heat water and 1 teaspoon salt to boiling in Dutch oven. Place 6 dumplings, 1 at a time, in boiling water. Cover and simmer until done, 8 to 10 minutes. (To test for doneness, cut 1 dumpling into halves; dumplings should be firm but not gummy.) Remove dumplings with slotted spoon. Repeat with remaining dumplings.

Cook and stir bread crumbs in 2 tablespoons margarine until light brown. Roll dumplings in crumbs. Mix sugar and cinnamon; sprinkle over dumplings.

Rhubarb Pudding
(Rabarbragrøt)

Rhubarb, the traditional harbinger of spring, was a favorite in China and the Middle East in ancient times. The Vikings may have introduced rhubarb to Norway from the Mediterranean during the Middle Ages. Today rhubarb is popular throughout Scandinavia.

6 servings

1¾ cups water
¾   cup sugar
1½ pounds rhubarb, cut into ½-inch pieces (4 cups)
¼   cup cold water
3   tablespoons cornstarch
½   teaspoon vanilla
1   cup chilled whipping cream
2   tablespoons sugar

Heat 1¾ cups water and ¾ cup sugar to boiling, stirring occasionally. Add rhubarb. Simmer uncovered until rhubarb is tender, about 10 minutes.

Mix ¼ cup water and the cornstarch; stir into rhubarb. Heat to boiling, stirring constantly. Boil and stir 1 minute. Stir in vanilla. Pour into serving bowl or dessert dishes. Cover and refrigerate.

Beat whipping cream and 2 tablespoons sugar in chilled bowl until stiff. Pipe through decorators' tube or spoon onto pudding.

Fluffy French Cream Sauce over Fruit

Fluffy French Cream Sauce over Fruit

(Crème Fraîche aux Fruits)

The noble crème fraîche *of France—literally fresh cream—is a rich, heavy country cream with a tart flavor—similar to our dairy sour cream but richer and sweeter. The French use* crème fraîche *for many purposes—from thickening and enriching soups and sauces to garnishing desserts and pastries. Our easy method of creating the cream enables you to produce a variety of fresh-fruit desserts in minutes.*

4 to 6 servings

⅔ cup whipping cream
⅓ cup dairy sour cream
2 to 3 cups assorted fresh fruit (see Note)
   Ground nutmeg or sugar

Gradually stir whipping cream into dairy sour cream. Cover and refrigerate no longer than 48 hours. Serve over fruit. Sprinkle with nutmeg.

Note: Suggested fruits are blueberries, raspberries, strawberries, sliced peaches or cubed pineapple.

Strawberries Romanov

Named after the imperial Russian dynasty whose reign began in 1613 and ended in 1917, Strawberries Romanov is truly among the royalty of desserts.

6 servings

1   quart strawberries
½   cup powdered sugar
3   to 4 tablespoons kirsch or orange-flavored
    liqueur
1   cup chilled whipping cream

Cut strawberries into halves, reserving 3 strawberries for garnish. Sprinkle with powdered sugar and kirsch; stir gently. Cover and refrigerate about 2 hours. Just before serving, beat whipping cream in chilled bowl until soft peaks form; fold in strawberries. Garnish with reserved strawberries.

Creamy Custard Sauce with Fruit

(Crème Anglaise aux Fruits)

Crème anglaise is France's traditional topping for berries and can be used to grace many kinds of fruits and pastries as well. For optimal eye appeal, layer the fruit in parfait or wine glasses, then spoon the cream on top. Serve with lacy cookies and garnish with candied violets (available at gourmet shops).

4 to 6 servings

3   egg yolks, slightly beaten
3   to 4 tablespoons sugar
    Dash of salt
1   cup milk
½   teaspoon vanilla
2   to 3 cups assorted fresh fruit (see Note)

Mix egg yolks, sugar and salt in heavy 2-quart saucepan. Stir in milk gradually. Cook over low heat, stirring constantly, until mixture coats a metal spoon, 15 to 20 minutes. (Do not boil; custard sauce will thicken slightly as it cools.)

Remove sauce from heat; stir in vanilla. Place saucepan in cold water until sauce is cool. Cover and refrigerate at least 2 hours but no longer than 24 hours. Serve over fruit.

Note: Suggested combinations are blueberries and sliced peaches, strawberries and cubed pineapple or raspberries and sliced peaches.

Almond Custard with Litchis

(Hsing-jen-tou-fu)

Our modern do-ahead version of a Chinese classic makes a graceful bow at an applause-winning oriental banquet. For gala celebrations (such as Chinese New Year's), begin the party with Egg-Drop Soup (page 30) as the first course and Mou Shu Pork (page 150) as the main course, accompanied by rice. For a special party touch, serve Deep-Fried Wonton Cookies (page 334) along with the custard.

4 to 6 servings

¾   cup water
¼   cup sugar
1   envelope unflavored gelatin
1   cup milk
1   teaspoon almond extract
2   cans (11 ounces each) litchis

Heat water, sugar and gelatin to boiling, stirring occasionally, until sugar and gelatin are dissolved. Remove from heat. Stir in milk and almond extract. Pour into loaf dish, 9 x 5 x 3 inches. Cover and refrigerate until firm, at least 4 hours.

Cut gelatin custard into 1-inch diamonds or squares. Place litchis (with syrup) in serving bowl; arrange custard around fruit.

Danish Rice Pudding

Danish Rice Pudding

A raspberry-and-currant sauce serves as the crowning glory on Denmark's rich, tasty rice pudding. On festive occasions, the Danes insert a whole almond in the pudding and award a prize to the lucky recipient! Both pudding and sauce can be made well in advance of serving.

8 servings

½	cup sugar
½	cup water
2	envelopes unflavored gelatin
½	teaspoon salt
2	cups milk
1½	cups cooked rice (page 253)
2	teaspoons vanilla
1	cup chilled whipping cream
	Raspberry-Currant Sauce (right)

Heat sugar, water, gelatin and salt in 2-quart saucepan, stirring constantly, until gelatin is dissolved, about 1 minute. Stir in milk, rice and vanilla. Place saucepan in a bowl of iced water, stirring occasionally, until mixture mounds slightly when dropped from a spoon, about 15 minutes.

Beat whipping cream in chilled bowl until stiff. Fold whipped cream into rice mixture. Pour into ungreased 1½-quart mold. Cover and refrigerate until firm, about 3 hours. Unmold and serve with Raspberry-Currant Sauce.

Raspberry-Currant Sauce

1	package (10 ounces) frozen raspberries, thawed
½	cup currant jelly
1½	teaspoons cornstarch
1	tablespoon cold water

Heat raspberries (with syrup) and jelly to boiling. Mix water and cornstarch; stir into raspberries. Heat to boiling, stirring constantly. Boil and stir 1 minute. Cool. Press through a sieve to remove seeds if desired.

Italian Wine Custard

Italian Wine Custard

(Zabaglione)

Marsala—the principal dessert wine of Italy—is a dark, sweet wine with a taste reminiscent of burnt sugar. It is made in northwest Sicily, is exported throughout the world and is essential to zabaglione—*one of the triumphs of Italian dessert making.*

To serve, spoon the sauce into crystal goblets or fine stemware. Often the custard is spooned over berries, fruit-filled crêpes or slices of poundcake.

4 to 6 servings

4	egg yolks
1	egg
⅓	cup sugar
⅓	cup marsala wine or sherry
	Dash of salt

Beat egg yolks and egg in small mixer bowl on high speed until thick and lemon colored, about 3 minutes. Gradually beat in sugar, scraping bowl occasionally. Beat in wine and salt on low speed.

Pour mixture into top of double boiler.* Add enough hot water to bottom of double boiler so that top does not touch water. Cook over medium heat, stirring constantly, until slightly thickened, about 5 minutes. (Water in double boiler should simmer but not boil.) Remove from heat. Serve immediately.

* A metal bowl placed over a saucepan of simmering water can be substituted for a double boiler.

Caramel Custard

(Flan)

Caramel Custard is one of the most favored desserts in international cooking. It is light, easy to make, can be prepared in advance and makes a suitable ending to nearly any meal you have in mind. In France the custard is called crème caramel.

4 servings

½	cup sugar
3	eggs, slightly beaten
1	can (13 ounces) evaporated milk (1⅔ cups)
⅓	cup sugar
2	teaspoons vanilla
⅛	teaspoon salt

Heat ½ cup sugar in heavy 1-quart saucepan over low heat, stirring constantly, until melted and golden brown. Divide syrup among four 6-ounce custard cups; rotate cups to coat bottoms. Allow syrup to harden in cups about 5 minutes.

Mix remaining ingredients; pour into custard cups. Place cups in square pan, 9 x 9 x 2 inches, on oven rack. Pour very hot water into pan to within ½ inch of tops of cups. Bake in 350° oven until knife inserted halfway between center and edge comes out clean, 40 to 50 minutes. Immediately remove from water. Serve warm, or refrigerate and unmold at serving time if desired.

Spiced Brandy Custard: Stir 2 tablespoons brandy, ¼ teaspoon ground cinnamon and ⅛ teaspoon ground nutmeg into beaten eggs.

Strawberry Trifle

Strawberry Trifle

Trifle has been called "the inevitable dessert." It appears on dessert carts and menus throughout Britain and is virtually impossible to miss when visiting England. There are many variations. Trifle can be as sublime or as forgettable as the ingredients that go into it. Our favorite trifle uses ladyfingers and strawberries—easy to make and fitting for all seasons.

8 to 10 servings

½   cup sugar
3   tablespoons cornstarch
¼   teaspoon salt
3   cups milk
½   cup dry sherry
3   egg yolks, beaten
3   tablespoons margarine or butter

1   tablespoon vanilla
2   packages (3 ounces each) ladyfingers
½   cup strawberry preserves
1   package (12 ounces) frozen strawberries, thawed
1   cup chilled whipping cream
2   tablespoons sugar
2   tablespoons toasted slivered almonds

Mix ½ cup sugar, the cornstarch and salt in 3-quart saucepan; gradually stir in milk and sherry. Heat to boiling over medium heat, stirring constantly. Boil and stir 1 minute. Stir at least half of the hot mixture gradually into egg yolks. Blend into hot mixture in saucepan. Boil and stir 1 minute. Remove from heat; stir in margarine and vanilla. Cover and refrigerate at least 3 hours.

Split ladyfingers lengthwise into halves; spread each half with strawberry preserves. Layer ¼ of the ladyfingers cut sides up, half the strawberries and half the pudding in 2-quart serving bowl; repeat. Arrange remaining ladyfingers around edge of bowl in upright position with cut sides toward center. (It may be necessary to gently ease ladyfingers down into pudding about 1 inch so they remain upright.) Cover and refrigerate.

Beat whipping cream and 2 tablespoons sugar in chilled bowl until stiff; spread over dessert. Sprinkle with almonds.

Carrot Pudding

(Gajar Halva)

The boldly seasoned foods that characterize Indian cooking linger most pleasantly in the memory when followed by sweets that soothe the tongue but do not disappoint the palate. India's Carrot Pudding is an excellent example—a touch of cardamom and a garnish of pistachios add just the right accent to the mild carrot-and-raisin mixture.

6 servings

6	medium carrots (about 1 pound), finely shredded
2	cups half-and-half
½	cup packed brown sugar
½	cup golden raisins
¼	cup margarine or butter
½	teaspoon ground cardamom
¼	teaspoon salt
¼	cup unsalted pistachios or slivered almonds

Heat carrots and half-and-half to boiling in 2-quart saucepan; reduce heat. Cover and simmer, stirring frequently, until half-and-half is absorbed, about 1 hour.

Stir in brown sugar, raisins, margarine, cardamom and salt. Cook over low heat, stirring constantly, until brown sugar is dissolved and mixture is desired consistency, about 15 minutes. Garnish with pistachios.

Noodle-and-Raisin Pudding

(Lukshen Kugel)

There are many variations on this creamy noodle pudding, which is featured in Jewish homes from Eastern Europe to Israel.

6 to 8 servings

1	package (8 ounces) wide egg noodles
2	eggs, slightly beaten
1	cup dairy sour cream
1	cup small-curd cottage cheese
½	cup golden raisins
½	cup sugar
½	teaspoon salt
¼	teaspoon ground cinnamon
⅛	teaspoon ground nutmeg

Cook noodles as directed on package; drain. Mix remaining ingredients; toss with noodles. Pour into greased 2-quart casserole. Bake uncovered in 350° oven until golden brown, 40 to 50 minutes.

Pistachio Nuts

Did You Know?

Pistachio nuts, sometimes called "green almonds," are the seeds of the fruit of the pistachio tree. The pistachio tree is a tropical evergreen grown principally in Iran, Afghanistan and Turkey. There the pistachio nut is a frequent ingredient in meat pies, pilafs, soups, cookies or puddings.

The shells of the pistachio nut are grayish white in their natural state, but they are often dyed red for eye appeal. Americans have learned to enjoy these nuts as a snack, for desserts, including ice cream and candies, and in cooking generally. Pistachio nuts keep best if stored, tightly covered, in the refrigerator. Freeze them for longer storage.

English Plum Pudding

English Plum Pudding

England's favorite holiday dessert, immortalized in Charles Dickens' A Christmas Carol, has delighted British food lovers since the Middle Ages, when it was often served with meats as a first-course "porridge." Suet—the layers of fat surrounding beef kidneys and loins—can be purchased from butchers and large supermarkets; it is inexpensive and can usually be purchased preground during the holiday season.

8 servings

½   cup all-purpose flour
½   teaspoon ground cinnamon
⅛   teaspoon ground nutmeg
⅛   teaspoon ground cloves
½   teaspoon baking soda
½   teaspoon salt
1   cup raisins
½   cup currants
¼   cup cut-up candied fruit peel
¼   cup cut-up candied cherries
¼   cup chopped walnuts
¾   cup soft bread crumbs
1   cup ground suet (4 ounces)
½   cup packed brown sugar
2   eggs, beaten
1   tablespoon brandy
¼   cup brandy (optional)
    Hard Sauce (right)

Mix flour, spices, baking soda and salt. Stir in fruit, walnuts and bread crumbs. Mix suet, brown sugar, eggs and 1 tablespoon brandy; stir into flour-fruit mixture. Pour into well-greased 4-cup mold; cover with aluminum foil.

Place mold on rack in Dutch oven; pour boiling water into Dutch oven to rack level. Cover and boil over low heat until wooden pick inserted in center comes out clean, about 3 hours. (Add boiling water if necessary.)

Remove mold from Dutch oven; unmold. Heat ¼ cup brandy until warm; ignite and pour over pudding. Serve with Hard Sauce.

Hard Sauce

Beat ½ cup margarine or butter, softened, 1 cup powdered sugar and 2 tablespoons brandy until smooth.

Pineapple Meringue Bread Pudding

(Kueh Prol Nanas)

Pineapple, cinnamon and coconut milk are the exotic ingredients that give this Indonesian delicacy its tropical flavor.

8 servings

3   cups ½-inch cubes French bread
1   can (15¼ ounces) crushed pineapple, drained (reserve syrup)
3   eggs, separated
⅓   cup packed brown sugar
½   teaspoon grated lemon peel
½   teaspoon ground cinnamon
½   teaspoon salt
1   cup Coconut Milk* (page 58)
¼   teaspoon cream of tartar
¼   cup sugar

Place bread cubes in greased oblong baking dish, 10 x 6 x 1½ inches, or square baking dish, 8 x 8 x 2 inches. Spread pineapple on top. Beat egg yolks slightly; stir in brown sugar, lemon peel, cinnamon, salt and the reserved syrup. Slowly stir in milk. Pour over bread cubes and pineapple. Bake uncovered in 350° oven until knife inserted halfway between center and edge comes out clean, 30 to 40 minutes.

Remove from oven. Beat egg whites and cream of tartar on medium speed until foamy. Beat in ¼ cup sugar, 1 tablespoon at a time; continue beating until stiff and glossy. Spread over pudding. Bake until delicate golden brown, 8 to 10 minutes. Let stand 5 minutes.

* 1 can (7¾ ounces) sweetened reconstituted coconut juice can be substituted for the coconut milk.

Pineapple Meringue Bread Pudding (page 311) and Mexican Bread Pudding.

Mexican Bread Pudding

(Capirotada)

Cinnamon and orange peel add fragrance to this unusual and inexpensive Mexican pudding. Shredded cheese is the surprise ingredient and bright flecks of apple peel add color.

6 servings

1	cup packed brown sugar
1½	cups water
2	tablespoons margarine or butter
1	teaspoon ground cinnamon
1	teaspoon grated orange peel
5	cups ½-inch cubes toasted French bread
½	cup chopped blanched almonds or walnuts
½	cup raisins
1	tart apple, chopped
1	cup shredded or diced Monterey Jack or Cheddar cheese (4 ounces)

Heat brown sugar, water, margarine, cinnamon and orange peel to boiling; reduce heat. Simmer uncovered 5 minutes.

Layer half the bread cubes, almonds, raisins, apple and cheese in ungreased 1½-quart casserole; repeat. Pour hot syrup over top. Bake uncovered in 350° oven until syrup is absorbed, 30 to 40 minutes.

Semolina Pudding

(Ma'mounia)

This nourishing pudding is popular in many areas of the Middle East, particularly Syria. Ma'mounia has many names and there are many recipes for it, but the basic ingredients remain constant. Syrians often serve the pudding for breakfast and traditionally use it as a restorative for young mothers after childbirth.

4 to 6 servings

2	cups water
¾	cup sugar
¼	cup margarine or butter
¾	cup semolina (couscous) cereal*
½	cup raisins
¼	cup slivered almonds
¼	teaspoon salt
	Ground cinnamon

Heat water and sugar to boiling; reduce heat. Simmer uncovered 10 minutes. Heat margarine in 1½-quart saucepan until melted; add semolina. Cook over low heat, stirring constantly, 5 minutes.

Stir in sugar syrup, raisins, almonds and salt. Heat to boiling. Cook, stirring constantly, until thickened, 5 to 8 minutes. Pour into serving dishes; sprinkle with cinnamon. Serve warm or cold with sweetened whipped cream if desired.

* ⅓ cup farina can be substituted for the ¾ cup semolina.

Semolina

Did You Know?

Semolina, the particles of wheat remaining in the bolting machine after the flour has been sifted, is more commonly used in Europe than in the United States. It can be prepared somewhat like farina and is used in making puddings and soups and in the manufacture of macaroni and spaghetti.

Little Salzburger Soufflés

(Salzburger Nockerln)

The pride of Salzburg, these remarkable "little soufflés"—distant relatives of our floating-island desserts—have enchanted visitors and native Austrians for many generations. The dish is favored both as an afternoon refreshment with coffee and for Sunday-evening dessert parties. Today Salzburger Nockerln appear on restaurant menus throughout Austria and Germany in a number of versions.

6 servings

4	eggs, separated
¼	teaspoon cream of tartar
	Dash of salt
⅓	cup sugar
2	tablespoons flour
2	teaspoons finely shredded lemon peel

Heat oven to 350°. Butter oblong baking dish, 11 x 7 x 1½ inches. Beat egg whites, cream of tartar and salt in large mixer bowl until foamy. Gradually beat in sugar, 1 tablespoon at a time; continue beating until stiff and glossy. Do not underbeat.

Beat egg yolks in small mixer bowl until thick and lemon colored, about 3 minutes. Beat in flour and lemon peel. Carefully fold egg yolk mixture into meringue.

Spoon meringue mixture into 6 distinct mounds in baking dish. Bake until golden, 18 to 20 minutes. Serve immediately. (Separate mounds by gently pushing them apart with backs of two forks.) Serve with sweetened sliced strawberries or Almond Praline (page 341) if desired.

Thousand Leaves Torte

Thousand Leaves Torte
(Tusenbladstårta)

A memorable do-ahead dessert from Sweden, Thousand Leaves Torte is as pretty as a picture and a real joy to eat. The alternate layers of Cinnamon Pastry, applesauce and custard will please the most particular guest. Serve the torte as your pièce de résistance *when planning a crowd-size smorgasbord!*

12 to 14 servings

   Cinnamon Pastry (right)
6 tablespoons sugar
   Custard-Cream Filling (page 315)
1 cup thick applesauce
1 teaspoon lemon juice
   Sliced almonds

Prepare Cinnamon Pastry. Divide pastry into 6 equal parts. Roll each part into 7-inch circle on lightly floured cloth-covered board; place on ungreased cookie sheets. Heat oven to 425°. Prick circles with fork; sprinkle each with 1 tablespoon sugar. Bake until light golden brown, 12 to 15 minutes. Cool on wire racks.

Prepare Custard-Cream Filling. Mix applesauce and lemon juice. Stack circles, spreading alternately with ⅓ cup applesauce mixture and ½ cup Custard-Cream Filling. Spread top layer with remaining filling. Garnish with Almonds. Refrigerate at least 2 hours before serving.

Cinnamon Pastry

¾ cup margarine or butter
2 cups all-purpose flour
1 teaspoon salt
1 teaspoon ground cinnamon
3 to 4 tablespoons cold water

Cut margarine into flour, salt and cinnamon until particles are size of small peas. Sprinkle in water, 1 tablespoon at a time, tossing with fork until all flour is moistened and pastry almost cleans side of bowl (1 to 2 teaspoons water can be added if necessary). Gather pastry into a ball.

Custard-Cream Filling

¼ cup sugar
1 tablespoon cornstarch
¼ teaspoon salt
1 cup milk
1 egg, slightly beaten
1 teaspoon vanilla
½ cup chilled whipping cream

Mix sugar, cornstarch and salt in 1-quart saucepan. Stir in milk gradually. Cook over medium heat, stirring constantly, until mixture thickens and boils. Boil and stir 1 minute. Stir at least half of the hot mixture gradually into egg. Blend into hot mixture in saucepan. Boil and stir 1 minute. Remove from heat; stir in vanilla. Cover and cool slightly; refrigerate until completely cooled. Beat whipping cream in chilled bowl until stiff; fold into filling.

Almonds

Did You Know?

The almond has been well known in the Mediterranean countries and western Asia for thousands of years. It has been a common ingredient in breads, cakes, desserts and candies from Scandinavia to the Orient. The versatile almond is available in many forms and can be used with almost any food. Sliced or slivered almonds are often used as a garnish for main dishes, salads, vegetables or desserts. Almonds are available in blanched or unblanched form. Blanched almonds are those from which the brown skins have been removed.

Toasting almonds seems to further enhance their flavor. To toast, spread slivered or sliced almonds in a shallow pan and place in a 350° oven until delicately browned, stirring frequently, 6 to 10 minutes. To preserve the freshness of almonds, store them in a tightly covered container in the refrigerator or freeze them for longer storage.

Canadian Butter Tarts

These very rich little tarts from Canada are perfect snacks for serving with tea or coffee as an afternoon or midnight snack. For a more substantial refreshment, serve the tarts with ice cream or sherbet instead of the whipped-cream topping.

24 small tarts

1 cup all-purpose flour
½ cup margarine or butter, softened
¼ cup powdered sugar
¾ cup packed brown sugar
¼ cup margarine or butter, softened
¼ cup dark corn syrup
1 egg, slightly beaten
¼ teaspoon salt
¼ cup currants or cut-up raisins

Heat oven to 350°. Mix flour, ½ cup margarine and the powdered sugar. Divide into 24 equal pieces. Press each piece against bottom and side of ungreased small muffin cup, 1¾ x 1 inch.* Do not allow pastry to extend above tops of cups.

Mix brown sugar and ¼ cup margarine. Stir in corn syrup, egg, salt and currants. Spoon scant tablespoonful mixture into each muffin cup. Bake until filling is set and crust is light brown, about 20 minutes. Cool in muffin cups 20 minutes. Remove from muffin cups with tip of knife; cool on wire rack. Top with sweetened whipped cream if desired.

* Medium muffin cups, 2½ x 1¼ inches, can be substituted for the small muffin cups. Divide pastry into 12 equal pieces. Divide filling among muffin cups. Bake about 30 minutes.

Do-Ahead Tip: Tarts can be wrapped and frozen no longer than 3 months. To thaw, unwrap and let stand at room temperature 30 minutes.

Apple Strudel
(Apfelstrudel)

Although quick strudel can be made with filo pastry leaves (page 7), taking the trouble to make your own Strudel Dough from scratch is well worth the effort. When you try our recipe you'll find out just why strudel has been so highly prized by Austrians, Germans, Hungarians and Czechs for so many generations.

16 to 18 servings

	Strudel Dough (right)
1	cup granulated sugar
½	cup finely chopped walnuts
½	cup raisins
1	teaspoon ground cinnamon
6	cups chopped apples (about 6 medium)
2	tablespoons lemon juice
¼	cup margarine or butter, melted
¼	cup dry bread crumbs
	Powdered sugar

Prepare Strudel Dough. While dough is resting, cover a 3-foot square space on counter or table with large dish towel or tablecloth. Tuck ends under; secure with tape. Sprinkle cloth with small amount of flour. Mix granulated sugar, walnuts, raisins and cinnamon. Toss apples with lemon juice.

Roll dough on floured cloth until ⅛ inch thick. Working quickly to prevent drying, place hands palms down and close together under dough; gently lift and stretch dough by moving hands apart until dough is paper thin and forms a 30- to 36-inch square. (See diagram.) Trim edges evenly with kitchen scissors.

Heat oven to 375°. Brush square with margarine. Sprinkle bread crumbs in 3-inch strip along one edge to within 2 inches of edge and ends. Mix walnut-raisin and apple mixtures; spread in 3-inch strip over bread crumbs. Lift edge of cloth nearest apples with both hands; roll up as for a jelly roll, lifting the cloth at the same time as an aid in rolling the strudel.

(See diagram.) Place roll seam side down on greased cookie sheet in a horseshoe shape. Tuck ends under to seal. Brush with margarine.

Bake until golden brown, 35 to 40 minutes. Remove from oven; sprinkle with powdered sugar. Cut into 1-inch slices; serve with sweetened whipped cream or ice cream if desired.

Strudel Dough

1½	cups all-purpose flour
½	cup lukewarm water
2	tablespoons vegetable oil
½	teaspoon salt
	Margarine or butter, melted

Mix all ingredients except margarine until flour is moistened and dough cleans side of bowl. Turn dough into lightly floured surface; knead until smooth and no longer sticks to surface, about 10 minutes, sprinkling with small amount of flour while kneading if necessary. Shape dough into a ball; brush with margarine. Cover and let rest in warm place about 30 minutes to make dough easier to handle.

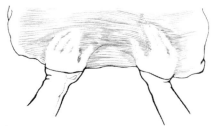

Place hands palms down and close together under dough; gently lift and stretch dough by moving hands apart until dough is paper thin and forms a 30- to 36-inch square.

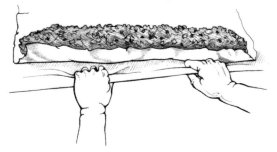

Lift edge of cloth nearest apples with both hands; roll up as for a jelly roll.

Baklava

Baklava

The Turks are credited with introducing Baklava to Greece and other parts of Eastern Europe—but the sweet, flaky pastry has been a favorite treat throughout most of the Middle East for many centuries. Some food historians believe the recipe may have been invented by the ancient Egyptians!

About 36 pieces

	Honey Syrup (right)
3	cups finely chopped pecans, walnuts, almonds or combination of nuts (¾ pound shelled)
2	teaspoons ground cinnamon
½	teaspoon ground nutmeg
¼	teaspoon ground cloves
1½	cups margarine or butter, melted
1	package (16 ounces) frozen filo leaves, thawed

Prepare Honey Syrup. Mix nuts and spices. Brush bottom and sides of jelly roll pan, 15½ x 10½ x 1 inch, with some of the margarine. Unfold filo leaves; cover with damp towel to prevent drying. Carefully separate 1 leaf; place in pan folding edges over to fit pan if necessary. Brush lightly with margarine. Repeat 6 times.

Sprinkle 1½ cups of the nut mixture evenly over top. Layer 7 more filo leaves in pan, brushing each leaf with margarine. Sprinkle with remaining nut mixture. Layer remaining filo leaves over nuts, brushing each leaf with margarine.

Heat oven to 350°. With a sharp knife, cut pastry into 6 lengthwise strips, ½ inch deep and 1¾ inches wide. Make diagonal cuts across strips ½ inch deep and 2 inches wide. Pour remaining margarine over top. Bake until golden brown, 1 to 1¼ hours. Place pan on wire rack; pour syrup over top. Cool. Cut along scored lines.

Honey Syrup

1½	cups sugar
1½	cups water
2	tablespoons lemon juice
¾	cup honey

Heat sugar, water and lemon juice to boiling; stir until sugar is dissolved. Boil 5 minutes. Remove from heat; stir in honey. Cool.

Honey
Did You Know?

There are five types of honey available on the market today—liquid, solid, comb, cut comb and chunk. Most people in America prefer honey in the liquid form. Solid honey is very popular in Canada and is also known as creamed honey or honey spread. To serve comb honey, cut into 1-inch squares and chill 30 minues before serving to prevent loss of honey from the comb.

Honey should be stored in a tightly covered container in a cool place. Refrigeration is not necessary and it may hasten crystallization of liquid honey. If honey does crystallize, it can be reliquefied by placing the container in a pan of warm water until the crystals dissolve.

Italian Ricotta Cheesecake

(Crostata di Ricotta)

This fruit-flavored cheesecake is one of the most ancient of Italian specialties, dating back to the early days of the Roman Empire. Slightly tart fruits, such as green grapes, orange segments and cherries, are often served as a flavor contrast to the rich pie.

12 to 16 servings

	Cheesecake Pastry (below)
1½	pounds ricotta cheese, well drained
½	cup granulated sugar
3	tablespoons flour
3	eggs
1	teaspoon grated orange peel
1	teaspoon vanilla
¼	teaspoon salt
2	tablespoons golden raisins
2	tablespoons finely cut-up candied citron
2	tablespoons chopped blanched almonds
2	tablespoons powdered sugar
½	teaspoon ground cinnamon

Prepare Cheesecake Pastry. Beat ricotta cheese, granulated sugar, flour, eggs, orange peel, vanilla and salt in large mixer bowl on high speed until smooth and creamy, about 4 minutes. Stir in raisins, citron and almonds. Pour into pastry-lined pan. Bake in 350° oven until center is set and top is golden brown, 1¼ to 1½ hours. Cool. Refrigerate 12 to 24 hours. Remove outer rim of pan. Mix powdered sugar and cinnamon; sprinkle over cheesecake. Serve with green grapes if desired.

Cheesecake Pastry

¾	cup all-purpose flour
⅓	cup margarine or butter, softened
2	tablespoons sugar
⅛	teaspoon salt

Mix all ingredients until blended; press evenly in bottom of ungreased 9-inch springform pan. Bake in 475° oven 5 minutes.

Cheese-and-Honey Pie

The Greeks were famous for their "cheesecakes" in ancient times. Modern Greek cooks continue to take pride in artful cheese pies and cakes such as this one, which features a fragrant Sesame Seed Pastry and uses cream cheese.

10 to 12 servings

	Sesame Seed Pastry (below)
2	packages (8 ounces each) cream cheese, softened
2	eggs
½	cup sugar
½	cup honey
½	cup whipping cream
1	teaspoon grated lemon peel
¼	teaspoon ground nutmeg

Prepare Sesame Seed Pastry. Beat cream cheese in large mixer bowl on medium speed until creamy. Add remaining ingredients; beat until light and fluffy. Pour into baked pie shell. Bake in 350° oven until firm, 40 to 50 minutes. Refrigerate until serving time.

Sesame Seed Pastry

1	cup all-purpose flour
⅓	cup margarine or butter, softened
1	tablespoon sugar
1	tablespoon toasted sesame seed
¼	teaspoon salt

Mix all ingredients until blended; press firmly and evenly against bottom and side of 9-inch pie plate. Bake in 475° oven 5 minutes.

Ricotta Cheese

Did You Know?

Ricotta cheese, a soft, unripened cheese made from milk or whey, has a bland semi-sweet nutty flavor. It is used extensively in Italian cooking, especially in ravioli, lasagne and desserts.

German Plum Cake

German Plum Cake
(Zwetschgenkuchen)

For best results, plan to make this homey German classic during the late summer, when fresh plums are in season. You'll find it tastes especially good after a spicy main dish, such as Sauerbrauten *(page 116) or* Choucroute Garnie à l'Alsacienne *(page 148).*

6 servings

Pastry (right)
2   pounds purple or red plums, halved and pitted (about 5 cups)
¾   cup sugar
2   tablespoons flour
1   teaspoon ground cinnamon
¼   cup slivered almonds

Prepare pastry. Place plum halves cut sides down and overlapping slightly in pastry-lined pan. Mix sugar, flour and cinnamon; sprinkle over plums. Sprinkle with almonds. Bake in 375° oven until pastry is golden brown and plums are bubbly, 35 to 45 minutes.

Pastry
½   cup margarine or butter
2   cups all-purpose flour
¼   cup sugar
1   teaspoon baking powder
½   teaspoon salt
½   teaspoon grated lemon peel
¼   teaspoon ground mace
1   egg, beaten
2   tablespoons cold water

Cut margarine into flour, sugar, baking powder, salt, lemon peel and mace until mixture resembles fine crumbs. Mix egg and water; stir into flour mixture. Gather pastry into a ball; knead just until smooth, 5 or 6 times. Press evenly on bottom and side of ungreased round layer pan, 9 x 1½ inches.

French Cream-Puff Cake (Gâteau Saint-Honoré)

Gâteau Saint-Honoré is named after France's patron saint of cooks and pastry chefs and is eminently worthy of the honor! This is not really a cake but a wreath of plump cream puffs arranged around a pastry ring and filled with a luscious vanilla cream. Feature the cake on a party menu that includes a clear French soup or first-course salad and a main-course masterpiece, such as Duckling with Orange Sauce (page 74), Chicken Fricassée (page 82) or Coquilles Saint-Jacques à la Parisienne (page 65).

	Vanilla-Cream Filling (page 321)
⅓	cup margarine or butter
¾	cup all-purpose flour
¼	teaspoon salt
2	to 4 teaspoons cold water
	Cream-Puff Dough (page 321)
1	cup sugar
¼	cup water
2	tablespoons corn syrup
1	cup chilled whipping cream
1	teaspoon vanilla

Prepare Vanilla-Cream Filling. Cut margarine into flour and salt until particles are size of small peas. Sprinkle in 2 to 4 teaspoons water, 1 teaspoon at a time, tossing with fork until all flour is moistened and pastry almost cleans side of bowl (1 to 2 teaspoons water can be added if necessary).

Heat oven to 400°. Gather pastry into a ball; shape into flattened round on lightly floured surface. Roll pastry into 10-inch circle. (Inverted 10-inch dinner plate or 10-inch pie plate can be used as a guide; trim uneven edges of pastry if necessary.) Place pastry round on ungreased cookie sheet. Prick with fork at 1-inch intervals. Bake until golden brown, 10 to 15 minutes.

Prepare Cream-Puff Dough. Using 1-inch plain tip and about 1 cup dough in pastry bag, pipe 9-inch ring about 1 inch wide on un-greased cookie sheet. (For a guide, place 7½-inch plate on cookie sheet and trace lightly around it; pipe dough just outside traced circle.) Press remaining dough through bag or use rounded teaspoonfuls to make 12 small mounds about 2 inches apart on ungreased cookie sheet. Bake cream-puff ring and individual puffs until puffed and golden brown, 25 to 30 minutes. Cool.

Open cream puffs partially on side; fill with 1 to 2 teaspoons filling. Heat sugar, ¼ cup water and the corn syrup to boiling in 8-inch skillet over medium heat, stirring constantly, just until syrup mixture turns light-golden brown, about 6 minutes.

Spoon thin ribbon of caramel syrup around edge of pastry round. Place cream-puff ring on top. Using tongs, dip bottom of each puff into syrup; place puffs side by side on ring. (See photograph.) If syrup hardens, reheat slowly until soft. Drizzle any remaining syrup over puffs. (See Note.) Fill center of puff ring with remaining filling. Beat whipping cream and vanilla in chilled bowl until stiff. Spread over filling. Refrigerate until serving time.

Using tongs, dip bottom of each puff into syrup; place puffs side by side on ring.

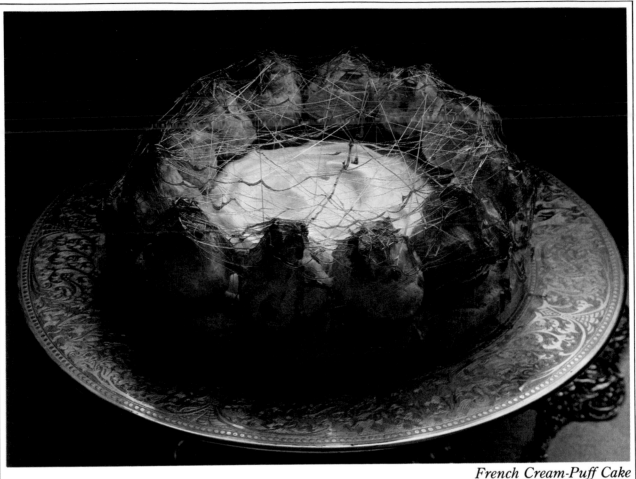

French Cream-Puff Cake

Vanilla-Cream Filling

⅔   cup sugar
¼   cup cornstarch
½   teaspoon salt
3   cups milk
4   egg yolks, slightly beaten
2   tablespoons margarine or butter
1   tablespoon plus 1 teaspoon vanilla

Mix sugar, cornstarch and salt in 1½-quart saucepan. Stir in milk gradually. Cook over medium heat, stirring constantly, until mixture thickens and boils. Boil and stir 1 minute. Stir at least half of the hot mixture gradually into egg yolks. Blend into hot mixture in saucepan. Boil and stir 1 minute. Remove from heat; stir in margarine and vanilla. Cover and refrigerate until chilled, about 1 hour.

Cream-Puff Dough

1   cup water
½   cup margarine or butter
1   cup all-purpose flour
4   eggs

Heat water and margarine to rolling boil in 1½-quart saucepan; reduce heat. Stir in flour. Stir vigorously over low heat until mixture forms a ball, about 1 minute; remove from heat. Beat in eggs; continue beating until smooth.

Note: To form caramel syrup threads as pictured, fill center of ring with remaining filling and whipped cream before drizzling puffs with syrup. Dip wooden spoon handle, wooden ice cream stick or chopstick into syrup, then draw quickly back and forth over filling and cream puffs. This step should be done just before serving as threads may soften with longer storage.

Dobos Torte

Dobos Torte

Dobos Torte competes only with strudel and goulash for top culinary honors in Hungary. The dessert was the tour de force of a legendary Hungarian chef who created the cake in the nineteenth century and won top honors.

6	eggs, separated
1½	cups sugar
1½	cups all-purpose flour
1	teaspoon baking powder
½	teaspoon salt
⅓	cup cold water
2	teaspoons vanilla
½	teaspoon cream of tartar
	Chocolate Butter Frosting (page 323)
	Caramel Glaze (page 323)

Grease and flour 4 round layer pans, 8 or 9 x 1½ inches.* Heat oven to 325°. Beat egg yolks until very thick and lemon colored, about 5 minutes; pour into large mixer bowl. Gradually beat in sugar. Beat in flour, baking powder and salt alternately with water and vanilla on low speed.

Beat egg whites and cream of tartar until stiff. Gradually fold egg yolk mixture into egg whites. Divide batter among pans. Bake until top springs back when touched lightly in center, 25 to 35 minutes. Cool cake 5 minutes. Loosen edges of layers with knife; invert on wire racks. Cool completely. Prepare Chocolate Butter Frosting.

Split cake to make 8 layers. (See diagram.) Reserve layer with smoothest top for top of cake. Fill 7 layers with ⅓ cup frosting each. Frost side of cake with remaining frosting.

Prepare Caramel Glaze. Place reserved layer on ungreased cookie sheet. Pour glaze evenly over layer, spreading to edges (glaze should be handled carefully when hot, but becomes brittle when cool). Working quickly, snip into 12 to 16 wedges with kitchen scissors. (See diagram.) Overlap wedges on filled layers.

* If you have only 2 round layer pans, cover and refrigerate remaining half of batter until first layers are baked.

Chocolate Butter Frosting

½   cup margarine or butter, softened
5   ounces unsweetened melted chocolate (cool)
5   cups powdered sugar
5   to 6 tablespoons cold coffee or water

Mix margarine and chocolate. Stir in powdered sugar and 3 tablespoons of the coffee. Beat until smooth. Stir in additional coffee until frosting is of spreading consistency.

Caramel Glaze

Heat ½ cup sugar over low heat, stirring constantly, until sugar is melted and golden brown. Remove from heat. Stir in 2 teaspoons margarine or butter.

Split layers by using a long, sharp knife.

Snip glazed layer into 12 to 16 wedges with kitchen scissors.

Greek Honey-Walnut Cake

(Karithopita)

The Greeks have as many recipes for their beloved walnut cakes as Americans do for apple pie. Like apple pie, the cake is served all year around and is especially popular during the harvest season, when walnuts are plentiful.

1¼   cups all-purpose flour
¾   cup sugar
1   teaspoon baking powder
1   teaspoon ground cinnamon
½   teaspoon salt
¼   teaspoon ground cloves
¾   cup milk
⅓   cup shortening
1   egg
1   cup finely chopped walnuts
    Honey Syrup (below)

Heat oven to 350°. Grease and flour square pan, 9 x 9 x 2 inches. Beat all ingredients except walnuts and Honey Syrup in small mixer bowl on low speed, scraping bowl constantly, 30 seconds. Beat on high speed, scraping bowl occasionally, 1 minute. Stir in walnuts. Pour into pan. Bake until wooden pick inserted in center comes out clean, 35 to 40 minutes.

Cool cake in pan about 30 minutes. Prepare Honey Syrup. Cut top of cake into diamond pattern; pour syrup evenly over top of cake.

Honey Syrup

¼   cup sugar
¼   cup water
¼   cup honey
1   teaspoon lemon juice

Heat sugar and water to boiling; reduce heat. Simmer uncovered 5 minutes. Stir in honey and lemon juice.

Black Forest Cherry Cake

Black Forest Cherry Cake (Schwarzwälder Kirschtorte)

Perhaps the most famous of all German desserts, this divine cherry-and-chocolate classic originated in the Black Forest region and quickly spread to all regions of Germany, eventually captivating Europe and America as well.

2¼	cups all-purpose flour or cake flour
1⅔	cups sugar
⅔	cup cocoa
1¼	teaspoons baking soda
1	teaspoon salt
¼	teaspoon baking powder
1¼	cups water
¾	cup shortening
2	eggs
1	teaspoon vanilla
	Cherry Filling (right)
1	bar (4 ounces) sweet cooking chocolate*
2	cups chilled whipping cream
¼	cup sugar
	Maraschino cherries

Heat oven to 350°. Generously grease and flour two 9-inch or three 8-inch round layer pans. Beat flour, 1⅔ cups sugar, the cocoa, baking soda, salt, baking powder, water, shortening, eggs and vanilla in large mixer bowl on low speed, scraping bowl constantly, 30 seconds. Beat on high speed, scraping bowl occasionally, 3 minutes. Pour into pans. Bake until wooden pick inserted in center comes out clean, 30 to 35 minutes. Cool 5 minutes; remove from pans. Cool on wire racks.

Prepare Cherry Filling. With a vegetable parer or thin, sharp knife, slice across chocolate bar with long strokes to form 12 to 14 chocolate curls for garnishing cake. (See photograph.) For best results, let chocolate stand in warm place 10 to 15 minutes before slicing. Refrigerate curls until ready to use.

Place 1 cake layer upside down on serving plate. Beat whipping cream and ¼ cup sugar in chilled bowl until stiff peaks form. Spread bottom layer with about ⅔ of the Cherry Filling and 1 cup of the whipped cream. Place other layer top side up on whipped cream. Spread with remaining Cherry Filling. Frost side and top of cake with remaining whipped cream.

If desired, coarsely shred enough remaining chocolate to measure ½ cup. Gently press shredded chocolate onto side of cake. Garnish top of cake with chocolate curls and maraschino cherries. Refrigerate until serving time.

Cherry Filling

½	cup sugar
3	tablespoons cornstarch
1	can (16 ounces) pitted red tart cherries†, well-drained (reserve liquid)
¼	cup kirsch
	Few drops red food color (optional)

Mix sugar and cornstarch in 1-quart saucepan. Add enough water to reserved liquid to measure ¾ cup; stir into sugar mixture. Cook, stirring constantly, until mixture thickens and boils. Boil and stir 1 minute. Stir in kirsch and food color. Cut cherries into halves; stir into filling. Refrigerate until completely chilled.

* Milk-chocolate candy bar can be substituted for the sweet cooking chocolate.

† 1 can (16 ounces) pitted dark sweet cherries can be substituted for the red tart cherries and the maraschino-cherry garnish; decrease sugar to 2 tablespoons.

With a vegetable parer, slice across chocolate bar with long strokes to form chocolate curls.

Brazil Nut Cake

Coffee and spices lend a remarkable flavor to this light, moist layer cake; a rich "frosting" of coffee-flavored whipped cream and a final sprinkling of Brazil nut curls make the dessert just right for a festive occasion.

6   eggs, separated
½   cup sugar
2   tablespoons vegetable oil
1   tablespoon brandy
½   cup sugar
¼   cup all-purpose flour
1¼   teaspoons baking powder
1   teaspoon instant coffee
½   teaspoon ground cinnamon
½   teaspoon ground cloves
1   cup fine graham-cracker crumbs (about 12 squares)

1   cup finely chopped Brazil nuts
1½   cups chilled whipping cream
¼   cup sugar
2   teaspoons instant coffee
     Brazil nut curls (see Note)

Heat oven to 350°. Line bottoms of 2 round layer pans, 8 or 9 x 1½ inches, with aluminum foil. Beat egg whites in large mixer bowl until foamy. Beat in ½ cup sugar, 1 tablespoon at a time; continue beating until stiff and glossy.

Beat egg yolks, oil and brandy in small mixer bowl on low speed until blended. Add ½ cup sugar, the flour, baking powder, 1 teaspoon instant coffee, the cinnamon and cloves; beat on medium speed 1 minute. Fold egg yolk mixture into egg whites. Fold in cracker crumbs and 1 cup nuts. Pour into pans.

Bake until top springs back when touched lightly, 30 to 35 minutes. Immediately invert pans, resting rims on edges of 2 inverted pans. Cool completely. Loosen edges of layers with knife; invert pans and hit sharply on table. Remove foil.

Beat whipping cream, ¼ cup sugar and 2 teaspoons instant coffee in chilled bowl until stiff. Fill layers and frost side and top of cake with whipped cream. (To decorate cake as pictured, frost side and top of cake with thin layer of whipped cream; place remaining whipped cream in decorators' tube or bag and, using star tip, make rosettes and pipe borders around cake.) Garnish with Brazil nut curls.

Note: To form Brazil nut curls, cut lengthwise slices from Brazil nuts with a vegetable parer.

Savarin

Savarin

Savarin is a yeast-leavened cake that is made in a savarin (or ring) mold and soaked with syrup or liquor. Perhaps the most famous variation on Savarin is Baba au Rhum *(see below). Often the center of the ring is filled with fresh fruit or with a sauce such as* Crème Fraîche *(page 304) or* Zabaglione *(page 307).*

1	package active dry yeast
½	cup warm water (105 to 115°)
¾	cup margarine or butter, softened
4	eggs, beaten
2	tablespoons sugar
½	teaspoon salt
2	cups all-purpose flour
	Savarin Syrup (page 327)
½	cup apricot preserves
2	tablespoons sugar

Dissolve yeast in warm water in 3-quart bowl. Stir in margarine, eggs, 2 tablespoons sugar, the salt and 1 cup of the flour. Beat until smooth. Stir in remaining flour until smooth. Beat 25 strokes. Spread batter evenly in well-greased 8-cup metal ring mold or tube pan, 10 x 4 inches. Cover; let rise in warm place until almost double, 50 to 60 minutes.

Heat oven to 375°. Bake until golden brown, 25 to 30 minutes. (If top is browning too quickly, cover loosely with aluminum foil.) Cool in mold 10 minutes. Remove from mold; cool slightly on wire rack.

Prepare Savarin Syrup. Place Savarin on serving plate. Slowly drizzle syrup on Savarin until all syrup is absorbed (see Note). Press apricot preserves through strainer. Heat preserves and 2 tablespoons sugar to boiling, stirring constantly; reduce heat. Simmer uncovered until slightly thickened, 1 to 2 minutes. Cool 10 minutes. Spread apricot glaze over Savarin. Savarin can be served with fresh berries or peaches and sweetened whipped cream if desired.

Savarin Syrup

Heat 1 cup sugar and 1 cup water to boiling; reduce heat. Simmer uncovered 2 minutes; cool to lukewarm. Stir in ¼ cup brandy, rum or orange-flavored liqueur.

Baba au Rhum: Stir ½ cup raisins into batter. Spread in well-greased 8- or 9-cup metal mold or 9-cup bundt cake pan. Bake until golden brown, about 30 minutes. Use rum in the syrup and omit apricot glaze if desired.

Note: A fine skewer can be used to make holes in Savarin or Baba au Rhum before drizzling with syrup to facilitate penetration of syrup.

English Cake Roll

A most unusual accent—whipped cream flavored with tea!—and a sublime marmalade filling make this British inspiration a real conversation piece.

10 servings

3	eggs
1	cup granulated sugar
⅓	cup water
1	teaspoon vanilla
¾	cup all-purpose flour or 1 cup cake flour
1	teaspoon baking powder
¼	teaspoon salt
¾	cup orange or lemon marmalade
	Tea Whipped Cream (right)
	Powdered sugar

Heat oven to 375°. Line jelly roll pan, 15½ x 10 ½ x 1 inch, with aluminum foil or waxed paper; grease generously. Beat eggs in small mixer bowl on high speed until thick and lemon colored, about 5 minutes. Pour eggs into large mixer bowl. Beat in granulated sugar gradually. Beat in water and vanilla on low speed. Add flour, baking powder and salt gradually, beating just until batter is smooth. Pour into pan.

Bake until wooden pick inserted in center comes out clean, 12 to 15 minutes. Immediately loosen cake from edges of pan; invert on towel sprinkled generously with powdered sugar. Carefully remove foil. Trim off stiff edges if necessary.

While hot, carefully roll cake and towel from narrow end. Cool on wire rack at least 30 minutes. Unroll cake; remove towel. Spread marmalade over cake. Cover marmalade with Tea Whipped Cream; roll up. (See diagram.) Sprinkle with powdered sugar. Refrigerate until serving time.

Tea Whipped Cream

1	cup chilled whipping cream
3	tablespoons powdered sugar
2	tablespoons instant tea
½	teaspoon vanilla

Beat all ingredients in chilled bowl until stiff.

Do-Ahead Tip: Before sprinkling with powdered sugar or spreading with filling, roll can be wrapped and refrigerated no longer than 48 hours or frozen no longer than 1 month (place in box to prevent crushing). Let stand at room temperature 15 to 30 minutes before filling.

While hot, carefully roll cake and towel together from narrow end.

Orange-Almond Cake

Orange-Almond Cake

(Torta de Almendra)

A sprinkling of orange-flavored liqueur and sugar moistens and enhances the flavor of this simple little cake, which originated in Spain and has won many admirers in Mexico. The cake makes a fine family dessert after a tasty meal of Spicy Sausage Burritos (page 159) or Tostadas (page 144).

1¼	cups all-purpose flour or 1½ cups cake flour
1	cup sugar
1½	teaspoons baking powder
½	teaspoon salt
¾	cup milk
⅓	cup shortening
1	egg
2	teaspoons grated orange peel
¼	cup sliced almonds
1	tablespoon sugar
2	tablespoons orange-flavored liqueur

Heat oven to 350°. Grease and flour round layer pan, 9 x 1½ inches, or square pan, 8 x 8 x 2 or 9 x 9 x 2 inches. Beat all ingredients except almonds, 1 tablespoon sugar and the liqueur in large mixer bowl on low speed, scraping bowl constantly, 30 seconds. Beat on high speed, scraping bowl occasionally, 3 minutes. Pour into pan; sprinkle with almonds.

Bake until wooden pick inserted in center comes out clean, round pan 40 minutes, square pans 40 to 45 minutes. Sprinkle with 1 tablespoon sugar; drizzle with liqueur. Cool 10 to 15 minutes. Remove from pan; cool completely.

into 4 rectangles, 10½ x 3¾ inches. Alternate layers of cake and ricotta filling, beginning and ending with cake. Frost with Chocolate Mocha Frosting. (Use decorators' tube and tip to make decorative swirls if desired, and garnish with additional candied fruit.)

Sponge Cake

3   eggs
1   cup granulated sugar
⅓   cup water
1   teaspoon vanilla
¾   cup all-purpose flour or 1 cup cake flour
1   teaspoon baking powder
¼   teaspoon salt
    Powdered sugar

Heat oven to 375°. Line jelly roll pan, 15½ x 10½ x 1 inch, with aluminum foil or waxed paper; grease generously. Beat eggs in small mixer bowl on high speed until thick and lemon colored, about 5 minutes. Pour eggs into large mixer bowl. Beat in granulated sugar gradually. Beat in water and vanilla on low speed. Add flour, baking powder and salt gradually, beating just until batter is smooth. Pour into pan.

Bake until wooden pick inserted in center comes out clean, 12 to 15 minutes. Immediately loosen cake from edges of pan; invert on towel sprinkled generously with powdered sugar. Carefully remove foil. Trim off stiff edges if necessary. Cool on wire rack at least 30 minutes.

Chocolate Mocha Frosting

2½   cups powdered sugar
⅓   cup margarine or butter, softened
2   ounces melted unsweetened chocolate (cool)
2   teaspoons instant coffee
3   tablespoons hot water

Beat powdered sugar, margarine and chocolate in small mixer bowl on low speed. Dissolve instant coffee in water. Add coffee gradually; beat until smooth and creamy. If necessary, stir in additional water, a few drops at a time.

Sicilian Cheese-and-Chocolate Cake

Sicilian Cheese-and-Chocolate Cake

(Cassata alla Siciliana)

Sicilian chefs have been famous for their sweets and pastries for many centuries. Crowning the culinary repertoire is the Sicilian cassata, *or layer cake—a joyous-celebration cake once served only at Christmas and Easter but now served at weddings and christenings, too.*

    Sponge Cake (right)
1   carton (about 16 ounces) dry ricotta cheese
¼   cup sugar
2   tablespoons milk
2   tablespoons orange-flavored liqueur
¼   teaspoon salt
⅓   cup semisweet chocolate chips, chopped
⅓   cup finely chopped mixed candied fruit
    Chocolate Mocha Frosting (right)

Prepare Sponge Cake. Beat ricotta cheese, sugar, milk, liqueur and salt in small mixer bowl until smooth, 2 to 3 minutes. Stir in chocolate chips and candied fruit. Cut cake

Honey Cake
(Lekach)

The traditional spices of the ancient Middle East mingle with the flavor of coffee in this Eastern European holiday cake that Jewish families traditionally serve on the first night of Rosh Hashanah and Simhath Torah.

1	cup sugar
1	cup honey
½	cup vegetable oil
4	eggs
1	tablespoon finely shredded lemon peel
3	tablespoons lemon juice
2	tablespoons brandy
3½	cups all-purpose flour
1½	teaspoons baking powder
1	teaspoon baking soda
½	teaspoon salt
1	teaspoon ground cinnamon
½	teaspoon ground ginger
¼	teaspoon ground nutmeg
2	teaspoons instant coffee
⅔	cup cold water
¾	cup chopped nuts
½	cup raisins
	Lemon Sugar (right)

Heat oven to 350°. Beat sugar, honey, oil, eggs, lemon peel and juice and brandy in large mixer bowl on medium speed 2 minutes. Stir in flour, baking powder, baking soda, salt, cinnamon, ginger, nutmeg and instant coffee alternately with water. Beat on high speed, scraping bowl occasionally, 2 minutes. Fold in ½ cup of the nuts and the raisins.

Pour into greased tube pan, 10 x 4 inches, or 12-cup fluted tube pan. Bake until wooden pick inserted in center comes out clean, about 1 hour 10 minutes. Cool in pan 15 minutes; remove from pan. Prick top of cake carefully with fork; drizzle with Lemon Sugar. Sprinkle with remaining nuts.

Lemon Sugar
Mix 1 cup sugar and ⅓ cup lemon juice.

Greek Honey Twists
(Diples)

The traditional way to serve these Greek cookies is to drizzle them with honey, then sprinkle with cinnamon, finely chopped almonds or walnuts. This is a very old country recipe, delicious with tea or coffee. The twists keep well in an airtight container.

About 32 twists

3	eggs, beaten
2	tablespoons vegetable oil
½	teaspoon baking powder
¼	teaspoon salt
1¾	to 2 cups all-purpose flour
	Vegetable oil
¼	cup honey
1	tablespoon water
	Ground cinnamon

Mix eggs, 2 tablespoons oil, the baking powder and salt in large bowl. Gradually stir in enough flour to make a very stiff dough. Knead 5 minutes. Roll half the dough at a time as thin as possible on well-floured surface with stockinet-covered rolling pin. Cut into strips, 8 x 1 inch. Tie strips loosely. (Cover with damp towel to prevent drying.)

Heat oil (2 to 3 inches) to 375°. Fry 3 to 5 twists at a time until golden brown, turning once, about 45 seconds on each side. Drain on paper towels. Heat honey and water to boiling; boil 1 minute. Cool slightly. Drizzle over twists; sprinkle with cinnamon.

Spanish Crullers

Spanish Crullers
(Churros)

To the Spanish and Mexicans, crullers (or churros*) are as necessary for coffee breaks and leisurely breakfasting as doughnuts are to Americans. For an invigorating winter refresher, try them with hot chocolate after an outing in the snow.*

About 24 crullers

	Vegetable oil
1	cup water
½	cup margarine or butter
¼	teaspoon salt
1	cup all-purpose flour
3	eggs
¼	cup sugar
¼	teaspoon ground cinnamon

Heat oil (1 to 1½ inches) to 360°. Heat water, margarine and salt to rolling boil in 3-quart saucepan; stir in flour. Stir vigorously over low heat until mixture forms a ball, about 1 minute; remove from heat. Beat in eggs all at once; continue beating until smooth.

Spoon mixture into decorators' tube with large star tip. Squeeze 4-inch strips of dough into hot oil. Fry 3 or 4 strips at a time until golden brown, turning once, about 2 minutes on each side. Drain on paper towels. Mix sugar and cinnamon; roll crullers in sugar mixture.

Clockwise from top: Greek Crescent Cookies (page 334), Dutch Fried Puffs (page 333) and Greek Honey Twists (page 330).

Dutch Fried Puffs
(Olie Bollen)

These "Dutch doughnuts" can be made in a number of ways. Often chopped apples are used and occasionally mincemeat replaces the currants. Olie bollen is traditionally served on New Year's Eve in the Netherlands.

About 30 puffs

	Vegetable oil
¾	cup milk
½	cup sugar
¼	cup vegetable oil
2	eggs
3	teaspoons baking powder
½	teaspoon salt
½	teaspoon ground mace
2½	cups all-purpose flour
½	cup currants or raisins (optional)
¼	cup sugar
½	teaspoon ground cinnamon

Heat oil (2 to 3 inches) to 375°. Beat milk, ½ cup sugar, ¼ cup oil, the eggs, baking powder, salt, mace and 1 cup of the flour in large mixer bowl on low speed, scraping bowl constantly, 30 seconds. Beat on medium speed, scraping bowl occasionally, 2 minutes. Stir in remaining flour and the currants.

Drop batter by teaspoonfuls into hot oil. Turn puffs as they rise to the surface. Fry until golden brown, 2 to 2½ minutes on each side. Drain on paper towels. Mix ¼ cup sugar and the cinnamon. Roll puffs in sugar mixture.

Mexican Honey Puffs
(Sopaipillas)

Sopaipillas are deep-fried pastries shaped like small pillows. They can be served plain (like bread), dipped in honey or sprinkled with cinnamon sugar and served as a sweet.

About 20 puffs

1	tablespoon shortening
2	cups all-purpose flour
1	teaspoon baking powder
½	teaspoon salt
⅔	to ¾ cup cold water
	Vegetable oil
	Honey Butter (below) or Cinnamon Sugar (below)

Cut shortening into flour, baking powder and salt until mixture resembles fine crumbs. Gradually add enough water to make a stiff pastrylike dough, tossing with fork until all flour is moistened and dough almost cleans side of bowl. Gather dough into a ball; divide into halves and shape into 2 flattened rounds. (Cover half to prevent drying.)

Heat oil (1½ to 2 inches) to 360°. Roll 1 half of dough ⅛ to ¼ inch thick. Cut into rectangles, 3 x 2 inches, or 3-inch diamonds.

Fry 3 or 4 rectangles at a time, turning once, until puffed and golden brown, 1 to 2 minutes on each side. Drain on paper towels. Repeat with remaining dough. Dip puffs into Honey Butter or sprinkle with Cinnamon Sugar.

Honey Butter
Heat ⅓ cup honey and 2 tablespoons margarine or butter until hot.

Cinnamon Sugar
Mix 3 tablespoons sugar and ¼ teaspoon ground cinnamon.

Do Ahead Tip: Puffs can be reheated uncovered in 350° oven about 8 minutes.

Deep-Fried Wonton Cookies

(Teem Gok)

A sweet, tasty filling of dried fruit and coconut provides still another use for wonton skins (page 10). The cookies will keep well in an airtight container and will serve you well at dessert time or for a midday snack.

About 48 cookies

1½	cups chopped prunes*
1	cup chopped dried apricots
1½	cups packed brown sugar
1½	cups flaked coconut
1	cup chopped almonds
24	wonton skins
	Vegetable oil

Mix prunes, apricots, brown sugar, coconut and almonds. Place about 2 teaspoons filling on center of each wonton skin. Moisten edges with water. Fold each skin in half to form triangle; press edges firmly to seal. (Cover to prevent drying.)

Heat oil (1 to 1½ inches) to 360°. Fry 3 to 4 wontons at a time, turning occasionally, until golden brown, about 1 minute on each side. Drain on paper towels. Store in airtight container. Serve with ice cream or sherbet.

* 1½ cups chopped dried apples can be substituted for the prunes.

Greek Crescent Cookies

(Kourambiethes)

These all-purpose cookies are served by the Greeks on holidays throughout the year. Ouzo—the Greeks' beloved anise-flavored liqueur—gives the cookies their distinctive flavor. French, Spanish or Italian liqueurs that are anise- or licorice-flavored will provide the same flavor as ouzo.

About 48 cookies

1	cup margarine or butter, softened
½	cup powdered sugar
1	egg yolk
2	teaspoons ouzo or brandy
½	teaspoon almond extract
2	cups all-purpose flour
	Powdered sugar

Mix margarine, ½ cup powdered sugar, the egg yolk, ouzo and almond extract; stir in flour. Shape dough by teaspoonfuls into crescent shapes. Place about 1 inch apart on ungreased cookie sheet. Bake in 350° oven until light brown on bottom, 12 to 15 minutes. Sprinkle with powdered sugar while hot. Cool on wire racks.

Storing Cookies

Did You Know?

Proper storage of cookies depends on humidity. In dry climates, storing crisp cookies in a container with a loose cover will retain their crispness. For longer storage, cookies should be frozen. To freeze cookies, place them in an airtight container or wrap in freezer wrap. Baked cookies as well as cooky dough can be stored in the freezer for 9 to 12 months. Baked cookies will thaw out very quickly at room temperature.

Brandy Snaps

heat. Stir in 2 teaspoons brandy. Mix flour and ginger; gradually stir into syrup mixture.

Drop dough by teaspoonfuls about 5 inches apart onto lightly greased cookie sheets. Bake until cookies have spread into 3- to 4-inch rounds and are golden brown, 6 to 8 minutes.

Cool cookies 1 to 3 minutes before removing from cookie sheets. Working quickly, roll each cookie on greased handle of wooden spoon; slip from spoon and place on wire racks. If cookies become too crisp to roll, return to oven to soften about 1 minute.

Beat whipping cream and powdered sugar in chilled bowl until stiff; fold in 1 tablespoon brandy. Using decorators' tube with plain tip, pipe whipped cream into each end of cookies.

Note: Store unfilled cookies in airtight container.

Brandy Snaps

These rolled cookies are served throughout England under a variety of names: In York-shire they're called Ormskir gingerbread; in Devon, honiton or west country fairings; and in Hampshire, mothering Sunday wafers. The old-fashioned names indicate that the cookies have been around for many centuries.

About 30 cookies

½   cup margarine or butter
½   cup dark corn syrup
⅓   cup packed brown sugar
2   teaspoons brandy
¾   cup all-purpose flour
½   teaspoon ground ginger
1   cup chilled whipping cream
2   tablespoons powdered sugar
1   tablespoon brandy

Heat oven to 350°. Heat margarine, corn syrup and brown sugar to boiling in 1½-quart saucepan, stirring frequently; remove from

Mexican Cheese Cookies (Palitos de Queso)

Shredded cheese makes these crisp Mexican cookies truly unique. Try them with Caramel Custard (page 307).

24 cookies

½   cup sugar
⅓   cup margarine or butter, softened
1   cup shredded Monterey Jack cheese (4 ounces)
1   cup all-purpose flour
1   teaspoon baking powder
¼   teaspoon salt
1   egg, beaten

Heat oven to 375°. Mix sugar and margarine; stir in cheese. Stir in remaining ingredients except egg. Roll dough by teaspoonfuls into sticks, about 3½ x ½ inch. Place on lightly greased cookie sheet. Press sticks lightly to flatten. Brush with egg. Bake until light brown around edges, 8 to 10 minutes. Immediately remove from cookie sheet. Cool on wire racks.

Vanilla Soufflé

(Soufflé à la Vanille)

Many expert chefs shy away from dessert soufflés because of the time required for preparation. Here is a recipe even novice chefs will find a pleasure to prepare. Once assembled, the soufflé requires a full hour of baking time. This should give you ample time to relax with your guests and enjoy your main dish while your extra-special dessert puffs and turns golden in the oven!

6 servings

¼   cup sugar
3   tablespoons all-purpose flour
⅛   teaspoon salt
¾   cup milk
5   eggs, separated
3   tablespoons margarine or butter, softened
1   tablespoon vanilla
¼   teaspoon cream of tartar
¼   cup sugar
    Chantilly Cream (right)

Mix ¼ cup sugar, the flour and salt in 1-quart saucepan. Stir in milk gradually. Heat to boiling, stirring constantly. Remove from heat. Beat egg yolks with fork; beat in ⅓ cup of the milk mixture. Stir in remaining milk mixture gradually. Stir in margarine and vanilla. Cool slightly.

Place oven rack in lowest position. Heat oven to 375°. Butter and sugar 2-quart soufflé dish. Make 3-inch band of triple thickness aluminum foil 2 inches larger than circumference of dish. Butter and sugar one side of band. Extend dish by securing band buttered side in around outside edge.

Beat egg whites and cream of tartar in large mixer bowl until foamy. Beat in ¼ cup sugar, 1 tablespoon at a time; continue beating until stiff and glossy. Do not underbeat. Stir about ¼ of the egg whites into egg yolk mixture. Fold in remaining egg whites. Carefully pour into dish. Bake until puffed and golden brown, about 1 hour. Serve immediately with Chantilly Cream.

Chantilly Cream
Beat ¾ cup whipping cream, 2 tablespoons sugar and ½ teaspoon vanilla in chilled bowl until stiff. Fold in 1 tablespoon orange- or almond-flavored liqueur, rum or brandy.

Liqueur Soufflé: Decrease vanilla to 1 teaspoon. Stir in 1 teaspoon grated orange peel and ¼ cup orange- or almond-flavored liqueur.

Russian Easter Cheese Dessert

(Pashka)

Orthodox Russians greet Easter with this molded cheese dessert, traditionally decorated with the letters XV (meaning Christ is risen). Kulich (page 290), the Russian Easter bread, is the time-honored accompaniment to pashka.

12 to 14 servings

3   egg yolks, slightly beaten
1   cup whipping cream
¾   cup sugar
⅛   teaspoon salt
1   teaspoon vanilla
6   cups small-curd creamed cottage cheese
¼   cup margarine or butter, softened
½   cup chopped mixed candied fruit
¼   cup finely chopped blanched almonds

Mix egg yolks and whipping cream in heavy 2-quart saucepan. Stir in sugar and salt. Cook over low heat, stirring constantly, until mixture just coats a metal spoon, 12 to 15 minutes. Remove from heat; stir in vanilla. Place saucepan in cold water until custard is cool. (If custard curdles, beat with hand beater until smooth.)

Place 3 cups of the cottage cheese and 2 tablespoons of the margarine in blender container. Cover and blend on medium speed, stopping blender occasionally to scrape sides, until smooth. Repeat with remaining cottage cheese and margarine. Stir custard into cheese mixture until smooth. Stir in candied fruit and almonds.

Line a 2-quart non-clay flower pot (with opening in bottom) with double layer dampened cheesecloth. Pour cheese mixture into pot; fold ends of cheesecloth over top. Place in shallow pan; place weights on top. Refrigerate 12 to 24 hours, pouring off any liquid that accumulates in pan.

To serve, unmold onto serving plate; remove cheesecloth. Garnish as desired with additional candied fruit and blanched almonds. Refrigerate any remaining dessert.

French Chocolate Custard (Pots de Crème au Chocolat)

This "cooked mousse"—France's inspired adaptation of a chocolate pudding—is the perfect dessert for a busy party-giver. Not only can the desserts be prepared a day before the party; the individual cups make service easy.

6 or 7 servings

1½	cups half-and-half
1	package (6 ounces) semisweet chocolate chips
3	eggs
⅓	cup sugar
⅛	teaspoon salt
½	cup whipping cream
1	tablespoon sugar
1	to 2 tablespoons brandy, orange-flavored liqueur or creme de menthe

Heat half-and-half and chocolate chips, stirring constantly, until chocolate is melted and mixture is smooth. Cool slightly. Beat eggs, ⅓ cup sugar and the salt; gradually stir into chocolate mixture. Pour into 6 ungreased 6-ounce custard cups or 6 or 7 ovenproof *pot de crème* cups.

Place cups in baking pan on oven rack. Pour boiling water into pan within ½ inch of tops of cups. Bake in 350° oven 20 to 25 minutes. Remove cups from water; cool slightly. Cover and refrigerate at least 4 hours but no longer than 24 hours.

Beat whipping cream and 1 tablespoon sugar in chilled bowl until stiff; fold in brandy. Top each serving with whipped cream.

Gingered Pear Sorbet

A French sorbet is a sherbet made only with fruit juice, sugar and sometimes egg white—cream is never used. The French serve their sorbets as elegant appetizers, as between-course palate fresheners and as desserts (but sorbet never appears on the menu more than once during a meal).

When serving this sorbet at an important party, dress it up for the occasion by garnishing individual servings with mint leaves, sliced crystallized ginger, fresh berries.

6 servings

1	can (29 ounces) pear halves, drained (reserve syrup)
¼	cup sugar
2	tablespoons lemon juice
1	to 1½ teaspoons finely chopped crystallized ginger or ⅛ teaspoon ground ginger

Heat 1 cup of the reserved syrup and the sugar to boiling, stirring constantly; remove from heat. Cool. Place pears, half at a time, in blender container; cover and purée until uniform consistency. Mix syrup, purée, lemon juice and ginger; pour into ice cube tray. Freeze until partially frozen, 1 to 1½ hours.

Pour into blender; blend on medium speed until smooth and fluffy. Return to ice cube tray. Freeze until firm, about 3 hours. Let stand at room temperature about 10 minutes before serving.

Biscuit Tortoni

To serve these delightful frozen desserts Italian style, look for the traditional decorative paper cups—you'll find them at Italian groceries and gourmet shops. If you can't locate them, use paper cupcake liners set in muffin pans.

12 servings

1½	cups chilled whipping cream
⅓	cup sugar
1	cup almond macaroon or vanilla wafer crumbs (about 24 cookies)
½	cup chopped toasted almonds
¼	cup maraschino cherries, drained and chopped
2	tablespoons rum or dry sherry
1	teaspoon vanilla

Beat whipping cream and sugar in chilled bowl until stiff. Reserve ¼ cup macaroon crumbs; fold remaining ingredients into whipped cream. Divide among 12 small dessert dishes or paper-lined medium muffin cups, 2½ x 1¼ inches. Sprinkle with reserved crumbs. Freeze until firm, about 4 hours.

Lemon Ice
(Granita di Limone)

This light, easy Italian favorite can be adapted to many uses. It's a fine treat for children and grownups on a hot summer afternoon (serve the ice in paper cups or cones when eating out-of-doors) or as a light dessert after a substantial family or party meal.

8 to 10 servings

2	cups water
1	cup sugar
1	tablespoon finely shredded lemon peel
1	cup lemon juice

Heat water and sugar to boiling; reduce heat. Simmer uncovered 5 minutes. Remove from heat; stir in lemon peel and juice. Cool to room temperature. Pour into loaf pan, 9 x 5 x 3 inches. Freeze 3 to 4 hours, stirring every 30 minutes.

Serve in chilled dessert dishes. (If ice is not to be served immediately, cut into ½-inch chunks; place in bowl. Cover and freeze until serving time.)

Coffee Ice
(Granita di Caffé)

This smart, easy Italian treat can be adapted to your personal taste in coffee. If you prefer, substitute instant decaffeinated coffee for the espresso in the recipe, or try one of your favorite instant-coffee party blends.

6 servings

1	cup water
¾	cup sugar
3	tablespoons instant espresso coffee powder
2	cups water
1	cup chilled whipping cream
2	tablespoons sugar
½	teaspoon ground cinnamon

Heat 1 cup water and ¾ cup sugar to boiling in 2-quart saucepan; reduce heat. Simmer uncovered 5 minutes; remove from heat. Sprinkle in coffee powder gradually, stirring until dissolved. Stir in 2 cups water. Pour into ice cube tray. Freeze until mushy in center, 1½ to 2 hours.

Stir mixture; freeze 1 hour, stirring after 30 minutes. Stir again before serving. (Mixture should be broken into tiny ice crystals but should not be solid.)

Beat whipping cream, 2 tablespoons sugar and the cinnamon in chilled bowl until soft peaks form. Alternate layers of whipped cream and Coffee Ice in chilled sherbet dishes or stemmed dessert dishes, beginning and ending with whipped cream.

Swiss Meringues

Swiss Meringues
(Meringues Schalen)

Keep this easy recipe in mind the next time you find yourself with several extra egg whites.

6 or 7 servings

3	egg whites
¼	teaspoon cream of tartar
¾	cup granulated sugar
¾	cup chilled whipping cream
2	tablespoons powdered sugar
1½	cups sliced fresh fruit

Cover cookie sheet with heavy brown paper. Beat egg whites and cream of tartar in small mixer bowl until foamy. Beat in granulated sugar, 1 tablespoon at a time; continue beating until stiff and glossy. Do not underbeat.

Drop meringue by ¼ cupfuls onto brown paper. Shape into 3-inch ovals. (See photograph.) Bake in 225° oven 1 hour. Turn off oven; leave meringues in oven with door closed 1 hour.

Press a hollow into bottom of each meringue with thumb. Finish cooling at room temperature. Beat whipping cream and powdered sugar in chilled bowl until stiff. Reserve ¼ cup fruit for garnish; fold remaining fruit into whipped cream. Fill meringues; place 2 together. Serve on sides (yo-yo fashion). Garnish with additional whipped cream if desired and the reserved fruit.

Drop meringue by ¼ cupfuls onto brown paper; shape into 3-inch ovals.

Frosted Meringue with Kiwis

Frosted Meringue with Kiwis

(Pavlova)

This seductive meringue from Australia honors the celebrated ballerina Anna Pavlova, who made extensive world tours in the early decades of this century. Any number of fruits can be used in preparing Pavlova. *Kiwi fruit (see page 341) is a typical New Zealand touch.*

8 servings

3	egg whites
¼	teaspoon cream of tartar
½	teaspoon vanilla

¾	cup sugar
1	cup chilled whipping cream
2	tablespoons sugar
3	kiwis,* peeled and sliced

Heat oven to 225°. Line bottom of round layer pan, 8 or 9 x 1½ inches, with brown paper. Beat egg whites and cream of tartar until foamy; add vanilla. Beat in ¾ cup sugar, 1 tablespoon at a time; continue beating until stiff and glossy. Spread in pan. Bake 1½ hours. Turn off oven; leave meringue in oven with door closed 1 hour. Finish cooling meringue at room temperature.

Loosen edge of layer with knife; hit pan sharply on table to remove meringue. Invert onto plate. (Meringue will be crumbly on bottom and around edge.) Remove paper. Beat whipping cream and 2 tablespoons sugar in chilled bowl until stiff. Frost side and top of meringue, building up edge slightly. Arrange kiwi slices on top. Cut into wedges to serve.

* 1½ to 2 cups fresh strawberries, cut into halves, raspberries, blueberries or a combination of these can be substituted for the kiwis.

Kiwi Fruit

Did You Know?

The kiwi fruit or berry has a fuzzy soft brown skin and firm green flesh dotted with tiny black seeds. The oversized-egg–shaped berries have a mild, melony flavor with a suggestion of tartness and are ready to eat when the skin feels soft to the touch.

Kiwi berries can be peeled and sliced for use in salads, fruit compotes, desserts and meat accompaniments; or they can be sliced in half, scooped out and eaten with a spoon.

Most of the kiwi fruit available in the United States comes from New Zealand, although it is native to China and is sometimes referred to as the "Chinese gooseberry." New Zealanders began to cultivate the curious-looking fruit several generations ago, naming it after New Zealand's national bird—the kiwi, famed for its oversized eggs.

Mocha Praline Torte

Imaginative Swiss and French chefs have invented many recipes for tempting meringue layer desserts filled with memorable creams flavored with nuts and fruit. This Swiss triumph is one of the easiest and best.

10 to 12 servings

4	egg whites
¼	teaspoon cream of tartar
1	cup sugar
	Almond Praline (below)
1½	cups chilled whipping cream
1	tablespoon sugar
1	teaspoon instant coffee
¼	teaspoon almond extract

Cover 3 cookie sheets with heavy brown paper. Heat oven to 225°. Beat egg whites and cream of tartar in large mixer bowl until foamy. Beat in 1 cup sugar, 1 tablespoon at a time; continue beating until stiff and glossy. Do not underbeat. Shape meringue into three 8-inch circles on brown paper. Bake 1 hour. Turn off oven; leave meringues in oven with door closed 1 hour. Remove from paper with spatula; cool.

Prepare Almond Praline. Beat whipping cream, 1 tablespoon sugar, the instant coffee and almond extract in chilled bowl until stiff. Reserve 1 to 2 tablespoons Almond Praline for garnish; fold remaining praline into whipped cream. Stack meringues, spreading whipped-cream mixture between layers and over top. Sprinkle with reserved praline. Refrigerate at least 2 hours.

Almond Praline
Cook and stir ½ cup sliced almonds and ¼ cup sugar over low heat until sugar is melted and golden brown. Pour onto greased cookie sheet; cool. Crush coarsely in blender or place in plastic bag and crush with wooden mallet.

Strawberry Praline Torte: Omit instant coffee; fold 1½ cups sliced strawberries into whipped cream. Garnish with additional strawberries.

The Metric System

We are gradually converting to the metric system in the United States, but it may take another ten years or longer before metric becomes an actuality. Since all metric measures are divisible by ten, the system won't be difficult to learn. Cooking under the metric system will be easy. Measuring will continue to be by volume, not by weight, and there will be metric measuring utensils available to match the metric recipes. You won't have to worry about complicated conversion tables. Test kitchens will have to retest and convert recipes, and you will probably have one set of measures for conventional recipes and another set for metric recipes.

Metric Weight
(Solids)

The gram (g) is the basic unit for measuring solids by weight. Over 500, the term for weight changes to *kilogram* (kg) and the decimal system is used. Meat, butter, cheese and packaged goods are sold by gram and kilogram.

Metric Quantity	Equivalent
30 g	1 ounce plus a large pinch
125 g	¼ pound plus about ¼ ounce
250 g	½ pound plus less than an ounce
500 g	1 pound plus 1⅔ ounces
0.750 kg	1½ pounds plus about 2½ ounces
1 kg (1000 g)	2 pounds plus about 3½ ounces

Metric Dimensions
(Length, Width, Depth)

The meter (m) is the basic unit for measuring length, width and depth. However, the centimeter (cm), .01 meter, is used most often. In addition, the millimeter (mm), .001 meter, will be used.

Metric Measure	Equivalent
6.0 mm	about ¼ inch
2.5 cm	slightly less than 1 inch
15.0 cm	6 inches
30.0 cm	slightly less than 1 foot
1.0 m	slightly longer than 1 yard

Metric Volume
(Dry and Liquid Ingredients)

The liter (L) is the basic unit for measuring dry and liquid ingredients. It is a little larger than a quart. Recipes will usually use the milliliter (mL), which is .001 liter.

Metric Quantity	Equivalent
1 mL*	slightly less than ¼ teaspoon
2 mL*	slightly less than ½ teaspoon
5 mL*	1 teaspoon
15 mL*	1 tablespoon
25 mL*	1 tablespoon plus 2 teaspoons
50 mL*	¼ cup minus 2 teaspoons
125 mL*	½ cup plus 1½ teaspoons
250 mL*	1 cup plus 1 tablespoon
500 mL	1 pint plus 2 tablespoons
1 L (1000 mL)	1 quart plus ¼ cup

* These are the measures expected to be available.

Metric Temperatures

Degrees Celsius (°C) is the metric unit of measure for temperature.

Examples of Metric Cooking Temperatures

120°C	very slow oven
142°C	slow oven
180°C	moderate oven
210°C	hot oven
230°C	very hot oven

Water boils at 100°C (212°F) and freezes at 0°C (32°F) at sea level. Room temperature is about 20°C; body temperature, 37°C.

Spices and Dried Herbs for International Cooking

Name	Form	Flavor	Use
Allspice	*Whole* *Ground*	*Blend of cinnamon, cloves and nutmeg*	*Fruits, cakes, pies, cookies, meats, stews, pickling*
Anise	*Whole seed* *Ground*	*Licorice flavor*	*Scandinavian and Italian coffee cakes and rolls, cookies, candy, salads*
Basil (sweet basil)	*Dry leaf* *Ground*	*Sweet with clovelike spicy tang*	*Soups, stews, tomato sauces, vegetables, meats, egg dishes*
Bay leaves (laurel)	*Whole*	*Aromatic*	*Pickling, meats, lamb, fish, stews, soups, sauces, vegetables*
Cayenne pepper	*Ground*	*Hot, peppery (use sparingly)*	*Meats, fish, gravies, eggs, sauces, vegetables*
Caraway seed	*Whole*	*Pungent and intense (use sparingly)*	*Rye bread, sauerkraut, cabbage, soups, meats, stews, pickling*
Cardamon (see page 287)			
Celery seed	*Whole* *Ground*	*Similar to fresh celery*	*Sauces, salads, dressings, pickling, vegetables, meats, tomato sauces*
Chili powder (blend of spices)	*Ground*	*Hot, spicy*	*Mexican cooking, eggs, cottage cheese, cocktail sauce, stews, vegetables*
Cinnamon	*Stick* *Ground*	*Pungent and sweet*	*Cookies, cakes, puddings, pies, fruit desserts, pickling*
Cloves	*Whole* *Ground*	*Strong, pungent and sweet*	*Ham, pork and meats, pickling, fruits, stews, gravies, desserts*
Cumin seed	*Whole* *Ground*	*Strong, dry taste, reminiscent of caraway*	*Mexican foods, meats, poultry, pickling, cheese, sausages, chutney*
Curry powder (see page 190)			
Dill	*Whole* *Ground*	*Tang resembling caraway*	*Pickling, soups, salads, sauces, meats, fish*
Fennel seed	*Whole* *Ground*	*Aromatic, sweet, resembling licorice*	*Sweet pickles, sausages, soups, sauces, fish, breads*
Ginger	*Whole* *Ground*	*Pungent and spicy, aromatic*	*Gingerbread, cookies, cakes, stews, fruits, oriental dishes, vegetables*
Mace	*Ground*	*Intense, similar to nutmeg*	*Soups, chocolate desserts, cookies, cakes, fruit, salads*

Name	Form	Flavor	Use
Marjoram	Dry leaf	Aromatic with slightly bitter undertone	Vegetables, lamb, stews, soups, cottage cheese, stuffings
Mint	Dry leaf	Sweet with cool aftertaste	Lamb, fish sauces, soups, vegetables, desserts, beverages
Mustard seed	Whole Ground	Hot, pungent and dry aftertaste	Pickling, relishes, salads, casseroles, vegetables, meats
Nutmeg	Ground	Sweet with warm and spicy undertone	Cakes, cookies, puddings, sauces, vegetables, beverages, meats, stews
Oregano	Dry leaf Ground	Strong, aromatic with pleasantly bitter undertones	Italian dishes, meat, fish, sauces, soups, eggs, vegetables
Paprika	Ground	Dry taste with slightly bitter undertones	Garnish, soups, salads, eggs, fish, meats, casseroles, vegetables
Parsley	Dry flakes	Mild and pleasant	Garnish, soups, fish, vegetables, salads, gravies, casseroles
Pepper	Whole (peppercorn) Ground	Penetrating odor; hot, biting and very pungent	Soups, meats, salads, sauces, vegetables, casseroles, eggs
Poppy seed	Whole	Pleasant, crunchy nutlike flavor	Sauces, fillings for pastries, breads, rolls, cakes, cookies
Rosemary	Dry leaf	Sweet aroma and fresh, sweet flavor	Lamb, soups, stews, fish, salads, vegetables, casseroles

Saffron (see page 233)

Name	Form	Flavor	Use
Sage	Dry leaf Ground	Aromatic, slightly bitter (use sparingly)	Pork, meats, sausage, fish, stuffings, salads, dressings, chowders
Savory	Dry leaf Ground	Aromatic and slightly piquant	Meats, chicken, soups, salads, sauces, stuffings, vegetables
Sesame seed	Whole	Rich nutlike flavor	Garnish, topping for breads and rolls, candies, cookies, salads, pastries
Tarragon	Dry leaf	Reminiscent of anise, piquant flavor	Pickling, sauces, salads, poultry, meats, eggs, tomatoes
Thyme	Dry leaf Ground	Aromatic, pungent flavor	Chowders, stews, meats, fish, poultry, tomatoes, stuffings

Turmeric (see page 233)

Pronunciation Guide to Foreign Titles

A

Adobo aw-*doh*-boh
Akwadu ah-*kwa*-doo
Albondiguitas ahl-bohn-dee-*ghee*-tahs
Antipasto di Funghi Crudi ahn-tee-*pahs*-toh dee *foon*-ghee *crew*-dee
Apfelpfannkuchen *ahp*-f'l-p'fahn-*koo*-kh'n
Apfelstrudel *ahp*-f'l-*shtroo*-d'l
Arroz con Carne de Cerdo ar-*rohs* kohn *kar*-neh deh *sehr*-doh
Asopao de Pollo ah-sah-*pow* deh *poh*-l'yoh
Asperges à la Gruyère ahs-*pehr'zh* ah lah gree-*yair*
Ata *ah*-tah

B

Baba Ghannooj bah-bah gahn-*oush*
Bacalhau com Tomatada bah-kahl-*yow* kohm toh-mah-*tah*-dah
Bagna Cauda *bah*-n'yah kah-*oo*-dah
Baklava bahk-lah-*vah*
Bangbangji bong-bong-jee
Barmbrack *barm*-brack
Beirocks *beer*-ochs
Betyár Fogas *bet*-yahr *foh*-gosh
Blomkaalssuppe blohm-kohls-*soh*-peh
Bobotie boh-*boh*-tee
Boeuf à la Mode en Gelée buhf ah lah mohd awn zheh-*leh*
Boeuf Bourguignon buhf bohr-ghee-*n'yahng*
Bogrács Gulyás *boh*-grotch *goo*-l'yosh
Bolitas con Pollo boh-*lee*-tahs kohn *poh*-l'yoh
Bonjan Borani bon-jon bohr-*ah*-nee
Borscht borsht
Bourride boor-*reed*
Bredie *bray*-dee
Brioche bree-*ohsh*
Bruna Bönor brew-nah *buh*-nohr
Bulgur Pilav buhl-*gahr* pee-*lahv*
Buljol buhl-johl
Bul-Ko-Kee buhl-*koh*-kee
Burritos boo-reet-tohs

C

Cacik *chudge*-chik
Camarones a la Criolla kah-mah-*roh*-nehs ah lah kree-*oh*-lah
Caneton à l'Orange kah-neh-*tawng* ah loh-*rawnzh*
Cannelloni kahn-nel-*loh*-nee
Capirotada kah-pee-roh-*tah*-dah
Caponata kah-poh-*nah*-tah
Carbonnades à la Flamande kahr-bohn-*nahd* ah lah flah-*mohnd*
Carciofi Ripieni con Prosciutto kar-*choh*-fee ree-*p'yeh*-nee kohn proh-*shoot*-toh
Carne Rellena *kahr*-neh reh-*l'yeh*-nah
Carottes Glacées kah-*roht* glah-*seh*
Cassata alla Siciliana kahs-*sah*-tah ahl-lah see-chee-*l'yah*-nah
Cassoulet kah-soo-*lay*
Challah kah-*lah*
Ch'ao Lung Hsia chow luhng shee-ah
Charlotte aux Pommes sharh-*luht* oh pohm
Cha Yun T'un jah yuhn tuhn
Chiles con Queso *chee*-lehs kohn *keh*-soh
Chi Tan Chuan jee don joo-ahn
Choucroute Garnie à l'Alsacienne shoo-*kroot* gar-*nee* ah lahl-zahs-*s'yehn*
Churros *choo*-rohs
Clafouti klah-foo-*tee*
Cock-a-Leekie cock-uh-*lee*-kee
Colcannon kohl-*can*-non
Coq au Vin Rouge kohk oh vahng roozh
Coquilles Saint-Jacques à la Parisienne koh-*kee*-yuh sahng-*zhahk* ah lah pah-ree-*zh'yen*
Coquilles Saint-Jacques Provençale koh-*kee*-yuh sahng-*zhahk* praw-vahng-*sahl*
Côtelettes de Saumon Glacées koh-t'*let* duh soh-*mohng* glah-*seh*
Coulibiac *coo*-l'yee-bee-ak
Couscous *koos*-koos
Crème Anglaise aux Fruits krem ahn-*glaze* oh frwee
Crème Fraîche aux Fruits krem fresh oh frwee

Crêpes Fruits de Mer krehp frwee duh mehr
Croissants krwah-*sawng*
Crostata di Ricotta kroh-*stah*-tah dee ree-*koht*-tah
Csirke Paprikás *cheer*-kah *pas*-pree-kosh

D

Dal dul
Daube de Boeuf à la Provençale dohb duh buhf ah lah praw-vahng-*sal*
Diples *thee*-plus
Dolmades dohl-*mah*-dehs

E

Eierkuchen *eye*-er-koo-kh'n
Empanaditas ehm-pah-nah-*dee*-tahs
Enchiladas ehn-chih-*lah*-dahs
Ensalada de Calabacitas y Aguacates ehn-sah-*lah*-dah deh kah-lah-bah-*see*-tahs ee ah-gwa-*kah*-tehs
Ensalada de Guacamole ehn-sal-*lah*-dah deh gwah-kuh-*moh*-lay
Ensalada de Noche Buena ehn-sah-*lah*-dah deh *noh*-cheh *bweh*-nah
Erwtensoep *ehrt*-tuhn-soop
Escabeche de Pescado Frito ehs-kah-*beh*-cheh deh pehs-*kah*-doh *free*-toh

F

Falafel fah-*lah*-fel
Fegato alla Veneziana feh-*gah*-toh ahl-lah veh-neet-*s'yah*-nah
Feijoada fay-*zhwah*-duh
Fettuccine alla Panna fet-too-*chee*-neh ahl-lah *pah*-nah
Filets de Poisson Florentine fee-*leh* duh pwah-*sohng* flaw-rawn-*teen*
Filets de Truite Amandine fee-*leh* duh trweet ah-mawn-*deen*
Finnan Haddie *fin*-nuhn *had*-dee
Flan flahn
Flatbröd *flaht*-bruh
Fondue Neufchâteloise *fawn*-doo neu-shah-teh-*l'wahz*
Fricassée de Poulet free-kah-*say* duh poo-*lay*
Frijoles para Sopear free-*hoh*-lehs *pah*-rah soh-peh-*arh*

Frittata di Zucchine freet-*tah*-tah dee dzook-*kee*-nee
Funghi alla Parmigiana *foon*-ghee ahl-lah par-mee-*jah*-nah
Fyldt Svinemørbrad fewlt *svee*-neh-mewl-brahl

G

Gado-Gado *gah*-doh *gah*-doh
Gai Ding guyding
Gajar Halva *gah*-jer *hul*-vuh
Gänsebraten mit Apfelfüllung *genz*-uh-brah-t'n mitt *ahp*-f'l-fuh-loonk
Gâteau Saint-Honoré gah-*toh* sant ohn-aw-*ray*
Gazpacho gah-*spah*-choh
Gebratene Hähnchen guh-*brah*-tuh-neh *han*-shen
Gefüllter Hecht guh-*fewl*-ter hehkt
Ghiveci gee-*vetch*-ee
Gnocchi alla Romana *n'yohk*-kee ahl-lah roh-*mah*-nah
Gnocchi di Patate *n'yohk*-kee dee pah-*tah*-teh
Gougère goo-*gehr*
Granita di Caffé grah-*nee*-tah dee kahf-*feh*
Granita di Limone grah-*nee*-tah dee lee-*moh*-nay
Gratin Dauphinois grah-*tahn* doh-fahn-*nwahz*
Grönsaksgratin gruhn-sahks-grah-*teng*
Guacamole gwah-kuh-*moh*-lay
Gugelhupf *goo*-g'l-hoop'f
Gul Ärtsoppa gewl *ehrt*-soh-pah
Gyuniku no Teriyake g'yoo-nee-koo noh teh-ree-ah-kee

H

Himmel und Erde himm'l oont *ehr*-deh
Houskove Knedliky *hoos*-koof ned-*leek*-ee
Hsia Ch'iu sh'yah chee-oo
Hsing Jen Chi Ting h'sing ren jee ding
Hsing-jen-tou-fu shee-ong-ren-dough-foo
Huachinango Relleno wah-chee-*nahn*-goh rel-l'*yeh*-noh
Huachinango Veracruzano wah-chee-*nahn*-goh vehr-ah-kroo-*sah*-noh
Huevos Rancheros *weh*-vohs rahn-*cheh*-rohs

Hummus *hum*-muss
Hung Shao Niu Jo hwung shah-oo nee-oh rwo
Hun T'un T'ang hwun tuhn tong
Hutspot met Klapstuk *huhts*-pot met *klahp*-stuhk

I

Inkokta Rödbetor *in*-cooked-ah *ruhd*-beh-tohr
Insalata di Fagioli e Tonno een-sah-*lah*-tah dee fah-*joh*-lee *toh*-noh
Insalata Mista een-sah-*lah*-tah *mees*-tah

J

Jollof Rice Ghana jaw-*lawf* rice *gha*-nah
Julekage yoo-leh-*kay*-yeh

K

Kabuli Pelau *kah*-boo-lee puh-*low*
Kaki no Nikomi kah-kee noh nee-koh-mee
Kalakasvisvuoka *kuh*-luh-*kuhs*-vees-voh-oo-kah
Kåldolmar *kohl*-doll-mahr
Kål· och Äppelsallad kohl-oh *eppel*-sah-lahd
Karithopita kar-ee-*dop*-ee-tah
Kartoffelpuffer kahr-*tohf*-f'l-*poof*-f'r
Ka Salun kah sah-loon
Kasha kah-shuh
Kedgeree *ked*-guh-rree
Keftedakia keff-teh-*thigh*-kee-ah
Kesäkeitto keh-sah-*kay*-toh
Khoshaf *hoh*-shef
Kibby bil Sanieh *kib*-beh bill sah-*nay*-uh
Kiev kee-ehv
Kimchee *kim*-chee
Kissel *kiss*-uhl
Knapwurst knahp-voorst
Koláče koh-*lotch*-eh
Kotopoulo Riganato tis Skaras koh-*toh*-poo-loh ree-gah-*nah*-toh tiss *skah*-rahs
Köttbullar *chutt*-boo-lahr
Kourambiethes kur-em-bee-*eth*-ehs
Kroppkakor *kropp*-kah-koor
Kueh Prol Nanas *koo*-en prol *na*-nes
Kulich *koo*-lickh
Kyinkyinga chih-*ching*-gah

L

Lanttulaatikko *lahn*-too-*lah*-tee-koh
Lasagne Verdi al Forno lah-*sah*-n'yeh *vehr*-dee ahl *for*-noh
Lefse *leff*-seh
Lekach *lek*-ah(k)
Lihakaalilaatikko lee-huh-*kall*-ee-*lah*-tee-koh
Limpa *lim*-pah
Linguini con Vongole Bianco ling-*gwee*-nee kohn vahn-*gho*-lee b'*yahn*-koh
Lukshen Kugel *luck*-shen *koo*-guhl

M

Ma'mounia mah-moo-*nay*-ah
Mancha Manteles *mahn*-chah mahn-*teh*-lehs
Melanzane con Due Formaggi meh-lahn-*tsah*-neh kohn *doo*-ay for-*mahj*-jee
Meringues Schalen *meh*-ring *shah*-lehn
Minestrone mee-nes-*troh*-neh
'Mjeddrah *m'jed*-duh-ruh
Moui Nagden moo-*ee* nahg-*den*
Mou Shu mow-shoo
Moussaka moo-sah-*kah*
Muckalica muh-*koll*-ee-kah
Mulligatawny mul-i-guh-*taw*-nee

N

Naan non
Nasi Goreng nah-*see* gohr-ring
Natte naht
Nkrakra n'krah-krah

O

Oeufs à la Florentine uhz ah lah flaw-rawn-*teen*
Olie Bollen *oh*-lee *boh*-len
Osso Buco *ohs*-soh *boo*-koh
Ostiones en Cazuela ohs-tee-*ohn*-ehs ehn kah-*sweh*-lah
Ovnsstekt Torsk med Sitron ovn-*stehkt* toschk meh see-*trohn*

P

Paella pah-*eh*-l'yah
Palitos de Queso pah-*lee*-tohs deh *keh*-soh
Panettone pah-neh-*toh*-nee

Paõ de Banano   pow day bah-*nah*-noh
Paõ Dôce   pow *doh*-say
Pashka   *pahsh*-kuh
Pasta al Tre Formaggi   *pahs*-tah ahl treh for-*mahj*-jee
Pasta con Pesto   *pahs*-tah kohn *pehs*-toh
Pasta e Fagioli   *pahs*-tah fah-*joh*l
Pastel de Choclo   pahs-*tehl* deh *chohk*-loh
Pastel de Pollo   pahs-*tehl* deh *poh*-l'yoh
Pasticcio   pah-*sti*-zoh
Pavlova   pahv-*loh*-vah
Pavo en Mole Poblano   *pah*-voh ehn *moh*-leh poh-*blah*-noh
Peperonata   peh-pehr-oh-*nah*-tah
Picadillo   pee-kah-*dee*-l'yoh
Piccata di Vitello al Limone   peek-*kah*-tah dee vee-*tel*-loh ahl lee-*moh*-neh
Pi Chi T'ang   bee jee tong
Pilav   Pee-lahv
Pipérade Basquaise   *peep*-eh-rahd bahs-*kehz*
Pipián Rojo de Ajonjoli   pee-*p'yahn* roh-hoh deh ah-hohn-*hoh*-lee
Pirozhki   pee-*roh*-zhkee
Poisson Bonne Femme   pwah-*sohng* bun fahm
Poisson Véronique   pwah-*sohng* veh-rawn-*eek*
Polenta   poh-*len*-tah
Pollo a la Chilindrón   *poh*-l'yoh ah lah chee-leen-*drohn*
Pollo a la Jardinera   *poh*-l'yoh ah lah hahr-dee-*neh*-rah
Pollo alla Cacciatora   *pohl*-loh ahl-lah kah-chah-*toh*-rah
Pollo con Piña a la Antigua   *poh*-l'yoh kohn *pee*-n'yah ah lah ahn-*tee*-gwah
Pollo en Jugo de Limones   *poh*-l'yoh ehn *hoo*-goh deh lee-*moh*-nehs
Pollo in Brodo con Tortellini   *pohl*-loh een *broh*-doh kohn tor-tehl-*lee*-nee
Pommes de Terre Anna   pohm duh tair *ah*-nah
Potage Crème de Champignons   poh-*tahzh* krem duh shawn-pee-*n'yohng*
Potage Crème de Laitue   poh-*tahzh* krem duh leh-*tew*
Pot-au-Feu   poh-toh-*fuh*

Potica   *poh*-tee-kah
Pots de Crème au Chocolat   poht duh krem oh shaw-koh-*lah*
Poulet a l'Estragon   poo-*lay* ah *leh*-strah-gawng
Poulet Cordon Bleu   poo-*lay* *kor*-don bloo
Poulet en Cocotte à la Paysanne   poo-*lay* awng koh-*koht* ah lah pay-*zahn*
Prosciutto   pro-*shoot*-toh
Psari Plaki   p'*sah*-dee plah-*kee*
Pulao   *poo*-low
Puris   poo-rrees

Q

Quesadillas   keh-sah-*dee*-l'yahs
Quiche à la Suisse   Keesh ah lah swees

R

Rabarbragrøt   rrah-barr-brra-groot
Raclette   rah-*klett*
Raita   *right*-tuh
Rakott Krumpli   *rah*-koht *kroom*-plee
Ratatouille   *rah*-tah-twee
Ravioli   rah-*v'yoh*-lee
Rinderrouladen   *rin*-der-rroo-*lah*-den
Risi e Bisi   *ree*-see eh *bee*-see
Riso e Formaggio   *ree*-soh eh fohr-*mah*-joh
Risotta alla Milanese   ree-*soht*-toh ahl-lah mee-lah-*nay*-seh
Risotto con Funghi   ree-*soht*-toh kohn *foon*-ghee
Rødgrød   rohl-grohl
Roesti   *ruh*-stee
Rollatini di Pollo   rohl-lah-*tee*-nee dee *pohl*-loh
Ropa Vieja   *roh*-pah *v'yeh*-hah
Rostélyos Ezterhézy   rosh-*teh*-yosh ester-*haze*-zee
Rumaki   roo-mah-kee
Ruskistetut Lantut   *roos*-kis-teh-toot *lahn*-toot

S

Saganaki   sah-gah-*nuh*-kce
Salade de Laitue   sah-*lahd* duh leh-*tew*
Salade Niçoise   sah-*lahd* nee-*swahz*
Salata Athenas   sah-*lah*-tah ah-*th'ee*-nahs
Salata Meze   sah-*lah*-tah *meh*-zah

Saltimbocca alla Romana sahl-teem-*bohk*-kah ahl-lah roh-*mah*-nah

Salzburger Nockerln *zalts*-boor-ger *nawk*-airl'n

Samak Tahini *sah*-mack tah-*hee*-nee

Sambal Goreng Udang sahm-*bahl* gohr-*ring* oo-*dung*

Same ki Bhaji *sah*-mee kay *bah*-jee

Samosas suh-*moh*-suss

Saté Ajam sah-*teh* eye-*yem*

Saucochi di Gallinja *sow-oh*-coh-chi dee gay-*een*-ha

Sauerbraten mit Kartoffelklössen *zow*-er-brah-t'n mitt kahr-*tohf*-f'l-kluhs-sen

Sauerkrautsalat *zow*-er-krowt-sah-*laht*

S'chee shee

Schinkenfleckerln *shink*-k'n-fleck-airl'n

Schwarzwälder Kirschtorte *shvarts*-veld-er *keersh*-tor-teh

Shao Pi K'u sha'ow bee koo

Shish Kabob *shish*-kuh-bahb

Sienisalaatti *see*-ehn-ee-sal-*ah*-tee

Sillsallad *sill*-sah-lahd

Smørdampete Nypoteter smuhr-*damp*-eh-teh new-poh-*teh*-tehr

Sopa de Pescados *soh*-pah deh pehs-*kah*-dohs

Sopa de Tortilla *soh*-pah deh tohr-*tee*-l'yah

Sopaipillas soh-py-*pee*-l'yahs

Sopa Paraguaya *soh*-pah pah-rah-*gwy*-yah

Sorbet sor-*beh*

Soufflé à la Vanille soo-*flay* ah lah vah-*nee*-yuh

Soufflé de Crabe Roulé soo-*flay* duh krahb roo-*lay*

Soupa Avgolemeno *soo*-pah ahv-ghoh-*leh*-moh-noh

Spaetzle *shpeh*-ts'luh

Spaghetti al Giardino spah-*gayt*-tee ahl jahr-*dee*-noh

Spaghetti alla Carbonara spah-*gayt*-tee ahl-lah kar-boh-*nah*-rah

Spaghetti con le Polpettone spah-*gayt*-tee kohn leh pohl-pet-*toh*-neh

Spaghetti with Amatriciana Sauce spah-*gayt*-tee with ah-mah-tree-*ch'yah*-nah sauce

Spanokopita spah-noh-koh-pit-ah

Sri Lanka sri *lahn*-kah

Stegt And steak ond

Stollen *shtawl*-len

Stovies *stoh*-vees

Stroganov *stroh*-gan-ohv

Suimono soo-ee-moh-noh

Sukiyaki skee-yah-kee

Suomalaisruisleipa soo-oh-mah-*lice-roo*-is-*lay*-pah

Sylta *sewl*-tah

Syltede Agurker *sewlt*-eh-deh ah-*goor*-kehr

Székely Gulyás *say*-kay *goo*-l'yosh

T

Tabooley *tah*-boo-leh

Tandoori Murghi tahn-*door*-ee *mur*-gee

Tan Hua T'ang don hwa tong

Tarator tahrr-ah-*tor*

Teem Gok teem gawk

Tempura tem-poo-rah

Terrine de Campagne teh-*reen* duh kahm-*pah*-n'yeh

Tien Shuen Yu dee-en shoo-wan you

Tiropetes tee-*roh*-peh-tes

Torta de Almendra *tohr*-tah deh ahl-*mehn*-drah

Tortilla de Patatas tohr-*tee*-l'yah deh pah-*tah*-tah

Tortoni tor-*toh*-nee

Tostadas tohs-*tah*-dahs

Tourtière tohr-*t'yehr*

Tou Shih Hsia Jen dough-sher shee-ah ren

Tusenbladstårta thew-sen-blahds-*tawr*-tah

V

Vatkattu Marjapuuro *vaht*-kaht-too *mahr*-yah-*poor*-oh

Vitello Tonnato vee-*tel*-loh toh-*nah*-toh

W

Wu Hsiang Chi woo shee-ong jee

Z

Zabaglione dzah-bah-*l'yoh*-neh

Zwetschgenknödel *ts'vetch*-g'n-*k'nuh*-d'l

Zwetschgenkuchen *ts'vetch*-g'n-*koo*-kh'n

International Food Terms

Al dente: term used in Italian cooking to describe the degree (barely tender) to which pasta, rice and vegetables should be cooked.

Antipasto: hot or cold Italian appetizer course including an assortment of vegetables, meat and/or fish.

Aspic: a flavored glaze for meat, fish or poultry, or a molded salad made from vegetable or meat stock.

Au gratin: food topped with bread crumbs and/or grated cheese and broiled or baked until brown.

Au jus: French term referring to the natural, unthickened juices of meat obtained in the cooking and served with the meat.

Baba: French cake made with a yeast dough and usually flavored with rum or fruit juice.

Béchamel: French term for a basic white sauce.

Bisque: thick cream soup, usually made from puréed vegetables or fish.

Bok choy: a variety of Chinese cabbage resembling celery.

Bombe: frozen dessert made by lining a mold with one kind of ice cream and filling it with another.

Borscht: Russian soup made with beef broth and several vegetables including beets.

Bouillabaisse: hearty French soup made with several varieties of seafood.

Bouquet garni: combination of herbs, usually bay leaf, thyme and parsley, tied in cheesecloth or placed in a tea ball and added to soups, stews and other foods for flavoring.

Brioche: slightly sweetened French yeast bun.

Chutney: spicy, somewhat sweet relish of East Indian origin, made from several fruits and/or vegetables and often served with curried foods.

Cannellini: white beans sometimes used in Italian cooking.

Cannelloni: hollow tubes of pasta, usually filled with a seasoned meat or cheese filling and baked in a tomato or cream sauce.

Caper: flower bud from a Mediterranean shrub; the bud is pickled and used as a condiment.

Cellophane noodles (bean threads): thin, translucent noodles made from mung beans and used in Southeast Asian cooking.

Coquille: shell or small dish in the shape of a shell. Used for baking and serving seafood and meat dishes prepared with a sauce.

Condiment: pungent substance, such as chutney, mustard or catsup, served with food to make it more appetizing.

Dal: the Indian name for all members of the legume family.

Demitasse: a small cup or serving of very strong black coffee, usually served after dinner.

Dolma: filling wrapped in cabbage leaves, grapevine leaves or hollowed-out vegetables.

En brochette: French term for cooked on a skewer.

Frappé: diluted sweetened fruit juice, frozen to a mushy consistency.

Frittata: Italian omelet.

Fromage: French word for cheese.

Garam masala: mixture of dried spices ground at home for use in Indian cooking (most Western recipes call for curry powder).

Gnocchi: Italian dumplings.

Goulash: thick Hungarian beef or veal stew

with vegetables and usually including paprika.

Hoisin sauce: brownish, sweet, spicy sauce used in oriental cooking.

Hors d'oeuvre: appetizer, usually finger food, served before or as the first course of a meal.

Julienne: cut into matchlike strips.

Legumes: vegetables which bear their fruit or seed in pods, such as beans, peas or lentils.

Marzipan: confection of European origin made from almond paste and often formed into fruit and other shapes.

Mocha: coffee-flavored, or a combination of chocolate and coffee.

Oyster sauce: thick, rich sauce made from soy sauce and oysters.

Pilaf: mixture of rice or other grains in which the rice is usually sautéed for a few minutes in fat and then cooked in a seasoned liquid. Meat, fish or poultry can be added for a main dish.

Pirozhki: Russian pastries with a variety of fillings, such as meat or cabbage.

Polenta: Italian cornmeal side dish, to which cheese is often added.

Praline: mixture of caramelized sugar and almonds that is ground or crushed and used as a garnish or flavoring.

Ragout: highly seasoned thick meat stew.

Ramekin: an individual baking dish.

Rice sticks: very thin noodles made of rice flour.

Rose water: flavoring, distilled from fresh rose petals, that is available in specialty stores and pharmacies.

Roux: cooked mixture of flour and butter used to thicken sauces.

Sake: rice wine used as a beverage or as a Japanese cooking ingredient.

Tahini: thick sesame seed paste.

Tamale: highly seasoned Mexican dish of ground meat, beans, olives and seasonings rolled in oiled cornhusks and steamed or boiled.

Tofu: soybean curd sometimes used in oriental cooking.

Torte: rich cake, usually made from nuts, crumbs and eggs, or a meringue in the form of a cake.

Tortilla: thin round Mexican bread made of cornmeal or flour.

Terrine: dish in which fish, poultry or meat pâtés are cooked. The term also refers to the food cooked in this dish.

Zest: the yellow outer peel of lemons and oranges, which contains a strong fruit flavor. The white part underneath is somewhat bitter and should not be used when grating.

Regional Index

General Index